The Final Victim of the Blacklist

The Final Victim of the Blacklist

John Howard Lawson, Dean of the Hollywood Ten

GERALD HORNE

University of California Press

BERKELEY   LOS ANGELES   LONDON

University of California Press, one of the most distinguished university presses in the United States, enriches lives around the world by advancing scholarship in the humanities, social sciences, and natural sciences. Its activities are supported by the UC Press Foundation and by philanthropic contributions from individuals and institutions. For more information, visit www.ucpress.edu.

University of California Press
Berkeley and Los Angeles, California

University of California Press, Ltd.
London, England

Library of Congress Cataloging-in-Publication Data

Horne, Gerald.
   The final victim of the blacklist : John Howard Lawson, dean of the Hollywood Ten / Gerald Horne.
      p. cm.
   Includes bibliographical references and index.
   ISBN-13: 978-0-520-24372-9 (alk. paper).
   ISBN-10: 0-520-24372-2 (alk. paper).
   ISBN-13: 978-0-520-24860-1 (pbk. : alk. paper)
   ISBN-10: 0-520-24860-0 (pbk. : alk. paper)
   1. Lawson, John Howard. 1894–1977.   2. Dramatists, American—20th century—Biography.   3. Screenwriters—United States—Biography.   4. Blacklisting of authors—United States.   5. Communism and literature—United States—History—20th century.   6. Theater—New York (State)—New York—History—20th century.   7. Motion picture industry—California—Los Angeles—History.   I. Title.

PS3523.A954Z69 2006
812'.52—dc22   2006007346

Manufactured in the United States of America

15   14   13   12   11   10   09   08   07   06
10   9   8   7   6   5   4   3   2   1

This book is printed on New Leaf EcoBook 60, containing 60% post-consumer waste, processed chlorine free; 30% de-inked recycled fiber, elemental chlorine free; and 10% FSC-certified virgin fiber, totally chlorine free. EcoBook 60 is acid-free and meets the minimum requirements of ANSI/ASTM D5634–01 (Permanence of Paper).

Contents

Prologue

John Howard Lawson was not pleased.

Here he was in the fall of 1947 not recumbent in his comfortable Southern California home but instead in a forbidding congressional hearing room on Capitol Hill. This year was to prove to be the "driest . . . in the history of Los Angeles";[1] meanwhile, a steady rain had descended on Washington. Lawson's trip east likewise had been a voyage from blue and sunny skies to what was to become dreary weather. The celebrated playwright and screenwriter who had penned tomes on the magic behind creating dramatic tension now found himself as the unlikely leading character in a bit of political theater not of his making.

He had been summoned to Washington ostensibly because of concern over the ability of Communist screenwriters—like himself—to insinuate their ideologically verbal wizardry into the mouths of stars on the silver screen, thereby providing the newly minted foe in Moscow with an incalculable advantage. Actually, what was driving this well-attended hearing was the specter of militant labor led by Reds like Lawson, who had organized writers a few years previously and had marched with studio carpenters, painters, and other workers when they had conducted a fierce strike two years earlier.[2]

It was no secret that affluent Reds like Lawson subsidized the Communist Party and its initiatives, as they provided living proof that being a revolutionary did not entail grim sacrifice. Putting Hollywood at center stage—in the person of the rumpled, tousled, hawk-nosed Lawson, he of the foghorn voice—was designed to dramatize the simple fact that a new day was at hand, a day in which Reds would receive no quarter, labor would be shellacked—and the progressive redoubt that Hollywood, notably the Screen Writers Guild (SWG), had become would be radically altered.

Certainly, Congressman J. Parnell Thomas—the conservative New Jersey Republican who presided over this political drama—treated this gathering as if he were Cecil B. DeMille, the Hollywood mogul who had helped to inspire this hearing, rather than an elected official. This was nothing new. Thomas's otherwise obscure national political profile was transformed after he launched a crusade against the Federal Theatre of the New Deal, a few years earlier; this led to "nation-wide publicity."[3] He well knew the political mileage to be gained by assailing performers and writers and their political patrons.[4]

Thomas, a hound for publicity, which he deemed a "politician's meat and drink," made sure that Lawson's star turn would receive maximum press coverage.[5] It was one of the "capitol's biggest shows," crowed one local newspaper, as "more than 100 reporters" assembled to make sure that the moral of this story reached far and wide. There were "at least four newsreel cameras trained on the witness chair . . . manned at all times. Six or more still photographers—often as many as 10 . . . crouched near the chair." A technician ensured there would be blinding illumination, holding "first one exposure meter and then another a few feet" from Lawson's nose, "checking the lighting for his shots." Klieg lights and other floodlamps bedecked the crowded room, causing several reporters to "wear dark glasses, adding another Hollywood touch to the proceedings."[6]

Thomas's committee was the epicenter of the gathering Red Scare storm.[7] With satisfaction he remarked subsequently that "the room was not only jammed with spectators, but it was crammed with newspaper correspondents, news camera men, movie cameras, . . . radio operators and their machines, even Washington society."[8] He had learned well from his predecessor, Martin Dies of Texas, whom he deemed primarily an actor. "He could dramatize any kind of situation," he remarked with no small envy, "and in the exposure of spy activity a certain amount of dramatization is required." One of the chief investigators for the House Un-American Activities Committee (HUAC) was "an actor born who was never happier than when he was slinking about in disguise. He smoked a curved-stemmed pipe a la Sherlock Holmes and was a real sleuth."[9] This congressional hearing was a form of guerrilla theater, a drama meant to instruct a wider audience about the arrival of a new political era. "Nothing is more significant," opined George Bernard Shaw sagely, "than the statement that 'all the world's a stage.'"[10] This was no less true in the early fall of 1947 on the banks of the Potomac River.

To be sure, the lights and cameras were not attracted solely by the prospect of recording a soliloquy by a man who came to be known as the

Communist cultural commissar of Hollywood and Broadway. In *Sahara* and *Action in the North Atlantic,* Lawson had crafted some of Humphrey Bogart's most memorable roles, and the actor with the sandpapered voice reciprocated by joining some of the brightest stars in Hollywood's firmament in attendance at the Washington hearing. Yet Bogart's evident anxiety foretold his subsequent quick defection from the ranks of Lawson's supporters: as he rose from his seat, "his tongue nervously curled to one side of his mouth." The woman with whom he was to spend his dying days, the lovely Lauren Bacall, stretched her neck in an effort to see past the sea of heads. Nearby, June Havoc and the carrottopped Danny Kaye watched fretfully.[11]

These stars had not seemed as apprehensive earlier when as the Committee for the First Amendment they had a "big meeting" at the home of the famed director William Wyler. There were "about sixty people" present, including "largely well-known stars, some writers, some directors and some producers."[12] They were seized with the idea—not inappropriately, as it turned out—that these hearings would have a chilling effect on the creativity of the industry, hampering the production of challenging films. Soon, as Bacall was to observe, a "disturbing and frightening period" arose in Hollywood. "Everyone was suspect—at least, everyone to the left of center." This was her "first grown-up exposure to a cause," and she became "very emotional about it." Bogart, noted Bacall, "felt strongly about it too, but at first I was the more outspoken."[13]

Thus, by the time Lawson arrived in the witness chair at 10:30 A.M. on 27 October 1947, he had managed to unite a powerful array of foes bent on his destruction. Thomas, Congressman Richard Nixon, and those interrogating Lawson were determined to get answers to questions about two organizations he had helped to build—the Communist Party and the SWG—and Lawson was equally determined to resist their inquiries. "It is a matter of public record that I am a member of the Screen Writers Guild," he shouted, but added quickly that "the question of whether I have held office is also a question which is beyond the purview of this committee. . . . it is an invasion of the right of association under the Bill of Rights of this country."[14] This was followed by a cacophony of interruptions and gavel pounding. Lawson's lawyers, said Thomas, were "popping up like jacks-in-the-box," and the similarly pugnacious congressman "carried on a three cornered debate as to whether or not Lawson should be allowed to make a statement"—a debate Lawson lost resoundingly amid the chaos.[15] In the "supercharged atmosphere little incidents provided light relief. As a movie flood lamp exploded with a soft 'plop' and showered glass down on the audience, one of the 31 Capitol police guarding the hearing room" reflected the palpable tension in the air when he murmured, "'I thought they had me for a minute.'" Meanwhile, "all day long, outside of the old House Office Building, sidewalks were sprinkled with waiting lines of movie fans yearning to catch a glimpse of the high-powered screen stars" present; it was a "movie fan magazine writer's dream."[16]

Undeterred, Lawson kept shouting as the cameras whirred and reporters scribbled furiously, capturing this moment of dramatic tension and bitter confrontation. It was "bare knuckles" combat and a "fishwife brawl," commented *Daily Variety*, as Lawson and Thomas were "screeching at each other."[17] "I am being treated differently from the rest," Lawson bellowed. "I am an American," he continued with passion, "and I am not easy to intimidate."

Finally, he conceded the obvious: "I was the first president, in 1933, and I have held office on the board . . . of the Screen Writers Guild at other times," and, yes, he worked at "practically all of the studios, all the major studios." But on the question of Party membership, he would not yield. "The question of communism," he instructed his interlocutors, "is in no way related to this inquiry, which is an attempt to get control of the screen and to invade the basic rights of American citizens in all fields." Thomas would not relent either, telling his obstreperous witness, "We are going to get the answer to that question if we have to stay here for a week." Lawson, a frequent teacher, resumed his professorial posture, noting, "It is unfortunate and tragic that I have to teach this committee the basic principles of American [life]." "I have told you," he said with exasperation, "that I will offer my beliefs, affiliations and everything else to the American public, and they will know where I stand." Demonstratively unimpressed, with a final flourish Thomas replied, "Officers, take this man away from the stand"—which they did, as the diminutive Lawson resisted forcefully and futilely their successful attempt to drag him away from the witness chair. Rather quickly, a nine-page memorandum detailing Lawson's radical and Communist ties was read into the record, then the committee cited him for contempt—a charge that was to derail his lucrative screenwriting career and land him in federal prison.[18]

Thirty years later, in the high court case of *Wooley v. Maynard*, Carey McWilliams, the prominent California progressive, observed that "by ruling that the First Amendment protects the right to refrain from speaking about one's political beliefs as well as the right to speak," the court vindicated Lawson's position. "Today," he added, "this point of view is not exceptional; then it was. In fact, it was regarded as heretical."[19] For his heresy, Lawson was placed in a tiny, clammy prison cell.

.   .   .

Lawson, a close student of the busy intersection where politics and theater collided, was probably not surprised about his starring role in Washington. Historically in Europe there had been "antipathy" toward the theater world, not least because of the "undeniable similarities between religious ceremony and dramatic performances." In prerevolutionary France men and women of the theater—these "immoral, incontinent vagabonds"—"possessed no civil status and along with Jews, Protestants and executioners, they were excluded from all forms of political life."[20] In a sense, Lawson—both Jewish and a man of the theater—was part of a larger historical cycle.[21]

In short, powerful breezes had blown Lawson into the witness chair in Washington that were not solely a matter of chance. For he was not only a Communist, he was also Jewish; further, he was also affluent and thus excited the febrile passions of the most dedicated anti-Semites.[22] Congressman John Rankin of Mississippi, who referred routinely to Jews as "'long nosed reprobates,'" also "blamed Jews not only for Communism but also for 'trying to undermine and destroy America.'" This unvarnished bigotry had played a role in radicalizing a number of Jewish Americans—including Lawson—which in turn gave more fuel to the Rankins. Thus, it was not long before Arnold Forster of the Anti-Defamation League of B'nai B'rith was complaining sourly that "'Jews were automatically suspect. . . . our evaluation of the general mood was that the people felt if you scratch a Jew, you can find a Communist.'"[23] Even Chairman Thomas, no cosmopolitan, found Rankin "unduly narrow-minded on certain subjects, bitter against the Jews"—a man who "never hesitated to show his disgust for Jews." On one memorable occasion, he had a "heated . . . argument" with the Mississippian, who "left the room with tears of rage streaming down his cheeks."[24]

Though scarcely mentioned at the time, the question of anti-Semitism haunted this 1947 confrontation and the subsequent "blacklist." "Six of the Hollywood Ten"—those in the dock with Lawson—"were Jewish." Weakening consideration of this explosive point was that raising it "put Jewish organizations in a difficult position." "They could not afford to oppose HUAC openly on the grounds that it was anti-Semitic, for fear of appearing sympathetic to Communism"—which they did not want to do, not least since by then they were about to purge "their own ranks of Communists."[25]

Of course, Thomas was not the only congressman who had grasped the intimate tie between entertainment and politics. Alongside him was a ski-nosed junior congressman with a rapidly receding hairline and an apparently permanent five o'clock shadow. He, too, had to combat repeated charges that he harbored deep-seated anti-Semitic passions.[26] Though some film critics and scholars were to accord directors the preeminent role in Hollywood, while the public dutifully idolized actors, Congressman Richard M. Nixon thought that Communists had a different pecking order, and that was what he was bent on pursuing. "So far as the Communists are concerned," he instructed one witness, "their primary aim in Hollywood . . . is to attempt to enlist the support first of writers, and second, of directors and probably a very poor third of actors."[27]

In a sense, Nixon was auditioning for a larger role on a larger stage. His performance here catapulted him into the Senate, then a heartbeat away from the presidency as vice president in 1952. It was then that a producer offered his aid in publicizing the campaign with Eisenhower, "theoretically as my leading man," and Nixon costarring, ably aided by a "skillful director and some fine writers."[28]

Nixon, who was to raise a small fortune in campaign contributions from Lawson's employers, the Hollywood moguls, jousted visibly with Thomas over who would be most prominent in the spotlight as Lawson was unmasked as the doyen of Communist writers. Lawson's radical lawyer, Ben Margolis, later recalled that Thomas and Nixon were virtually arm wrestling as they competed for the microphone and the opportunity to star in this congressional production. Nixon was so "eager" to "get into the act" that Thomas was "trying to keep [him] still."[29] But the future U.S. president refused to be restrained. Behind the scenes he was courting Lawson's counterpart in the Screen Actors Guild. A few weeks before the 1947 hearing commenced, the wily Nixon had a "long conference" with Ronald Reagan and "was particularly impressed by his attitude" to the point that he rued the fact that "the committee did not contact him," since Reagan "would make a particularly good witness in view of the fact that he is classified as a liberal and as such could not be accused of simply being a red-baiting reactionary."[30] Nixon later said, speaking of Reagan, that their friendship dated from the pivotal hearings of 1947 where Lawson starred.[31]

In addition, Nixon was quite close to Harry Warner of the filmmaking family, the mogul having once expressed to Nixon "the regret that you were not my own son."[32] Jack Warner raised a small fortune for Nixon's various campaigns.[33] Another mogul, Spyros Skouras, who produced *The Nixon Story*, told the subject of this hagiography that "our male stars are becoming a little concerned with your attractive and virile appearance."[34]

In sum, in 1947 and thereafter Nixon was hammering Lawson—a man who had organized labor employed by those who were soon to be the congressman's chief supporters. Nixon's own sterling performance at this time earned him the enduring gratitude of these extraordinarily affluent men who happened to be dominant in an industry where Reds were—for a while—far from impotent, a process that in turn helped to generate the congressman's own trailblazing anticommunism. "If you want to scare a country," said the writer Victor Navasky, "scare its royalty and Hollywood is America's royalty."[35] Another way to put it is that the grilling of Lawson was orchestrated by his employers and friendly congressmen in order to send a bold signal to artists and others in the culture of celebrity that their magnetism—and their often healthy incomes—should not be used on behalf of left-leaning causes. Thus was marked the beginning of the end for "Red Hollywood," a community of cultural workers headed by Lawson—and a step backward for Liberal Hollywood.

Nixon, Lawson, and the moguls all hailed from a region—Southern California—that was rapidly becoming the economic and cultural dynamo of the entire nation. Shortly after Lawson's capital ordeal, *Time* magazine—already the arbiter of emerging trends—was agog in speaking of L.A. as if it were truly the land of Oz: "It lands more fish than Boston or Gloucester, makes more furniture than Grand Rapids, assembles more automobiles than any other city but Detroit, makes more tires than any other city but Akron. . . . its port handles more tonnage than San Francisco."[36] By targeting Hollywood, Nixon and his comrades also happened to be targeting a booming region: yes, the profitable film industry with its attention-gathering "stars" was in the bull's-eye—but so was the increasingly wealthy city where it was sited.

The man who was to be perceived ultimately as Lawson's polar opposite in this boomtown—Reagan—then was seen in defined circles as being something more than a mere liberal. The actor John Garfield remembered a popular front meeting, a "meeting of about 150 actors at a private home." "As a matter of fact Ronald Reagan was there," he said with some bemusement, and the B-actor reacted as if he had been jerked out of the closet, for "when he saw me he was surprised, and when I saw him I was surprised."[37] In those different days, Reagan was regarded as a reliable man of the left, which—in Nixon's mind—increased his value as a witness against Communists like Lawson.

No doubt during their confab the two future presidents shared intelligence about their joint antipathy to Communists in Hollywood—and particularly their leader, John Howard Lawson. Certainly Reagan needed no prompting when the subject was denouncing Lawson: Lawson, a "shadowy figure," was a "competent playwright," he thought, who was essential to the "communist plan for Hollywood," which was "merely to take over the motion picture business. Not only for its profit, as the hoodlums had tried"—referring to organized crime's often shrouded interest in the industry—"but also for a grand world-wide propaganda base." Reagan had clashed openly and vocally with Lawson at a postwar meeting where the issue was whether an organization to which they both belonged would "repudiate Communism." Lawson, he recalled with asperity, was "most vehement"; he "persisted in waving a long index finger under my nose and telling me off. One woman of liberal leanings actually had a heart attack and had to be taken home, the emotional atmosphere was so strong."[38] This episode was a critical way station on the epochal journey that led Reagan to the embrace of conservatism and away from the kind of popular front liberalism that he once had exemplified. It also sheds light on why Reagan, as FBI "informer T-10" chose to monitor Lawson's activities.[39]

. . .

There was a larger meaning embedded in this political drama—or so thought one insider. The anticommunist Hollywood union boss Roy Brewer was exultant with the results of Lawson's bravura performance before the cameras. "You will remember the general hostility of the press—you will remember our apparent inability to break through the wall of disbelief" about the alleged evil of the Communists, he began glumly. "And then John Howard Lawson testified," he recalled, brightening. "As they dragged him screaming from the witness stand the world took a new look at our problem." Triumphantly he concluded, "Lawson had achieved for us something which we had been unable to do for ourselves. . . . [The] American people were convinced that Americans did not act the way Mr. Lawson acted that rainy October morning." Moreover, it all "came as a great shock to Hollywood." Yet, even as he spoke in 1953, when it appeared that the Reds had been routed thoroughly, the resolute Brewer conceded that the "question of how the Communists were so successful has not been fully answered and until it is we will not be out of danger."[40] Thus, Lawson had to be crucified further, it was thought.

Brewer's view of Lawson had become the consensus, with few willing to concede publicly what the prototypical L.A. writer Raymond Chandler said privately. He found the "Hollywood show in Washington . . . pretty awful. . . . I do not think the Founding Fathers intended this sort of investigation to be conducted with microphones, flash bulbs and moving picture cameras."[41] What this fabricator of mystery did not perceive is that Lawson had been subjected to a "show trial" designed to provide a political lesson borne by the dynamics of theater and, therefore, more difficult to forget. This is something that the blunt and crude Brewer nonetheless detected.

But Brewer did not detect a perhaps larger point of this political drama. It was not only that Lawson had been the pivotal figure in the organizing of Hollywood labor in the 1930s and now was paying the price for his gumption; it was also that he and other writers had been in the vanguard of this venture, and diluting the strength of writers was an essential part of this process.[42]

"For some reason," Lawson wrote quizzically two decades after his congressional tribulations, "we all have been remarkably reluctant to grant that the Hollywood screenwriter was as responsible as the Hollywood director for the quality and expressiveness of the films made there."[43] Lawson's puzzlement would have dissolved if he had considered momentarily the point—which he actually knew better than most—that the fear of the potential and actual power of writers generated a corresponding movement to pound them into submission and dilute the rightful credit and income they should have received for being "creators" of modern motion pictures.

Raymond Chandler argued that "the basic art of the motion picture is the screenplay; it is fundamental; without it there is nothing."[44] Edmund Hall North, former head of the Screen Writers Guild that Lawson founded, and writer of the screenplays for *The Day the Earth Stood Still*, *Patton*, and other acclaimed films, declared bluntly that "the auteur theory"—or the idea that the director is "author" of the film—was, "to put it at its kindest, not useful." Once he tried to "get scripts mimeographed and sent—a broad spectrum of scripts—to reviewers. So they would see just what we're talking about, they would [see] that a lot of these 'directorial touches' are written."[45] More to the point, Howard Koch, screenplay writer of *Casablanca*, suggests that "film being a collaborative art (auteur theory to the contrary). . . . a good movie will seem to have been made by one person when actually it will be a felicitous fusion of the work of many contributors"—though it all started with a blank page to be filled by a writer.[46]

The left-winger Adrian Scott wrote the screenplay to *Mr. Lucky*, produced both *Murder My Sweet* and *Crossfire*, and worked on *The Boy with Green Hair*, so he had a vaster range of experiences than most. But in 1949 he held "neither to the old-fashioned precept that the director is all, nor the current precept that the director is an errand boy whose chief responsibility is to get the actors on and off a set at the proper time." Scott declared that he, along with the renowned director William Wyler, believed "that 80% of direction takes place with the perfection of a fine script before a production goes on the floor."[47] Quite typically, Arthur Miller and Elia Kazan were shooting on location, and the prominent director began tinkering with the script, to which the equally renowned writer replied, "'Where the hell were you when the page was blank?'"[48] Even the Paramount executive George Weltner observed that "in our business of dreams, everything starts with an idea and generally speaking the idea is the story."[49] Yet nowadays film is seen as a "director's medium," and a film is said to be "by" the director, not the writer, though few have speculated on what impact the writer's role in agitating the moguls at a time of widespread unrest in Hollywood—at a time when directors were comparatively quiescent—may have played in this designation.[50]

Thus, years after Lawson was manhandled in Washington, a concerted attempt to root out all traces of Communist influence in Hollywood—a crusade that often resembled a campaign to extirpate all manner of non-conservative influence—continued. Weeks after standing up for Lawson, Bogart retreated after not-so-subtle coercion from the moguls. The actress Jane Wyatt had been at Bogart's side—then suddenly found herself unemployable. "I couldn't get a job," she moaned. "It was just after I'd played with Gary Cooper and had been in a Goldwyn picture and was getting parts all the time. Suddenly my agent called up and said, 'I don't know what's the matter.'" As one scholar observed, "Virtually overnight the atmosphere in Hollywood became one of terror. Lives were wrecked, careers destroyed, marriages and families shattered as friend betrayed friend, sometimes after swearing devotion the night before."[51]

Few were to adopt the viewpoint of actor and dancer Gene Kelly, who when asked his reaction to Lawson's 1947 performance lamented the "denial of free speech" to which the screenwriter had been subjected and posed the question that so few did—"What if he is a Communist?"[52] Kelly at that moment did not seem to recognize—or, perhaps, he did—that the era of the "blacklist" and the "witch hunt" and "friendly witnesses naming names" before congressional committees had been kicked off in the fall of 1947 with the summoning of Lawson, then well past fifty years of age. Later Reagan was to instruct the affluent smut merchant Hugh Hefner that "Hollywood has *no blacklist*,"[53] but this bit of verbal legerdemain hardly accounted for the vertiginous drop in Lawson's screenwriting jobs in Hollywood. His career, which had been on a steady ascent since he had burst onto the Broadway scene in the 1920s, came to a screeching halt. Though he was to write a series of critically acclaimed books and anonymously pen various screenplays—including the acclaimed *Cry, the Beloved Country*—thereafter until his death in 1977 he was to be persona non grata in Hollywood, a man with whom one should associate only if one cared not a whit about one's well-being. He was "dean of the Hollywood Ten," said his good friend Paul Robeson admiringly, referring to his fellow persecuted cineastes, but such verbal bouquets could not obscure the ignominy Lawson suffered in the latter stage of his life.[54]

This was quite a turnabout for Lawson, who had led something of a charmed existence to that point, enjoying a kind of celebrity status while maintaining credentials as a staunch radical. The novelist John Dos Passos, with whom Lawson became quite close in the aftermath of World War I, described him as an "extraordinarily diverting fellow, recently out of Williams [College], with bright brown eyes, untidy hair and a great beak of a nose that made you think of Cyrano de Bergerac. There was a lot of the Gascon in him at that. He was a voluble and comical talker. He had drastic ideas on every subject under the sun. He was never away from you for ten minutes that he didn't come back with some tale of . . . adventures that had happened in the meanwhile." He was a "socialist," said Dos Passos, "who greatly added to the vivacity of the scene."[55]

Lawson's restless intelligence, conversational glibness, and penchant for "adventures" had combined to make him one of Hollywood's most politically minded storytellers. He was one of the few screenwriters capable of penning one of the few movies that addressed what may have been the chief real-life moral drama of his era: the Spanish civil war. His *Blockade*, which brought him a coveted Oscar nomination, soared above its competitors—including *Love under Fire*, an incongruous comedy, and *Last Train from Madrid*, a routine melodrama that aped *Grand Hotel*[56]—though contemporary viewers may justifiably wonder why it was considered so daring. Yet today's minds find it hard to recall a time when cinematic reinforcement of antifascism was considered to be a bold breakthrough. Conversely, audiences in 1930s Shanghai, then under siege by Japan, gave this film "prolonged applause . . . after nearly every showing," something that was "unprecedented." For, said one journalist, "an audience of Chinese is easily the most blasé and even at the very exciting classical dramas the patrons sit talking, sipping tea, munching lichee nuts and wiping off their faces with hot towels thrown to them from a distance by attendants parading [in] a continuous stream up and down the aisles." But rapt attention was the byword when *Blockade* was screened, since "its essential truths were just as applicable to China as to Spain."[57]

Lawson was that rare U.S. intellectual with global reach. When he visited the Soviet Union in the early 1960s, he discovered that the renowned filmmaker Sergei Eisenstein had a copy of Lawson's *Theory and Technique of Playwriting* and "that almost every page [was] marked with comments and notes in his handwriting."[58] The director Elia Kazan attained lasting notoriety when he "named names" of Communists before a congressional committee. Yet when he was conceiving the cinematic version of *East of Eden*, he, too, resorted to Lawson's writings on the "importance of unity in a work of art." Lawson, he recalled, "said in his book on screenwriting that unity comes from the climax. That is a very fertile thought. Every element in your story should lead up to the climax. Using that idea as sort of an aesthetic guide, I thought"—correctly, as it turned out—"that a good film could be made out of the last part of Steinbeck's book."[59]

Lawson was caricatured as a Red who crudely sneaked propaganda onto the screen, yet Carl Foreman, one of his former comrades who confessed to having learned much from him, then went on to write the screenplay for the classic *High Noon*, recalled that "one thing I learned in the Party was about myself"—and not falling in love with a tractor or even the power of the collective or other such clichés about Red writing. No, said Foreman, "I learned that the things I wrote best were about the conflict of the individual against the mass. . . . 'High Noon' was the apotheosis of the theme of the individual against the mass. I knew it."[60] Abby Mann, who wrote the screenplay for *Ship of Fools* and received credit for the story for the award-winning *Judgment at Nuremberg*, said Lawson "meant more to me than any other writer." His book "saved me," he confessed. "I . . . could not have finished my screenplay without that book." Lawson was deemed by many to be "doctrinaire" and "inflexible," but Mann thought him a "giant." For without Lawson, he argued, there would have been no "Clifford Odets, Lillian Hellman, Arthur Miller," for Lawson "founded a whole new genre of realistic drama." Deeply touched, Mann "started to cry" as he contemplated this. When his wife asked why, he responded that the "lack of greater recognition" of Lawson, his "not being in the mainstream," was a loss for the nation, for the culture.[61]

Lawson's war drama *Sahara* received high praise from James Agee, one of the era's leading critics.[62] The film exuded a premature antiracism.[63] This was the kind of "propaganda" that Communist screenwriters like Lawson had brought to the screen, and this is what had brought him obloquy in 1947 and thereafter—not cinematic paeans to Moscow.

Lawson's ability to inject antiracist themes was facilitated by the nation's wartime need for unity in the face of Japan's powerful appeal to the "colored."[64] Indeed, Lawson was probably the premier cinematic critic of white supremacy—a factor often lost in discussions about his Communist ties. Thus, in *The Pagan*, a 1920s movie, he "presents European civilization as indisputably the villain—an uncommon approach in films of the period"; it concerns the "subversion of the island's way of life by white invaders, from their belief that the value of nature lies only in pounds and dollars to their imposition of an alien and unsuitable religion." In this silent movie, Lawson was "responsible for the perceptive inter-titles."[65]

In fact, on the practical level, Lawson's disruption of traditional "race relations" was what inflamed the ire of so many—and enticed others. Charlotta Bass, publisher of the black weekly the *California Eagle*, recalled that the "little people . . . knew [Lawson]. He had often visited and spoken in their churches, other civic and religious organizations. They marveled over his knowledge of early Negro history in this country. Often there were whispers, 'he knows more about our history than we do.'"[66]

Though Cecil B. DeMille was to become a hostile and unforgiving ideological foe of Lawson, he had high praise for the film on which they collaborated in the 1920s. *Dynamite*, said the portly mogul, was "one of the best stories I have ever done."[67] Moreover, it was *Cry, the Beloved Country*, also written by Lawson, that made South Africa "highly visible among Afro-Americans," thereby providing a dramatic jolt to the antiapartheid movement and compelling Pretoria's then close ally in Washington to begin an agonizing retreat from the powerful illogic of de jure racial discrimination.[68] Regarded by one critic as "one of the cinema's finest statements about the necessity of racial understanding," in 1952 it won both a British Film Academy United Nations Award and the Silver Laurel Award.[69]

Lawson was not just writing powerful political tracts. His movies paid obeisance to Hollywood's god—profit. *Action in the North Atlantic*, for example, was "successful at the box office" and almost broke "*Yankee Doodle Dandy*'s opening day record in New York."[70] This further undermines the basis for the congressional flyspecking of Lawson's screenplays, that is, the allegation that he had used movies as a tool of Communist subversion. For given their relative success at the box office, perhaps there was an audience in the "free market" for this kind of "propaganda," and Lawson should have been left undisturbed. Or, more precisely, perhaps the idea that a screenwriter—who had to answer to producers and executives too numerous to mention—could deceive them all into following his "line" was risibly ridiculous. As one authoritative study put it, "Whatever writers did, they were under the strict supervision of a top-heavy, usually conservative, studio hierarchy."[71] The threadbare rationale for his Washington interrogation led Lawson and his comrades to avoid answering inquiries that they had reason to believe were ill-motivated.[72]

His formidable gifts notwithstanding, it is important to recognize that Lawson did not stand alone. He was not a solitary "Hollywood Red" but instead an essential component of "Red Hollywood." Fellow Communist screenwriters—and members of the "Hollywood Ten"[73] who followed him in the witness chair in Washington in 1947—like Ring Lardner Jr. and Dalton Trumbo may have had more talent. However, as leader of Hollywood Communists, Lawson spent more time organizing and campaigning, to the detriment of his writing.[74] It was Lawson, for example, who reached out to a stumbling F. Scott Fitzgerald during his days of ennui and anomie in Hollywood. Howard Fast, another writer who was influenced by Lawson, recalled that the Princeton-educated novelist had "long talks" with the Hollywood Communist leader: "At a low point in Fitzgerald's despair, Lawson had opened a new direction for his work, which led in time to the writing [of] *The Last Tycoon*. Fitzgerald had been ready to embrace the [Communist] party I was told."[75] Later Fast was more definitive. "Sure," he said, "Fitzgerald was a member of the Party. John Howard Lawson, the cultural dean of the Party, finally convinced him that his only way to salvation—especially literary salvation—was to join the Party."[76] In what may still rank as the leading novel about Hollywood—and based on the life of Irving Thalberg, with whom Lawson worked intimately—there is one of the most favorable depictions of a Communist found in U.S. literature, a character who provides a sound thrashing to a Hollywood mogul.[77] As Fitzgerald put it after this radical departure, "To bring on the revolution . . . it may be necessary to work inside the Communist Party."[78]

In these different days, Fitzgerald's was not an isolated example. Ernest Hemingway, with whom Lawson also conferred, "always had a positive attitude about the [Cuban] Communists and had given considerable economic aid to the cause." Of "all the foreigners," it was said, "Hemingway contributed the most to the Communist Party in Cuba." Said one Havana Red, "the sum" from the hirsute writer "was never lower than five hundred dollars, and he gave it as a natural thing to do"; moreover, "he sponsored the Party's Central Committee in the district of Guanabaco when the Cuban Communist Party became legal on the island. He paid their rent, lighting and telephone."[79] Orson Welles also circulated in left-wing circles, which brought him unwanted attention from the U.S. authorities.[80] Sean O'Casey, the celebrated Irish playwright whose ideological predilections were similarly pro-Communist, was cited as remarking, "'Lawson, that's a talented playwright' and there was a world of warmth and respect in his voice."[81]

Lawson also influenced the rebel playwright Clifford Odets, who acknowledges that his mentor's work "had a very decisive influence on me. I began to see what you could do." Lawson's play *Success Story* "showed me a great deal. It showed me the poetry that was inherent in the language of the street. There was something quite elevated and poetic in very common scenes, in the way people spoke. I would say that Jack Lawson is definitely one of those people who gave me a push, in this play particularly."[82] It was Lawson who was the main speaker at the funeral of his Communist comrade Theodore Dreiser, whom he had recruited to the Party,[83] and with whom he had worked closely on converting his novel *Sister Carrie* into a screenplay.[84]

Charles Chaplin was also present at this funeral, which represented something of a dirge for Red Hollywood as well; this brightest of stars was likewise part of this radical circle.[85] Lawson was the keystone of the arch of Red Hollywood, the center of a left-wing spiderweb that also included Paul Robeson.[86]

Lawson in turn was influenced deeply by the famed writer and intellectual Edmund Wilson,[87] who acknowledged that Lawson had a "wit and fancy which have found their proper vehicle in the theater."[88] Their fateful encounter led directly to Lawson joining the Communist Party and, therefore, his 1947 rendezvous with destiny and subsequent discomfiture.[89]

But perhaps even more than Lawson's decision to throw in his lot with the Communists, it was his energetic effort to organize screenwriters in Hollywood that led to his own Waterloo. The "opening speech" he made at the convocation of the Screen Writers Guild, where he "opened with the words: 'the *writer* is the creator of motion pictures,'" in a real sense sealed his fate in Hollywood. As Lawson later acknowledged, "Those words were sufficient to insure the eternal enmity of the producers against writers"— and himself personally. "I don't think you can possibly understand the situation that developed around the Hollywood Ten and why the attack was made at that particular time in 1947 without this perspective. . . . I regard that meeting at the Knickerbocker Hotel in 1933 as really the beginning of a cycle of my life, a determination, a commitment to give my life and my professional activity to this cause."[90]

Screenwriters were the sparkplugs of labor organizing in Hollywood and were overrepresented in the Hollywood Communist Party.[91] As the Depression began to bite, Lawson was successful in organizing the Screen Writers Guild and becoming its first president. Hence, "many in Hollywood have argued that producers simply used McCarthy and the HUAC as a vehicle for re-establishing their control in the industry," elevating the role of the director—an elevation ratified by "auteur theory"—and converting writers to what Lawson's comrade Lester Cole termed "'the niggers of the studio system.'"[92]

Lawson's commitment to this cause of organizing of Hollywood labor and, ultimately, betterment of the lives of the downtrodden generally, was exacted at enormous personal sacrifice, including a prison term, infamy, and huge financial loss. Though during his "early career many observers considered him one of the first American-born playwrights likely to achieve international artistic stature," by the time of his death in 1977, he was laboring in virtual obscurity.[93] Yes, Lawson made blunders—huge ones—especially in politics. And, yes, some of his films, even those hailed when they were first released, have not withstood the test of time: *Action in the North Atlantic*, for example, seems contrived, even boring, nowadays. However, the life of this Hollywood Red—when viewed in the context of Red Hollywood—provides one of the most captivating stories of twentieth-century cinema and politics. Moreover, his life is a useful prism through which to view another trend, for the writer and producer Adrian Scott is largely correct when he suggests that the 1947 hearings starring Lawson led directly to the poisonous trend encapsulated in the term "McCarthyism," which was responsible for "producing among other pollutions the 'silent generation.'"[94]

But what about Lawson and his rather steady devotion to the now disappeared Soviet Union? Does that discredit him or his critique of the society in which he lived? I do not think so. Professor Leon Friedman of Hofstra School of Law replied sharply to cultural critic Hilton Kramer when this ideologically driven conservative insisted "he will not listen to anyone condemning the blacklist unless and until he first condemns Stalin." "In short," concluded Friedman, "one must take a loyalty oath of anti-communism before criticizing injustice in the United States."[95] I agree with this eminent constitutional scholar and with the similar words of the equally eminent historian David Brion Davis, who has reminded us that "the deadly failure of communism in no way lessens the historical and contemporary crimes of capitalism."[96] Devotees of a nation that benefited from the horrors of the African slave trade—which is responsible for my presence on these shores—above all should be hesitant about sweeping condemnations and, above all, should be guarantors of nuance.

Though fellow members of the Hollywood Ten, for example, Lawson's former cellmate, Dalton Trumbo, were liberated from the pain of the "blacklist" early on, at his death in 1977 Lawson was still a pariah. Obviously his failure to quit the Communist Party—a legally constituted entity with respected counterparts from South Africa to Chile to Vietnam to Japan to India to France—had much to do with his being banned. Even today Lawson's reputation continues to suffer because of the perception of his ties to the former Soviet Union, though the forces that assisted the United States in helping to destabilize Communist Party rule there—so-called Islamic fundamentalists during the war in Afghanistan and China, in the wake of President Nixon's epochal journey to Beijing more than three decades ago—are the same forces that are bedeviling Washington mightily in the twenty-first century.[97] It is more than idle speculation to suggest that the United States might be in a more advantageous position today if the nation had not been so single-minded in its focus on Moscow during the cold war—in other words, following Lawson's path should have been given more serious contemplation. But, sadly, this remains a ticklish question to raise in a nation where John Howard Lawson remains the final victim of the "blacklist."

Introduction

It happened so often that it seemed to be a new Hollywood ritual. Contrite, often ashen, a penitent would sit in the witness chair in a hearing as members of Congress, often on an elevated platform, stared strategically downward. Then, with eyes often downcast and heart often heavy, the witness would proceed to unburden himself—or herself—of the names of others who also had once strayed down the wrong political path toward the Communist Party or its ill-defined "fronts." Often the name relinquished was Lawson's. He was "named 28 times (more than twice as often as anyone else) by the various 'friendly' witnesses and informers."[1] Expiation completed, the witness could then resume a—presumably—lucrative career.

As with Lawson's 1947 appearance, there was something more than vaguely theatrical about this variety of congressional investigation, often suggested by the presence of cameras, particularly those from the newly powerful television networks that broadcast these minidramas into living rooms nationally.[2] When the barrel-chested, prematurely graying Budd Schulberg appeared before Congress, the results were similarly dramatic—albeit for different reasons. Though a fluid and fluent writer, he had something of a speech impediment, which led him to speak in a "hop-skip-jump manner—a few words, then a pause, then another rush of four or five words and another pause." This, said one analyst, "gave the impression of great earnestness and obviously made a deep impression on the Committee" as he "piled up fact on fact" as to "why creative writers should not be Communists." In his "halting" and "intense manner," Schulberg, "speaking with almost no prompting, . . . concentrated the interrogation on the relationship between the witness' experiences with the Communist Party in Hollywood and the pattern of control in Russia."[3] The villain of this set piece, as so often during this political ritual, was John Howard

Lawson, in this case his attempts to squelch Schulberg's intriguing—and still compelling—novel about Hollywood, *What Makes Sammy Run?* Here as elsewhere, Lawson's alleged approach—his "dogmatic, ad hominem style of argument," which, in the words of one historian, "became the rule, not the exception, in the Hollywood party"—was analogized to the kind of pain inflicted on Soviet writers during the darkest days of Stalin's rule. Or, as Martin Berkeley put it during his testimony, Lawson was the "'grand Poo-Bah of the Communist movement'" who "'speaks with the voice of Stalin and the bells of the Kremlin.'" His "official job description," it was said, was the "enforcer position."[4] Lawson, according to the former Communist director Edward Dmytryk, was the "Gauleiter of the Hollywood section of the Communist Party."[5]

These hearings were latter-day morality plays, with Lawson often playing the role of the reviled off-screen presence, the object of fear and loathing. As the screenwriter Walter Bernstein once said, "the Soviet Union was the Great Satan," and Communists like Lawson populated its "American coven," doing the "devil's work, taking the place formerly occupied by witches, warlocks and occasionally goats."[6]

Hence, to the extent that he is remembered at all, John Howard Lawson is constructed as the epitome of the humorless, rigid, dogmatic, unsmiling, doctrinaire Communist, mixing ruthlessness promiscuously with insensitivity. Certainly, despite stiff competition from the likes of Theodore Dreiser and W. E. B. Du Bois, Lawson may very well be the most notorious U.S. Communist; therefore, the inexorable gravity of anticommunism may help shed light on why this screenwriter's image has been so tarnished. And, since Lawson spent much more time in the Communist Party than either Dreiser or Du Bois, the filings of anticommunist hatred clung to him magnetically.

Yet Lawson was made to take the weight for traits that were not so much his own as they were components of the industry he served. For it is well known, as the *Los Angeles Times* once noted, that Hollywood was "so competitive that people routinely root for friends to fail," with "bad behavior . . . permanently embedded in showbiz DNA," generated by a "briar patch of feuding moguls, narcissistic movie stars and egomaniacal directors." Routinely "the miscreants kowtow to the powerful and let fly at their inferiors." Hollywood, it was said, was "teeming with unhappy, insecure people with a lethal combination of big egos and low self-esteem," while the "analysts' couches" received "quite a beating in this business." Rudeness was rewarded; "in fact, the 'hip' Hollywood insult" as the twenty-first century dawned was "for someone just before slamming down the phone in a fit of rage, to bellow, 'you should die!'" Yet in the alchemy of anti-communism, somehow it was Lawson who seemed exotically unique in his ability to dole out invective.[7]

The portrait of Lawson presented to Congress was not fabricated wholly, however. His family upbringing, his personality, his "commitment," all combined to create an individual who often jangled nerves in a Hollywood otherwise known for insecurity. Moreover, his Jewishness in a nation not adverse to anti-Semitism, his advocacy of communism in a nation where its demonizing was exalted, his evident treason to his class contributed immeasurably to his negative image.

On the other hand, Lawson's own son—Jeffrey—has done his share to substantiate the negative portrayal of his father. His father, Jeffrey says, was "raised by nurses and caretakers," and "his father didn't spend much time with him. My father was deeply affected by the suicide of his older brother, due in part to my grandfather's insisting that Wendell go into business and give up his aspirations to be a violinist." One of Lawson's early successes, the play *Processional*, bore the earmarks of this upbringing; "first performed in 1914," it was "experimental and pre-Brechtian in form and showed a Victorian, overbearing, overcontrolling, angry, capitalist father." Thus, Jeffrey Lawson recalls an "aloof, very, very angry and riven man who seldom spoke to me, who was not affectionate, and toward whom I felt fascination and awe but also fear. He was not a disciplinarian but was emotionally distant, filled with a frightening ire, and apparently inwardly afraid to be warm and loving to a child." As his son sees it, John Howard Lawson "hated the Victorian period and revolted against it," which was part and parcel of his revolt against U.S. capitalism. Jeffrey also discerned a "connection between the Victorian way of turning a blind eye to sexual reality and my father's way of turning a blind eye to Soviet reality."[8]

Jeffrey Lawson was also impressed with his father's intense power of commitment, a strength that could compel him to not give in to the powerful, even as others in Hollywood were bending to this reality. "He had tremendous will power," Jeffrey recalled at his father's death, and "the concept of the conscious will was very important in his thinking, in his concept of man, in his theories of drama." When his son was quite young, Lawson "smoked a great deal. He smoked about two packs of cigarettes a day and pipes and cigars in between." "I'd go into his studio," he recollected, "and see him madly typing and these clouds of smoke rising up about him. He had even, at times, a voracious quality. He ate, for instance, with great gusto," just as he smoked with abandon. "But one day a doctor told him to quite smoking [and] just like that he threw away his pipes, cigars, the fragrant tobacco, the cigarettes and never smoked again." "He could do that," Jeffrey remarked almost wondrously, "make a decision like that. That always impressed me, the will power he had."[9]

This power of the will allowed Lawson not only to abandon smoking but also to stick to unpopular causes as others fled. Lawson, like many other productive individuals, had the ability to compartmentalize, to stay focused on political and creative tasks amid domestic turmoil that would have destabilized most.

Lawson had an older brother, Wendell, who committed suicide as the future screenwriter was still growing to maturity. At this fraught moment, Wendell Lawson sent letters to his father and sister—but not his brother. As one analyst put it, the "letters imply by omission—some sibling rivalry of longstanding," which happened to be "one of Lawson's most persistent themes" beginning with his earliest plays, including *Roger Bloomer*.[10]

It was not just his difficult relationship with his son, and perhaps his brother, that made for a complicated family, it was also Lawson's often troublesome relationship with Jeffrey's mother, his second wife, Sue. A few years before he passed away, he confessed to one friend the details of how "Sue tried to commit suicide with sleeping pills and came perilously close to succeeding. We got her to the hospital but she had stopped breathing, had to insert an oxygen pipe, etc. She has been disturbed by wild hallucinations for years. She insisted that she was fine, and the fantasies were real." He had been "battling this thing for years," and it had "been acute for about a year." Finally, he said with palpable relief, "[I] can now tell people what's wrong and I am released, or seem to be from this lonely battle which has been killing me." He had enlisted "two able psychiatrists" and felt "an awful sense of hopelessness," but with a steely determination, the elderly Lawson, who had his own debilitating medical problems, was able to persevere.[11]

Persevere was also the watchword in his decades-long relationship with the Soviet Union. Long after his friends and fellow screenwriters like Dalton Trumbo and Ring Lardner Jr. had deserted the banner of Moscow, Lawson persevered, helping to prolong his presence on the "blacklist" and his image as "doctrinaire." Though it is unclear what this latter term actually means, whatever its connotation, it hardly does justice to the malleability of Lawson's views, suggesting that he recognized that "commitment" did not mean dogmatism. He was deeply affected by the many months he spent in the former Soviet Union in the early 1960s, speaking movingly of the "crimes of the Stalin era. The whole life of the country was affected by the violations of socialist legality during these dark years. It is difficult for anyone who has not lived in the Soviet Union to realize the depth of feeling aroused in the people by their experience."[12] Though Lawson has been derided for his presumed unwillingness to criticize the Soviet Union, in 1965 he lamented "the joke" that his book *Film: The Creative Process* "is quite opposed to the official 'line' regarding film art in the Soviet Union and its publication there is regarded by many of the most serious and dedicated film artists as an important step toward liberating film from certain restrictive influences." "I have just received a letter from a publishing house in East Germany," he continued regretfully, "refusing the book on the ground that it does not accord at all with their views there." During his extended visit in the Soviet Union he proclaimed, "I don't like many of their present films and told them so, much more sharply in conversation than in the book. I had very mixed impressions of the Soviet Union. I make clear in the book that I do not approve of much of their present film work. . . . my main emphasis in the book is on the recent development of film in Italy and France, which I find far more interesting than anything in the Soviet Union." He emphasized, "I do not follow a Russian Communist 'line' or any other line but my own." Again and again—especially after the 1956 revelations of Stalin's crimes—he railed at the "ravages of the Stalin period." "I don't think that the full story of those crimes and oppression has yet been told and its effect on the arts has been disastrous," he concluded balefully. But this realization—unlike that of most others who had soured on Soviet developments—did not "change my basic 'commitment' to socialism." His "commitment" was too strong for that. Still, he acknowledged, "I am constantly changing and developing my view of the creative process," conceding that he did not have all the answers to this often mysterious praxis. "Marxism has never dealt effectively with aesthetic questions," he argued, "because it has not taken account of the subtleties and psychological difficulties of the creative act." Though he had "done a tremendous amount of reading, not only in philosophy and aesthetics but in all related fields," he still had more questions than answers, even in his final years.[13]

The shame was that his critics were unwilling to allow for a Communist with complex views. One of Lawson's contemporaries, the writer John Steinbeck, made such an allowance.[14] Yet this Nobel laureate's ability to see plasticity in Communists was both rare and perceptive, as Lawson's example suggests. Certainly this flexibility in Lawson's thought was largely a product of his searing experiences after 1947—imprisonment, the "blacklist," a severe drop in income, metastasizing family problems, and so forth. Yet it remains true that he continued being a card-carrying Communist, even as his thinking belied the image that continued to dog him.[15]

Moreover, on the burning issues of the day—including those that brought Lawson so much grief, such as his support of Soviet foreign policy—there is room for reassessment. His comrade and former prison cellmate, Dalton Trumbo, remarked with typical sarcasm and precision that in the welter of attention devoted to the Soviet-German Nonaggression Pact of 1939, lost in the discussion were the "French-Italian agreement of January 7, 1935; the Anglo-Nazi Naval Treaty of June 18, 1935; the British-Italian accord of April 16, 1938; the Munich Pact of September 29, 1938; the Anglo-Nazi Non-Aggression Pact of September 30, 1938; or the French-Nazi Non-Aggression Pact of December 6, 1938—all of which preceded and considerably affected the one pact they cherish and recall."[16]

Even Lawson's heavily criticized reluctance to acknowledge his party membership in congressional hearings and elsewhere has been subject to retrospective reevaluation. "The idea that real radicals," said Lawson in 1973, "are obligated to adhere to the rules of open disclosure imposed by their oppressors seems too fantastic to merit serious discussion."[17] The North Carolina Communist leader Junius Scales, in a bout of premature glasnost, "hoped that he could humanize the image of the Communist Party and help to stem the tide of anti-Communism locally by giving the Party a public face" by openly declaring his membership—a gesture he took during the momentous year of 1947. But according to the scholar Robert Rodgers Korstad, this was a "vain and even naïve gesture: Scales's announcement created a firestorm that engulfed him and his entire family, jeopardized his friends and ended his plans for a scholarly career. It also alienated liberal allies who had known and respected him all his life. Many, it seemed, blamed him more for announcing his affiliation than for his beliefs; almost everyone preferred public silence and personal discretion."[18]

·   ·   ·

When the young writer Howard Fast traveled to Southern California in the early 1940s to visit John Howard Lawson, he was taken aback by the lushness of the lifestyle enjoyed by the radical screenwriter. "It was wonderful indeed," he reminisced. "There were still barley fields sweeping down to the left [on] Sunset Strip [and] oil derricks among the fields." Fast drove over Laurel Canyon into the San Fernando Valley to Laurel Canyon Road, hard by Lawson's residence. It was then "unsurfaced, a dirt road cutting through endless acres of orange and peach and pear and almond orchards, and a scent so strong and delightful that one had visions of paradise. There was no smog." There was a "fifty-acre spread" among the rampant beauty that constituted Lawson's estate, and there amid the splendor he encountered "bright and fascinating people," all of whom were Communists. Suitably impressed, Fast had reason to feel that his own Marxist leanings required no severe challenge.[19]

More than this, Lawson symbolized the affluent radical who seemingly contradicted his own class interests by subsidizing subversion of an order that obviously had brought him immense material benefit. This apparent contradiction seemed to further inflame the animus toward him; after all, it was easier for some to accept the radicalism of, say, a Negro or the poor, but the radicalism of a rich—and "white"—man like Lawson seemed to suggest a peculiar kind of betrayal or, worse in a sense, ineradicable flaws in the status quo.

Or, alternatively, it led to quixotic searches for the source of Lawson's commitment. As the befuddled journalist Victor Riesel put it, "It would take several teams of psychiatrists and a huge Rockefeller grant to explain why the $5000 a week actors and writers and some producers go left."[20] What did they really want?[21]

The ability to raise large sums of money was one major reason congressional investigators pursued the chief Hollywood Communist—Lawson—with such vigor.[22] Four years after Lawson's appearance in Washington, Congressman Donald Jackson of California concluded that "Hollywood Communists paid an estimated $8,000,000 to $10,000,000 into the treasuries of Communist Party and front organizations during the war and shortly after,"[23] though it is unclear how he arrived at this figure. As late as 1957, testimony at the Subversive Activities Control Board indicated that "while the Communists are not numerous" in Southern California, "they are still able to raise large sums of money," with this region continuing to be "identified as a lush grazing ground for Communist fund-raisers."[24]

Inevitably, more feverishly agitated minds concluded that Lawson's ethnoreligious heritage had something to do with his attraction to the left and his ability to raise substantial sums for these forces. According to one account, when Lawson sat down in the witness chair in Washington in 1947, "a heckler audibly grumbled 'Jew.' It was an uncomfortable but apt prelude."[25] Apt indeed. Hollywood was thought to be dominated by Jewish Americans, while the Communist Party was thought to be similarly oriented. Lawson as a Jewish Communist—an affluent one at that—seemed to confirm the worst nightmares of those favorable to anticommunism, particularly the anti-Semitic variety. These prejudices did not abate when a "1934 United States Chamber of Commerce publication cited a congressional investigation listing Jews as the group 'of foreign origin' with the greatest 'Communist membership.'"[26] No doubt the chamber took note of the allegation that "Jews were the second largest ethnic group" in the Soviet Communist Party, "with a high proportion, fully thirty-five percent in the 'core revolutionary elite.'"[27] When one high-level U.S. military official averred that MGM "is known to be 100 per cent Jewish as to controlling personnel," this was not deemed an overly unusual comment; nor were many eyebrows raised when he averred that "agents of the USSR had contacted motion picture companies in California and contributed to some of them with a view to insuring propaganda and support of USSR policies."[28]

Hollywood, of course, was in Southern California, and, predictably, this esoteric region seemed to have as many rabid polemicists as palm trees, mud slides, and deadly fires. In 1940 the Jewish organization B'Nai B'rith of Los Angeles was curtly informed that "some day when the real Americans awake, these smarty-alecs [i.e., "Comjewnazis"] will find themselves in concentration camps where they belong."[29] This Jewish organization was urged to lead a "very necessary anti-Communist crusade," since "every Jewish Communist living in the United States is an ingrate and should [be] deported to his beloved Russia. . . . to me, American Jewish Communists are like rats; with apologies to the rodents."[30]

Inevitably, part of the hostility directed at Lawson stemmed from his conforming to the worst of anti-Semitic stereotypes—he was an affluent Communist, who was Jewish.[31] This was living proof, thought the most obsessive minds, of the canard put forward in the notoriously libelous *Protocols of the Elders of Zion*, which floated the idea of a conspiracy between wealthy Jews and Jewish Communists to dominate the world.

To be sure, like a number of Jewish Americans, Lawson no doubt was propelled leftward by the rise of fascism. By his own admission, Lawson was "very emotional about my Jewish background, although I was brought up in total ignorance of that background." "I have enormously strong feelings about this," he declared passionately, "about the Jewish temper or soul."[32] His boss Harry Cohn, the head of the Columbia studio, was of a different opinion. "When approached for a donation to a Jewish charity, Cohn, himself Jewish, exploded: 'Relief for the Jews? What we need is relief from the Jews. All the trouble in the world has been caused by Jews and Irishmen'"[33]

Jewish moguls like Cohn were under a particular stress.[34] Their non-Jewish counterparts like DeMille were suspected of being less than favorable toward Judaism, while the flourishing anti-Semites of Los Angeles targeted men like Cohn. As unemployment in Depression-era L.A. escalated, one ultraright grouping distributed "12,000 handbills" proclaiming that "unemployment in the motion picture industry is reaching tremendous proportions . . . while the Jewish monopoly of the motion picture industry brazenly discharges non-Jewish men and women and replace[s] them with refugees from Europe." Lawson's *Blockade* was also targeted, assailed because it was "saturated with vicious, war-provoking propaganda."[35] One particularly obnoxious handbill depicted a Jewish man with a nose resembling Lawson's in intimate contact with a blonde beauty with the headline "Christian Vigilantes Arise. Buy Gentile, Employ Gentile, Vote Gentile, Boycott the Movies! Hollywood Is the Sodom and [Gomorrah] . . . Where Young Gentile Girls Are Raped." Another etching showed a big-breasted woman having her teat sucked by yet another large-nosed man as other men similarly endowed wait in line, presumably to have a go as well.[36] High on this group's list of "objectionable people in the motion picture industry" was producer Walter Wanger's "favorite writer," that is, Lawson, whose "real name," it was said, is "Jacob Levy."[37]

The alleged confluence between Jewishness and the Communist Party was not just glimpsed in the person of Lawson, however. It was not just a trait of this "Hollywood Red" but also of "Red Hollywood."[38] In the pivotal prewar year of 1940, some Jewish leaders were concerned that the high profile of Red Hollywood would bring unwanted attention to Jewish Angelenos, confirming the basest of anti-Semitic stereotypes.[39]

Just as the rise of fascism radicalized some Jewish Americans like Lawson, the vitality of antifascism, which morphed easily into leftism and Communism, sparked apprehension among other Jewish Americans, leading some to suspect that their entire community could suffer because of the activism of some. Simultaneously, a form of anticommunism got a real boost from anti-Semitism. Moreover, this complex battle was occurring on the unique turf of L.A., rapidly becoming a city crucial to the fortunes of left and right alike.[40] All this led ineluctably to a heightened assault on John Howard Lawson.

. . .

Lawson was convinced that the "blacklist"—that is, the ouster from influence of left-leaning film workers like himself—played a major role in Hollywood's manifold postwar problems. There were other problems surely: in the first place, the rise of television and an antitrust lawsuit that compromised the vertical integration of the industry. Still, it is noteworthy, as Hollywood's chief spokesman, Jack Valenti, put it, that "1946 was the high water mark for moviegoing at 4 billion admissions. The low was 1971 with 820 million"[41]—this peak and valley roughly covering the most intense years of the "blacklist." Ruling certain writers out of bounds likewise excommunicated certain ideas, facilitating the rise of trite and formulaic cinema, "beach-blanket fluff" and the like, just as this "blacklist" also allowed for an assault on writers perceived to be overly powerful in the industry and a culling of their ranks.

This was an idea that Lawson believed deeply. In 1952, just after emerging from prison, he argued that the "decline of Hollywood" was reflected in "falling box office receipts." With grim satisfaction he observed that "the period of witch-hunts in the industry and fascist propaganda on the screen has witnessed a spectacular decline in attendance." The previous year, he said, "100 theaters had closed in Philadelphia, 32 in Cleveland, 134 in [the] state of California"; in "1944 90 million tickets were sold each in the United States," while "in 1952 weekly sales dropped to 35 million!" And "because film is more than a commodity—it is propaganda—the film crisis is serious culturally as well as financially." This crisis was tied, he suggested, to the crisis in race relations. Negroes were "not permitted to appear even in street scenes or crowds. Negro actors are employed so rarely and irregularly that it is in most cases impossible for them to earn a living from their profession." They were also "excluded from all other skilled, technical or professional jobs," while "degradation of women on the screen" was accentuated by "an attitude of tolerant amusement toward the [industry's] mockery of women." With evident disgust he concluded, "Hollywood's vulgarities cannot be dismissed as adolescent sexuality, or even as senile decay."[42] How could Hollywood hope to be profitable when it routinely maligned such large groups of potential customers, a malignancy driven, he thought, by the efflorescence of conservatism in the industry?

The fear that drove Bogart, Bacall, and others to fly to Washington in October 1947 was not misplaced.[43] Days after Lawson's tempestuous appearance in the halls of Congress, the director William Wyler confided worriedly to the eminent film critic Bosley Crowther, "Film-making will be, and in fact already is, seriously complicated by the 'Un-American probers.' . . . [I]n going over my mind the great films of the past twenty years, it shocks me to realize how many of them couldn't be made today in the same way."[44]

Certainly he would have to be careful about his cinematic portraits. Wyler said flatly about the limiting of portrayals on screen that "'bankers are out. Anyone holding a mortgage is out. Crooked public officials are out. All I've got left,'" he continued wryly, "'is a cattle rustler.'" This "scarcity of roles for villains" had "become a serious problem, particularly at studios specializing in Western pictures." *The Treasure of the Sierra Madre* "ended with the subtitle 'gold, mister, is worth what it is because of the human labor that goes into the finding and getting of it.' The line is spoken by Walter Huston in the course of the picture. John Huston, who directed it, says that he couldn't persuade the studio to let the line appear on the screen. 'It was all on account of the word "labor,"'" he said, a term redolent with

Marxist implications, it was thought. "'That word looks dangerous in print, I guess,'" he concluded morosely.

Wyler reportedly said during the HUAC hearings that "it was clear he would be unable to make a picture like 'The Best Years of Our Lives' if the Thomas Committee won." He was right in that "he was denied the right by Paramount Studios to hire Lillian Hellman" because "not only was she suspect but so was 'Sister Carrie' by Theodore Dreiser[,] the book she was to adapt to the screen."[45] Frank Capra was shooting *State of the Union* as the 1947 hearings unfolded. "'I haven't seen the town so panicky since the banks closed in 1933,'" he declared. Capra was "panicky" too; he "pulled his punches" in this film as a result.[46] How many Capras were similarly affected in Hollywood?

Adrian Scott, a skilled producer and graduate of Amherst who had served in Naval Intelligence and the National Guard before being "blacklisted,"[47] thought there were "whole categories of ideas which normally would be in preparation if the Thomas Committee had not held its hearings."[48] Months after the stormy 1947 congressional hearing, Scott spoke of a "friend" who "attended a story meeting at a major studio. The purpose of the meeting was to determine studio policy toward story purchases. At this meeting it was held that even the Bing Crosby–Ingrid Bergman picture, *The Bells of St. Mary* could be construed as subversive," since the "nuns succeeded [in] getting a new building to house some orphan children [but] only after instituting a series of pro-Marxian and anti-Christian arguments! (This was the way it was described by the executives in the meeting.) It was pro-Marxian to suggest that a rich man shouldn't have a building to make profits where there were orphans who could live in it!" The meeting "ended in uproar." The conclusion reached by those assembled? "One way for studio executives to achieve immunity from the Committee is by the production of anti-Communist pictures."[49]

Scott had taken an option on a book about the "racially" charged subject of "restricted covenants" in housing. "I have tried a number of times to secure a release on this picture but none of the companies will touch it," he wailed. "I have tried to get money to do the picture independently [but] people are afraid to invest in the picture." RKO executive Dore Schary "approved the idea in principle," but this "was about the time the subpoenas were served upon" those who were to become the Hollywood Ten.[50] Robert Rossen, the former Communist, faced another kind of dilemma. When Columbia previewed an "expensive" film, *The Brave Bulls*, which he directed, "one local reviewer who praised the picture disclosed that he had been privately charged with Communist sympathies as a consequence."[51] The actor

Edward G. Robinson, who for the longest time operated at the intersection of Red and Liberal Hollywood, began to retreat after the saying became popular that "Little Caesar" (one of his most popular roles) was actually a "Little Red." The same attack was launched against Orson Welles, "for the records show," said one stern critic, "that both Robinson and Welles have been connected with various Communist fronts and still are."[52]

There was a "panic" in Hollywood, said Scott in late 1947, just after the hearings.[53] Scripts were "subject to the closest sort of scrutiny"; thus, "the most subversive pictures which have been made are the Gene Autry . . . westerns," since there "you'll find the bank owner or the ranch owner always characterized as a very mean hombre." Now "awkward characterization of the rich as mean, rapacious and blackguards is just goddam corny and I would (and intend to) avoid this like the plague," said Scott. "But it is awful tough to function with this new censorship. You couldn't even begin to consider a film like 'Crossfire' today," referring to the classic condemnation of anti-Semitism. "If ideas are blackballed," he predicted, "the industry, facing a rapidly declining box office cannot possibly survive." "In a year or two," he announced with prescience, "you'll be able to buy RKO for a dollar down and even then it might not be a good risk."[54]

Scott's spouse felt that his film's condemnation of anti-Semitism led to his being harassed by the authorities.[55] Perhaps this film's reluctant producer, Dore Schary, had a point when he reportedly "disapproved the idea of making a film about anti-Semitism. He was a member of that school (at that time) of 'let sleeping dogs lie,'" said Dmytryk.[56]

Huston and Wyler, even Schary, were far from being Communists—but that was precisely the point. For although the "blacklist" supposedly targeted full-fledged Communists like Lawson, the actual dragnet swept within its ambit a much broader array of political forces.[57] Liberal Hollywood needed to be punished severely for being—supposedly—insufficiently harsh toward Red Hollywood and insufficiently conservative.

The deforming of the creative process that resulted was the long-term price paid for the 1947 inquisition in which Lawson starred. The Motion Picture Alliance for the Preservation of American Ideals, a conservative lobby, demanded in its "Screen Guide for Americans" that writers should not "smear industrialists" or "wealth" or "success" or "deify 'the common man'" or "glorify the collective."[58] The influential columnist Hedda Hopper carped in 1951 that "we've had many pictures pointing up our racial problems, political corruption in government, the evil of wealth, men driven to crime because of the supposed pressure of our capitalistic system." These were no more but "devices which the Commies could use to get inverse propaganda in our films."[59] While Lawson boldly challenged racial stereotypes in *Sahara*, after he was barred, Sol Siegel, production chief of MGM meekly declared, "'Racial films alienate too large a portion of the box office to justify making them.'" Naturally, this also meant "lack of hiring of Negroes for films and also the lack of membership of Negroes" in the talent guilds.[60]

This imposition of thought control may be why Charlton Heston—who has been viewed justifiably as the reigning symbol of opposition to Red Hollywood—nonetheless termed HUAC's "exploration of Communist influence in Hollywood" an "appalling exploitation of many public reputations." These "hearings abused the democratic process and provided nothing useful to the country's confrontation with the Soviets." It was an "unsavory page in our history." "Of course," he adds correctly, "there were Communists in Hollywood, some of them no doubt politically educated. But none of these people were positioned to channel crucial intelligence to the Soviets." "I can't think of one film made during that time," he concludes accurately, "that could be described as politically radical, let alone anti-American."[61]

But these sage words were uttered long after Red Hollywood—and Lawson—had disappeared into oblivion. Yet one cannot comprehend the ferocity unleashed against this man and his community unless one begins to understand how both came to be.

1   Beginnings

John Howard Lawson's father, Simeon Levy, was the son of Jewish immigrants who arrived in the United States in the 1840s from Poland, driven by an outburst of anti-Semitism. The family settled in Springfield, Massachusetts, where Levy was born in 1852. Lawson's grandfather profited handsomely during the U.S. Civil War and was able to pass a good deal of this wealth on to his son. By 1880, Lawson's father was in Mexico City, where he started a newspaper, the *Mexican Financier*. He sold the paper after he met Belle Hart, Lawson's mother—who was from a well-to-do family—and moved to New York City, where he was an executive with Reuters. To escape the ravages of anti-Semitism, he changed his name to S. Levy Lawson. John Howard Lawson was born in New York City in 1894, the youngest of three children, named after a famed prison reformer (his brother, Wendell Holmes—named after the well-known jurist—committed suicide when Lawson was a young man, and his sister, Adelaide, was a habitué of the art world). His mother died when he was five years old—of breast cancer, just before Christmas—and given his father's lack of warmth, Lawson grew to maturity without the comfort of a parent's affection. This death, said Lawson, had a "devastating effect on my father," but the same could be said of Belle's younger son. Schooling began for him at a "progressive 'play school' financed by his father"; later his family moved to Yonkers, where Lawson and his sister "boarded at Halstead School," then to Seventy-second Street and Riverside Drive in one of Manhattan's most fashionable neighborhoods.[1]

Lawson's early educational experiences made a permanent impression on his consciousness. Later he recalled fondly his "nursery school," which was "dedicated to the principle that a child learns through self-expression and imaginative play." His teacher, on the other hand, recalled Lawson as "quite self-centered and self-employed."[2]

"My father was a complex man," says John Howard Lawson's son Jeffrey. "I believe his mother's death [also] had a deep effect on him and was part of his anger. But I think what also helped to make him so angry and radical was having a family that tried so hard to gain approval and yet was not totally accepted."[3] Anti-Jewish bias contributed to this lack of acceptance.

Still, the son's words must be read cautiously, since it is evident that he is resentful of his father and mother. Jeffrey Lawson "began to resent his parents for indulging in their Utopian views. 'I kind of broke down under it,'" he admits. "'I sort of fell apart psychologically.'"[4]

One of the son's "earliest memories is of his father blushing whenever Jeff tried to kiss him goodnight. 'My father was pretty aloof, he didn't know how to relate to children . . . he never touched me or held me.'" As Jeffrey Lawson recounted as an adult, still pained by the memory, "He was emotionally blocked. But he would talk to me for hours about movies and theater.'" Was there a connection between John Howard Lawson's difficulty in expressing emotions to his son and his powerful imaginative ability to manufacture emotion on a blank sheet of paper?[5]

John Howard Lawson was single-minded. "In our house there were thousands of books," his son recalled. "My father devoured books. Yet many were read only partly through," as he had gleaned whatever it is he wanted and had no need to see it through to the end. When Jeffrey Lawson was twelve, he and his father went to see *The Count of Monte Cristo,* but "after 20 minutes, my father informed me that it was obvious from [what] had already appeared on the screen how the plot would turn out and therefore [there was] no point in staying for the rest of the film. I ranted and raged, but he insisted we leave." The younger Lawson "couldn't understand how all he wanted from that film was an intellectual grasp and as soon as he had that he wished to go on to something else." His father "never knew the baseball scores or who was in the World Series. . . . I'm not sure he really knew there was a World Series."[6]

Jeffrey Lawson describes his father in terms akin to how John Howard Lawson describes his own. The expressive screenwriter asserts that his father "maintained an angry silence about everything connected with his childhood," a period evidently replete with angst. Just as Jeffrey Lawson describes his father in less than complimentary terms, John Howard Lawson says of his grandfather that he was "dissipated and irresponsible," not least since he "deserted his wife and children, leaving them in straitened circumstances." Just as Jeffrey Lawson felt a kind of abandonment, John Howard Lawson's father felt "unwanted" and "ran away at the age of fifteen. He went to the Far West where he spent more than a decade of hungry wandering." He encountered his father again in the late 1890s, "destitute and in rags, dying in a Bowery lodging house." By that time Lawson's father, rather affluent, "had become the main support of his mother and sisters and brothers."

Lawson's father had become "comparatively wealthy"—which meant that Lawson grew up with few unfulfilled desires, at least materially. This was accomplished in the face of formidable anti-Jewish barriers. For example, Halstead, the school Lawson attended in Yonkers, "had never had a Jewish pupil"; Lawson's "father found that [his daughter] was snubbed by her class-mates and he reacted in the only way that was open to him." He bought a carriage to further impress, or perhaps intimidate, the bigots; it was a "stupendous vehicle," and the "fairy coach wrought its magic. Every child in the school wanted to ride in it."

In their eye-catching carriage, Lawson and his family would travel from their huge apartment. "The whole ground floor, running through from Seventy-second to Seventy-first Street, was a big foyer, with Oriental rugs and massive furniture, never used by anyone and empty except for the uniformed attendants. . . . [O]ur apartment on the eleventh floor had a wonderful view of the New York Central railroad yards and the river." There was a governess, of course, and "dinner was a Victorian ritual." Lawson's abstemious father "never smoked or drank" but "insisted on strict observance of the [Jewish] dietary laws."

Lawson did well in school, particularly "in elocution," though his "failure to make close friends may have been due to" his "Jewish background," though he "was hardly aware" of this explanation at the time. He was consumed, however, with a round-robin of attendance at "concerts, art exhibitions, operas and theatres."

In 1906, the eleven-year-old Lawson made the grand tour of Europe, visiting London, The Hague, Amsterdam, Berlin, Dresden, and other metropolises. A visit to Shakespeare's grave seemed to have left a deep impression, for upon returning home he began to read plays and "see productions." At the age of thirteen—he gives the date precisely as 22 January 1908—he began writing his first play, though he later claimed that his career as a playwright had begun at the age of six. Whatever the case, there is little question that Lawson was precocious in his taking up the pen, keeping an extensive diary of his European tour, maintaining detailed notes on drama and dramatic construction at the age of thirteen, sending evocative letters to his governess at the age of ten.[7]

By the age of fourteen he had also written a thoughtful play, *Savitri*.[8] He continued to pursue this fascination with India in *A Hindoo Love Drama*, written a few years later,[9] though he conceded the plot was derivative.[10] Even early in his teen years, John Howard Lawson was determined to become a successful writer.

.   .   .

Nestled comfortably in the picturesque Berkshire Mountains of western Massachusetts, Williams College provides an outstanding balance of natural splendor and cultural vitality. Lawson enrolled in this posh school at the age of sixteen. However, Williams was a rather homogeneous environment: there was "one Negro student." "Jews were not admitted to fraternities," in addition to being subjected to quotidian indignities. Most of Lawson's friends were "not Jewish," though this did not spare him from the lash of discrimination. At the first meeting of the leading student publication, "the editor in charge of the competition remarked that Jews were not wanted on the paper." Lawson was furious—he was "seized with icy fear." "It forced me to admit my Jewish identity," something that theretofore had not been foremost in his consciousness. This also was a boost to his budding political-mindedness, for it was then, in 1912, that he "joined a campus group supporting Teddy Roosevelt and his Bull Moose Party." Shortly thereafter he joined the Socialist Club.

He also was developing other interests. In 1913 he began to pay attention to a rapidly developing art form: cinema. The "time will come," the teenager announced portentously, "when the Nickelodeon will have its classics, no less prominent than their theatrical rivals." His discoveries also included romance. At the age of eighteen he dated a French-Canadian girl—a new experience in more ways than one, since to that point he "had never been in a working class household." Later he was engaged to a young woman who eventually joined the Ziegfeld Follies, but this romance did not end well. The woman rejected him, creating a "lasting effect" on his "character, creating an ambivalent attitude toward sex."[11]

That year, 1913, was also pivotal in another way. A prelude to his joining the Socialist Club occurred that fall when his brother, Wendell, just back from a voyage to Germany, brought him a copy of Karl Kautsky's *The Class Struggle*. According to one account, "This book gave Lawson his first knowledge of Marx and Marxism, with which he first disagreed, though he brought Kautsky's book to Socialist Club meetings and, to the faculty sponsor's annoyance, quoted from it as a basis for discussion."[12]

But Lawson was not just attending political meetings and citing daring literature. He was a prolific and ambitious writer, penning poems, plays, and papers, often writing under the assumed name "Vox Literatuae," shrouding his identity, just as years later he shrouded certain controversial political affiliations.[13] After leaving college, graduating at the age of nineteen in 1914, he was "employed for several months in the New York branch of Reuters"—his father was helpful here, of course—while he "employed his free time in writing plays."[14] His play *Standards* (1914) "presented the first condemnation in the American theatre of the cult of efficiency, of the antihuman aspects of the rigid old-time religionists and a critique of the harmful influence of advertising in American life."[15]

As a budding writer, Lawson learned early on how to deal with rejection. Though Budd Schulberg and others were to spear him for his often acidic evaluations of their work, a tendency that was ascribed to his Leninism, the fact is that the literary culture from which he emerged was dripping with tartness. The American Academy of Dramatic Arts was not happy with his "three act play called 'Souls,'" rebuking not only the play but the playwright as well.[16]

By 1916 he was in Los Angeles complaining sourly about the "criticisms" of his latest play, which were "merciless." But, unlike some who were later subjected to his barbs, he was "far from being discouraged" but was convinced of something else. "I am a good playwright," he said with confidence. "I'm wide awake to my difficulties"; the problem was "the leading parts are acted badly." Lacerating actors for misinterpreting and misunderstanding his work was to become a staple for Lawson—and other writers, for that matter.[17]

Around the same time he had finished his first full-fledged play. Appropriately given his later trajectory, it concerned a "dramatist about to be evicted." He was "not yet twenty-one" and was attracting attention from producers. That same year, 1915, he finished another play, *The Spice of Life*, whose action occurs on a "wealthy woman's wedding day: the first act is drawing room comedy." Another drama, *Servant-Drama-Love*, about an "Irish Cinderella" of the slums, brought him face-to-face with the political economy of the theater. "A few minutes before the curtain rose," a bemused Lawson recounted, "[the director] asked me for a percentage of my royalties, as payment for his help on the script. We argued as if millions were involved. I have often regretted that I refused to give him anything. Two hours later, I offered him half my royalties and he accepted without enthusiasm."

On another occasion a director of one of his early plays "gave me a tumbler of whiskey and said he would give me any amount of money if I would withdraw and sign over all my rights in the play to him. . . . I told him he could have it for one hundred thousand dollars. We bargained gravely and finished several bottles of whiskey." Then the two agreed on "eighty thousand dollars." Lawson knew "of course" that his interlocutor "did not have eighty cents." Still, Lawson's "lifelong concern with the function of the author, with his rights and responsibilities," stems from these experiences; these experiences compelled him to stray from having "accepted other people's values" for "it turned out that they had no values."[18]

Getting this play off the ground also led Lawson into intriguing places. Producers took one look at the work and asked him to rewrite it. Rapidly becoming inured to criticism, Lawson was still "hurt" but in search of enlightenment nonetheless. He took the bus to Santa Barbara. Once there, he recalled, "I climbed a steep hill to a country club where [his producer] and [actor] John Barrymore were spending a few weeks. They were surprised but courteous. They gave me dinner [and] a great deal of whiskey." A bit tipsy, Lawson was determined to share his manuscript, although his voice "was fuzzy after dinner." The producer listened while Barrymore "snored." The producer then stated the play needed revision, as Lawson "tried to persuade him" otherwise. "His voice became cold," and this may have jolted Barrymore out of his snoozing, because he then "began his own soliloquy on the unspeakable state of the theatre."[19]

Writing plays may have been intellectually, creatively, and alcoholically stimulating, but at his level, it was far from being exceedingly profitable. Barely twenty, Lawson signed a contract in 1915 that called for a flat payment of $500 for production of his play *The Butterfly Lady* in the United States and Canada; in addition, he was to receive 5 percent of the weekly gross of the first $5,000, 7.5 percent of the next $3,000, and 10 percent of anything over $8,000—not too shabby given the times, but it definitely helped that Lawson had a father who could subsidize his muse.[20] This lack of income was surpassed by the attention that Lawson the wunderkind was beginning to attract from the press.[21]

He was consorting with the brightest lights of Broadway, a golden route laid out before him. But, barely twenty-one, he gave it all up for the adventure of going to Europe to aid his nation's war effort, as an ambulance driver.[22] Taking out a passport, the five foot seven Lawson, a man with large eyes and square chin, repaired to Italy, then France, working on behalf of the Red Cross.[23] He joined the ambulance corps, he argued later, to "avoid the draft." He was, he said, "opposed to the war," though "public refusal to serve would have jeopardized [his] father's position with Reuter's." When he arrived in France, "the smell of death changed to the bitter-sweet smell of mustard gas." As for many other intellectuals, the war—supposedly fought to make the world "safe for democracy"—had a transforming impact on his consciousness, accelerating his rapid movement to the left, just as it provided a larger storehouse of ideas for his dramas. Lawson, in fact, was a charter member of the fabled "Lost Generation." In western Europe he met John Dos Passos, who for a while was his boon companion, before he went on to fame as a leading novelist, then conservative. They had "become close friends," not least because of "similarities in our backgrounds," though at that juncture "in politics as well as art, Dos was far beyond me."[24]

The critic Alfred Kazin described Dos Passos, a prolific writer of Portuguese descent, as "diffident, shy, elaborately hesitant, an elusively upper-class man who had passed through Choate and Harvard"; he was the "illegitimate child" of a man who "became one of the favorite lawyers of the rich" and a "Republican stalwart" besides. He was made to order for rebellion, but unlike Lawson's, his did not last.[25]

"Like all the men and women of my generation, the first World War was the matrix of my creative life. I remember," Lawson noted later, "sitting on a haystack behind the lines of Northern France in the golden fall of 1917. The thunder of the front was a distant rumbling. Three young men had just bought three clean notebooks. And each of us opened his book at a blank page. John Dos Passos wrote the words, 'one man's imitation.' Robert [Hillyer] began a poem. I wrote the words 'Roger Bloomer' the imagined name of a young man coming out of the American Middle West in search of life." At that juncture, Ernest Hemingway was "already in Italy," and e. e. cummings "was imprisoned." They "were to follow different roads but for all of us," he observed, "the experience of war brought us face to face with the breakdown of the values which [we] had been taught to regard as the stable and permanent foundations of our society."[26]

Lawson also entered into a passionate relationship during his sojourn abroad. Kate Drain was a scant year older than he and from a similarly privileged background. She was from a prominent Spokane family—her father was a lawyer and banker—and she too had traveled widely abroad. They married in November 1918 and divorced in 1924, producing one son, Alan Drain Lawson, a sculptor and stage technician. Her relationship to the "blacklisted" Lawson did not prevent her from attaining heights of her own in Hollywood, appearing as an actress as late as 1951 in *How to Marry a Millionaire* and serving as a costume designer for the notorious right-winger Bob Hope for his 1950s television show. In fact, she spent more than two profitable decades with Hope.

When Lawson and Kate Drain met in Europe, she was a "volunteer nurse's aide," a move facilitated by her powerful father, the "adjutant general" of the state of Washington. "Dos" was a "very dear friend" of hers, as well as a friend of her soon-to-be spouse. She had a "little apartment in Paris, a little sort of a room and a cuby [*sic*] corner, and [for] some reason," she was "allowed in the gang" led by Dos Passos and Lawson. She met Lawson in Rome. "He was the head of a little magazine that they were doing. We were very much in love," she recalled wistfully.

Their marriage was rather surreptitious; Lawson still under his thumb, "didn't want his father to know me at all." The Lawsons' son was born in 1919 and it seemed that they were well on their way to marital bliss. But the youthful Lawson rapidly lost interest in his new bride. "He didn't care much for me," she confided later. Lawson, she said, "was restless and he didn't like being married after he got home." He was "quite definite about it and wanted to be free. He said I stultified his creative urge, which is a pretty fancy line, [so] he just one day came in and said, 'I don't like being married and I'm leaving. . . . I want a divorce. I want to be free.' And I had such confidence in him at that time, such faith in him, that I thought, 'well, if I'm blocking anything, I better get out quickly because it's too good a man to miss, to lose in the shuffle.'"

Then there was Sue Edmonds. She often found Sue "sitting on the door[step] of the apartment we had in New York"—"quite a lot before he threw me out." Still saddened by it all decades later, Kate Drain conceded that "it broke my heart, incidentally. I've never gotten over it." Despite the peremptory manner in which Lawson treated her, she admitted candidly months before his passing—when they were both well into their ninth decade—"I'm still in love with the man, which is kind of ridiculous but charming."

She was also with him when his life was indelibly marked. They were working on a play, collaborating with Augustin Duncan, "brother of Isadora." "[W]e were living—we lived in the summertime," recalled Kate Drain Lawson, "up near Haverstraw. . . . [W]e were all driving in an automobile one night and the car went off the road . . . and threw us all out into a field and broke Jack's leg very badly. . . . [H]e spent that summer in the hospital with a very badly broken upper leg or something or other. And I kept house and took care of the baby which had arrived a short time before."[27]

From that point forward, John Howard Lawson—Jewish, left-handed, short, big-nosed—had another distinguishing characteristic: he walked with a noticeable limp. These distinctive characteristics, like the defective eye of the novelist Alice Walker,[28] or the halting speech of the writer Budd Schulberg, helped to provide Lawson with a sense of being different and with it a sensitivity to humanity that often shone through in his fictional creations. But Kate Lawson's recollections of her former husband also capture another critical element of his life, for he did go on to marry Sue Edmonds, and they remained together—despite numerous travails—until he took his last breath.

A Texan who attended Baylor University, Sue Edmonds then had a "beautiful mop of red-gold curls" that sat as a crown on an "expression of a certain rebellious and innocent deviltry."[29] She was from a rough-and-tumble frontier family, her grandfather in the mid–nineteenth century was part of a wagon train west—that came into sharp conflict with Native Americans.[30]

His own conflicted love life aside, these few years spent in Europe had left a lasting imprint on Lawson, not only because of the birth of his son Alan and early friendship with a man, Dos Passos, who turned out to be one of the major U.S. writers of the century. It was in January 1920, shortly after his return from Europe, that he sold his play *The Spice of Life* to Paramount for $5,000—a sum that convinced him, if there had ever been any doubt, that he could survive as a creative writer.[31] Even if he had not been so blessed, Lawson retained other options. He had "no money problem" at that time, since his "father was . . . glad to advance whatever was needed." Hence, when he returned from his European jaunt he rented temporarily from painter Rockwell Kent an "apartment on the parlor floor of a brownstone on Fifteenth Street near Seventh Avenue" in Manhattan. His plan was to make his "permanent home in Paris." Lawson was "not unhappy" in the City of Light. He "wandered about the city. [I] danced in small taverns and in the streets. [I] dined well and picturesquely." He made friendships, two of which—with Edna St. Vincent Millay and Ezra Pound—"had a memorable effect" on his thinking, though he found the future fascist "difficult to understand," whereas Pound found Lawson's questions "stupid," as he felt literature was the "answer to all problems."[32]

Lawson's recollections encapsulate another aspect of his persona: his restlessness, especially in his early years, which contrasted with—and may have perversely generated—the deep sense of commitment he developed as a mature adult. He was trying to ride simultaneously two different horses going in different directions. Thus, in the summer of 1918 he and Kate Drain "were together constantly," not least since he desired a "rich emotional life"—yet he "feared marriage as a loss of 'freedom'" and "felt constricted by domesticity." At times he left her, as when he decamped to Le

Havre "and found a room in a house on a cliff above the sea a few miles north of the town" to work on a play. When he was away from her, which was often, his "marriage . . . began to go to pieces."

Lawson gave all appearances of being a self-indulgent and confused scion of a prominent family; certainly, he gave little indication of becoming what some viewed as a dogmatic, doctrinaire Marxist. He was in Paris at the same time that W. E. B. Du Bois was there on behalf of his Pan African Congress, but Lawson, an intellectual dabbler, a man who hailed from cosmopolitan Manhattan and considered France a second home, had "never heard of Du Bois or of the meetings he organized."[33]

Thus his wife may not have been surprised by Lawson's subsequent choice to flit around Europe in the aftermath of the war, soaking up both ideas and atmosphere. Groucho Marx once quipped that "every American who has gone Communist or anti–United States should and would be cured by spending a few years in Europe. I have met ever so many expatriates over here, who would give years of their life could they go back home again."[34] It was unlikely that Lawson was on Marx's mind when he crafted these words, since Lawson's transatlantic journey was far from enervating. Just before his twenty-sixth birthday, in 1921, he was in Antwerp—en route to Liverpool—and enjoying himself immensely.[35]

Lawson spent "three desolate weeks in Vienna," desperately seeking a meeting with Sigmund Freud, but "he was away." He walked "mile after mile through working class districts" in an Austria not far from being on the cusp of the Holocaust. At that point in his life "the only entertainment that interested" him there was "presented in a small theatre," where he was shaken by his encounters with "the Futurists."[36] The theatrical innovation for which he became notorious—with the debut of *Processional* particularly—was influenced profoundly by his jaunts around Europe.

While Lawson's relationship with his first wife seemed to be troubled from its inception, it seemed that his ties to Dos Passos were of a radically different character. A shy man well on his way to baldness, Dos Passos "had a long puffy face that made him look like an 'elongated squirrel'"; he also suffered from a speech impediment that caused him to lisp slightly. He was straitlaced and bookish and took himself quite seriously.[37] It "wasn't long," said Dos Passos, "before Jack and I were telling each other how, when we got home from the war, we would turn the New York theater inside out." Like literary roustabouts, they caroused around Europe together. Dos Passos, whose Portuguese origins paralleled the outsider status of his friend's Jewishness, recalled that Lawson was so taken by the "Neapolitan ladies," found them so fascinating, "we had to leave him behind when we started out on foot to Pompeii." They were departing "when a horse cab drove up at a gallop. There he was, chipper and shaved and bursting with a whole Arabian Night's entertainment . . . of Neapolitan adventures." The peripatetic Lawson migrated from the ambulance corps to a "Red Cross publicity job that kept him in Rome in some splendor during the rest of the war." While in France, Lawson had a room on the Quai de la Tournelle. "I don't remember what his putative occupation was," said Dos Passos, "but most of his energy was going into writing a play. Before and after dinner I'd read him parts of *Three Soldiers* and he'd read scenes from what was to turn into *Roger Bloomer*." At that juncture, Kate Drain, a "handsome strapping girl" with the "finest brown eyes and level brows you ever saw," was part of this threesome. At this point, Dos Passos was "absolutely intoxicated with Lawson's dramatic style and swore he would turn out the greatest playwright ever." Confident of the future, they "ate well and drank well and loaned each other money when we ran out." They "led a fine life," as "Paris was full of music that spring." They "listened to the chansonniers at the *boites de nuit.*" They "raved over Charpentier's opera *Louise* and suffered at the Comedie Francaise." Yes, said Dos Passos, still savoring the experience years later, "we led a fine life."

The revel was hardly interrupted when they all decamped across the Atlantic to Manhattan. Lawson "with his plays and his lady friends"—of which there seemed to be a profusion, both before and after his marriage—"and his enthusiasms and outré convictions and his willingness in those days to argue any topic on any side at the drop of the hat, was a three-ring circus. His sister, Adelaide, roamed in and out in her Gypsy way, paying no attention to all the pretentious nonsense talked around her, interested only in putting how things looked to her on canvas." Dawn Powell, the underrated writer who was to become Lawson's loving muse—and vice versa—was part of this enchanting circle. According to Dos Passos, she was "one of the wittiest and most dashingly courageous women I ever knew." There was a time when "Whittaker Chambers, . . . then a spooky little guy on hush-hush missions as a Communist Party courier, flitted in and out." Ernest Hemingway, F. Scott Fitzgerald, and other founding members of the Lost Generation were hovering about. It was almost as if they were all consciously seeking to provide each other with material for their various novels and plays. They sat around dinner tables and in taverns engaging in witty banter, since "conversation in the early twenties had to be one wisecrack after another. Cracks had to fly back and forth continually like the birds in badminton."[38]

Such an ambience seemed to be tailored with Lawson in mind, as his plays, then screenplays, came to be known for their scintillating dialogue.

Such was the case with the play that helped to cement his early celebrity. *Roger Bloomer* hit Manhattan in 1923 like a thunderclap. Lawson had returned to the United States from a trip abroad in the late summer of 1923, and, as he observed later, "it seemed as if a door closed behind me on Europe and another door opened on the universe. . . . I was ignorant of history and I was ill-informed about time and space." He spent most of his "time on the ship returning to the United States reading *The Waste Land* and *Ulysses*" and found that "both books offered me technical lessons for drama"—many of which found their way into *Roger Bloomer*.[39]

The eponymous lead character of this play runs away from his prosperous Iowa home to New York after failing his college examinations. He falls in love with a woman accused of theft at a place where she works—and she commits suicide. He is arrested for murder, and his father hurries to the big city to rescue him.[40] The parallels to Lawson's own life—moving to New York, suicide, the protective father—are evident.

Lawson had written of what he knew, but reviews were mixed[41]—though one critic implicitly compared him to theatrical giants: "Every healthy movement in creative literature begins with 'storm and stress . . . its wildness and overwrought passion and excess.' So the young Marlowe began, so the young Goethe."[42] And so the young Lawson. Similarly aroused were Edna St. Vincent Millay and John Dos Passos, who rallied to his side.[43]

Slightly autobiographical, the play depicts a well-raised country boy whose father owns the one big apartment store in an Iowa town of thirty-five thousand inhabitants, who finds his surroundings too provincial, too uniform, too conventional, and thus departs for Manhattan. Once engulfed in this metropolis, which is pictured as more forbidding than it actually is, he goes to pieces and has visions of witches, biers, and goblins.[44] The play offers presentiments of Lawson's future. Bloomer's father remarks, "Anybody who's a little different from everybody else gets it in the neck. That boy is fixing up to get it in the neck." Another character notes that there were "not too many Socialists at these State colleges." A Yale student blares, "Look at me! Senior year, I'm sure of the best club. Simple rule: I always kept away from Jews, highbrows and guys that eat with their knives." Later he flashed his class credentials, chirping, "This year I'm traveling with a society girl, a sort of society girl." Capitalist society is portrayed as robotic, soulless. Says one character, "There are only two things in New York, Sex and Money—if you get one, you get the other." A judge asks Roger Bloomer, "Are you a socialist?" He replies no and is hit with the rejoinder "Lucky for you . . . [for] a man of your age. . . . It's anarchical: where is our young manhood going?"[45] The blunt airing of ideological laundry hit Broadway like a bazooka. The play consisted of "thirty or forty short scenes. Some of these are acted in front of drops painted in distorted fashion, some against black velvet."[46]

Almost instantaneously, Lawson's drama was associated with the nascent school of expressionism, then gaining popularity in Europe.[47] It was the "first American expressionist drama," says the analyst Bernard Dick; it "might even be called modified expressionism: it has the basic features— short scenes that flow into each other, sometimes giving the impression of concurrent action; aphoristic dialogue that barely avoids being apocalyptic; fragmented plot; half-formed thoughts and unfinished sentences of a phantasmagoric ending." Lawson's deep knowledge of the arts was revealed here, as in this work "the ghosts of Wedekind, Kaiser, Stravinsky's 'Rites of Spring' and Aeschylus hover in the background." *Roger Bloomer* was cinematic in its sparkling dialogue and its quick cuts from scene to scene— virtually a movie on stage and a signal to the movie industry that would soon require such talent. It also displayed a theme that was to mark much of Lawson's later work and support an "indefinite variety of plots: boy/girl, rendered not so much in romantic as in social terms," a theme that would emerge in his movies, for example, "heiress/miner *(Dynamite)*, adventuress/peasant *(Blockade)* and femme fatale/thief *(Algiers)*." Lawson the theorist would describe this as a "root idea," which could "branch out in enough directions to create a varied system."[48] Decades after this play's production, Lawson continued to insist that "the thing that always concerns me deeply" was the "form or structure" of a work.[49]

Lawson was steaming ahead. Having tasted the best that Europe had to offer and having savored the sweet success of Broadway, he was brimming with confidence, writing with a "consciousness of my class, as one who was in it and not outside it." He was drawing lines, too, feeling a "kinship" with the future Communist poet Walter Lowenfels that he "could not feel with [e. e.] cummings because cummings seemed to offer a false picture of himself—the I in lower case concealing the colossal ego."

Before *Roger Bloomer*, Lawson was a "cipher," but "now it was taken for granted that sooner or later [he] would become an important person in the theatre establishment." He was being seen in all the "right" places, socializing on the Upper East Side of Manhattan, not far from where he had been raised. Greenwich Village, south of these environs, and a bastion of avantgarde artists living amid winding streets, had become his habitat. There a "continuous party that was either in progress or about to be started again" was the norm. Lawson "drank immoderately," also the norm. He was still a buddy of Dos Passos, though he "came and went relentlessly," but "when he was in New York, he spent a great deal of time" with his old friend. "Abstractly," the novelist with a growing reputation "hated money people, but he got along better with them" than Lawson did. "He was also ready to escape whenever he faced complications which threatened to become onerous. He was likely to hurry away on a moment's notice. On one occasion, he announced as Sue and he and I were riding in a taxi that he had to take a ship leaving in an hour. He had an appointment he explained 'to take tea with some old ladies in London.'" Lawson and his companion waited while Dos Passos "packed his bags and rushed . . . to the boat. He did not have enough money for the ticket, so Sue loaned him a hundred dollars."

But Lawson seemed as odd as Dos Passos, at least to some. Success had not brought him peace of mind. He confessed to having "plagued Sue with my frantic instability. . . . [A friend] consulted William Carlos Williams about me, asking him if he could suggest any medical or psychological clues to my ambivalent conduct."[50]

He was grappling with James Joyce's *Ulysses*, attracted in part— seemingly—because studying it "seemed like a gesture of rebellion. It was banned in the United States and the book had to be hidden when I passed the customs." But traipsing through Joyce's word puzzles seemed to leave him even more unsettled. He fled for Pittsburgh, simply "because" he "wanted to encounter an American reality that was not visible in New York." Yet he found no key to his ennui there, returning to Manhattan in late 1924 to be a "member of an Honorary Committee at the laying of the cornerstone of the new Guild Theatre on 52nd Street." This recognition signified his growing importance as a playwright, though neither that nor rubbing shoulders with Governor Al Smith, who gave the main address, brought him a settled state of mind. He and Sue Edmonds were having their ups and downs; dumping Kate Drain had brought no particular happiness either, since the new "relationship was not free from emotional tensions." By his own admission, Lawson was "moody and somewhat cruel," continuing to "feel 'threatened' by a love that gave promise of lasting a lifetime." Kate Drain, now the "other" woman, was living near him in the Village with Alan; she "had no objections and no demands," which was fortunate, since Lawson probably would not have been capable of meeting either.[51] He was now smitten with Sue Edmonds, just as a few years earlier he had been taken with Kate Drain. Sue Edmonds had her own problems. Her parents "emigrated from Scotland, lived in Virginia and then moved" to Texas. Her son, Jeffrey Lawson, recalls his mother as being "very sensitive"; she "had problems accepting the rough-hewn macho world dominated by Texas males. At about twenty she went to New York City, attended Columbia University," and, like, her future husband, "became friends with e. e. cummings."[52]

Lawson was restless, roaming socially (marrying one woman, then dropping her for another) and otherwise (traveling almost aimlessly to Pittsburgh, then back to Manhattan). But through it all, he remained anchored—committed—to his desk and typewriter, continuing to tap his creative muse. While waiting for his next play, *Processional*, to debut, he "wrote six or eight hours of every day in Patchin Place," his residence in southern Manhattan. It was then that he "developed the plan of *The Pure in Heart.*" He was ransacking his experiences and his mind for other play ideas; as he listened to Governor Smith ramble on at the laying of the cornerstone of the Guild Theatre, he "wondered" about Otto Kahn, soon to be his benefactor, "running for governor, and a play came to mind fully formed and titled; it was a glib idea for a play" concerning a millionaire seeking this high office. This turned out to be *Loudspeaker*. This fertile imagination was bringing Lawson no settled mind, however. He "thought of the play as a mad tea party," but "the question to which there was no answer was—what was I doing there?" (i.e., listening to Smith). "I would ask the same question in Hollywood several years later," he added. "Everything I had written had been a protest against authority," befitting an artist deemed to be the epitome of the avant-garde. Yet "here I was in the lap of the establishment," on Broadway, hailed in the bourgeois press, rubbing elbows with Governor Smith and Otto Kahn. He was consorting with those against whom he was supposedly rebelling—and doing it inconsistently at that. He "had voted in the presidential election of 1916 to celebrate" coming "of age"—but "never again until 1932." What manner of rebellion was this?[53]

Wrestling more definitely with this knotty problem would come later. For now it was enough that *Processional* was debuting. Again, by his own admission, Lawson was expanding the bounds of dramatic form, seeking to "lay the foundations of some sort of native technique, to reflect to some extent the color and movement of the American processional, as it streams about us. The rhythm is staccato, burlesque, carried out by a formalized arrangement of jazz music." Originally presented in January 1925 with George Abbott, Lee Strasberg, and Alvah Bessie in the cast, it also contained elements that would cause Lawson some discomfort later. Revealing an underdeveloped political mind, there was an offensively stereotypical Negro character, Rastus Jolly ("one lonesome nigger Boss, wid a heart full a' care an' desecration") and another ethnically questionable figure named "Dago Joe". A Ku Klux Klan character, not portrayed favorably, nonetheless wails provocatively, "Clean up the dirty foreigners, make 'em kiss the flag! Skin the Jews, lynch the niggers, make 'em kiss the flag!" But Lawson

FIGURE 1. At one time, Lawson—who had been one of the closest friends of the novelist John Dos Passos—was considered the "hope" of the theater and an avant-garde dramatist. After he began writing screenplays, however, he correspondingly wrote fewer plays. (Courtesy of Library of Congress)

was groping for something else, with references in this play to an "Armenian Bolsheviki" and a "new sun risin.'" "What's that?" was the question posed by one of his characters. "The proletariat," was the quick reply.[54] Lawson admitted that "a writer often creates himself or part of himself in his characters," and this work was exemplary of this tendency, reflecting as it did Lawson's divided heart.[55]

It was a "jazz" play in its free form, and it was also radical in its blunt invocation of class conflict as a theme. It "created an enormous sensation and had an enormous impact on the theatre," Lawson conceded decades later. It "marked a break with the conventional theatre. I set to 'push out the walls of the theatre.' In a way there's some resemblance to the work that Bertolt Brecht has done. . . . the use of music, the use of jazz is very striking." Then there was the subject matter, "the labor movement," "material [that] had never before been brought into the theatre in that way, especially with the violence and crudity with which the strike situation and the struggle around it is treated." *Processional* included the "use of almost a film technique in the chase [which] was also very striking in the play." Opening night for this extravaganza was "an absolute uproar. The audience was literally swept off its feet," though it played "only 14 weeks."[56]

While visiting Vienna, Lawson had sought vainly to meet Freud. Here Freud appeared as if by magic on stage, represented by the "many elements of Freudian symbolism" in this work.[57]

Lawson's own personal drama continued as the play opened. He had been allocated "six seats in the balcony, and six or eight in the orchestra." He "gave the upstairs seats to people who were closest to me, including Sue [Edmonds] and Dos [Passos] and my sister; the orchestra tickets were given to influential or wealthy friends." Sue Edmonds was "deeply hurt and told me so." Lawson was "upset by the argument, because it exposed weaknesses in me which went far deeper than the foolish disposal of first-night tickets. " Lawson, the rebel, the avant-garde writer, wanted something quite conventional: "I wanted success; I wanted prestige; and the uproar over *Processional* fed my vanity and at the same time posed my creative problem." Lawson was trapped within a contradiction, and it was only less squishiness about commitment that would lead to his being released. "I proclaimed my opposition to people who held power, including those who controlled the theatre. Yet I was dependent on them and in my personal contacts I liked them and tried to conciliate them. . . . Sue saw that I deceived myself and she was angry at the deception." Lawson "could not resolve the conflict between my ambitions and my ideals and so I deceived myself about both." His idealism was empty, simply "pretension and romantic." Flagellating himself, Lawson cried, "I pretended that I could fulfill my ambition without paying the price. . . . my creative problem was related to the concrete question of money." He was now thirty, yet "there had only been brief periods when I had supported myself and my family." The roaring rebel was "dependent on my father," while "Sue earned a good income in department store advertising." He was "shamed" by it all, particularly the "generosity" of his father. "I could find no way to talk to him about my writing or its future course. . . . we could never bring ourselves to speak of it, or of anything else that was close to our hearts." His angst caused him to strike out at the person he loved: "Sue was the storm-center of my miseries. I made life intolerable for her. Since I held that the intensity of my feeling for her interfered with my writing, she decided that a separation would be good for both of us," so "she left for Europe."

The night of her departure was filled with gloom for him that a "wildly intemperate party on the forward deck of the 'Homeric'" could not hide. "Yos Kuniyoshi and his wife, Katinka, were on the same ship and my sister and Dos and everyone we knew were there to celebrate," but symbolizing his unsteady state, Lawson "almost fell off the boat." "I woke up in Jack Cowles' apartment," he recalled, still embarrassed, "with a devastating hangover and a feeling that I had made a fool of myself."

His life resembled a chaotic "processional"—"eight hours of work, dissipation in the evenings, week-ends at rich houses." It was this state of disordered bewilderment that was reflected in his play *Nirvana*, which he then began writing. The play concerned in part "an American intellectual facing the total collapse of moral values," the dilemma of the Lost Generation, though he was "less manic than [F. Scott] Fitzgerald." Yet he "was caught in the same maze of money and the imminence of hysteria" as was e. e. cummings. One evening the two "knocked on the wall that separated our room in Patchin Place" in Manhattan, "and we proceeded to spend a wild night together." Finally, like a man reaching out for a life raft, Lawson made a stab at commitment, marrying Sue Edmonds after her return from Europe; "for me it was a refuge and a hope," though he "made the first years difficult." His father handed him a hefty $12,000, "telling me it was mine and I could buy any property I wanted," and a similar amount to his sister. These gestures made Lawson think his father "had an inexhaustible supply of money," but "actually his only income came from the house he owned on Fortieth Street near Sixth Avenue," prime real estate to be sure. "He also [owned] the ten lots near the ocean at Belle Harbor." Lawson "used the money for a down-payment on a house on Waverly Place near Washington Square. The total price was $60,000."[58]

Patchin Place had been no prize. Peaceful and picturesque with iron-gated mews nestled just off Tenth Street and Sixth Avenue in the bawdy, rowdy Greenwich Village, it was variously the home of Djuana Barnes and Theodore Dreiser, among others. There were ten narrow row houses in a tiny, gloomy court snuggled beside a central shopping district. The neat oyster gray row houses were guarded by gaslight lampposts and ailanthus trees, serenely removed from the cacophony of the streets. They were built in 1848 as cheap boardinghouses for local workers before becoming residences for the chic. Though Lawson was only a sojourner there, cummings was to reside there until his death in 1962.[59] The buildings lacked utilities, with metered gas flares for light and heat, pumps for running water, and outhouses, "but the life there was shared and furniture emblazoned in fauve colors." There was a massive courthouse near Patchin Place, where like sentries gaudy prostitutes provided a nightly spectacle. The creative artists who flocked to Patchin Place could easily surmise—even though they were a short subway ride from munificence—that they were enduring the suffering that animated their fictional creations.[60]

Stumbling, bumbling, Lawson's inchoate life was reflected in an inchoate play. Despite its conspicuous weaknesses, *Processional* understandably excited audiences accustomed to much tamer fare. Sited in a West Virginia mining town in the throes of a strike and writhing under martial law, it features Rosie Cohen, daughter of a local merchant who succumbs to the lure of jazz and screeching horns. Still, the conservative writer, Kenneth Lloyd Billingsley was singularly unimpressed with this work, recalling sourly how it "featured children in overalls and masks ranting about the 'monster of capitalism' and screaming lines such as 'Dynamo! Dynamo!' and 'kill Henry Ford!'"[61]

Such carping was not accepted universally. One critic, after terming Lawson a "theatrical iconoclast," predicted boldly that "he may some day be a theatrical god."[62] Another felt the "awe of genius" after watching this play.[63] Robert Benchley may have gone too far in comparing him to Shakespeare.[64] Upton Sinclair was enthusiastic,[65] which Lawson found heartening.[66]

Lawson's friends Edna St. Vincent Millay, Donald Ogden Stewart, and John Dos Passos took out an advertisement as they sought to "urge everybody to see" this work. "We consider it one of the most thrilling plays ever written," they concluded unabashedly.[67] Sherwood Anderson told the world that this play "had inspired him to write for the theatre."[68] Another eminent critic called *Processional* "a Rhapsody in Red. . . . I had been present at the first performance of 'Rhapsody in Blue' in 1924 and I found it impressive as the personal statement of a serious art."High praise from such literary luminaries was thrilling—and an antidote to the pointed shafts of criticism about this innovative work.[70] Walter Winchell, the increasingly influential journalist, was aghast: "I have never seen anything so bad," adding that he was "being kind."[71] George Jean Nathan with derision called Lawson "the latest young playwright to parade the Rialto in his underwears with his Hemschweif hanging out." The *New York Times* was less hostile,[72] though Lawson felt compelled to register a "protest vote of one against your (to say the least) extravagant estimate."[73]

Overall, reviews were mixed, though the impact was large.[74] When the Theatre Guild staged a "public discussion" of the play in February 1925, "every seat was taken thirty minutes before the program began and many of the [Guild's] own subscribers had to be turned away." Reflective of the high esteem in which Lawson was held, Elmer Rice, Dorothy Parker, and Fanny Hurst spoke "most favorably as its champions"—but the "debate ranged strongly" as "there were violent speeches from the balcony [with] volleys of applause for both sides."[75]

Lawson, who was profoundly influenced by the theatrical experiments then coursing throughout Europe, sought to explain to the U.S. audience what was on his mind. Readers of the *New York Times* were instructed that "in the theatre more than in any other field, the experiment must be a living entity, move and quiver in the calcium glare. . . . I have endeavored to create a method which shall express the American scene in native idiom, a method as far removed from the older realism as from the facile mood of expressionism." This was not an "abstract theory"; it was driven by his perception that "the legitimate theatre seems without warmth or richness of method." It "has become the fashion," he lamented "to forget that the history of theatrical entertainment is a tradition of crowded movement, violent physical vitality." Already a close student of theatrical history, he reminded his readers that "if this outer movement ceases to exist a play might just as well be phrased in terms of sonnet sequence or a grammar of Esperanto. And, indeed, the average drawing room play"—then all the rage—"has about reached this point of absolute nullity—three walls with footlights on the fourth side, lifeless dialogue and improbable enunciation—these have become a fixed standard." Lawson had a different vision. "The blood and bones of a living stage," he thundered, "must be the blood and bones of the actuality stirring around us." The status quo meant a withering theater: "The floundering method of production," said Lawson, "makes the producer a lucky man if one out of five productions brings a reasonable profit. This gigantic game of chance can hardly be called a legitimate business. On the other hand we have the art theatre existing in a feeble trance totally removed from the rush and roar of things as they are, a sanctuary with doors barred against the world." But this "avant-garde" was no remedy, since "art as an escape from life is no better than morphine, rotary clubs, murder, speech-making, or any of the methods used by hundred-per-cent Americans to escape from actuality." Now his *Processional* was seeking to be the advanced guard of an accessible avant-garde: "The rhythm is staccato, burlesque, carried out by a formalized arrangement of jazz music." In this work Lawson sought to "lay the foundations of some sort of native technique, to reflect to some extent the color and movement of the American procession as it streams about us."[76]

Years later and despite its abject weaknesses, Lawson refused to repudiate *Processional* altogether. It was, he said in 1968, "still an important play, related to Brechtian drama and all the complex developments since that time—including 'happenings' and all the rest of it."[77] He was largely correct—and he could have added that his recognition of "jazz" was quite significant and important for this art form, which at that juncture was hardly given a respectful hearing and had yet to shake altogether its origins in brothels. Lawson had not been able to shake altogether, however, prevailing biases of the time, as he too conceded later, noting correctly that "the characters are stereotypes . . . the Negro playing his banjo, the Jewish storekeeper and his dancing daughter, the Polish radical talking about Marx." And, yes, the fact that there was "not a plot in the usual sense" was quite daring, liberating, and all that,[78] but this nonlinear approach could also leave theatergoers lost in a sea of confusion. This may shed light on why in 1966 Lawson concluded that it was "better not to include" this work in a published collection. "I have thought about it a great deal because it is a play of great and neglected significance," he said, "but the vaudeville or cartoon method I use includes caricature of Negro and Jewish personalities: this is presented as part of the raw crudity and violence of American life in the middle twenties, but it is so exaggerated that it has a very different and possibly unfortunate meaning in our world of the middle sixties." "I feel," he concluded, "I cannot publish a work which suggests racist stereotypes."[79]

But this Sargasso Sea of confusion that *Processional* represented was symptomatic of the floundering of Lawson himself—a man of no small material means who was becoming ever more critical of the system that had produced this wealth, a man with a felt desire for emotional engagement but who found it difficult to maintain a loving relationship with a woman. Yet his marriage to Sue Edmonds, a union that lasted for almost half a century, was a gigantic step toward a commitment that was to encompass all realms.

2 Toward Commitment

By the age of thirty, John Howard Lawson was something of a celebrity, an enfant terrible of Broadway, with critically celebrated productions generating a buzz of publicity and acclaim. But he was dissatisfied—with the state of the world and his ability to influence it. His marriage to Sue Edmonds was a landmark on his journey toward commitment, and his joining the Communist Party and organizing the Screen Writers Guild were to enhance this process: they were to bring him grief years later.

Yet that crucial turning point was years away, and in the meantime, Lawson was navigating life in pre-Depression New York, often in the company of similarly groping members of the Lost Generation, including Dos Passos and Hemingway. "The shock of the war had a profound effect on my thinking," he confessed, and he was particularly "moved [by] the early short plays of Eugene O'Neill." This combination had led him to write *Roger Bloomer*, whose "sensation" was encapsulated when "it almost caused a riot," and *Processional*, which deployed "techniques from vaudeville and even from burlesque." But tweaking the bourgeoisie was becoming stale rather quickly, especially since instead of being outraged, this powerful force seemed to absorb his blows by welcoming him as the latest celebrity—or freak show.[1] Lawson was becoming a regular on the lecture circuit, and publicity material meant to elicit invitations billed him as "the iconoclast among the current American playwrights. Probably no contemporary writer has been more extravagantly praised or more violently attacked."[2]

All true—but the radical as trained seal, performing for tossed coins, was insufficient for Lawson's gargantuan ambitions.

It was then that he "talked at some length with Ernest Hemingway on the last night before his departure for Europe. We were in the middle of a noisy party, and we were not sober, which made our conversation more intimate than usual. He was enormously pleased with himself, that evening he had concluded arrangement for publication of *The Sun Also Rises* and the taste of success was in his mouth. Yet he was insecure; his lack of confidence was embarrassingly manifested in rough talk about his own virility and the [women he hoped to bed]." The inebriated Illinoisan "spoke of his trans-Atlantic voyage as if it were a journey to Cytherea; he had even provided himself with an aphrodisiac and he showed me the small bottle." Lawson, who had spent a fair amount of time and effort of his own tracking down the fairer sex, may not have been in Hemingway's league but was hardly in a position to disapprove. Still, Lawson "took a rather dim view of his early work and had argued with Dos [Passos] about the short stories." Lawson, who had spent part of his youth literally in search of Freud, had little problem unpacking Hemingway's id. Reading Hemingway's just-completed novel, Lawson "recalled" their conversation and "related Jake's impotence to the bragging talk about sex. It made me realize how deep and shallow Hemingway was, how peculiarly American in his innocence and strength."[3]

Lawson's intimate encounters were at times vexed as well, though not taking the same route as the bedeviled Hemingway. Vivacious, quick-witted, and talented, Dawn Powell was the kind of woman who could easily excite the imagination. Dos Passos, with whom she, like Lawson, shared an intense friendship, called her "one of the wittiest and most dashingly courageous women I ever knew."[4] She was born in 1897 in Ohio and was of Welsh ancestry. One relative described her accurately as "pert, petite and devastatingly witty and astute." She may not have "enjoyed the same popularity with boys" as her sister, "the Gloria Swanson–like Mabel," but she was not pining for company either. "From the time she was quite small"— and remarkably like Lawson—she was "constantly writing her thoughts and ideas in notebooks and on the backs of old letters."[5] Like Lawson, she too was friendly with the protean intellectual Edmund Wilson, and also not unlike the radical screenwriter and playwright, her often pungent and poignant novels, as Wilson has observed, "are so much less well known than they deserve to be," not least due to her "almost complete indifference to publicity."[6] Her most authoritative biographer asserts that "one person in particular dominated Powell's thinking" in the 1920s: this was Lawson. He adds, "It is my own belief that the two had a passionate but highly secretive love affair between 1925 and 1929; at the very least Lawson influenced Powell's life profoundly in those years, for good and for ill." Yes, Lawson was married during the height of this operatic romance, which is why his decision for marriage was merely a stab at commitment. And, yes, Lawson was a man of many secrets—and not just his Communist Party membership. He was a man whose emotions were run ragged by the pre-mature death of his mother, then the suicide of his only brother, and the ex-pressive distance maintained by his father. He was then thrust into a dis-satisfying marriage and then—at least initially—an unsatisfactory one. He was intensely self-critical and disdained the unexamined life. This was not the ideal prescription for creation of a man of gentle probing—as some on the receiving end of his barbs in the Communist Party were to discover.

Lawson, it is said, "adopted, or strove to adopt, the position of the learned man, the sage, the thinker, the supreme analyzer who recognized the complex nature of situations and saw through, beneath and behind him." In "another era he might have been described as a sort of guru and he made an enormous impression on the distraught, insecure Dawn Pow-ell." This was a different Lawson from the one who emerged. He was to symbolize for some the epitome of Stalinism, but back then he had a "deep admiration for Leon Trotsky." A hatibué of the most bohemian sectors of Manhattan's Greenwich Village, his apartment just off Sixth Avenue and Tenth Street allowed him to cross paths frequently with the likes of his friend e. e. cummings, Djuana Barnes, and other imaginative artists and nonconformists—a list that decidedly included Powell. He had "become a mantric refrain in Powell's appointment book by late 1925"; in fact, his "was far and away the most common name in Powell's diaries for 1925, 1926 and 1927." This overlap with Lawson's marriage "made for some awk-ward moments," as the "two women evidently hated one another pretty much from the start."

This fiery love triangle was further inflamed, since Powell and Lawson "saw each other almost every day for several years." Lawson's son Jeffrey recalled later that when the family was living on Long Island, "'my father was always taking [a] train to New York and my mother was quite upset about it.'" The extremely self-assured Lawson, says his son, "'was a real ladies' man, combining a strong intellect with enormous vitality and ani-mal energy.'" Jeffrey Lawson, among his father's sternest critics, observes that as he grew older, John Howard Lawson "'felt very guilty about all he had put my mother through. By then, due in part to Communist discipline, he had become mechanistically moralistic.'" The complete rupture with Powell did not occur until "the mid-1930s," after he had joined the Com-munist Party. Moreover, the guilt he felt about this affair and the intense self-criticism he exhibited as a matter of everyday practice combined to cre-ate a man who often was as harsh with others as he was with himself.[7]

Mike Gold, Lawson's future Communist comrade, observed that "Com-munists are not Puritans. They have no false shame about sex, because it is a normal activity of human beings, it is a natural process, the device of sane, healthy old Mother Nature for continuing life on this planet."[8] There was something to Gold's confabulations that directly contradicted notions about Red prudishness—but the fact remained that the embryonic Communist Lawson had made a vow of sexual exclusivity that he was having difficulty in keeping.

Dawn Powell was not exactly the retiring type, in any case, and her tempestuousness merged with Lawson's own peculiar issues to make for a volatile combination. At one memorable and festive party in 1926 that she attended with "Sue and Jack," she "got drunk and amorous with Carl Van Doren." Months later, there was another "party at Sue Lawson's," with more liquor flowing abundantly and resultant drunkenness. "Jack brought [her] home," her diary records, with no indication of what further ensued.[9]

Hence, the dialectic that Lawson had discerned in Hemingway could also be detected in himself, given his halting steps toward commitment, his unchained libido, and his simultaneous desire and disdain for bourgeois prestige. Dawn Powell was to be a recurring presence in his life at the same time he had "committed" to marriage. His next play, *Nirvana*, reflected similar tensions; it was a pastiche of nonlinear drama, à la *Processional*, with no discernible plot, though it bowed to convention in other ways.[10]

As in a hall of mirrors, the sad devolution of this play reflected the moral chaos in Lawson's own life. "When I saw a dress rehearsal," he moaned, "my heart sank. The raggedness of the performance, the lack of any style in a play that depended on virtuoso interpretation forced me to see that the first night would be a disaster." Lawson fled to the lobby and phoned the hugely talented director and actor George Abbott and "begged him to come down and help me." In half an hour, he had arrived and "stayed . . . practically the whole time until the opening." Speaking later, the self-abnegating Lawson asserted that "my actual situation, socially and economically, made me turn from the material riches of New York to a spiritual quest among the stars," to "Nirvana" in other words.[11] His personal philanthropist, Otto Kahn, "provided at the request of the producers, some $4000 toward the production" of this "religious, mystical drama."[12]

It opened at the Greenwich Village Theatre in Manhattan on Tuesday evening, 2 March 1926.[13] The playbill for this opening performance must have seemed forbidding to some in the audience. "Freud has dragged strange monsters from the bottomless sea of the unconscious. Einstein has deposed the straight line. Viewing the mental uncertainties of today," Lawson stated with certainty, "I am convinced that there is a religious need, not satisfied by any of the current forms of worship"—a need filled by Marxism, said Lawson's harsher critics subsequently. He explained, "I do not mean that a new religion can be invented. . . . I am merely asking a question," though he could not resist adding, "suppose that even now a faith were stirring in the depths of the crowd subconscious?"[14]

Later he was to dismiss this play and its companion, *The Pure in Heart*, as being "swamped in mysticism." In his oft-consulted text *Theory and Technique of Playwriting and Screenwriting*, it is cited as an example of what not to do on stage. "While poetry, painting and music have moved toward the abstract and subjective," he argued in 1949, when his commitment to the radical left was firm and unquestioned, "dramatic technique has tended to become narrowly 'practical,' dependent on tricks and repetition of tested effects. The theatre has drifted technically because it has drifted socially." And, yes, his "own plays"—particularly *Nirvana*—did "exhibit these tendencies in their most malignant form." Yes, "the more rebellious spirits in the theatre talked of breaking down the walls of the playhouse," but this play may have accomplished the perhaps related goal of breaking down the walls of significance.[15]

Describing *Nirvana* remains difficult, even years after it was unveiled.[16] Lawson referred to it as a "comedy in a very unhappy sense and upon a rather cosmic scale. . . . [I]t is the delicate convolutions of this mind, which the author has desired to probe and consider—a task which he realizes to [be] so difficult and ungrateful that the tide of laughter, in the last analysis, sweeps back upon himself."[17] It was "the most confused play I ever wrote," said Lawson, "the most characteristic of the chaotic philosophical and creative life of the decade. It is an eclectic combination of incompatible theatre styles. It is closest to the theatre of the absurd."[18] Yet his comrade the Marxist poet Walter Lowenfels took to the pages of the *New York Times* in its defense.[19]

Eugene O'Neill also hailed *Nirvana*. He was "deeply impressed" by it "when he saw it," recalled Lawson, not least since there was a "very close relationship between . . . 'Nirvana' and O'Neill's 'Dynamo.'"[20] This was a turnabout, since privately O'Neill was dismissive of Lawson.[21]

But Lawson's latest "was the first play" of his that O'Neill "had praised." Perhaps this was a cruel trick on O'Neill's part, seeking to mislead the competition, Lawson, into serving up more hash so O'Neill could excel even more in comparison. When, with a group of friends, Lawson drove out to a New York City suburb to see O'Neill, seeking support for this floundering production, they "were not welcomed with enthusiasm, especially by Agnes. Gene was not drinking and we brought a good deal of liquor with us and proceeded to drink it." They also "talked a good deal of the theatre," and

O'Neill "agreed with me in principle that a new kind of theatre was needed, but he seemed aloof and timid; he feared art almost in the same way that he feared drinking," and, unlike Lawson, "the question of style was not of deep interest to him." This was just before the birth of Lawson's son Jeffrey, otherwise a time of joy, but Lawson returned from his tête-à-tête with O'Neill in a profoundly "discouraged mood."

Lawson could be disturbingly harsh in evaluating his own work, something his critics consistently failed to recognize when they denounced him subsequently for his ripping of writers like Budd Schulberg. As he put it later, his "errors of judgment, which run through my whole career in the theatre, are flagrantly displayed" in this play. The "actor who played the writer—carrying the main burden of the play's meaning—seemed to lack emotional depth." This actor was Frederic March, soon to establish a sterling reputation, but here when Lawson "told him that I had decided to replace him, he displayed more emotion than he had in his performance."

Worse, Lawson received yet another rude introduction to the political economy of the modern theater. "We faced an invasion of bill collectors. The first act takes place in the doctor's office. The company which rented the medical equipment had been given a bad check: in the middle of a run-through, truckmen entered from the wings, stripped the stage and departed. It took complex negotiations, a frantic search for money and a dangerous waste of time, to get the equipment back."

The central premise of this play was "the moral imbecility of the American intellectual," who—announced the immensely self-critical Lawson—"was myself." In search of deeper meaning for this play and himself, Lawson made a pilgrimage to the office of Dr. Smith Ely Jeliffe, "one of the leading psychiatrists of the time," where he "discussed Freudian meanings," a preoccupation of this play and of Lawson's life at that time. The doctor, however, seemed to have another agenda in mind. He had attended the first performance and "invited" Lawson to "spend an evening" with him. Lawson "went with the intention of asking him for money to keep the show running." Hour after hour Dr. Jeliffe "discoursed" on "latent homosexuality in the American male," a subject, apparently, of more than theoretical interest in this circumstance. "He treated this as the theme of the play," recalled a baffled Lawson; "the idea had never occurred to me and it made me furious (which possibly tended to prove the doctor's point)." Dr. Jeliffe was insufficiently impressed with this play—and Lawson—so he "refused financial aid." Lawson requested a "statement supporting the play and he scribbled a note which was evasive." Otto Kahn, who was to become a financial angel of Lawson, was "cruising on his yacht off the Florida coast," and Lawson "appealed to him by wireless." He was turned down flat . . . again.

How long could Lawson continue to square the circle of posing as a rebellious writer, one clenched fist raised skyward while in his other clenched fist he held a tin cup for contributions from the very men whose system he was rebelling against? This tension between these two roles was fomenting further tension in his relationship with the woman to whom he had only recently pledged devotion. When he finished the manuscript of *Nirvana*, "I read it to Sue and it caused the most serious quarrel we ever had. She was angry, not because she failed to understand it but because she understood it too well." She "was repelled by it, with good reason," and "she responded with anger and vexation." The play "exposed" the "darkness in my soul that had threatened our relationship. The play had tortured me and it was inevitable that it would hurt Sue. But . . . she refused to surrender."[22]

Something had to give.

The increasingly frustrated Lawson, shortly after *Nirvana* had its premiere, met the wealthy Otto Kahn on the top floor of a Wall Street building, accompanied by some of his comrades. Lawson described Kahn as "looking 'a bit like the White Rabbit in 'Alice in Wonderland,' a brisk, alert, hurrying man.'"[23] The gathering between the radical writers and the man they were importuning was "rather awkward and comical."[24] Yet Kahn was known to be a devotee of the arts and was not adverse to the avant-garde, of which Lawson was a reigning symbol. With Lawson was Em Jo Basshe, who "wore old clothes because he had no others," and Mike Gold, the Marxist firebrand, who "had a sock in one of his pocket[s] under the impression that it was a handkerchief and he kept taking it out by mistake and blushingly returning it to the pocket." Kahn, who was to be asked for a subsidy for radical theater, nonetheless "did his best to make us feel at ease." Those across the table from Kahn "had never discussed the details" with him, and thus "our statements were not clear. I became aware as the lunch proceeded that we had not reached the most elementary agreement. Our fever to get started was all we had in common." Surprisingly, Kahn "asked no probing questions."

Why would Otto Kahn, a pillar of the financial establishment, support theatrical rebels? As it turned out, Kahn "took more than a fatherly interest" in some of the young actresses in this troupe—but, presumably, he could have sated this voracious appetite more easily than by subsidizing budding and actual Communists. Even Lawson acknowledged later that "critics" found Kahn's role "puzzling," but those who did, he suggested, "ignore the state of the theatre at the time." The "sickness" of the theater "in 1926 was no less evident," wrote Lawson almost forty years later, "than it is in 1962"; the difference was that "there was more hope and ferment in the middle twenties." Kahn was no rube; he had "taste, intelligence and a good knowledge of European developments in the arts." The "neurotic fear of communism was common enough in the twenties but it was not characteristic of the intelligentsia and had not become an official requirement of the dominant culture." Lawson could have added immodestly that it was his own dramatic celebrity, which accelerated spectacularly in 1947, that helped to alter thinking about whether artists should be considered dangerous radicals or mere fops and poseurs. He did grant that "I am inclined to suppose that I was the key figure in Kahn's estimate of the undertaking: I had more theatre experience and had attained more prestige than the others," and, tellingly, "my associates deferred to me on most matters."

At the end of the luncheon, Lawson and his comrades left with appetites sated and pockets full. Kahn "promised to give us $30,000 for our first season." He sought to include O'Neill, but the competitive playwright sent a missive that "seemed to me ice-cold." Increasingly, "I was accepted as the leader of the group; my manner was convincing and I dealt with figures as if I were a certified accountant." As they left the meeting, giddy with the prospect of making theater history, Lawson and company "were all in a state of hypertension, vacillating between euphoria and anxiety."[25] Kahn had reason to be satisfied also—though, thought Lawson, he "certainly . . . did not think we were threatening the status quo."[26]

Later Lawson was told that Kahn "offered the idea that art was a way to control radicalism, for it was the catharsis of such notions. For instance he observed that art contained 'the ingredients for one of the best antidotes against Bolshevism and similar pernicious excrescences.'" Was it "also not possible," asked a Lawson interlocutor rhetorically, "that Kahn, being Jewish, enjoyed backing bright . . . Jewish boys who seemed to promise great things in the arts?"[27]

Whatever Kahn's motivation, the "New Playwrights," as they were christened, despite their avowed radicalism and au courant attitude, were touchingly innocent of what they should have known—even about theater. As Lawson later confessed, "We were aware of the work being done along similar lines by Piscator in Germany and by Meyerhold in the Soviet Union but we had heard nothing of Brecht or Mayakovsky. When I read Mayakovsky years later, I found he had used almost the same words that we had used." Sergei Eisenstein "had spoken in much the same way."[28]

The formation of the New Playwrights was one step Lawson made to resolve the tensions that inhered in his complicated role as theatrical rebel seeking favors from those he was pledged to challenge. Of course, that he was being subsidized by Otto Kahn suggested the impossibility of his quest. That Lawson was accompanied on this journey by two fellow travelers, particularly the combative Gold, meant that he was slowly recognizing that collective action could be the Rosetta stone answering the question of how to move forward effectively in the capitalist society that he abhorred even while it benefited him materially, not to mention assuaging the dilemma of the isolated writer whose activism was often limited to sitting alone at his desk banging on typewriter keys. As it turned out, "the whole sum" contributed by Kahn "was used up on the first three productions," and though he "contributed generously" to the "second season" of New Playwrights, it did not take long for this noble experiment to die in its cradle.[29]

This did not still Lawson's seemingly inexorable march toward the left. Another step in that direction was his taking to the streets of the Massachusetts he had abandoned years earlier, this time in vocal support of Nicola Sacco and Bartolomeo Vanzetti, the Italian immigrant anarchists accused of a felony murder—though Lawson and many others had reason to believe they were framed.[30] Participation in this political campaign was transforming and liberating for Lawson, providing him with a sense of rebellion beyond the stages of Broadway.[31] Edna St. Vincent Millay "was a good friend" of his first wife, Kate Drain Lawson, and Lawson himself, and she helped convince him to join this crusade.[32] It was a "turning point in my life and work," he conceded later; "it helped to transform my anarchic discontent into a clearer recognition of the nature of American society and the need of fundamental change."[33]

Those "seven years that they spent in jail," Lawson recalled wistfully, "covered the seven years of my struggle to revolutionize the theatre." It was his old friend, Dos Passos, soon to be a reliable mainstay of conservatism, who—with Millay—dragged him into this case. Dos Passos had hurried to Massachusetts "in response to the appeal." The otherwise engaged Lawson could not then be convinced to do so. But "a few days later," Dos Passos, "wired me begging me to join him." Lawson "talked it over with Sue" but remained reluctant, for at that point he was an activist at the keyboard alone: "I did not want to interrupt my writing." But then he yielded and traveled a few hundred miles northward to the main site of protest. He "arrived on a Sunday morning" and immediately "went to the headquarters of the defense committee," where he "was told to be on the Boston Common at three o'clock." There Dos Passos, Edna St. Vincent Millay, Malcolm Cowley, and "many other writers, scholars, artists . . . walked gravely at the head of our line" as, symbolically, Lawson followed.

The scene that then unfolded was like the denouement of one of Lawson's dramas, propelling the arc of his own life forward as it clarified his immediate future. "Mounted police surrounded" this verdant, postage stamp–sized oasis in the middle of Boston's urban landscape to "prevent any demonstration." Lawson and others assembled "assumed that the police would hesitate to attack the holiday crowd. But they made a furious charge, riding down women and children, striking out indiscriminately with their clubs in the effort to reach the sign-bearers." Lawson was stunned. More than that, he was "frightened." He knew "abstractly" that "power" was "sustained by force." "But this was concretely what it meant to oppose the ruling power in our country," he recollected later, still digesting the weighty meaning of what he had witnessed.[34] The noted civil libertarian Roger Baldwin was Lawson's attorney for the "trial in Boston" arising from this incident and, fortunately for the playwright, it eventuated in an "important victory for civil liberties."[35]

Like his marriage, this Boston tryst with destiny accelerated Lawson's march toward a more fulfilling commitment. The same held true for the New Playwrights. As a producer, Lawson was in a new role now, one he found infinitely more complicated than the comparably prosaic responsibility carried by a playwright. "Dear Sinclair," he was compelled to address the writer Upton Sinclair, "we feel it would [be] disastrous to make a Spring production of *Singing Jailbirds*," referring to a play the Californian felt strongly about. Part of the problem was lack of a decent venue, though the newly minted impresario, Lawson, hoped to soon have a "slightly more practical theatre, possibly the Grove Street downtown which seats 299 people." At that moment, the New Playwrights were in a "fairly bad position," though they were "determined to go on under any difficulties." And Sinclair should also realize that he should not expect a nifty profit, "unless you have a public success. Our plays were not in any sense financial successes this year, and receipts ran from a lowest of $500 weekly to a highest of $1600. That high figure was reached only in two weeks." They had a "plan to safeguard our income next year in two ways: by putting on a campaign for a solid subscription list" and "by canvassing labor and other organizations to buy the whole house at half price ($200 flat this year) to sell to their members for their own benefit. This system worked so well during the latter part of last season that we had sold out nine complete nights" for Lawson's controversial play *The International*. Actually, Lawson was hoping that Sinclair, who he had reason to suspect had a stash of ducats stashed away, could "help in this vexed question of financing."[36]

Perhaps Sinclair's fortune could also help to bring one of Lawson's plays into production.[37] Lawson's highly praised play *Loudspeaker* was "first presented by the New Playwrights' Theatre at the 52nd St. Theatre" in Manhattan on 2 March 1927.[38] This political satire takes place at the home of Harry Collins, a millionaire who decides to run for governor. His wife, in turn, falls under the spell of a bearded stranger, a devotee of a new religion. His daughter falls in love with a reporter who breaks into Collins's house in search of documents. Collins, all the while, is being pursued by the winner of an Atlantic City beauty bathing contest with whom he had indiscreetly spent quality time. Lawson's lack of regard for bourgeois politics and religion—two of the mainstays of U.S. society—was apparent.[39]

It was, said one critic, a "satirical epic on American fakery"—"fake religion, fake romance, fake politics, fake news, fake women, the fake 'younger generation', fake booze, fake newspaper confessions, fake radio speeches." That was not all. There was also "the bathing beauty sweetheart, the sob sister, the tabloid reporter, the political campaign manager, the black bottom dancer, the amorous couple warbling songs in the spotlight." It "tells of the rise to fame of Henry U. [*sic*] Collins," who, "having salted away his millions," has "political aspirations." It had the absurdities embedded in *Processional* and *Nirvana*, with the more linear approach of *Roger Bloomer*. One critic gushed, "Nobody before has done the voodoo orgy of an American election the justice it is done in this farce." Just as Lawson had pioneered in introducing expressionism to U.S. audiences, *Loudspeaker* had "the first Russian constructivist setting used in America"; "scenes dovetail, actors flow from one episode into another." The rhetorical query was posed: "Is it true" that some "have been 'laying for' this new theatre of . . . young radical playwrights"? "Is it because *Loudspeaker* bites, because it doesn't make compromises, . . . because he says our governors are asses and our 'Miss America' whores?"[40]

Certainly, Lawson was at his acerbic best in this play. But it was not only a slashing assault on bourgeois politics; it was also an affirmation that another path was available, and this was a step forward in Lawson's personal evolution. When one character remarks, "I have a fully developed philosophy of life," his interlocutor replies, "A damned socialist, eh? Believe in government ownership?" The riposte—"Well, there's a lot in it"—reflected Lawson's tentative steps toward a firmer engagement with the organized left.[41]

Yet, despite the praise heaped upon this work by some critics, Lawson himself was less than pleased with the final product. The problem here was structural and dogged many of his plays and screenplays—or so he thought. Unlike the work of a novelist, Lawson's words could not stand on their own; they had to be expressed through an actor and orchestrated by a director. Now it was one thing for the lion's share of praise to be aggrandized by these figures—this was a blow to the ego but could be survived—but it was another matter altogether for what transpired in *Loudspeaker* to take place, that is, a performance that was wanting. An irate Lawson could hardly contain his ire. "The performance of Mr. Seth Kendall" was "shamefully incompetent," he cried. "A fine play with great chances is being crippled by one performance." To cite one example among many, "On the opening night while playing a scene downstage with Miss Hilda Manners, Mr. Kendall suddenly turned to her and said, 'Look out for my make-up.' This was audible." Then, "last Friday night having forgotten a line while playing a scene, Mr. Kendall stopped to beg the pardon of the other performer." The furious Lawson reported this malfeasance to Actors' Equity, seeking to ensure that Kendall would not be inflicted easily upon another playwright, concluding majestically that "such mishaps are not in the best interests of the acting profession."[42]

There was a discernible "tension" between Lawson and the director, Harry Wagstaff Gribble. During one noticeably difficult rehearsal, "Lawson . . . interrupted a scene and Gribble, in a fury, told him to shut up. Lawson went to the office feeling that the whole concept of playwrights' control of the theatre was at stake. He sent his secretary to ask Gribble to come upstairs and then sat biting his nails and wondering whether he had gone too far." According to one analyst, "Inevitably the play suffered. It was greeted with puzzlement and derision for the most part."[43]

The mishap with Kendall was only one among many, making New Playwrights appear to be a "comedy of errors." The then astonishing sum of $5,000 was pledged to the middling Robert Milton to direct Mike Gold's *Fiesta*. "I was blamed by everyone," Lawson observed disconsolately. "Milton insisted I had reached an understanding with him. The board accused me of proceeding without their authority."[44]

It was not easy to carve out a revolutionary enclave in a sea of commercial theater.[45] But New Playwrights tried valiantly, desperately. It sought to give "special inducements to trade unions." Sadly, however, "only a few unions responded." Yet when they did, magic ensued. Lawson recalled vividly an "evening when the Union of Window Cleaners occupied most of the house to hear and see" his latest production. Lawson "moved to strategic points around the theatre, studying their faces," and observed with dismay that "they would have been happier at a movie. Those faces of workers were the measure of our failure."

Lawson plodded on, however, but even he could not stanch the bleeding alone. After "2½ seasons and eight extraordinary productions," New Playwrights folded its tent.[46] Harold Clurman—a well-known producer and dramaturge in his own right—saw this experience as "the decline of [Lawson's] first period. He is unable to support himself by his earnings as a playwright either in the big theaters of Broadway or in the little theaters of Greenwich Village. He adapts himself to Hollywood and, one might say, he enjoys it!"[47]

Lawson thought that the importance of New Playwrights was underestimated. "It had an indirect but considerable effect on theater ideas," not least in highlighting the "conflict between the aspirations of the artist and business control of the arts," which had "existed throughout the Twentieth Century," not to mention before and after.[48] Lawson insisted repeatedly that the New Playwrights was a sound initiative.[49]

The Sacco and Vanzetti case and the New Playwrights experience were transforming events for Lawson.[50] They moved him a step closer to the commitment he so desperately sought, and these tormented feelings were poured into his next play, *The International.*

It was a breakthrough—of sorts—for its time. More linear and conventional in form than some of Lawson's earlier works, in content it is more overtly "revolutionary." It concerns a future world war that begins in Tibet and spreads to China where the Soviet Union supports a revolution. As Lawson remembered it, "This was drawn directly from the newspaper headlines in the spring of 1927," suggesting how the press of events—along with his own experiences—was influencing him. The second act of this turbulent piece of theater, which, rather adventurously, "shows the Soviet Union aiding the people of China," was written just before he left for Boston in support of Sacco and Vanzetti. Suggesting the direction of Lawson's thinking, the action of this play that concerns revolution commences in a Wall Street office.[51] The play had its debut in January 1928.

Perhaps a greater adventure was Lawson's often difficult interaction with those intermediaries who were so essential to his ability to transmit his message: actors. He chose to direct this work, and it was not long before "'the actors came to a point almost of revolt because they thought I didn't know what I was doing—and I must say they were largely right.'" Also masquerading as a "Renaissance man" was Dos Passos, who did the sets. Unfortunately, his "gifts as a novelist were perhaps no qualification for scene design. And the theatre itself was small and uncomfortable with hard seats."[52] There were "difficulties," which "multiplied from the beginning of rehearsals." It was not entirely the actors' fault. "Actors are long-suffering and loyal," Lawson said gallantly, "but I drove them to rebellion. One afternoon after a long day, I expressed dissatisfaction with a scene we had just done, and said we would do it over. Lionel Ferrand, the Stage Manager, was sitting with his script at a table on the stage. He looked at the people around him, deliberately closed the script and left the stage. He returned with his hat and coat, descended to where I was sitting in the front row, handed me the script and left the theatre." His revolt was "supported by the performers." Ferrand considered Lawson to be "incompetent," and "most of the actors felt the same way." Contrite, Lawson "begged" him to stay, Ferrand agreed, and all seemed hunky-dory—at least for the time being.

But that storm seemed placid compared with the gusts of opprobrium unleashed by the critics. The play "was attacked from the left as well as from the right." Then somewhat taken with Leon Trotsky, well on his way to becoming an archfoe of Joseph Stalin, Lawson included in his play "unflattering portraits of Soviet officials," which infuriated the Communist left, and pictured the Soviet Union as aggressively fomenting "world revolution"— which infuriated the right. Joseph Freeman, then an editor of the left-wing journal *New Masses,* "paid me an official visit to chide me on the political errors in the play," though the "discussion was long and friendly"—at least to a degree.[53] Lawson agreed later that it was an "imaginative and incoherent vision of coming war, which would start in Central Asia and spread around the world,"[54] but Sender Garlin in the *Daily Worker* "denounced" the play.[55]

This, said one analyst, was "perhaps the most painful review for Lawson." New Playwrights itself was conflicted about this work. The group's members promoted this play as "the first Communist play to be produced in an American theatre. On the other hand, they did not wish their theatre to be labeled a Communist group and risk alienation by the more conservative New York establishment"—a circle that was terribly difficult to square.[56] Freeman, the caustic critic of the left, later was to put forth Lawson—and Dos Passos—as exemplars of what was wrong with the arts. "Shall we revolt blindly," he asked rhetorically, "or with full, bold, hard consciousness[?] John Dos Passos says blindly. And he and John Howard Lawson and others formulate a vague aesthetic creed of impressionism—of sensationalism—of empiricism. They try to shut their eyes to the main drifts of American life" as "they hug chaos to their bosoms" and as "all the heroes of their fiction wind up in chaos and failure."[57]

Lawson was aware of the critical grenades exploding all around. Later he did argue that *The International* "went much further in trying to create a new theatrical and social reality," not unlike Brecht and Meyerhold and Piscator but with "experiments with multi-media, music, dance, pantomime"—not unlike "the theatre of the seventies." Yet, he admitted sadly much later, he found it "impossible" to "break through the web of bourgeois consciousness"—in fact, this play was "full of it."[58]

But Lawson was no innocent, not least since his politics were so befuddling. It was in late 1927 that the future Communist told the press, "I can imagine being tremendously excited by a Fascist play or a Catholic play or an anti-Red play—if it contained the precious spark of exciting theater." He added quickly, "I don't think I am exaggerating when I express my grave doubts that such a play will ever happen," but, in any event, "it is not the business of a theater to be controlled by any class or theory."[59] His future comrade Lester Cole argues that even as late as 1933, when Lawson was on the verge of joining the Communist Party, he was a "liberal, middle-of-the-roader and a unifier" and "by no means a leftist." This is why it was "no wonder that Jack Lawson was regarded as the most liberal of all liberals when he was unanimously elected President of the [Screen Writers] Guild."[60]

It was ironic—perhaps, foreordained—that Lawson, often flayed because of his "liberal," bohemian, and avant-garde tendencies, became a scourge of those similarly situated, or so it was said. After he became a Communist—at least for a while—he seemed to have minimal tolerance for the kind of vacillation and confusion that he exhibited before he opted for firmer political commitments. It was as if scrutinizing other writers was like looking in the mirror and being repulsed by the reflection.[61]

But as his relationship with the New Playwrights was unraveling, another attraction beckoned. "I saw the crass vulgarities of Hollywood," he concluded much later, but "on the other hand, I was fascinated by the technique and potentialities of film."[62]

3 Hollywood

John Howard Lawson loved trains. As his son Jeffrey recalled, "He loved to stand in the station while the monstrous locomotives roared down on us. I've seen him drive say 30 miles down a lovely desert road, just to see for a minute, say the Super Chief, roar by, then turn around and drive back to the main road."[1] Father and son "traveled the continent dozens of times; a big part of my early childhood was spent hearing the clack of wheels as a crack continental train, the Chief or the Twentieth Century Limited, sped west or east." They "often made the crossing by car," too, "taking a week, stopping for lunch in small town cafes and spending the night in motels in small towns."[2]

Perhaps Lawson's fondness for trains was generated by his fondness for Hollywood, where he traveled in the iron horse from Manhattan to toil as the film industry was enduring a wrenching technological change—the progressive introduction of sound—that was to bring Lawson the kind of notoriety that most radicals could only muse about.

By that juncture, Lawson was more than ready to turn his back on New York and the theater. His "recognition of defeat" with the New Playwrights "was so strong" that he "left for Hollywood in the summer of 1928." The "negative lessons" he "learned" were "so overwhelming" that Lawson's "career as a dramatist was gravely affected and almost crushed."[3] Lawson's desire to make radical statements on the stage was constrained by the economics of theater production, the lagging political consciousness of his intended audience, and various other factors too complex to disentangle. He was disappointed in his comrades in New Playwrights, too, one of whom, he thought, was "acting like a combination of an efficient executive and a person in the last stages of dementia praecox."[4] On more sober reflection he admitted that the New Playwrights' importance has been "underestimated. It had an indirect but considerable effect on theater ideas." In a larger sense, this episode illuminated for him what was a fundamental issue of the epoch: "the conflict between the aspirations of the artist and business control of the arts."[5] This conflict was exacerbated by the fact that as Lawson was grappling with philosophical queries about mammon and art, he was "dead broke" and had "heavy debts."[6]

Propitiously, as Lawson—now well into his thirties—was wrestling with what to do with his life and where and how theater fit into his dreams, Hollywood beckoned. For at that precise moment, Hollywood was wrestling with demons all its own and desperately needed the talent of those few who could craft glistening dialogue. For it was in the summer of 1928 that a "panicked mood" gripped Hollywood, an industry reeling "under siege." At that time one could not "pick up a daily paper, walk along Hollywood Boulevard, attend a meeting of any kind or even sit at a table" at one's favorite bistro, one could not "do any of these things or follow the routine of his daily life, without reading, hearing a little matter of interest and a lot of nonsense on the 'talkies' and without being questioned on their past, present and future." The "silent" film had reached an impasse, and "talkies" were the wave of the future. It was not only the actors whose skill rested with their pantomime— not with speaking expressively—who would have to retool; the studios would have to invest heavily in technology with no guarantee that audiences would be swayed by this fundamental change in movies. Different skills were also required for "scenario writers." A silent film, according to one analyst, "was like writing a novel, and a script [for a talking picture] was like writing a play." "Silent screenplays could be likened to a skeletal map, pointing the direction, without specifying the route," whereas "sound screenplays" were "exhaustively complete road maps, providing all sorts of suggestive routes and signs by which the dramatic trip could be made."

Likewise, anxieties about the impact on audiences notwithstanding, "average weekly attendance" for films "increased from 50 million in 1926 to 65 million in 1928 (and would skyrocket to 90 million in 1930)." In 1928 Paramount had "released seventy-eight movies, all silent. In 1929, it would release sixty-seven, only twenty of them silent." Net profits grew accordingly—Warner Brothers' "asset base had grown from slightly more than $5 million in 1925 to $230 million by 1930, a 4600 percent increase in five years."[7]

In sum, this transition to sound was akin to a cinematic earthquake. Later Lawson was to have a hand in drafting an analysis of this intoxicating moment. "There is very little that can be said for the screenwriter of the silent days," it was said. "It was a crude, vigorous, bawdy, blatant sort of business" that "resembled a sideshow in a honky-tonk circus; in fact, most of the people who controlled its destinies had come up from these sideshows and still carried with them their philosophy that 'audiences were suckers and had to be taken.'" Similar disrespect was accorded writers, since "the writer was practically non-existent" and certainly "not a creator. His function was merely to execute and organize the ideas of the director. Pictures were 'made up' as they went along. In fact, there are few written records, in terms of scripts, of the early silent days"; the "first time a writer's work became perceptible was in the introduction of titles on the screen." By "the late twenties, a period which reached boom proportions the like[s] of which America had never seen, the motion picture was dying."

So, what happened? "The discovery and application of sound to motion pictures revolutionized the entire industry." For there were "hundreds of millions of dollars which were needed to install new machinery," and the moguls "found it necessary to go to the banks, and in so doing they were forced to relinquish their control," as "the patents controlling sound and electrical devices were all in the hands of great monopolies." Sound meant "an influx of ideas" in the heads of those like Lawson, which meant a "transformation of Hollywood from a provincial to a cosmopolitan town." Amid this upheaval, "in the early days of the readjustment . . . confusion reigned. The old silent directors found themselves bewildered. Their supreme power was slipping out of their grasp," and the industry "turned to the writer in desperation." At the same time, fear of the power of the writer meant "an attempt was made to reduce the writer to the status of the early silent days," which was hardly possible. Thus, "each successive attempt by the producer to lower the economic and artistic status of the screenwriter" was to be met with "stronger organization on the part of the screenwriter."[8] When V. I. Lenin, architect of the Bolshevik revolution, declared, "'You must consider that of all the arts, the motion picture is for us the most important,'"[9] the notion of the special role of the left and cinema was cemented.

At this fraught moment, as the industry zoomed from ordinary wealth to untold riches, Hollywood craved desperately those with the skill to pen the new kind of scenario writing required. This panicked desperation also entailed a willingness to overlook the studied radicalism of writers like Lawson. Thus, it was in that pivotal year of 1928 Lawson was employed by MGM "as one of the first dramatists imported from New York to meet the need of dialogue."[10] It was not only Lawson that a frenetically anxious Hollywood sought to recruit. Soon Dorothy Parker, John O'Hara, Maxwell Anderson, and many others had decamped to California.[11]

The industry was befuddled by this technological turn of events and began to toss buckets of cash at the nearest writers. The moguls found themselves more dependent on speech, which led to a hunt for writers of dialogue. It was through trial and error, stops and starts, that an audiovisual language was developed—and Lawson was present at the creation and continued to be a principal theorist of this fundamental question, even after he had been "blacklisted." "Film," he wrote almost four decades later, "is especially effective [in] portraying external reality, while drama excels in characterization and the expression of thoughts and ideas." Yet he also felt "intensely that poetry, verbal poetry is an essential aspect of cinematic expression and that the present lack of poetry in film impoverishes and depletes the art."[12]

Lawson was in the mood to devote time to pounding his keyboard. He had "felt the sting of defeat" in New York—what with the biting reviews of his plays and the failures of the New Playwrights—and "as always" when faced with such setbacks, he "wrote with furious energy." Again, Lawson took criticism not as the prelude to execution—as some of his more draconian assailants suggested two decades later—but as the prelude to accelerated striving for improvement. "A good lively shower of critical disapproval," he told readers of the *New York Times* in that pivotal year of 1928, "can be as refreshing as a cold bath"; "even torrid abuse can be valuable," he argued. In fact, "maybe a lot of it isn't torrid enough." On the other hand, the less than hypersensitive Lawson also looked "in vain for a useful or constructive word, for criticism which takes the slightest account of intention." For, he asserted, "if criticism is not concerned with the relation between intention and the complete product, it isn't criticism at all, but merely the snap judgment of an observer who is too bored to think, feel and consider." In a wildly erroneous—though whimsical—prediction, he posited that "for sane and proper criticism of this whole field of dramatic effort, I fear one must eagerly await the daily press of 1949."[13]

But Lawson did not err in forging a key relationship. Theodore Dreiser, who later was to join Lawson in the ranks of the Communists, was a novelist respected by Lawson, and it was then that the playwright "went to see [him]," though he knew the famed novelist "only slightly." Lawson was also moved by praise and was "surprised to learn that [Dreiser's] admiration for *Processional* led him to select" the radical playwright "as the only dramatist who could be trusted with the adaptation" of *Sister Carrie.* Lawson was to receive the then handsome sum of $250 per week for three months' labor in writing a screenplay in which Paul Muni would star. "MGM insisted that I leave for the coast immediately," Lawson recalled, and he was loath to reject their entreaties, not least since he "felt that closer knowledge of cinematic technique might help me in the theatre."

So he boarded the Santa Fe Chief for the long ride west. He "sat on the open observation platform" as the train bolted "through Missouri," then "went indoors and spent the rest of the night re-reading *Sister Carrie*." Arriving in downtown Los Angeles, he "dined with Sam Ornitz," then "spent the night at his home." Ornitz's novel *Haunch, Paunch and Jowl*, had a "decisive influence" on Lawson, who respected his fellow radical highly. They "talked for hours," and Lawson "listened carefully" and "began to take notes on slips," which he "fished" from his pockets. Lawson had been an "inveterate note-taker from childhood," and his first briefing on Hollywood was no time to ditch this potent habit: "If I care about a conversation, I feel that the exact words (and sometimes the tone of voice) must be recorded."

Sufficiently educated by Ornitz—who was to join him in the infamous ranks of the Hollywood Ten years later—Lawson rose early the next morning and "took a long hot bus ride from Hollywood to Culver City." Though he was "given an office," he was "told" that studio boss Irving Thalberg "could [not] see me for three or four days." Thus, Lawson strolled through the lot, "about a mile to the western end of the enclosure, where there were medieval castles, renaissance palaces, colonial mansions, corners of Parisian streets, vistas of American frontier towns, trains of various periods." Lawson then "left the studio, bought a car from a second-hand dealer in Culver City, returned to Hollywood and searched for a home." He quickly "found a one-room shack in a scrubby canyon at the bottom of the Hollywood Hills." There he settled down to write.

He came home from the studio each night to a "delicatessen dinner and then worked on the script until two or three in the morning." Converting Dreiser's overstuffed, prolix novel into a screenplay was posing intractable problems "of form and content" that eventually defeated Lawson. Meanwhile, he finally secured a meeting with the elusive Thalberg "after several days of waiting" and "found him remarkable in his courtesy, his ability to say exactly what he meant and his willingness to listen"; "he was genuinely interested in surrounding himself with people he could trust," not least since there was stifling "friction between him and Louis B. Mayer," the big boss of MGM. On the other hand, Thalberg had a "childish taste," befitting a "boy genius." There was a "cruelty and lack of scruple" there that "were essential to his job." The "basis for a relationship with Thalberg—the relationship of a disciple or servant"—was bruited in their initial discussions. Lawson acknowledged this to the point where he ascertained early on that

"I could have remained at MGM and eventually secured a large salary and control of a production unit—if I had conformed to Thalberg's notion of unconditional loyalty."[14]

According to Lawson, his supervisor was a "really thoroughly interesting soft-spoken young Jew named Thalberg, who is twenty-nine years old and whose powers of life and death over the inhabitant makes Nero look like a Confederate letter-carrier—to all intent and purposes nobody is allowed to spit, piss or perform any of the other natural functions without his permission." Yet "through all this bedlam he displays unusual and continuous good sense (if he didn't we'd all be even nearer the mad-house than we are) and has never been known to raise his voice, swear, openly criticize or act discourteous to anybody. This interests me so much that (if we ever get drunk together again, which is extremely unlikely) I'd like to find out what in Hell he thinks about." Lawson found the Hollywood moguls more congenial than their counterparts in New York:

> It really differs extraordinarily from Broadway theatrical circles in that all the officials (taking their cue from Thalberg—and if they didn't they'd wait in the wings till doomsday) are extremely nice, good-natured and soft—instead of the roaring Broadway type—which makes it all the more odd they can stir up such a steam of hatred—for I've never been in a place where people are both so lazy and so Goddam sore—you can't walk from building to building without being pulled aside and being given a string of imprecations and complaints that burn your ears—of course, a lot of dirty tricks are pulled, but anybody who didn't expect that would be a moron— but the only reason I can see for the burning hatred is that there's just too much money lying around loose but slightly given to disappearing in smoke when you try to pry it off—and too many people trying to get it— so that you gradually find out that the place (in spite of appearing sane) is really Bellevue after all—and suddenly office boys who appear to be going about their business will come into one's office and break into hysterical weeping, screaming "for God's sake teach me to be a writer—for God's sake," etc.

In the midst of this controlled frenzy, Lawson appeared as an isle of serenity. "Due to a curious phobia which is part of my constitution," he remarked, "I don't play this game very much and really do a Hell of a lot of work—a habit which is very dangerous and will probably eventually cause me to slip and lose my footing on the heaving decks of this ship of state." "At the present moment, however," he announced in late 1928, "I am right on the bridge scanning the horizon with the practiced eye of a moving picture specialist and shouting through a megaphone at the myriad tugs which swarm in the putrid waters below."[15]

Much of this intelligence was being reported to his close friend John Dos Passos, then struggling to establish a stable income and typically seeking to borrow sizable amounts from Lawson. Lawson usually complied as he casually—and typically—reminded his friend of his comparative dearth of such a problem. "The ridiculous thing about money," said the well-paid writer, "is that you get adjusted to it so quickly that it means absolutely nothing and five hundred shining smackers each week seem like a bare pittance." The golden manacles that bound him to MGM rested more easily than others he had borne. "Being a slave to Metro-Goldwyn-Mayer," he commented, "is a lot pleasanter and more entertaining than being a slave to the Theatre Guild." Lawson was speculating wryly that he might receive a salary "calculated in platinum and Marion Davies thrown in" as a extra.[16]

Lawson was basking in the penetrating sunshine of Southern California and coming to know an industry that was to be his preoccupation in coming years. And he was grappling—not too well—with Dreiser's book, an ostensible reason for relocating three thousand miles westward. In the early fall of 1928 he was "deep in work" on the adaptation of the novel.[17] He had known Dreiser casually before being tapped for this assignment, seeing him "occasionally through the swirling smoke at parties" in Greenwich Village.[18]

However, it would take more than his admiration for Dreiser to complete his first Hollywood job. By late 1928 Lawson was enjoying the warm winter of Los Angeles—but not enjoying the novel-to-screenplay conversion that had ensnared him. It was a "terrific tangle of moving picture work," he said at the time. It had been preoccupying him "during the past fortnight," and though he had "continued to spend several hours each day" on this project, he had "not been satisfied" and "was trying to clear [his] mind on it."[19] He was compelled to tell Dreiser that a "violent delirium" and "haste" were complicating his assignment.[20]

Sister Carrie defeated Lawson. As he observed later, the project "fell through largely because of my inability to provide an effective dramatization of Dreiser's massive and subtle novel. We discussed the use of a symbolic device—a series of interludes in which a tramp, a man destroyed by society and wandering in its lower depths, would give a poetic and prophetic sense of the fate awaiting Hurstwood,"[21] but nothing seemed to work. His producer "wanted a conventional three or four act play," while Lawson—he of *Nirvana* and *Processional*—"had rather wild ideas of an experimental production." But "unfortunately" he was "not really able to give dramatic life to Dreiser's novel," since "he did not understand it well enough. Dreiser wrote encouragingly and felt sympathetic" to Lawson's "general conception," but "time ran out and nothing came of it." Yet a lily arose from the mud of this setback—he got to establish a firmer relationship with Dreiser. By then, said Lawson, Dreiser "had arrived at some very strong inner convictions," and "he and I had some sharp arguments," though the bouts were "not 'unpredictable.' He could be very emotional about ideas but also generous in admitting mistakes (a quality which is fairly rare in artists)."[22]

Bonding with Dreiser was not the only result of Lawson's initial Hollywood venture. His increased—and regular—income meant that he could do more for friends, such as Dos Passos, who had a knack for borrowing money from him. "I assume as a matter of course," Lawson told him, "you're as broke as I was before I came to the land where dollar bills are used to stop bung-holes and all God's chillun got Packards—anyway, here's two hundred bucks on account, to be followed by several more in a week or so. . . . I can offer you more a volonte as the occasion arises." "Of course," he said still marveling, "the amazing thing about getting a lot of money is that in some mysterious way one spends a lot too." As for many New York refugees, his appreciation for the lucre of Hollywood was leavened—at least initially—by a certain contempt. It was an "amazing dump" that "would give you hydrophobia in short order."

His plans then were to stay in the region until the fall of 1929, which would allow him to "save up eight or ten thousand"—that is, if he could subdue the "well-known California Lethargy (or Cinema Palsy as it is sometimes called)." An episode of this malady had overtaken Lawson, and he "sank into one of those Studio Comas in which people sometimes remain for weeks." The "Gold Rush" brought in by "talkies" had generated this sapping wealth. It was all so

> grotesquely easy and not at all unpleasant—in fact most of the people around here are extremely jolly—except for a curious psychological atmosphere which one could cut with a knife. The way this five million dollar a year business is run makes the American Red Cross during the war look like a sternly efficient enterprise. Everybody vies with everybody else as to who shall do the least work, everything is completely irregular except the pay. By a little skill and delicate lying one could lock oneself up in one's office day after day and work on one's own plays and nobody would be the bit wiser: in fact there's one story extant of a man who went to New York for a year and came back and walked into the accountant's office and collected his salary for the entire time. Now that you bring it to my attention, I may try that myself.

That was an unlikely prospect, for he railed against the "lethargy which eats into one like a creeping sickness." Yet he "could arrange" his "time easily to do a lot of [his] own work but somehow the days pass and very little gets accomplished."

Easy money was not the only emolument offered by Hollywood. On one afternoon in late 1928, a not atypical drunken revel was unfolding. There were "forty bottles of Scotch and an equal amount of champagne" being guzzled "in the executive offices," though "the only result of that was that Jack Gilbert kissed Louis B. Mayer's hand and called him 'Papa' and a stenographer named Goldie threw a full glass of liquor in Mr. Thalberg's face." In an industry where sexual seduction via the "casting couch" was becoming de rigueur, Lawson the libertine "was eventually found" by his spouse "(who had been searching the premises for hours) in a rather obscure location in the arms of a woman whose name turned out (after exhaustive investigation) to be Camille P. Pyburn." Then there was nearby "Tia Juana" in Mexico, which "alone is worth the price of admission, being the lowest, swellest, noisiest Hell-hole on this or any other continent."

Riotous parties, dissolute getaways, easy money, liquor flowing like the Nile—though this was not an everyday pattern by any means—it was a wonder that any movies got made in Hollywood, though Lawson was quick to debunk the idea that this industry was notably different from any other. "I think the people who regard the movies as a special and queer phenomen[on] are damn fools—as it is exactly like every other American industry, except slightly exaggerated and made grotesque—the methods here are just like those in a factory or cloak-and-suit house—and Hollywood is exactly like any American village." Actually, "the grotesque elements are of no importance," he confided to Dos Passos, though "to be sure, there are some five thousand fallen (or falling women) hanging on the edges of the picture precipice and some ten thousand nephews of General Wrangel trying to wedge in and some fifty thousand Frenchmen who (in spite of the old adage) have been completely wrong in thinking this would be an Elysian field for them." Sure, Hollywood had its peculiarities, but at root it was "exactly like any other American industry, it's extremely comic, inefficient, and not violently unpleasant. Personally I think the work at times can be thoroughly interesting (though that's fairly rare) and all this rub-adub-dub about 'isn't it Hell to debase our Art' should be tied outside." Early on Lawson was taking a hard-boiled view of this "industry" and dismissed the soon-to-be venerated idea about Hollywood debasing artists.

"It's true," he admitted, that "the psychology is queerly depressing, but the state of really tragic nerves and the complicated protective coloring into which so many alleged authors get out here is simply ridiculous. People like Sam Ornitz get a sort of hurt pride about it all which develops into a regular neurosis—there is a curious and completely subconscious method which exists in the picture business of breaking down an author's self-confidence by a series of the most subtle and complicated events."

At one juncture, Lawson had to "hastily read a lot of books on India before four o'clock," since he had just received a "phone call for a conference." That's "how we are around here," he mused, "things spring out of the nowhere into the here full blown and magnificent—well, said this eminent official, 'I got something that'll knock 'em all cold—Lon Chaney in 'Gunga Din'—can't you see it.'" Nonplussed, Lawson

> admitted bashfully that it gave me a glow—'getting a glow' is such a by-word around here that just to mention it will send any little group of serious thinkers on the lot into gales of laughter—well, the next step is to confer for four or five days, during which time the eminent executive sits with his feet on his mahogany desk smoking cigars, having his nails manicured and telling the story of his life—somewhere toward the end of that time, having worked up to it properly I throw out dark hints about a brand-new idea of a white girl held prisoner in a Hindoo [sic] temple: if this thought is decked in skillful phraseology it produces the desired glow, whereupon I retire to write the thought, which is the last seen of me for three weeks at least, at the end of which time I send out a brief inter-office communication saying that I fear I have been on the wrong track. As you see, brains are what counts in this business. As a matter of fact, it's much more interesting, but considerably more trouble, to set out to convince them that the proposition is all wet to start with.[23]

The process of making movies frequently lacked prettiness. "The actual mechanics of shaping a movie up and trying to get an audience story out of a lot of disjointed scenes which have been shot by an intoxicated director can be enormously interesting," he said; "in fact the basic theory is that if a lot of highly paid people are told to do and then not to do things with lightning rapidity, and if each of them is allowed to achieve a maximum of interference with the others, the result will be cosmic perfection." At that moment he had just written "some unbelievably stultified dialogue for *The Bridge of San Luis Rey*," and "when we sat in the monitor room (a little glass chamber [where] you hear the terrifying results of your labor) and heard the same recited by two aged actors," well, "it was like a nightmare . . . in a Shakespearean Hell"—though it "comes for some obscure reason under the head[ing] of ART." Now he was writing a "sentimental story about a song writer named 'Lord Byron of Broadway.'" Further conflict ensued as "we argued about that for two solid days of conference, and will no doubt for three days more." This was typical of this group approach to writing, somehow different from the theater, which was more of a writer's medium. "When I first arrived here," Lawson said, speaking of Hollywood, "those conferences used to frighten me into a green stupor, but I've found they can be made quite enlightening. I used to try to be real congenial and nobody would listen to a word I said, but now I've reached a point of importance where I can hold them spellbound with the weariest blah—and that's what we're paid for, the real duties are solely oral, and if you can keep a conference in a state of expectancy for ten hours or so, you're a made man." "Dorothy Farnum," he insisted, "a little washed-out blonde with the manner of a nosey sob-sister, gets fifteen hundred a week and I don't believe she's ever been known to put a word on paper." Lawson could only marvel at the enormous sums exchanged for so little labor as "with each cable his artistic conscience gets more delicate and has to be salved with an offer of ten thousand more dollars. I think it will come to no good."[24] It was "enough," he ruminated, "to give any earnest economist the heeby-jeebies to see [MGM] turn all its wild inefficiency and madly wasteful production methods and impossible stories into more and more millions." Somehow, "the damn pictures keep coming out" and "they keep coining money (in spite of the fact that they are so messy that the audience would frequently not know the difference if the projection machine [ran] backward and the synchronization went sideways)." "Perhaps," he inquired of Dos Passos with no small amazement, "you can explain this at your leisure—I give . . . up."[25]

From Lawson's accounts, it was a wonder that any movies made it to theaters or that those that did would attract paying customers. Continually, in his early years in Hollywood, he griped about the process whereby scenes were shot, then magically converted into movies. "It's a hot day," he informed Dos Passos, "and I've been arguing three hours about a story I wrote for Greta Garbo, the only objection to it being that she starts the story as an innocent girl, and they say she does best as a fallen woman (as so many people do)."[26]

He was writing titles for silent films, in addition to his other tasks, such as adapting *Sister Carrie*. He made an "attempt to introduce Freud in *Flesh and the Devil*," something he was able to accomplish in *The Ship from Shanghai*, and for his troubles was "assigned to do titles for *The Pagan*."[27] *The Flesh and the Devil* was typical of the challenges presented by the transition to sound. Its stars, Greta Garbo and John Gilbert, were not "ready to undertake the ordeal of speech." So Lawson was brought in after this silent film had been finished because the studio was wary of releasing it as sound was debuting. "Since the stars could not speak," said the inventive Lawson, "I prepared a fantastic dream sequence" with "sounds and voices coming from a void. The director glanced at the script and tossed it aside. But Thalberg read [every] word, slowly and then spoke with genuine surprise:

'there's an *idea* in it.' The scene was not used, but my future at MGM was assured." Thalberg, Lawson stressed repeatedly, had a naive but genuine respect for the "idea." He was "gifted and dedicated" and "worked feverishly," though "his taste was mediocre." This realization dawned when the eminent producer would "call all the writers together—there were sixty or seventy of them at the time—and plead with puzzled urgency, 'Why are there so many writers and so few ideas?'"[28]

The Pagan was a sensation globally. Even here Lawson managed to make the indigenous woman character "socially conscious, unable to betray her people, and the visiting American unable to betray his way of living."[29] Yet in spite of his progressive politics, by his own admission, the future bête rouge of Hollywood was "the fair-headed boy, due largely to the fact that Cecil B. DeMille"—a future prime red-baiting antagonist—"has crowned me with laurel and has taken to talking about religion with me."[30]

DeMille may not have changed his stripes. He may have latched on to Lawson like a drowning man to a life raft, so stunned was he by the transition to sound. Mr. DeMille would "grouse about the demands of early talkies; 'to leaf through my shooting script of *Dynamite*,'" he said of a work actually written by Lawson, "'is to see at a glance what sound had done to films.'" This was DeMille's first venture into these uncharted waters, and he was none too tranquil about it.[31] So DeMille—"an intelligent reactionary," in Lawson's apt phrasing—found himself at a turning point in film history having to rely upon a radical writer. He countenanced *Dynamite*, which Lawson asserted "introduced the class struggle in terms of a sex triangle," a frequent dramatic device—or "root idea"—of his. DeMille went along with what he would persecute writers for two decades later.[32]

Dynamite was adapted from Lawson's *Processional*. Here "the coal-miner protagonist played by Charles Bickford is sentenced to death for a crime he did not commit and agrees for a cash settlement, to marry a frivolous society girl . . . who needs a husband fast in order to receive her family inheritance. The miner, finding himself suddenly surrounded by the amoral rich who are Johnson's social circle, returns alone to the coal patch in Pennsylvania, leaving both the dame and the money behind." Lawson's ability to inject such thinly disguised political "dynamite" into movies is why he was deemed "the originator of the class-conflict film" in Hollywood and an adept "avant-gardist" who was also a "skillful practitioner of the genuinely cinematic radical film."[33]

DeMille was concerned about this production, since his "lavish spectacles" were not "especially suited to silent presentation" and the advent of sound threatened his empire. He found their collaboration on films such as *Dynamite* "intimate, successful and reasonably satisfying." Lawson also collaborated with the director Charles Brabin—better known as the spouse of the megastar Theda Bara—on *The Ship from Shanghai*. "They sat in the garden of his Beverly Hills house" and chatted: "They wanted to understand and conquer the new Hollywood of the sound era." Lawson "came to them as the symbol of the change," the man who could put words in the mouths of the previously voiceless. This radical transition in moviemaking seemed to cry out for an actual radical as a midwife, and Lawson's appearance on the scene, thus, seemed to be magical, foreordained. That is, the anxiety generated by this transition to sound caused some to overlook the obvious direction of Lawson's radical politics, allowing him to make a ground-floor entrance to the wealth that Hollywood was to generate.

Nevertheless, there were blips on this otherwise placid screen. Thalberg "bowed before the Golden Calf with all the ecstasy of a true believer," and though Lawson was made to understand that he was going to receive a hefty $500 per week, this was whittled down to $350. This had occurred after Thalberg "passed me" in his "chauffer-driven limousine" and Lawson was trundling along in his "dilapidated topless car." Lawson "cursed the old car which showed [Thalberg] exactly what I was worth." A quick study, Lawson "calculated how quickly" he could have been "reimbursed" if he had "invested in a showy automobile" and "resolved to [do] so immediately." He did so and, consequently, came to meet his wife and son at the train station "with an open Packard, second hand but with shining chrome and expensive leather and de luxe accessories." This was followed by his move to "an attractive house at 7440 Rindge Avenue in Playa Del Rey," just a "few blocks from the ocean on a hill above the sea."[34] Lawson now understood that in Hollywood in order to be paid handsomely, one had to live handsomely—form, appearance, was the trump card, though he remained a casual, even sloppy dresser.

He would be paid well as long as he was able to produce compelling plots, as he did for Theda Bara. *The Ship from Shanghai*, one of her first "talkies," had a "crackling plot about a 'hairy ape' captain who leads a rough crew taking a millionaire's wife and friends" from the celebrated Chinese port of sin to its counterpart across the Pacific—San Francisco. The captain, who has his own designs on the attractive wife, leads a mutiny against the passengers, based on class resentment and—befitting Lawson's desperate search for Freud during his earlier stay in Vienna—"murkier Freudian impulses." Here and elsewhere, Lawson had managed to meld two powerful human impulses—class struggle and romance.[35]

Lawson was becoming a fixture on the Hollywood scene, moving from one "attractive house" to another—one was in Santa Monica at 628 San

Vincente—and figuratively holding the hands of those spooked by the "sense of a distant but gathering doom" and "private rumors of disaster" generated by the uncertain transition to sound. "Everybody is running around like chickens with their heads off," he remarked, a condition exacerbated by an illness afflicting the omnipotent Thalberg, who was "seriously ill." "Nobody can go the toilet without consulting him. So there are some bad cases of arrested bowels," Lawson added with a dash of sarcasm.[36]

Having developed bonds with Thalberg and DeMille, it was easier for Lawson to examine with bemusement the nervousness of others. "Come get yourself a little home with eight or ten Japanese servants in Holly Vista," he said somewhat invidiously to Dos Passos, adding with faux irritation, "it's really a Hell of a place—you can't imagine how disgusting, enervating and nerve-wracking the dump can be!"[37]

He did complain about not receiving the credit to which he felt entitled for his work on the Joan Crawford vehicle *Our Blushing Brides*. The future star was "one of three department store employees" and "roommates who hate their miserably low salaries, long hours, rat-hole apartment and cheap meals." One of them "becomes the mistress of a department store scion who pays her rent (and obviously takes her sexual favors) but will desert her for a woman of [his] own class; another gets married to a swindler who hides from the police and is finally sent off to jail; according to the film's harshest critics, Crawford alone triumphs because she fends off the capitalist playboy played by Robert Montgomery." However, on closer inspection, she is "far more intent on preserving woman's prerogatives generally, utterly repelled by upper-class men's manipulations on every side, at every pretext."[38]

Lawson was the rare radical who was able to communicate his vision to thousands—while being compensated well for doing so. He had settled into a comfortable routine of writing at his MGM office and tending to family matters. His mother-in-law visited from Waco in time to greet the birth of his daughter, though this elderly woman was "bashful" and—like many subsequently—"somewhat afraid" of him. Lawson "accepted" this "formal relationship which," he acknowledged, "prevented me from knowing her intimately." Such snits were alleviated by "occasional journeys" to the "tawdry streets" and "plush gambling tables" of "Tia Juana and Agua Caliente." Evenings were spent playing bridge and reading. Lawson at this pre-Communist moment "read the accounts of Trotsky's downfall and exile" with "mild interest and respect for Trotsky's position." He was spending a considerable amount of time with Samuel Ornitz, who was influencing him deeply as the Great Depression loomed. In the "weeks after Black Friday" [*sic*] in November 1929, they "studied the falling market," and Lawson "took to visiting a stock brokerage firm in Hollywood every morning at seven"; he disposed of surplus income by buying "on margin . . . shares of General Motors, Southern California Edison and Montgomery Ward." The fall in the market meant a further influx of writers seeking work; thus Stephen Vincent Benét came to Hollywood, since "like others" he "had lost money in the stock market." And there were those fabled Hollywood parties, some of which involved "casual intimacies; men and women disappeared briefly into offices, which were locked and unlocked again within minutes." But, above all, there were the lessons learned. His stay at MGM "deepened" his conviction that "social conservatism is inimical to art," as the "almost hysterical fear of experimentation at the studio" was quite frustrating to him.[39]

This was one reason he was so disappointed about MGM's attempt to produce a film on the Soviet Union. Reportedly, Thalberg—before his illness—had remarked, "'People are sick and tired of being told how terrible Russia [is], and pictures that attack it have been box-office failures; if we go half-way we're sure to have a mess; we can't come out in favor of their politics, so let's make them heroic!'" The script, thought Lawson, was "violently pro-Soviet." By 1929 it was "under way in a form which is really about as revolutionary as any Soviet picture" he had seen. It was about a "big dam" and was to be "shot at Boulder," and it "ends with what reads like a very effective crowd scene in which the sluice tunnels are stopped up and the dam is to be ruined—an old Bolshevik raises his clenched fist, recites the Communist oath and goes down in the tunnel to save the dam. One after another people in the crowd raise their fists, chant in chorus and go in to die." Yes, this was "a bit Hollywood, but the ideology," he thought, "seems . . . about eighty-two Proletarian, which isn't a bad average." Lawson was prophetic when he commented that "whether it will see the light in this surprising shape remains to be seen." Thalberg, who Lawson thought had "'the best and most clear-headed third-rate mind in the American show business,'" was unable to pull the trigger.[40] The benefit of this failed project was that it brought Lawson into closer contact with a man who was to influence him. Lawson "quickly fell in with Albert Lewin—a former Marxist who remained personally affable while politically distant and, above all, useful as a right-hand man of all-powerful producer Irving Thalberg, who himself claimed to be a former adolescent socialist street corner speaker." This may help explain why the commanding Thalberg "was personally fascinated with Lawson the intellectual."[41]

But Lawson had another problem. She "dislikes it more than I do," he said, referring to his wife's opinion of Hollywood. Yet, he thought, "it seems ridiculous . . . [to] spend a winter in a little apartment in New York." How could he turn his back on the blinding sunshine and potential riches of Hollywood for the uncertainties of Broadway? Again twitting Dos Passos, who as usual was trolling for a huge loan, he boasted, "At the rate of my present popularity (and such popularity must be deserved!) I can have almost anything I ask for in this Hell-hole next winter and the effort consists solely in mild shooting of the face and nodding of the head like a wise old owl." "However," he said, wisely aware of the vicissitudes of an industry that already had developed a well-deserved reputation for fickleness, "come November, the taking may not be so good—who knows but one [of] those terrible spasms of disorderly head-chopping may again sweep over the lot like a Pogrom—in the last one, three months ago, twenty writers met the axe in a single day, while the rest of [us] sat back secure and applauding the uncanny skill of the executioners." "Well," he added discerningly, "politics are mysterious, complicated and all-powerful and who knows that my smiling head may not face the block long before I get the magical Thalberg signature."[42]

Sue Lawson had itchy feet not only because of the heat emerging from the warm pavement of Los Angeles. Her husband's Hollywood carousing was inimical to his marital vows; even New York was not free of problems, from her perspective, for there resided Dawn Powell, who remained a fixture in her firmament. Sue Lawson had run into her and, "'being full of hooch, got in quite a state because she knew you were having affairs in Hollywood and knew I must be upset.'" The perceptive Powell was correct—which only served to inflame Sue Lawson's ire. "'The way that girl carries on about you is simply disgusting,'" she spat out to her husband, referring to Powell. Powell was suggesting that more was involved than simple adultery. No, said Sue Lawson, "'she not only boasts that you influence her entire [literary] career, which is the only thing that means anything to her now, she says, but she intimates there is still a [hot] romance'" raging with Lawson. Adding pain to injury, "'all this was shouted in a most casual manner,'" though Sue—who had been driven to tippling herself—"'was so affable'" in her gin that she "'didn't know she was even trying to pull anything until the next day.'"[43]

New York? Los Angeles? The Lawsons had choices of where to reside as the Damocles of the Depression hovered over most. For the next few years they would bounce between the two metropolises. But this trampoline-like odyssey and instability would eventuate in Lawson conclusively deciding to make a commitment—not only, finally, to his spouse but, in a life-transforming maneuver, to the Screen Writers Guild and the Communist Party.

4 From Hollywood to Broadway

When John Howard Lawson arrived in Hollywood in 1928, he was "dead broke" and "had heavy debts." After spending about a year doing what he deemed to be "a number of very bad but very important pictures which made a great deal of money, including *Our Blushing Brides*," he left, finances partially restored. He and his wife and family "were determined not to return to Hollywood"; with their newfound wealth, they "bought a house out near the Sound on Long Island." Ties with movies had not been severed altogether, for Lawson had made a "very unusual" and "very unsatisfactory arrangement with RKO" that "allowed" him to "write three original film plays in New York, not at the studio and just come out to the studio for two weeks consultation on each of the film plays." As it turned out, of the five scripts Lawson wrote for RKO, only one was produced—*Bachelor Apartment*.[1]

Why leave the sultry comforts of Los Angeles for the bone-chilling winters of New York? As one of the characters in his play *The Pure of Heart* put it, "It's no use going to Hollywood anyway, 'cause it's full of extras. You gotta get a reputation in New York."[2] Even Lawson's initial foray into Hollywood was premised on the idea that it was a "means of gaining cinematic knowledge which would be invaluable for future work"—on Broadway.[3] This condescending attitude toward the young film industry was au courant—particularly in certain precincts of Manhattan—and it would take a while before Lawson disabused himself of it. This attitude was even more remarkable, since, according to one critic, Lawson's experience in Hollywood actually improved his playwriting, making his "dialogue . . . much more fluent than ever before—almost slick; the plot more straightforward."[4]

The hamlet of Moriches on Long Island, where the Lawsons resided, was a stunning tableau of sand dunes, cool ocean breezes, and gentle waves—

certainly comparable to the pulchritude of Santa Monica that he had come to enjoy, winter aside. But pulchritude was not the term used to describe *Bachelor Apartment*. This movie was neither creatively nor financially successful. The best that can be said is that it anticipated *The Tender Trap*, produced decades later, with "women dropping into the bachelor flat to look for their shoes or change their rain-drenched clothes."[5] Nevertheless, Lawson felt that he had suffered the screenwriter's blight of not receiving proper credit for his work. He had "written the whole screenplay" in New York and "mailed" it to RKO, which "produced" it "exactly as I had written it." He "came out to the studio when the film was ready for release." When he "saw the credits," he went to the studio head "and made quite a scene" and was told that proper accreditation "was done only in the cases of famous authors whose plays or novels had been bought." Lawson considered the explanation "preposterous," but absent a powerful countervailing force such as a union, he was "helpless." Lawson's "response to these indignities was a main factor in [his] role in founding the Screen Writers Guild."[6]

Now Lawson was no ingénue or naïf when it came to moviemaking. "There's nothing sacred about a book per se," he once told John Dos Passos; "when you write a book or a play, you're responsible and you control it." Yet "when you sell it for a movie, it's out of your hands and everybody knows it." Hence, when Hollywood "made an unprecedented hash out of 'Success Story' which I adapted myself," Lawson reminded, he was not altogether shocked, since the "hash" emerged "largely through [his] own fault in handling the movie version stupidly and expecting stuff that was effective in the play to get over with picture actors." Despite this debacle, Lawson "certainly didn't suffer over that." In fact, he "got a good laugh out of [it],"[7] which was typical of his lack of touchiness about his work.

Bachelor Apartment was different, however, so he went to see David O. Selznick. But this soon to be famed producer was not enthusiastic about Lawson's request.[8] Still, Lawson's screenwriting career probably was not helped by this movie. This story of a Park Avenue man-about-town struggling with a raft of nubile and aggressive young lovelies contains a by now conventional plot device that actually was somewhat new and daring in Hollywood's infancy, namely, the carefree unmarried man being chastened from his rollicking ways by being intertwined with romantic love. This plot, of course, also contained more than a hint of Lawson's own predicament, for though he had committed to marriage in a formal sense, he was far from being dedicated to his marital vows.

Returning to New York meant rekindling the flame of his relationship with Dawn Powell; or, to put it another way, neither Broadway nor Hollywood was particularly good for long-term marriages, and bouncing between both only magnified the danger. Indeed, it is possible that part of the attraction of the Hollywood left was the perception that this was an entry point to a life of carnal pleasure. For example, Ring Lardner Jr., the Communist screenwriter, felt that it raised the self-esteem of Reds to have lovely women as comrades.[9] He once ruminated, only half jokingly, that "all the most beautiful girls in Hollywood belong to the Communist Party."[10]

Powell and Lawson had fallen into—indeed, had helped to set alight—a ring of fire. It seemed that he could open up with his mistress and fellow writer in a manner he found difficult with others. He confessed to her, for example, his discomfort in being turned down by the student newspaper at Williams College "because of Jewish prejudice," by which he meant anti-Semitism. "He and I," confided Powell, "both have ways of not facing things we don't want to. The only way of ever surmounting obstacles is not to see how big they are." Apparently Powell had little difficulty in seeing the "big obstacle" to capturing Lawson's complete affections—his wife. Sue Lawson was, she opined, a "pleasant, comfortable woman, shallow and lazy and scatterbrained." She was bad for her husband, and, of course, Powell was just the tonic he needed. "I hold it against her that she is dulling Jack to her level, making a rather average person of a very extraordinary genius." Dumbing down Lawson, she thought, was to Sue Lawson's "advantage"; it "keeps him from being desirable to better women than herself"—a "sad spectacle."

This was not the healthiest of love triangles. At one tumultuous party, Powell "in parting . . . socked her" and "also Jack." On another occasion, "Sue threw things around and started beating up Jack—a habit she has which always makes him look so ridiculous. But he told her this time to go to hell." The threesome were spending considerable time together in New York. Sue Lawson was an albatross, concluded her chief competitor, dragging down a brilliant man into a state of such mediocrity that he would not leave her.[11]

There were other domestic ructions that, at least, could provide fuel for Lawson's creative imagination. After arriving in New York, Lawson hurried out to "Belle Harbor to see [his] father." He "found that he had aged and seemed to have shriveled a little. But he walked with a springy step," and they "spent hours on the boardwalk talking about politics and the Depression; he had moved further to the left than I had and foresaw troubled days ahead." That was not the only surprise presented by his father. The RKO contract had guaranteed Lawson thousands of dollars per script—a gargantuan figure. He could write a "film in about two months," which meant he had entered the stratosphere of "affluence." Yet this roseate out-look could not conceal the gloom of the elder Lawson's revelation, as he "was forced to confess his own financial troubles." Worse, "there was a tone of worry or pleading in his voice that" Lawson "had not heard before"; he was "in debt: money had been his main means of proving his love to" his son, and with the disappearance of his money, it was as if the scant parental love Lawson had experienced since the premature passing of his mother had plummeted further. The newly affluent Lawson "opened" his "check-book and wrote him a check for over four thousand dollars"—though "a few months before this" he "could not have written a check for one tenth of this amount,"[12] a testament to his altered income and changed relation with his father.

On the other hand, another brewing relationship had captured Lawson's fancy that was to be much more revolutionizing and less replete with angst. On the train to Hollywood, Lawson was mesmerized by *Sister Carrie,* though he proved unable to convert it into cinematic form. On the train ride back to New York, Lawson read Dreiser's account of the Soviet Union and immediately was transfixed by the idea of writing a play concerning this vast land. Shortly thereafter Vladimir Mayakovsky, one of the founders of Russia's futurist movement—a trend that influenced pro-foundly Lawson's early plays—committed suicide, an event that shook Lawson to his core, for he identified with the passionate poet who was com-mitted to politics and revolution, frustrated by love, assailed by critics. Lawson was "shocked by the news" of this untimely death and "intended to make [Mayakovsky's] suicide"—a self-inflicted wound not unlike what had befallen Lawson's brother, Wendell—"the climax of a play which would cover the history of the Soviet Union." At that time he "knew very little about Lenin but wondered whether he could have met James Joyce when they were both in Zurich during the first world war." He "decided to begin" this "play with an imaginary meeting between the author of 'Impe-rialism' and the author of 'Ulysses.'" Lawson "regarded both as great in-tellectual leaders, representing opposing forces—the power of politics and the power of art," the animating forces of this screenwriter's own life.[13] Symptomatic of the drift of his thinking was the title of the play he con-ceived, *Red Square,* which also "dealt with an American writer's disillu-sionment with the Soviet Union." It was based loosely on another author he respected enormously—John Reed, the revolutionary writer who rode with Pancho Villa and communed with V. I. Lenin.[14]

The anomaly of his own increased wealth at a time of economic break-down was pushing Lawson further to the left. He was "heartily in accord"

with Dreiser, a growing influence, "about the importance of political persecution in the United States." Yet, at a time when the Communist Party itself felt that a revolution might be nigh and that certain pusillanimous elements on the "left" might be a roadblock, Lawson too found "the liberal
protests against this sort of thing to be so weak and confused as to be almost useless." "The liberal attitude," he sputtered, barely able to contain
his disdain, "is genteel, reasonable, and totally unrealistic." Tougher stuff
was needed, he told Dreiser. "I am saying this because I know your own
attitude is far from liberalism," yet, he conceded—not yet smitten by the
Communists—"I know of no means of opposition to persecution (which
really means opposition to the whole system) which is forceful enough
or organized enough to merit support,"[15] a point with which the novelist
concurred.[16]

These shifting currents were affecting Lawson. At this moment he was
"tremendously interested" in this "difficult question of mysticism." As he
told Dos Passos, "the detailed way in which the philosophical ideas of the
whole bourgeois era have penetrated the middle class mind—this is *your*
mind and *my* mind, as well as Eugene O'Neill's mind," was something of
which he was now acutely aware. Yes, he conceded, his "thinking" earlier
"was extremely confused; it is correct to call it mystical, because I consciously opposed the *rationalism* of the pre-war era, of which I felt [George
Bernard] Shaw was an example—and I had an idea that 'pure emotion' (a
'thing-in-itself' if ever there was one) was the basis of experience. This came
to a head in *Nirvana* but the vestiges of it in *all* my plays are important."[17]

Lawson, the proud avant-gardist, was now moving toward Marxism-
Leninism. In Hollywood he had written scripts that revealed his growing
interest in class conflict as a motive force of life. Now his plays were taking
on a similar stance.

.   .   .

When the renowned producer Harold Clurman first read Lawson's *Success
Story,* he was not impressed. The play concerns Sol Ginsberg—ironically a
precursor of Budd Schulberg's "Sammy Glick," a Jewish character who was
criticized so sharply by Lawson that Lawson became a subject of congressional debate. Like Glick, Ginsberg is an ambitious climber, clawing his way
from office boy to the executive suites via shady dealings and partner buy-
outs. In the final scenes with the girl he has loved and deserted, he draws a
revolver and is killed in a struggle for the gun.[18] The play included such
lines as "The Russian Jews are the world's most gifted and most difficult

people." Another says, "Gee, I like Jews, they're all poets or sugar daddies—or both!" His interlocutor responds, "You can't generalize, there's all kind." Politics is not absent either as Ginsberg remarks, "The way I figure it out, all this Capitalist graft is gonna bust up sooner or later." "Workers of the world unite," he adds sardonically, "you got nothin' to lose you but your chains—an' all you [got] to gain is bologney!"[19]

Success Story did not impress Clurman. "The play fails to click as a whole," he instructed condescendingly.[20] This was an auspicious start for one of Lawson's few plays to be translated to cinema. The play, directed by Lee Strasberg and featuring such luminaries as Luther and Stella Adler and Franchot Tone, was a production of Clurman's legendary Group Theatre, which was to feature Clifford Odets, Maxwell Anderson, Waldo Frank, and Aaron Copland.[21] The critic for the *New York Times* was not moved, however, by this display of star power.[22] The *New York Post* critic John Mason Brown was likewise ambivalent about this work.[23]

From the other shore, the Communist polemicist Mike Gold was similarly unmoved. In a critique that proved decisive in pushing Lawson further to the left, Gold was unsparing.[24] But, as so often happens, paying customers were not necessarily swayed by the critics. It was "doing such excellent business" that "300 people had to be turned away from the box office" during one "Saturday matinee."[25] Perhaps the sight of all those customers warmed the cockles of Clurman's heart—and changed his mind; subsequently he was effusive in his praise of both Lawson and this play. For Clurman, praise for Lawson was as pronounced as the latter's proboscis. He was "the hope of our theatre," he intoned, and the sparkplug of a Group Theatre hardly in need of sources of energy.[26]

Further, according to another analyst, *Success Story* deeply influenced a budding left-wing playwright who became something of a Lawson protégé. Clifford Odets, "far from finding Lawson's play hackneyed, would sense in it a cultural permission to unlock doors within himself he had hitherto not dared even to acknowledge." Odets was "significantly emboldened by Lawson's example." He felt that Lawson was "like some medieval figure, a Borgia, with a good strong chest and great vitality," and was sufficiently adroit, to "write with any sort of noise around him." He was, said Odets, a "good man indeed."[27] Clurman linked the dual avatars of radical theater, comparing Lawson's *Success Story* to Odets's *Awake and Sing!*[28] Cecil B. DeMille, who had become one of Lawson's most influential supporters, wrote him on Paramount stationery, on which he effused that *Success Story* "was the best written play that I saw in New York."[29] The success of *Success Story* was mirrored when it was serialized in the *New York Daily Mirror*.[30] It was viewed as not merely a play but a commentary on larger questions involving Jewish Americans, as a "reply to the Zionists" by some.[31]

What some found striking about this play—and ironic given Lawson's subsequent comments about Schulberg's Sammy Glick—is its "Jewishness" and the grasping, craven nature of Sol Ginsberg, which made him seem to be Glick's brother-in-law.[32] Lawson recalled that he had written this play with a "profound emotional involvement. He was wrestling, he believed, with 'the problem of my identity,' an important aspect of which was to come to terms 'with the Jewish aspect of my personality. . . . I could not be American without also being Jewish,'" thought Lawson. "'Sol Ginsberg has my idealism, my interest in social struggle. He also has my driving desire for recognition and money and success, which can be won only by spiritual bankruptcy and death.'"[33]

Interestingly, when the play was converted to cinema as *Success at Any Price,* the producers surgically removed this Jewish element, and the lead role was given a star turn by Douglas Fairbanks Jr. Lawson wanted Paul Muni—with whom he had collaborated previously—for this part, but RKO insisted otherwise. The increasingly popular screenwriter was disturbed about this "omission of the Jewish theme, which was the soul of the play," and how the lead character was "transformed into a Gentile."[34] However, the scalding and coruscating class politics remained, as this film—released as economic crisis loomed—was "one of the most bitter of the early Depression anti-business dramas," offering a "fascinating depiction" of a "fanatically determined working-class . . . mug rising from the bottom to become a successful advertising executive and abandoning all his morals in the process," including discarding his "childhood sweetheart."[35] Another analyst concurred, adding that this film "crystallized the era's anti-business sentiment and was precisely the sort of movie that could not be made once the Code"—Hollywood's system of self-censorship—"was enforced. The Code arrived just three and a half months after the release of the picture."[36]

Actually, Clurman's critical turnabout on this work may have been motivated by the fact that—as so often happens—the work improved as the performances improved. As a playwright and screenwriter, Lawson was irrevocably dependent upon actors. When Dawn Powell witnessed a first reading of *Success Story,* it "sounded confused and miserable," though even she—who at times could be Lawson's harshest critic—found it "magnificent" ultimately.[37] Powell realized more than most why *Success Story* became one of his signature works. It had obvious echoes of his own life: a Jewish man in New York torn between mammon and politics who treats women questionably.[38]

At the time this play was making waves, Lawson was driving home from Provincetown and gave a lift to W. Horsley Gantt, a "leading American authority on Pavlov's work." They conversed about this Russian genius, and Lawson was moved. He dropped Gantt off in New London and "immediately bought the volume of Pavlov," yet "found it almost as incomprehensible as Gantt," though it did provide "insight into the possibilities of a more scientific knowledge of human behavior." He compared these notions to what he had gleaned from "Freud's 'Civilization and Its Discontents' and the large conclusions he drew from his theory seemed to me to offer no explanation of the events which I realized were taking place around me." Like Pavlov, Freud now too proved to be ultimately dissatisfying. Bereft, scrambling for huge conceptions that would shed light on the human misery that stalked the planet—including the anti-Semitism which global events were forcing into his line of sight—Lawson began "thinking a great deal about communism."[39]

Dawn Powell was struck by this turn. "Jack," she acknowledged in her diary, "is thinking and talking so much more clearly and directly than ever before owing, he says, to Trotsky and a study of Marxian theories applied to creative work."[40] Powell's perception was a reflection of Lawson's systematic study. As he approached the pivotal age of forty, he had done an exacting inventory and emerged dissatisfied. What he later said about Herman Melville, seemed to apply to himself. "Melville's tragedy," he declared, "is the perennial tragedy of the intellectual: unable to achieve an integrated life devoted to rational social aims, he decided that social integration is neither possible nor desirable. But his despair made him a victim of the power he hated." He had not gone as far as Melville's story "Benito Cereno," however, which was little more than "a pitiful attempt to accomplish the task which Shelley rejected—to reconcile 'the Champion with the Oppressor of Mankind.'" Lawson, by his own admission, had a "superficial acquaintanceship with American literature and an almost complete ignorance of American history." He had begun to study these subjects, along with "Marxism," and "found it difficult but enormously rewarding as a revelation of the development of human society and the possibilities of a more rational order." His work on "dramatic history" made him "painfully conscious" of his own "historical illiteracy."[41]

Lawson's "first step toward any sort of serious political commitment" came in June 1932 when he first met the critic Edmund Wilson; under his "tutelage," Lawson began to delve deeper into Marxist literature. Then he met Louise Silcox, secretary and treasurer of the Authors League; of her Lawson said, "There was no one with the possible exception of Edmund Wilson who had such an influence on my becoming a Communist."[42]

This systematic study and the rushing currents that swirled around him—Depression, the rise of fascism and anti-Semitism, his changing relationship with his father, marital tensions—were pushing him inexorably toward firmer commitments. It was then that he became "increasingly convinced of the revolutionary function of literature" and began "continually trying to orient" himself "toward such an approach." He was not yet a "Communist," though he had "given much thought to the theory of it."[43]

Intriguingly, as he moved closer to unyielding commitment, Lawson became more accepting of Hollywood, perhaps viewing it—correctly—as an invaluable medium for massaging consciousness. Taking to the pages of the authoritative *New York Herald Tribune* in 1932, he pooh-poohed the common idea that "Hollywood is the death of art; that it kills the creative impulse in any artist." Yes, it was true that "the present function of the author in the motion picture industry is an extremely unsatisfactory one," and, yes, "the industry has many fantastic faults." Though creative writers routinely lamented the butchering of their words in Hollywood, Lawson, to the contrary, felt that "my own craftsmanship, my ability to give form and substance to my own ideas, has been enormously improved by my work in pictures. I have learned facility; I have learned conciseness in development of character and situation," and "I have also acquired new knowledge of audience reactions and box-office psychology." Where once he had adopted the common view of the superiority of stage drama, now he felt that "Broadway is bankrupt because of its lack of vision," whereas Hollywood inspired "new ideas" and "new vitality," which "inevitably require a new method of presentation." The power and infancy of Hollywood meant that Lawson was "still learning. One goes on learning until one dies. But for an author to say that Hollywood will kill his creative impulse is simply for him to admit that he is dead already. Many authors talk and think of their creative art as a delicate flower which must be nurtured and watered in order to bloom." He was leery of the writer spending "his whole life turning out a standardized product in a Hollywood cubicle"; in such a case, "it's obvious that [the writer] isn't going to be much of an artist." Yet, he countered, "the case is approximately the same if he spends his career grinding out stories for the pulp magazines, or pandering to higher class tastes with nicely written intellectual novels for the highbrow trade." Hollywood writers tended to be spoiled, he suggested. They were "an army of high-priced and eminent privates who are in general thoroughly discontented"; this future leader of writers argued that "more than half the blame for this condition lies squarely on the writers themselves; they do not approach the industry in a business-like or cooperative spirit." Unlike himself—presumably—he lamented that too many writers "make little or no effort to learn the technique with which he is dabbling," though the advent of sound had transformed the art of "scenario writing."[44] Strikingly, Lawson was not the only writer thinking along these lines.[45]

Yet this fascination with the screenplay had not distracted Lawson from writing plays. He was virtually unique in his ability to bounce between Broadway and Hollywood and maintain prominence in both. Lee Strasberg directed, and Stella Adler and Lloyd Nolan starred in Lawson's *Gentlewoman*. Elia Kazan was the stage manager of this Group Theatre production, which opened in the spring of 1934 at the Cort Theatre at Forty-eighth Street and Sixth Avenue in Manhattan.[46] Subway cars roared below, and brutish traffic snaked through narrow streets nearby as audiences piled into this cozy theater to witness Lawson's latest. It "possessed real qualities of emotional eloquence and social understanding," according to one analyst. Lawson had "presented a resolution in which a sensitive, wealthy, educated and neurotic woman is strengthened by an affair with a strong, daring, radical young poet who is both envious and contemptuous of her; the courageous man shows the in-turned, egocentric woman that one must confront the real, the objective world." This plot not only had obvious parallels to Lawson's storm-tossed relationship with Dawn Powell, as he continued to ransack his own life for dramatic material; it also continued what one critic termed his "awkward synthesis of Freud and Marx," a "kind of halfway house on a nameless road leading to an unknown destination."[47] Clurman was moved by the depiction of Lawson's protagonist, this "sensitive, educated woman of wealth who had grown neurotic through emotional disuse and lack of connection with the world." The poet—perhaps Lawson—she is attracted to is "both envious and contemptuous of her class; they have an affair in which both hope to resolve their lack of fulfillment."[48] The critic of the *New York World-Telegram* was likewise impressed.[49]

Brooks Atkinson, perhaps the most important critic, did not disagree.[50] In general, however, "the press was bad," recalled Clurman; "the reviewers had no idea what the play was about and didn't care."[51]

Amid the cogitation about the fate of a modern woman, Lawson managed to insert ruminations about his current preoccupations. One character noted, "I recently spent a year in Russia." Another observed, "Democracy can't swallow capitalism any more than a goat can swallow a five-ton truck—what happens? The truck runs over the goat. What's the result? Fascism!" Class conflict and romance—Lawson's principal fixations—were encapsulated in a line given to one leading character, who says, "Sure, the capitalist class is just going to shake hands all around and hand over the works—and you see your own husband doing it?"[52] Again, suicide—a theme since his brother's passing—was prominently featured.

As Lawson accelerated his steady march to the left, his methodical and analytical acumen—never dull—sharpened further and was turned on his critics. Then as now, Broadway critics were more powerful than those of Hollywood, with the effective ability to make or break productions. This was maddening to Lawson, no less so since he could comparably witness how these writers had a lesser impact on his movies. Thus, in publishing two of his works, he issued what he termed a "reckless preface," assailing drama critics in no uncertain terms. This was after *Gentlewoman* was performed a mere twelve times before closing, and another of his plays, *The Pure in Heart*—another story about a woman: a pretty girl from a small town who comes to New York and falls in love with a gangster—closed after seven performances.[53] This work fared no better at the hands of detractors.[54]

These "plays were not closed by the public," Lawson charged hotly in angry response. "They were closed by an irresponsible dictatorship" of "critics" with too much "control." One critic said that one of Lawson's plays was "'inflated with the poison gas of sheer noise and petulance and [the] shoddiest language.'" Another said, "'Compared to this sort of playgoing, a sinus attack is a welcome relief.'" With Olympian reserve, Lawson responded, "I have tried to present this problem from the professional Broadway point of view, without emphasis on the Marxian economics which offer the only reasonable explanation of the motives of the critics." What was to be done? Seeking to revive the kernel of the New Playwrights, he argued that "the only answer is to turn resolutely to the building of the revolutionary theater." On the other hand, despite his defensive tone, quite extraordinarily Lawson allowed Harold Clurman space in this book to assail—further—his plays, again suggesting that his blistering and searing experience on Broadway notwithstanding, he was far from being thin-skinned.[55]

More remarkable is that this critique of Lawson—appearing in Lawson's own book—was not far off the mark. Lawson *was* moving relentlessly toward a coherent social philosophy to which he would pledge undying commitment. Part of this evolution was the widening breach developing between himself and Clurman's Group Theatre, which had been essential in bringing a number of Lawson's plays to the stage. According to Clurman, "Lawson felt the Group viewed him as a Greenwich Village bohemian, well intentioned but lacking in the firm resolve the times demanded," while "he found the Group politically naïve and theatrically conventional." They were wedded—seemingly irretrievably—to the "Stanislavsky system" of acting, "still the core of the rehearsal process despite all their experimenting"; but to Lawson this "seemed old-fashioned to [a] man deeply influenced by the European avant-garde."[56] Clurman nonetheless "believed in Lawson's talent. To prove it, [he] advanced him a thousand dollars on his next play."[57]

Lawson tried to be firm. "I want freshness, excitement and poetry in the theatre," he maintained. "All the greatest tradition is one of violent contrasts and intensely vigorous movement. This was true of Shakespeare and Aristophanes, and please don't think I am cockily placing myself in their class." But something had changed—for the worse. "The whole growth of the theater through Ibsen and Shaw in recent years has intellectualized and devitalized it"; there was "the unbelievable repetition of the same plot, the same jokes, the same characters dished up each year with pitiful lack of showmanship. On the other hand, we have the art theater existing in a feeble trance totally removed from the rush and roar of things as they are, a sanctuary with doors against the world." This was no remedy, he said, since "art as an escape from life is no better than morphine, speech-making, murder or any of the other methods used to escape from reality."[58]

Nevertheless, a number of critics were not amused by Lawson's "reckless preface" or his tart analyses of contemporary theater.[59] Even Dawn Powell, one of his biggest fans, found *The Pure in Heart* "tawdry, incredibly stale," a "cheap, dull show. I was ashamed of Jack for having written it but more ashamed for his stupidity in thinking he could put such crap over on even the most moronic audience."[60]

The critics unsheathed their daggers and assaulted Lawson with relish.[61] Lawson fired back, arguing fervently that some critics "misrepresented" his work and "expressed a personal dislike of him more than an objective criticism of the [plays'] faults." But they disagreed even more stridently.[62]

Dustups between writers and critics were—and are—nothing new;[63] that others were similarly assaulted was small consolation to a wounded Lawson, though his own barbed commentaries on others rarely rose—or, better, descended—to this level of invective. The Communist newspaper, for example, "denounced" *Success Story* as "belonging to 'the Eugene O'Neill bourgeois reactionary variety, in which the audience is asked to weep over the sexual problems of a finance-capitalist swindler.'" Perhaps the Reds were aware, as Clurman put it, that "'from time to time, [Lawson] vented opinions that led us to believe that though he was definitely of progressive, even radical opinion, he was violently opposed to official Communist doctrine.'"[64]

Clurman also recalls that Lawson "interested the radicals, who nevertheless trounced him as mercilessly as the uptown boys. While the latter deplored his confusion, the former were positively enraged by it. Lawson accepted the invitation extended by a literary club to speak to them on his plays. Before he could take the floor, he was bombarded by a host of indictments, the burden of which [was] that though undeniably a writer of [merit], he was *confused*. The word 'confused' was repeated so often by so many it took on the quality of anathema." "When Lawson rose to speak," recalled a still dumbfounded Clurman, "I was shocked to find him not only humble but apologetic. He talked like a man with a troubled conscience, a man confessing his sin, and in some ways seeking absolution." One participant "hinted that what Lawson needed was closer contact with the working class. Lawson readily admitted this and soon went on a trip to cover the Scottsboro case for a left paper."[65]

Lawson was numb and benumbed. He was "radical" but derided by those of that ilk. He had few organic connections to the avant-garde—particularly in its most vital global iterations—of which he was a leading representative. He wanted recognition but was critical of the bourgeois forces that could deliver it, not least since challenging them was part of his raison d'être. The rejection of *Gentlewoman* and *The Pure in Heart* "within two days of each other" was particularly bracing. He had reached the peak of opening two plays simultaneously but had descended to the depths of having both being panned unremittingly. This "double rejection made him conscious of his own ideological as well as artistic limitations that ultimately led to his final acceptance of Communism."[66] His personal life was equally messy. His mistress, Dawn Powell, was beginning to turn against him. It was "very queer about material things and avarice," said this sharp-eyed critic. "There are people whose lives are dedicated to acquiring what they never had, then there are those who are only active in a greedy way in hanging on to what they have." "Jack," she said dryly, "has a little of both." She was still spending time with "Jack and Sue," but "we are in no sense on easy terms," she conceded. "Sue seems definitely a closed page—we scream at each other through carefully locked doors [and] can establish no semblances of our former friendship"; of course, that does tend to happen when one sleeps with the husband of a "friend." Still, this provided no comfort for Lawson, the frequently angry object of torment from the two torn women. Said Powell, "I vary in hating and despising Jack (for his mental and emotional cowardice in his work and in his life) to admiring him beyond reason (for his occasional flashes of heroic courage or strength). Both phases are beyond the power of most men." Yet she found it "curious how different, how devitalized," Lawson and his spouse were, "and as he grows older his Jesuitical logic becomes more unforgivable."[67]

Lawson was near the pinnacle of success but nonetheless was anguished, distressed, and under siege. Something had to give.

5 Commitment

By the early 1930s, John Howard Lawson was a bicoastal pioneer, a frequent traveler on trains shuttling between midtown Manhattan and downtown Los Angeles. He was compensated amply and had attained a critical acclaim, being viewed by some as the "hope" of the stage and an important voice of the screen. Yet he was torn with conflict and inner doubt, though like one of his well-made plays, his life was driving inescapably to a resolution. Those who perhaps should have been shouting support for him from the rooftops were among his most caustic critics, thereby contributing to his self-doubt. Harold Clurman "watched with shock and anger" as Lawson was upbraided by Communists and leftists at a meeting of the radical John Reed Club.[1]

Lawson's labor—pecking on a keyboard as he conjured up tales from his fertile imagination—was isolating, and that was hardly assuaged by collaboration with producers, directors, actors, stagehands, and others. With the advantage of hindsight, he later admitted that Clurman's critical evaluations of him were "not altogether wrong." "In my enthusiasm I oversimplified complexities and creative problems," though he was correct in "feeling that the Group could not establish a Broadway theater that would be genuinely creative." Many "days and evenings" were spent "when the whole company of the Group gathered to discuss what kind of theater should be built." The Adlers, Strasberg, Clurman, Odets, "Elia Kazan and Franchot Tone" discussed this issue interminably. Lawson—perhaps the most celebrated member of the Group—"argued that Clurman's plan was unrealistic, that one could not serve art and Mammon at the same time." Events proved, said Lawson with no hint of satisfaction, "that I was right."[2]

The fissures between Lawson and the Group may have been as harmful to the latter as the former, for he wielded wide influence on their brightest star, Clifford Odets, and his absence was not helpful to Odets. Clurman admitted that it was Lawson who "brought Odets an awareness of a new kind of theatre dialogue."[3] Odets scrutinized Lawson's *Success Story* assiduously, "studying the part[s] and writing down how I thought I would approach it as an actor."[4]

Lawson had first met Odets at the "Group's summer headquarters at Dover Furnace, New York in the summer of 1932." Thus began an intense friendship that continued keenly "about a decade after 1932." They "met many times." Toward the conclusion of this decade of upheaval, "there was quite a clash" between the two on the matter of "art and social responsibility," and Lawson "warned" his protégé that "the present trend of his work," specifically *Golden Boy* and *Rocket to the Moon*, "was weakening his art." Though not unsympathetic to the aims of the Group, he accused its members of "misinterpreting Stanislavsky" since they "wanted to find the true emotion in everything—but it was the false emotion, the tragic-comic pretense, that was the heart of Chekhov as it was of Brecht." "Odets," Lawson lamented, "was never able to see this rich contradiction in American middle class life, the only [life] he knew."[5]

"One of the difficulties with Odets, I should suppose," mused Lawson, "is that he was not an analytical or intellectual person."[6] Like Richard Wright and James Baldwin, these two writers who had so much in common clashed abrasively. At the "Third Congress of Writers" in New York in 1939, "there was quite a clash between us about art and social responsibility," recalled Lawson, and once more he warned his erstwhile protégé "that the present (psychological) trend of his work . . . was weakening his art." Again, this proved to be a "shock" to Odets.[7] "Can *Waiting for Lefty* be considered seriously as a work of dramatic art?" Lawson asked rhetorically, then answered, "I believe the answer must be no," it "was not a good play." By way of contrast, Lawson consistently praised another contemporary, Lillian Hellman, referring to her as "the most significant playwright of the later thirties."[8]

Odets was near the center of Lawson's dispute with the Group, for during this period, he recalled, "when Odets was turning from his first attempt to deal with working class material to a more natural and more honest use of middle-class material (which in turn led him into a cul-de-sac) I was having a bitter argument with the Group." Lawson "argued that there had to be a Left-wing theatre," yet "the dilemma of the writer in the thirties (a dilemma which continues into our day)," he proclaimed in 1961, "[was] we couldn't go to the left, we couldn't really be creative in these terms and we couldn't be creative in any other terms. So what to do? This is the dilemma that Arthur Miller faces at this very moment. He has no solution for it, and certainly there was no solution in the 1930s." The Group did not like his *Marching Song*, a play he himself later criticized, so he "stopped writing plays and the Group broke up" after increasingly "bitter discussions,"[9] a development that pained him greatly.[10]

Thus, though Lawson and the Group had a mutually advantageous relationship, ultimately it proved unsatisfying, as he was moving steadily to the left and—despite their fire-breathing rhetoric—Odets, Kazan, and company were not doing the same. And though Clurman had become not only a staunch supporter but one of his severest critics, it was scathing criticism from another corner that pushed Lawson definitely and defiantly toward a more unbendable commitment.

The Communist writer Mike Gold was well known as a prickly polemicist even before he criticized Lawson in 1934 for being a "bourgeois Hamlet," unsteady, unsure, unreliable.[11] Lawson confessed that this assault "made me angry," but remarkably—and in stark contrast to those who subsequently were censured by this well-spoken screenwriter—he went on to "unhesitatingly admit the truth of 70 percent of Mike's attack."[12] In his own defense, Lawson said, "prior to 1933 I know of no novels or plays in English which can be called completely successful from a proletarian point of view," but that was no excuse. For "five years ago," said Lawson, "I had similar tendencies toward confusion"—that word so often used to describe his work—"because I . . . had not made a disciplined study of the issues." Yes, said Lawson, "I readily admit that my plays have not achieved . . . real clarity." Thus, "after the childish high spirits of *Processional*," he "turned to a confused religious escape in *Nirvana*; that was the inevitable next step considering my background and intellectual processes; *The International* was a serious attempt to portray a world revolution, but my lack of theoretical background betrayed me into many inexcusable errors and a general air of anarchistic sentimentality." *Success Story, The Pure in Heart*, and *Gentlewoman* were the casus belli as far as Gold was concerned: Lawson meekly defended this work, since "in spite of faults," it "shows a considerable ideological advance." This could be seen, ironically, in the "unanimous antagonism with which these plays were greeted in the bourgeois press," for they depicted an "uncompromising and correct picture of bourgeois decay." "Mike's case," said the besieged Lawson, "simmers down to the fact that I ask a 'monotonous question': 'Where do I belong in the warring world of two classes?'" Well, said the aggrieved Lawson, "I'm sorry the question bores him, but I intend to make my answer with due consideration and with as much clarity and vigor as I possess."[13]

This disconcerting experience with the Group Theatre combined with a similarly unfortunate dalliance with Gold and the New Playwrights had drained Lawson.[14] One characteristic of insanity, it is said, is doing the same thing over and over again and expecting different results each time. From the New Playwrights to the Group Theatre, it seemed that Lawson was trapped in a cycle of insanity, reeling from one unsatisfactory stage experience to another.

Lawson's critics were deploying similarly strong language to describe him—and his work. Finally, he bent. As he saw it, the dramatic resolution of the dilemma of the role of the artist, trapped between mammon and politics, was to opt decisively for the latter. It was shortly thereafter that Lawson—nearing forty—joined the Communist Party. And this commitment led to others—a reaffirmation of his marital vows, organizing the Screen Writers Guild, and a further dedication to political struggle generally.

This was not a smooth or seamless transition, however. Lawson's "first reaction to Mike Gold's attack" was "blind rage." He "trusted him as a friend" and felt betrayed. How often is a writer attacked so witheringly in a journal—*New Masses*—on whose editorial board he serves?[15] What Lawson found particularly distressing was that he was under siege from all sides of the political spectrum. At the same time he was locked in a polemic with Mike Gold, he was facing down mainstream theater critics over the same issues. He reproached Percy Hammond of the *New York Herald Tribune,* accusing him of being part of a "rigid dictatorship of the reviewers" that warped theater.[16] Bernard Sobel of the *New York Daily Mirror* was likewise rebuked.[17]

Licking his wounds,[18] Lawson was "very anxious" to discuss this matter of his injured reputation and his future trajectory with his good friend and fellow writer Dos Passos, "particularly as it concerns the proletariat. Mike Gold made a bitter and exceedingly dirty attack on me, which I have just answered with what I think is a reasonable statement of my position." "I feel very strongly," he added, crystal ball in hand, "the necessity of a much closer contact with Communism, and much more activity in connection with it."[19] It was ironic that Lawson, who was to be accused of unfairly excoriating various writers during his time in the Communist Party, actually joined the Party after he was unfairly excoriated.

Being the perpetual student he was, Lawson was compelled by the sour critique to address more fundamentally the question of criticism itself—a subject and praxis with which he became associated intimately.[20] Gold's battering had not plunged him into suicidal depression or compelled him to question his own bent toward radicalism but to extend his own commitments, political and otherwise.

Actually, another important intervening event pushed Lawson into the embrace of the Reds. For in that decisive year of 1934 Lawson decided to venture south to investigate the horrific conditions that had catapulted the names of Angelo Herndon and the Scottsboro Nine into headlines globally.[21] This was not just a geographic journey but a political and ideological one because placing his celebrity at the disposal of a movement for justice was an essential aspect of Lawson's renewed commitment. For an entire generation these cases, which implicated racism and political repression, were captivating and transforming, deepening understanding of the plight that afflicted so many, particularly African Americans. Certainly this was the case for Lawson, who was beginning to tire of writing fantasies for actors when increasingly more dramatic events were playing out on a global stage.

Hence, in the midst of the critical assault upon himself, his reputation, and his work, the bedraggled and chastened Lawson decided that he would train his formidable rhetorical skills not on the theater but on life itself. He would venture south to write about these matters. He went to meet with Communist Party leader, Earl Browder, about this, after having "visited *The New Republic* and *The Nation*," whose "editors had given me letters introducing me as a prominent author." Browder, however, "was cautious." The avuncular, pipe-smoking bureaucrat with a shock of dark hair across his forehead, patiently "explained that the party in Alabama was underground and it might be dangerous for me to make contact with them." The party in this cradle of the former slave-owning Confederacy was an outlaw, subject to brutal harassment and casual gunplay. This chilling "conversation" with the blunt Browder "unnerved him"—but not enough to deter him.

Lawson's train was to depart from Manhattan into the southern heart of darkness at "eleven o'clock at night." Still ridden with anxiety after his exchange with Browder, Lawson "dined alone at an Italian restaurant and ate a huge dinner with too much wine and more than too much brandy." He was "in a coma" as his "train pulled out of the Pennsylvania station." He had a "vague notion" that he was "in a space capsule on my way back to the stars." Arriving in the South, he met with another son of affluence—the Harvard-trained lawyer Ben Davis, who also was a Communist and happened to be a Negro—who had served as a counsel in the Herndon and Scottsboro cases. From there Lawson repaired to the "parlor of an old mansion in Atlanta" on a "tree-lined avenue"; the "room was old-fashioned, furnished with nineteenth century taste and the walls were pock-marked"—ominously—"with bullet-holes." There the eminent Broadway playwright met with the state's hard-bitten, gnarled segregationist governor, who did not retreat an inch in defending the treatment of Angelo Herndon, jailed for his protest of economic misery. Then he met with the prisoner of conscience himself, as Herndon "sat under a glaring light, surrounded by four guards with guns," bewildered, "nervous and afraid."

This occurrence was sufficiently terrifying, but it hardly prepared Lawson for Alabama, his next stop. Browder had "instructed" him to "go to one of the best hotels and wait" until "someone came to see me." He waited—and waited some more. Lawson "felt conspiratorial and as the second day wore on, a little foolish." Finally there was a knock on the door; when Lawson answered apprehensively, he found a "girl, white and obviously southern. She was the wife of the district organizer of the Communist Party." From there, the prominent visitor from New York was whisked off to meet with the Scottsboro Nine. They "were somber and aloof, staring" at Lawson through metal bars—treated like caged animals. "They were not talkative," perceptively fearing that to be too forthcoming might lead to further medieval punishments after Lawson departed. Lawson himself "expected to be seized and thrown into one of the cells."[22]

This was not hyperbole. Brazenly, an advertisement in a local newspaper observed that Lawson was "no ordinary jackass. Mr. Lawson is a professional jackass. He makes it pay." He was a clear-cut case "for the psychoanalytical clinic." Lawson, it was said, "has an overdose of martyritis [*sic*]"; he "thrives on abuse," and his opponents were not averse to testing his limits of tolerance.

Lawson had traveled south on behalf of the National Committee for the Defense of Political Prisoners. Contrary to his enemies' assertions, this was no Red delegation; it did include one party member, but it also included a representative of the American Civil Liberties Union and a Yale student. This arduous and grueling experience helped to deepen Lawson's relationship with that political party—the Communists—whose alleged presence had sparked such consternation in Alabama. He was deeply affected by this astringent taste of southern Grand Guignol. Understandably, he viewed this unsettling experience through the lens of his own Jewishness and concluded that a deeper commitment by himself—and others—would be required if disaster were to be averted. "The course of embryonic Fascism in the South," he warned portentously, "was exactly analogous to its course in Hitler['s] Germany." He scoffed at what he perceived as less than full-bodied responses to this threat. "Liberals who think they are immune will soon find that the wiping out of 'radicalism'" would include "wiping out all independent thought and culture."[23] He took to the pages of the *New York Post* to present this foreboding warning directly.[24]

His encounter with Alabama Communists intensified his own rapport with the party. He sat in a "crowded courtroom" awestruck as he heard young Reds "from the North proclaim the right of national self-determination for their black brothers and predict a Soviet Alabama." "It was magnificent," thought Lawson, "and it made no impression on Judge Abernathy who sat on the bench rocking sleepily and chewing tobacco; now and then he spat accurately in a spittoon some distance from his seat." Lawson, simultaneously apprehensive and energized, found himself "surrounded by muscular men with gangster faces."

As he was leaving the courtroom, a "police car drove up to the curb. A cop jumped out and pulled [Lawson] away from the crowd and ordered [him] into the car." He "protested loudly," shouting as he was being manhandled, "'I'm the playwright from New York.'" Singularly unimpressed, the officer responded, "'All you trouble-makers come from New York,'" and the unsympathetic crowd laughed uproariously. The police questioned Lawson "for several hours. They wanted to know whether I was a Jew." When the resolute Lawson admitted that, yes, he was Jewish, his questioners "exchanged looks and peppered the conversation with anti-Semitic jokes." He was instructed to "get out of town." Not waiting for further elaboration, Lawson immediately "packed and checked out of the hotel."[25] It seems that the authorities had heard that Lawson had wired dispatches to the Communist newspaper the *Daily Worker*.[26]

Lawson was blunt in revealing that "my adventures in Alabama were a turning point in my life: I was confronted, suddenly and irrevocably, with the reality of class relations in the United States; I saw the heroism of the Negro people, and I saw the faces of their oppressors."[27] Later, in reflecting on these events as dramatic as any of his most febrile plays, Lawson still seemed awestruck by the sight of the "courtroom crowded with White Legionnaires who looked and behaved like motion-picture gangsters. I had never witnessed anything like the open terror, supported by the police power of the state, that was practiced in [Alabama]." But Lawson refused to back down. He did scram from Birmingham "but returned a few weeks later with a delegation to investigate." For his troubles, he was "arrested again, and on this occasion, accused of 'criminal libel.'" He was "released on bail and again given a peremptory order to leave town. The case was never brought to trial." Yet the imprint left on his consciousness was ineradicable. Organizing writers and sojourning in the South deepened his "conviction that *commitment* is essential to the artist's creative growth; what we call the *sensibility* of the artist is deadened if he does not respond generously to the human reality that surrounds him; to observe and report, to laugh or weep, are not enough." Lawson refused to stay away from Birmingham. In July 1934 he was arrested there "for the third time within two months." The *New York Times,* which described Lawson as a "self-styled radical leader," reported on his attempt to "intercede for the Negro defendants in the 'Scottsboro case'" without comment. Lawson, on the other hand, denounced the "'straight censorship'" to which he had been subjected, which was "'something that strikes directly at freedom of speech and press.'"[29] Years later he still recalled vividly the "rumor that the notorious White Legion was going to run me out of town so we moved at night to the little hotel where an electric fan stirred the turgid air and we listened as the creaky elevator made its occasional ascent."[30] It was easy for fear to drive him out of town but not away from radicalism.

News of Lawson's adventure "attracted national attention to civil liberties violations" in the South.[31] Lawson had now attained another kind of celebrity to accompany his notoriety on stage and screen. Returning to New York, he met with I. F. Stone and editors at the *New York Post.* His series for this paper "aroused national interest" and led to a protest by President Franklin Roosevelt and others by well-regarded activists, including Oswald Garrison Villard, Roger Baldwin, Corliss Lamont, and Waldo Frank. A radicalizing moment had seized the time. "Kazan, Odets and others joined the CP and," said Lawson, "I suppose a main influence was their participation in the presentation of the short play, 'Dimitroff'"—a dramatization of the story of the Bulgarian Communist who faced down the fascists in Europe, in a manner somewhat more heroic than Lawson's escapade in Alabama.[32] In such a hothouse environment, Lawson's own newly forged political commitments seemed ordinary. For it was in Alabama that Lawson saw the enormous strength—and commitment—of common, ordinary folks confronting forces more formidable than anything he had encountered in his own comparably uncomplicated life. It was in Alabama that he heard an "'older' comrade explain to a young recruit the importance of patience, humility and study: 'There ain't one of us here was born a Communist; we learned it and it ain't easy to learn.'"[33]

This pedagogical aspect of the Communist life appealed overpoweringly to Lawson, something of an autodidact with an intense need for study. Marxism-Leninism provided him with an entire library of volumes to pore through on all manner of topics. It provided him with a collective with which he could share experiences and thoughts, wisdom and inanities, just as his marriage, he came to find, could provide a haven in a heartless world.

Yet it was not just this eye-opening experience in a retrograde Alabama—not to mention the critical assault on his plays and reputation, his collapsing affair with Dawn Powell and resultant marital strains, his transformed relationship with his father, and his morphing ties to Dos Passos—that was pushing Lawson steadily leftward to firmer political commitments. Though he was compensated well for his creative labor, his more unyielding commitment came with a price—more straitened economic circumstances that also were radicalizing.

For one unavoidable aspect of his more expansive political involvements was that they pulled him away from his imaginative writing. Moreover, his increased political celebrity may not have endeared him to movie moguls, who could tolerate parlor radicalism more easily than that manifested on the front lines of struggle. He was still shuttling between Broadway and Hollywood, but he had not "done so well with jobs" in the latter, and by the mid-1930s his "return East was motivated by the scarcity of jobs" in movies and his "desire to return to the theatre." Indeed, the Lawsons "were so low financially" that when he finally "got a call to work on *Blockade*," perhaps his most celebrated film, he "waited most of the night at the Federal Arts Project for a special dispensation to get [his] last week's pay of $21.50 before it was due." His "political activity" had meant "no more jobs for a while"; besides, "Sue's deep dissatisfaction with Hollywood life and lack of outlet for her creative abilities" (she painted) was complicating life further—particularly since his more unswerving political commitments were accompanied by more steadfast marital ones.[34]

Another factor should be considered when divining Lawson's 1934 decision to join the Communist Party. Put simply, anti-Semitism seemed to be spiraling out of control globally, and Lawson, as a man who felt being Jewish intensely, could not be indifferent. In the first place, the obvious influence of Jewish Americans in Hollywood had attracted bigots like flies to honey. Among them was the industry's official censor, Joseph Breen, whose job was to make sure that certain kinds of propaganda were not allowed in movies. In this role he and his minions scrutinized scripts—which, inter alia, exposes further why the idea of Lawson smuggling Red views into movies was so laughable. A man so congenial to anticommunism—and anti-Semitism—as Breen would hardly allow a Jewish Communist like Lawson get away with much; to the contrary, he would be more likely to seek to bombard him out of the industry.[35] This calcified bias did not take a holiday after Breen assumed power in Hollywood.[36] As one analyst put it, as early as the 1920s "antagonism toward Jews increased alarmingly" in the United States, while the following decade witnessed "an explosion of unprecedented anti-Semitic fervor."[37]

Los Angeles, the epicenter of the film industry, did not escape this trend; it was a hotbed of pro-Nazi sentiment of a kind that could only profoundly affect one with Lawson's sensibilities and background.[38] "It seems hard to believe," recalled Carey McWilliams, the eminent chronicler of the region, "but there were headquarters here in Los Angeles" for "Nazi propaganda."[39] It was not unusual for them to make a "disgraceful scene" at events that did not meet their fancy.[40] It was not uncommon for mass rallies of Nazis to occur in Los Angeles with "'brown shirts' with the Swastika on the left arm."[41] As early as mid-1933, the press was reporting that "Nazis" were managing to "hold [their] first open meeting" in L.A.; there were an "estimated 150,000 Germans" in the city.[42]

It was hard for Lawson to be indifferent to such developments. Particularly after his visit to Alabama, where he came face-to-face with officially sanctioned anti-Semitism, he felt a passionate need to commit himself further to the struggle against bigotry. As he saw it, the Communists were the only global, well-organized force willing to dole out bitter medicine to the fascists. Hence, he deemed *Success Story* to be his "best" and "most powerful play." It was a "powerful play because it grew very much out of my personal emotional experiences," he said. He could feel the dull pain expressed by Sol Ginsberg because, like him, he too was Jewish in a world where anti-Semitism was far from absent.[43]

Thus it was that he arrived in the mid-1930s at the "ornate mansion" of a man he admired, Theodore Dreiser, on a mission that was somewhat discomfiting. Accompanying him to this plush section of Mount Kisco, New York, were Communist leaders Mike Gold and James Ford, along with the philanthropist Corliss Lamont. They had come to confront the eminent writer about anti-Semitic comments he had made—broad and disreputable generalizations about those who were Jewish.[44] By his own avowal, Lawson "was probably more emotional about the meeting than the others," though Gold was known to have a quick temper about such matters as well. As the discussion became more heated, one participant charged that Dreiser was becoming "senile." Because "age was more troubling to him than anti-Semitism," he "stood up in wrath and ordered us out of the house. There were apologies and he finally agreed, not very gracefully to disclaim his words."[45]

In what was becoming a pattern, Lawson then confronted the Nobel Prize–winning Italian writer Luigi Pirandello after he damned Ethiopia in its conflict with Italy, denouncing the "'prostitution of a writer to the service of destructive reaction.'"[46] Perhaps not expecting what was to occur, the visiting writer "entertained a group of . . . American dramatists and writers [in] his suite in the Waldorf-Astoria." This time the avenging screenwriter was accompanied by Clifford Odets. Lawson's denunciation followed on the heels of his attempt "to get Mr. Pirandello to disavow imperialism, fascism, reaction, war and Italy's intended invasion of Ethiopia." Pirandello greeted Lawson's torrent of words with the reply that "art and politics were entirely divorced, that politics and social questions 'are of the moment' but that 'an artistic moment lives forever.'" Lawson guffawed at this notion. The meeting ended in "rancor," which only increased when Pirandello realized that the "press" was "present."[47] The hard-boiled Lawson considered the Italian's thinking "fatuous," recalling later that "when we started to argue about fascism he almost collapsed." As Lawson recalled, "I suppose it was unfair, [but] we were brash in those days and I was the leading spokesman of the occasion—but the confrontation under such painful circumstances of the author of *Six Characters* and the author of *Lefty* has a sort of historical meaning."[48]

Lawson was also present when the German consulate in Manhattan was picketed. At this raucous gathering of one thousand protesters, organized by the Communist-led International Labor Defense, he demanded the release of the Communist leader Ernst Thaelman and "'freedom for all political prisoners.'" Lawson was a "principal" speaker to this assemblage at "Rutgers Square," which "broke up shortly before midnight."[49] Demonstrators had taken to the streets, since earlier consular officials had refused to meet with a Lawson-led delegation. In fact they were "'roughly' ejected" from the premises, with the officials "threatening their arrest."[50]

Lawson was becoming a familiar presence on the picket lines of Los Angeles and, particularly, New York, joining three thousand workers at a midtown rally protesting slashing of relief rolls; "a girl dressed as Santa Claus led the main body of demonstrators" as they marched "for two hours in the cold rain." The "block became choked with demonstrators, marching two abreast" to Columbus Circle, where they heard the now driven writer declaim.[51]

But even with this riveting escalation of chauvinism and resistance and the none too muffled roar of war, the actual conditions at the studios also impelled Lawson away from his typewriter and toward grappling in the political trenches. There was nothing magical about the exploitation of studio labor.[52] This was apparent to Lawson upon his arrival in 1928.

Studio executive Edmond DePatie later acknowledged that unions "developed because people were exploited en masse. There is no question about that," he explained. "I saw the exploitation of people in our business, until it was just almost sickening." Still seemingly distraught years after these heinous practices had been curbed, he said, "It was not uncommon to work people as late as eleven and twelve o'clock at night and give them a seventy five cent dinner check. And it was not uncommon to work them every Saturday night, fifty two weeks a year, until five or six o'clock in the morning." This, he declared, "was a very, very common practice."[53]

Writers and actors did not elude this kind of exploitation. Almost gleefully, Joseph Breen said in 1932, "There are 25,000 actors out of work in this town. You can imagine the reaction upon all these of such a stupid display of money" as the studio ad budget.[54] The actor James Cagney, who also became a union activist, was among those who were outraged.[55]

Writers may have been worse off. The comic Groucho Marx remarked sarcastically, "It looks like Paramount is determined to save some money, for they have chopped off about a dozen high priced writers in the past week, those that remain have all been forced to take a generous cut. I don't feel particularly anguished for any of them as they were all overpaid, including me."[56] The Oscar-winning screenwriter-director Robert Pirosh did not find this situation humorous at all, recalling the mogul, Daryl Zanuck as a "dictator." "I was in conferences with him," he recalled "and he would just pace up and down with his polo mallet . . . swinging it, and you're always wondering if he's going to hit you with it."[57]

Lawson was not immune. "I am working like a dog at the studio," he announced as the union was getting under way, as he also had to endure the mental strain of "political upheaval, full of plots for palace revolutions" that routinely afflicted MGM.[58] Long hours in a frenetic working environment were the order of the day.

Yet what drove the famously independent and solitary writers into a union was the drive to deprive them of their role—in Lawson's words—as the "creator" of the motion picture. The routine attempt to exploit writers took on new dimensions—again—with the advent of sound, as the blueprints from which movies were made, replete with dialogue, were clearly the foundation of the motion picture and clearly the product of the writer's imagination. Making a movie from a blank sheet of paper was more than a notion. But habitually writers' contribution to the making of movies was disregarded—and this pattern did not avoid Lawson. "In a good percentage of my pictures," he said later, "the credits on the screen bear no relationship to the work accomplished. This was especially horrifying (a whole system of manipulating credits) before the first Screen Writers Guild contract" was finally ratified "in 1941." Thus, "the credits for 'Dynamite' read:

'story by Jean Macpherson, dialogue by Jean Macpherson, John Howard Lawson and Gladys Unger.'" Well, said Lawson, "I was outraged when I learned of the credits and I protested to DeMille. He knew and admitted I had done the major work on the film. He did not change the credits but he did something quite unusual at the Carthay Circle theatre at the gala opening. He was in front of the main entrance, at a microphone, introducing stars, and he stopped me and introduced me in the rather florid DeMille manner—this was almost unheard of for writers, but it did not change the credits." He was embarrassed by *Our Blushing Brides*—a "horrid picture and a smashing success"—but, again, even more disturbing was the deprivation of his credit for the screenplay. Credits read, "'Scenarists, Bess Meredyth and John Howard Lawson. Dialogue by Bess Meredyth and Edwin Justice Mayer.'" This separate category, "'dialogue' was common in the early days of sound. Since Bess Meredyth and I had collaborated on the screenplay and had written the dialogue together, my designation solely as 'scenarist' deprived me of major credit." The producer, Hunt Stromberg, had "been very angry because I had argued with him about some of the dialogue he wanted—which I told him was artificial and absurd. This argument made him feel I was not 'cooperative' which was quite enough to cause a change in credit."[59]

This matter of "credit" was a prime reason that compelled screenwriters to organize. "Prior to the founding of the [SWG] in 1933," recalled Lawson, "Hollywood writers were treated with contempt; it was not uncommon for 8 or 10 writers to work on one script with screen credit whimsically distributed among the producers' in-laws, golf partners, or bookies."[60]

Lawson "did think that writers should have more participation in production." Why should writers be barred from the set when their creations were being acted out? It was almost as if there was fear that writers would desire to claim the wealth their imaginations were producing on the spot and, thus, had to be barred from sets.[61]

Initially Lawson sought to revive the "now moribund screen writers subsidiary of the Dramatists Guild," so they could better seek "royalties" and "a minimum percentage of the gross revenues of the pictures."[62] They sought to "set up a voluntary association to take the place of the present Academy" of Motion Pictures, formed, as they saw it, as an antiunion maneuver. "The name of the Academy has received such opprobrium among the employees," it was said, and should be replaced by the "Motion Picture Institute."[63] These were all fighting words as far as the moguls were concerned.

Defending the basic interests of the writers was the mission of the SWG. As so often happens, impending economic misery drove the famously atomized writers to flock together. The newly elected president, Franklin D. Roosevelt, had delivered his inaugural address, and "on that Saturday evening" Lawson held a festive "party in our home on San Vincente Boulevard in Santa Monica"; there was, as he recalled, "a tension, a vibration, a rumor of things impending and unknown that made the party different from other Saturday nights." The famed anarchist Carlo Tresca and his wife, Margaret de Silver, were his house guests. She "had been one of our dearest friends ever since the early twenties and her marriage to Tresca made him like a member of the family." Tresca and Lawson "differed" in their "estimate of Roosevelt," and "the party on the night of the inauguration was divided into two groups—Carlo led the group which held that Roosevelt would bring a revolutionary change, while [Lawson] held that only the groundswell of popular protest could persuade the nation's rulers to grant serious concessions." This "became a matter of passionate partisanship. The guests gathered around . . . attracted by the unexpected intensity of the discussion."[64]

The intensity of the discussion paled in the wake of Roosevelt's freighted words. As Lawson recalled later, early in Roosevelt's first term, "at one o'clock on [a] Monday morning" he "proclaimed the closing of all the nation's banks and the prohibitions of dealing in gold." The insouciant band of studio writers "responded to the crisis in accordance," smirked Lawson, "with our 'way of life.' We left on Monday afternoon for Agua Caliente, a plush gambling resort near Tia Juana." A small group of writers had been meeting informally airing grievances about their plight, but even FDR's thunderbolt had not shaken them out of their reverie.

Yet whatever naïveté had driven this reveling came to an abrupt halt that Wednesday, when MGM "called an emergency meeting of all writers, actors, directors and producers," who were told that they "must accept a fifty percent cut" in their salaries. Instantly, this "produced a mood of militancy among screenwriters that had never before been possible."[65] Lawson "was sitting close to Mayer" and "saw tears begin to flow down his cheeks as he explained that he too would receive half his usual income. Mayer's tears moved me and others" said Lawson derisively, but "possibly not in the way he would have wished. I was not weeping but I was thinking—studio workers who had union protection were not subject to the fifty percent cut." So almost instantaneously, Lawson and other like-minded writers decided to "announce a meeting of all screen writers at the Hollywood Knickerbocker Hotel. The committee asked me to deliver the main report, which proposed that each member sign a pledge to strike."[66]

Their goal—"building a powerful organization among the writers"—could "best be done by working slowly and by holding a series of meetings

to which each enrolled member should bring one guest at the next and subsequent meeting." Another goal—which "was brought forth with a great
deal of highly favorable criticism"—was "placing the screen writers remu-
neration on a royalty basis." This "could best be done by embodying in a
standard writer's contract a minimum percentage of the gross revenues
of the picture, the writer to have a specified drawing account against such
royalties."[67]

The whipsaw of economic distress globally, nationally, and in Hollywood itself was raising the consciousness of writers. A consensus had developed among many in the industry that there was a "rottenness, a complete disregard of the human factor" in Hollywood. "Men and women"
were "not considered as highly as the raw material that goes into any other
manufactured goods," said one union publication.[68] But this anger was particularly heartfelt among writers, who had good reason to believe that the
entire industry rested heavily on their often narrow shoulders.[69]

Simultaneously, producers often had contempt for the earnest grievances of writers.[70] Lawson was among those who was "particularly in-
censed at the fifty percent cut." "However, one good thing," he reported to
Dos Passos, "has been accomplished by it. We are now actively forming a
screenwriters union." "I've been very active in this," he confided, "with in-
numerable secret meetings and a lot of insurrectionary atmosphere"; there
was "the opportunity of tying up the studio if an issue arises." Best of all,
"it *may* enable writers to get a very much larger share of the creative end
of the stick" and "to work in pictures as freely as one does in the theatre."
Forming the Screen Writers Guild was "going to be a very tense and comical fight before we're through," he predicted.[71]

Shortly thereafter, the promised meeting of writers was convened at the
Knickerbocker Hotel, attracting a crowd of two hundred. Lawson was the
principal force in forging an agreement to be presented to the moguls. "I
read the contract and explained its [meaning]," he said later. "There was no
stormy applause." Nervously, Lawson surveyed the packed room and detected "tension and fear." Seeking to lead by example, he announced that
he "would be the first to sign the contract and asked who in the hall would
join me. Slowly, one by one, hands were raised. When about half those
present had raised their hands, people rose to their feet and everyone's
hands were in the air." Lawson was "unanimously chosen president."

Emboldened writers began to sign up, including another leader of the
guild, the screenwriter Frances Marion, a "wonderful and noble person,"
thought Lawson. She was among "about seventy-five writers at the meeting" who "signed the contract," though "many of the others scurried away,

shamefaced in their escape." Undeterred, Lawson then spent "the next six hours, until dawn," engaged in a unique form of labor organizing, traipsing from "house to house from the Hollywood Hills to the sea."[72] He recalled one writer "opening his front door, clad in pajamas, asking wistfully—'Must I sign?'"[73]

Lawson was not yet a Communist, his energy expended on door-to-door organizing notwithstanding, and he had reason to "doubt whether there were any Communists in the Guild at that time." Samuel Ornitz, a good friend and weighty influence upon him, was "more familiar with Marxist theory than anyone" Lawson knew, but he "was a mystic at heart." So, contrary to the jaundiced view of subsequent analysts, this union was no Red invention.

Still, the formation of this guild was a concrete step in Lawson's march into the arms of the Communists. "The first weeks of my presidency," he recalled later, "marked the beginning of a new personal development." Though there was "no change in the friendly attitude of Thalberg," Lawson acknowledged "I was being watched at the studio." The papers in his desk were examined during his "absence." Apparently aware of Lawson's proclivities for the sensual, "an attractive young woman who was a bit-player in films made an effort to attract me which was so naïve that I felt obligated to tell her that she too was a worker and should not lend herself to the dark schemes of the producers." A reinvented Lawson, with firmer commitment, was the moving force when the SWG was formed on 8 July 1933.[74] "I believe I am right in thinking that I am the only President elected in that way," he said proudly of his unanimous victory.[75]

Later Lawson expressed bafflement at the relative lack of attention to this labor organizing in Hollywood. "I had never before placed any great confidence in other writers," he proclaimed, "except for those who were my friends." He had "not been interested enough to attend a meeting of the Dramatists Guild in New York," but now he was "arguing with passion for faith in my fellow writers."[76]

Suggestive of the influence of playwrights in the organizing of screenwriters is not only the early tie to the Dramatists Guild but their desire—in the dramatist Lawson's words—to achieve "sane and intelligent adaptation of plays, which will have an effect in increasing the price of the material." "Protection against plagiarism, which is at present rampant in the studios," was also stressed. With breathtaking impudence, Lawson demanded a "revolution in the writer's position in the industry," and to that end he repeatedly "advised our entire membership to withdraw from the Academy of Motion Pictures Arts and Sciences, a producer-controlled organization which functions as a company union." Those who doled out the coveted "Oscar" did not approve. But driven by exploitation, by mid-1933 the nascent guild had attained an "extraordinary accomplishment: our membership, including both active and associate [had] passed the four hundred mark," although "those actually employed as writers in Hollywood studios is only two hundred and sixty eight."[77]

"I feel intensely," proclaimed Lawson, "that the fundamental interests of all writers are similar, that a closed shop of all writers in the United States is realizable and a magnificent protection for us."[78] This bombshell was dropped before Lawson became a Red—but it was no less unsettling to those who benefited from the labor of journalists, technical writers, scholars, novelists, poets, playwrights, and screenwriters. This was no rhetorical flourish either. In addition to the Dramatists Guild, the SWG sought a tie-up with the Authors League of America (ALA), where Lawson served on the council with Oscar Hammerstein II and Elmer Rice. The ALA had four thousand members, and the SWG perhaps 12 percent of this total. As Lawson saw it, screenwriters could only increase—deservedly so—their heft in the industry by allying with other writers. "I need hardly point out," he affirmed, "that writers are the foundation stone of this industry," for the "motion picture business is essentially the business of exploitation of the creative ideas of writers."[79] The guild, in Lawson's words, was seeking a "binding unity with the Authors' League so that, if the screenwriters went on strike, all authors in the U.S. would refuse to work or sell material to movies."[80]

Of the so-called talent guilds—for example, directors and actors—it remains striking that it was the writers who blazed the trail in organizing and, concomitantly, bore the brunt of repression when the political climate toward unions was altered for the worse. For the "formation of the [SWG] was a factor in ending the fifty percent cut" proposed by the studios and "restoring normal pay checks. It inspired the actors to follow our example and we advised them in the founding of the Screen Actors Guild," said Lawson. The newly energized writer-cum-organizer "spent most of the year [1933–34] in Washington trying to get recognition of the Guild under provisions of the newly enacted National Industrial Recovery Act." "When a contract was finally negotiated" about six-seven years later, Lawson "was one of those who sat at the bargaining table." Speaking of these historic events decades later, Lawson acknowledged that "there were many people who doubted whether" the guild "could live." Thus, keeping the SWG afloat was no mean task in the face of draconian opposition from the moguls. Hence, his "year as the first President of the Guild means so much to me," he announced in 1964, "that I cannot write about it without emotion."[81]

Effectively, Lawson was "fired" from MGM because of his union organizing. Still, he was "popular" as a union leader. "Even at that time," said Lawson, "there was a left-wing and a right-wing in Hollywood but I was almost the only person who was totally trusted by all groups within the Guild. They all felt they could rely on me, that I would serve only the interests of the writer." Hence, though moguls were outraged by his notion of organizing "one big union of writers," his colleagues saw the union as providing them with unparalleled leverage in prying higher fees and improved working conditions out of the studios. Lawson knew that "one big union of writers" was "fighting words as far as the producers were concerned."[82] "I had organized the first trade union of professional people in a big industry controlled by finance capital," boasted Lawson.[83] This was an accomplishment that his enemies would find hard to swallow and even harder to forget.

Worse from their point of view was that Lawson did not just stop with the writers but, as noted, spurred the organizing of actors, too. The Screen Actors Guild was "founded in 1933 just a few weeks after we founded" SWG, he said. It was "founded very largely with my advice and under my guidance," he asserted accurately. "I sat with the committee and we talked over all the arrangements." Actors, unlike writers, were "not feared in relation to the control of material," though they "had an advantage in that they were essential immediately to production."[84] Together and united, writers and actors were more than a match for the studios.

"When I made the opening speech at the writers' meeting" at the Knickerbocker Hotel, recalled Lawson, "I opened with the words: 'the *writer* is the creator of motion pictures.'" With grand understatement, he asserted, "I think people have failed to recognize the significance of those words." Lawson's words, as he saw it, were a classic expression by those whose talent was exploited seeking to reclaim the fruits of their labor—a cardinal and central aspect of human society that both transcended and animated the rise of the Communist Party, as evidenced by the fact that he was not a party member when those powerful words emerged from his mouth. He also realized that "those words were sufficient to insure the eternal enmity of producers against the writers." "It still exists," he remarked, just before he passed away in 1977. "I don't think you can possibly understand the situation that developed around the Hollywood Ten and why the attack was made at that particular time in 1947 without this perspective." The organizing of the SWG was also a personal watershed. "I regard that meeting at the Knickerbocker Hotel in 1933 as really the beginning of a cycle of my life, a determination, a commitment to give my life and professional activity to this cause."[85]

6   Theory and Practice

Lawson's commitment came with a steep financial price. His initial "black-listing" came in the 1930s with the organizing of the Screen Writers Guild, though the intervention of courageous producers like Walter Wanger and conditions at that point that were not favorable to ostracizing of left-wingers precluded his being totally banished. When he returned to Hollywood in 1936, he was—according to his longtime comrade and fellow screenwriter Lester Cole—a "very different man." "Always brilliant, with the keenest intellect," he had returned with an even sharper intellect, having "devoted himself to a study of Marxism, challenged, he told me, by Mike Gold."[1]

Lawson's interest in the literature of revolution had not dulled his taste for the good life. Thus, as his son Jeffrey recalls it, life in Hollywood in the mid-1930s was magical, akin to a fairy tale. During the Christmas holidays, the Lawsons would "visit well-off left-wing friends in their beautiful homes." This list included the family of Albert Lewin, a "small man with a sweet manner" whom they usually visited in the afternoon on Christmas Day. He had "started his career as a schoolteacher but through some important connection with Irving Thalberg, he ended up a very successful and important producer at MGM." He "owned a huge modern mansion that had been designed by the son of Frank Lloyd Wright in the early '30s." The "setting was luxurious, one suited to a sophisticated wealthy household of the time: deep, comfortable couches, displays of expensive glassware, the latest radio and record-playing equipment, fine wines and liquors." Lawson was Jewish but of the secular type: "Though surrounded as a child by Jewish people, I never participated in a celebration of a Jewish holiday in anyone's home," his son recalled. Lawson was also a Communist, but for his son, "at school, the question of being from a Communist family never came up."[2] Lewin was something of a radical himself; he was "named for Albert Parsons, the eloquent anarchist martyr of the Haymarket affair in Chicago in 1886, and grew up in an anarchist colony."[3]

Lawson often could be found on sun-drenched tennis courts in the most stylish neighborhoods in Southern California. Philip Barber worked with Lawson at the studios then. "I looked him up and we played tennis," he recalled later. "I liked Jack, but he had a limp, quite a decided limp. I never realized it hardly until he played tennis and then you'd see him limping as he would cover the court. But he was pretty good," making up in energy what he lacked in mobility.[4]

Party membership was not then the issue that it was to become. In any case, Lawson was not exactly shouting from the rooftops about this affiliation—and for good reason. "My only contact with the Communist Party in Los Angeles," he declared, referring to the mid-1930s, "was through a man who called on me at the studio. He wore dark glasses and gave an assumed name, he asked me for money and he returned each week for another donation." This was not a precursor of film noir. Nor was it an "affectation," said Lawson. "The Communist Party was condemned to an underground existence in Los Angeles: its legality was almost as tenuous as it was in the Deep South. Its meetings were broken up, its members were harassed and beaten." When Lawson and his wife "went with Sam and Sadie Ornitz to a meeting advertised in a downtown hall," they "found the building guarded by police who ordered people to disperse."[5]

The studios were akin to company towns, with the moguls in the role of omnipotent overlords. Unsurprisingly, Lawson's audacity in organizing writers, and then actors, was viewed as akin to a rebellion of peasants with pitchforks. The moguls' skittishness reached a frantic pitch when Lawson's fellow writer and colleague Upton Sinclair made a serious challenge for the governorship of California in 1934. The moguls had reason to believe that Sinclair's campaign to "end poverty" in California might make a dent in their own wealth. Thus, with no apologies or embarrassment they knocked on the door of Lawson—and others—and asked for "voluntary contributions" to combat this menace. "The element of duress was present in all cases," Lawson remarked, and "a definite threat was implied." He was irate at their brazenness. "I consider myself a writer and not (at least at the moment) a member of a chain-gang." So, he "gave nothing" and, above all, "did my best to persuade others from giving, and shall follow the same course in the future." "I am vigorously opposed to Sinclair," said Lawson, reflecting a then redolent sectarian strain among Reds: "a year from now Governor Sinclair will be lunching with Louis B. Mayer and shivering crowds will be standing in the same old breadlines."[6] Thus, as he later conceded with embarrassment, "I accepted the extremely foolish view of the Communist Party that Sinclair was an unreliable liberal."

This failure to embrace Sinclair did not spare him from being pressured. Harry Cohn of Columbia studios beckoned him to his inner sanctum for a talk after Lawson and a fellow left-wing writer, John Wexley, "decided to refuse" to contribute to the studios' campaign to stop Sinclair. Cohn, as deft a performer as those on his payroll, "was on the verge of tears," which then led to a "metaphysical argument about political and personal loyalties." Unembarrassed, the affluent mogul said tearfully, "'I'm asking you as a friend, I'm begging you, to give me just one measly dollar.'" Lawson still said no. So, "when it became apparent that my heart was in the wrong place, Cohn abandoned pleading" for blunt threats. "He told me I would never work at Columbia again." But it was easier at that time to fabricate threats than to find talented writers, so "it turned out" that Lawson "was back at the studio within a year."[7]

This retreat on the part of Cohn did not signal any lessening of the pressure on writers at the studios. At this juncture, Lawson—after his unceremonious ouster from MGM—was toiling at Columbia, where "on one side" was Wexley "and on the other side was Sidney Buchman." As Lawson recalled, "Our doors opened on a balcony and across a courtyard were the windows of Harry Cohn's executive suite. The three [writers] visited each other a good deal and when Cohn saw us enter one of the other two offices he would open his windows and shout at us to get back to work. His voice was strident and we hastened to obey."[8]

Writing for the studios may not have been akin to working on a chain gang but it was also far from heaven, particularly after the SWG was organized—then remained in limbo before a contract with the studios was finally ratified. Of course, there were differences among the studios. Columbia was probably the most friendly to Reds and the "home" of the "screwball comedy"—and also happened to be "cheap, dingy and heartless"; boss Harry Cohn "seemed to relish being the rudest and meanest, a cheat of cheats." This kind of comedy was "unruly" and "subversive," like many of its Red writers, and the "studio itself" was equally "disorderly." Warner's was more likely to produce films with a political theme, whereas MGM "glamorize[d] the shopgirls' ambition" and Paramount "just wants to get everyone into bed."[9]

John Lee Mahin—one of the most prolific scribes in Hollywood history, with credits ranging from *No Time for Sergeants* to *Tortilla Flat* to *Dr. Jekyll and Mr. Hyde*—was among those who thought the problem was not necessarily the studios but Lawson himself. Mahin was involved in the organizing of the SWG. "I put up money, a lot of us put money up, and then," he noted angrily, "we found out who was really running the thing, with Lawson and his minions. We used to call him George Washington Lawson, who was going to lead us into a great rebellion, but we found out they had other interests." What were they? The Communist Party, he charged, "was in there heavy. Then we split and formed the Screen Playwrights Incorporated [SPI]." "They called us a company union," he recalled years later but no less vinegary about it all. "Yes," he asserted defiantly, "we were a company union. . . . [W]e went cloak-and-dagger and we found out that all the heavy, leading, hard-working guys in the Guild were members of the Party." How did he know this? "We sent guys to [their] meeting. Frankly, we spied on them." The moguls did not form the SPI, he alleges. Mahin knew which way the historical winds were blowing. "I used to kid Dalton [Trumbo] and Jack Lawson. I'd say, 'you're gonna get in trouble because the American Legion and the Catholic Church are gonna have you blacklisted. You're gonna scare these guys to death, and you're gonna get blacklisted.'"[10]

With due respect to Mahin and his memory, the formation of the SPI was part of a massive counterattack against SWG—and Lawson—by the studios. Dudley Nichols, who led the guild in 1937–38 and is widely regarded as one of the most fecund writers the industry has produced, with credits for *Stagecoach, Pinky, The Informer,* and many others, declared in 1936 that "now the threat is promulgated that the producers will import thousands of newspaper men and other writers to take our places. Why not?" Nichols was all too aware of another reality; "many writers in Hollywood," he said, "already appear to be frightened out of their wits. A man may have the physical courage of a lion and yet run like a rabbit when his income is threatened."[11]

At one point it seemed that there were more rabbits than lions in the SWG, as this union was "tottering from the effects of its first batch of resignations" and absorbing a vicious "solar plexus blow."[12] The moguls were taking seriously Lawson's vow that the formation of the SWG was a mere prelude to forge "all pen pushers in one combine."[13] Lawson, by contrast, was roaring like a lion. He had made his way to Washington, D.C., to lobby legislators on behalf of labor law reform that would smooth the path for the SWG; in fact, he spent almost an entire year in Washington on behalf of the guild, draining valuable time from his creative labor—and draining his pocketbook, too. Something of a celebrity, he had little trouble in meeting face-to-face with William Green, the crusty leader of the American Federation of Labor, who "gave him fatherly advice and pledged the full support" of his organization; this "meant nothing," however, because this group seemed more allergic to radicalism than some of the moguls.[14]

Back in Hollywood some writers and almost all moguls viewed Lawson's remarks at a congressional hearing as veritably seditious, akin to going to Moscow—or Paris—and criticizing U.S. foreign policy. Already Hollywood had become something of a punching bag, routinely pummeled and blamed for declining standards in everything from literacy to morals. Lawson rode this wave, laying into "repetitious jokes and indecent allusions" in movies. Moguls, he charged, "know nothing of creative writing" and "refuse to take advantage of the technical ability of writers they have employed who have proven their ability in the book and magazine field." In words that brought him grief from some screenwriters, he asserted that "the position of the motion picture writer has none of the dignity a writer has in other fields" since "well-known writers are treated like office boys." An author, it was said, has "no rights to protect his works against 'mutilations.'" He described this situation as "one of the basic difficulties of aesthetic and moral standards in the movies." From Lawson's point of view, what was at issue was control at the point of production in a manner no less important than what was unfolding at steel or auto plants. He told "the committee that the director was formerly the dominant figure in picture production." However, "'with the advent of sound, the author became important because the director could no longer pick a story off his cuff as he went along, but the writer did not benefit because the industry went into the period of domination of executives who are ignorant of creative values.'"[15] Yet despite their power, screenwriters were virtually compelled to "inject smut into scripts."[16]

Some writers took heart from Lawson's bold words, but others took umbrage at his reference to them as "office boys." The "claim that I had insulted writers by calling them 'office boys,'" Lawson later recounted, led to a "furious and disruptive argument in the Guild, which centered around me and my radical politics." There were "days of wild charges and countercharges," and Lawson "spent about five hours each day on the phone discussing strategy with the directors of the Guild."[17] These dissidents had launched an attack against him, charging that he had demeaned the profession before powerful outsiders. SWG "split wide open" as a result of Lawson's spirited testimony. A wire was dispatched to the congressional committee signed by sixty-four writers—a hefty percentage of the guild's extant membership—"denouncing Lawson's testimony."[18] Lawson in turn was "bitterly hurt and offended by the failure of the [SWG] board to back me up immediately and unequivocally." It was "not only a betrayal of me but a betrayal of everything the Guild stands for."[19]

Lawson was not without support. Dorothy Parker, Nathaniel West, and S. J. Perelman also deemed the "conduct of local Judases shameful": "we are only several of hundreds of writers who are deeply grateful to you," they added.[20] Later the SWG formally "commended" Lawson and "expressed regret" at the "hasty action of some members in condemning Lawson with reference to his comments about Hollywood writers."[21]

Lawson thought he knew what was behind these hurled missiles. "The attack on me," he warned, "is incidental to the attempt to wreck the Guild." It was not just his remarks in Washington that were stirring resentments but his assumed political ties too. Lawson declared that to "Mayer and Thalberg and others," anyone "who fights for a closed shop for writers is as red as Stalin." The "attack on me," he warned the SWG prophetically, "was the first step in the battle to discredit all of you." Asking a question that was answered decisively and not in his favor about a decade later, he said, "If you run into your cellars and hide in the coal bin when your enemies fire the first shot, what are you going to do in the thick of the fight?"[22] Later Lawson argued that this assault was a harbinger of what befell him approximately a decade later. "The blacklist," he maintained, "was initiated for the first time in Hollywood—that was in 1936, not in 1947 or 1950. . . . I was definitely blacklisted in the industry, as were many other people too because of their known record as supporters and activists in the [Guild]. The Screen Writers Guild went completely underground; nobody could admit they carried a card." A producer with whom he was to collaborate—Daryl Zanuck— "was really the leader of the producers in suppressing the Guild and he was very open and frank about it."[23]

The moguls had banded together—Zanuck, Cohn, Mayer, Selznick, Jack Warner, and others—and threatened the guild. "A few agitators among screenwriters," they cautioned, "are determined to establish a closed shop for the writing profession." "For years," they said, exuding pain, "the producers have ignored the many false, malicious, defamatory and inflammatory articles and stories circulated by a few malcontents and disturbers among the writers." Listen well, they said. "The producers will not accept a closed shop for writers on any basis whatsoever"; in fact, "producers will use every resource at their command to defeat it." There was, they said, a "wide distinction between labor unions properly organized as such, and organizations of creative employees," such as the SWG.[24]

In the meantime, the moguls were fighting the guild as their counterparts nationally were combating unions in their workplace. On the other hand, the writers had not taken sufficient advantage of inherent rifts that divided the bigger from the smaller moguls. As mini-mogul David O. Selznick once remarked, "The problems of the members of our society"— speaking of the small fish—"with writers are quite different than those of the major studios." The "great majority of the writers of the larger companies are under long term contract, whereas our writers are engaged for the individual jobs." This meant that "the viewpoint of the larger studios" tended to "predominate and a deal [could] be made without regard" to Selznick's "problems."[25] Yet such a rudimentary fissure was not capitalized upon effectively by writers.

Meanwhile, amid the jousting and turmoil engendered by the backwash of labor organizing, Lawson still found time to sharpen his critical facilities. The first edition of his celebrated *Theory and Technique of Playwriting* emerged during this era, a book hailed by his former colleague and ever-present critic Harold Clurman.[26] Writing this book was a journey of self-discovery for Lawson, helping him to understand what he now thought in light of his heightened commitment.[27]

Allardyce Nicoll, a professor at Yale and chair of its School of Drama, termed Lawson's tome "an important volume" that was both "unique" and "outstanding."[28] Another critic enthused that this book "contains some of the most brilliant and vital dramatic criticism in English since Shaw's inimitable prefaces." Lawson, it was said, "is the first American critic to point out that to date we have had no systematic study of the history and tradition of dramatic technique," and "with his Marxist searchlight, Lawson has lit up many corners."[29]

Such high praise from such elevated circles did not persuade Lawson to retreat from his own considered criticisms.[30] The critics—and others besides—were not keeping up with rapidly changing events and, thus, in a real sense, were losing touch with the realities reflected by radical writers. "Revolution is no longer a mysterious and frightening reference to something incomprehensible that once took place in Russia," Lawson instructed readers of the *Times,* "but something clearly going on in at least three countries and imminent in at least three more." The "soundest and most exciting playwright," he proclaimed, "is the one who is most uncertain of the rightness of things as they are and seeks a finer, truer living." Critics, he charged, increasingly had lost touch with this point; Lawson, by way of contrast, declared, "I do not merely say that the experiment is a good thing: I say it is the only thing."[31]

Lawson's formal affiliation with the Communist Party seems to have emboldened him as a theorist. "The necessity of being *specific* in regard to party and political questions," he decreed, "is the first obligation of the revolutionary writer; the propaganda effect of his work depends on his ability to grapple in strictly dramatic terms, with the detailed reality of economics and politics." Yet the milieu in which he toiled, "the Broadway-Hollywood school of expression," was not up to the task, characterized as it was by "turgidity" and "emotional vagueness." In fact, he chortled, "one may reasonably say of the bourgeois theatre—the greater the confusion, the greater the artist! The aim of this sort of theatre is perfectly realized in Eugene O'Neill who attains great heights of confusion and pretentiousness." The revitalized Lawson thought it "absurd for any writer to attempt to write about the class struggle in *general* terms. The Communist Party," in contrast, "is playing a definite role in every strike, in every activity of the working class." Now "this does not mean that the playwright's approach should be narrowly sectarian," since "the theatre is an emotional experience, and the essential value of clarity lies in the heightening of this experience." "Nor do I mean to infer," he added quickly, "that the playwright must take a purely communist point of view." But the newly committed Lawson expected something similar from others, since "whatever the writer's liberal or radical point of view, his first duty in attacking working class subjects is to clarify his own attitude," that is, "he must face the problems which the working class itself faces."[32]

Lawson had good reason to be sensitive to the phenomenon of criticism, given the bashings he had absorbed. He could be penetratingly critical of his Communist comrades—a notion contrary to the idea that Reds were akin to ideological robots programmed by Moscow propagandists to march in lockstep. Thus, when the journal *New Theatre* went belly up, he announced without chagrin that this was "due to bureaucratic interference with cultural activity, an intolerable interference for which the party was to blame and in which I played a regrettable part." The critics were correct about this demise: "I was largely responsible for this, along with V. J. Jerome," the Communist leader. There were harsh "personal clashes," and though the Reds had not made a "direct attempt to dictate to the magazine," it was evident that some had good reason to think so. There was a noticeable "lack of democratic procedure," and this debacle, said Lawson, "haunted me when I returned to Hollywood later in the year. The whole progressive film community was indignant at my miscalculation and mismanagement. It was part of a complex of events that accounted for my enforced abandonment of the theatre."[33] The controversy over *New Theatre* was complicated. This journal was often unsparing in its scorching critiques of left-wing theater, no matter how well-intentioned.[34] There were those—Communist and non-Communist alike—who found these criticisms overly one-sided, but it seemed that only the integrity of the former was rebuked.

These sharp admonitions did not halt the process of radicalization that had seeped into Lawson's every pore—though it was beginning to create rifts between Lawson and others with whom he had grown close. In the first place this included John Dos Passos. Lawson was not impressed with his friend's play *Fortune Heights,* for example. Lawson continued to send Dos Passos funds but fewer sparkling compliments. Frankly, he "was disappointed" in this work; now he did not "take a stiff Marxian Stalinistic attitude—but Christ Almighty," he spluttered, "it seems to me obvious that if you undertake certain revolutionary problems—evictions, the hunger march, things that are part and parcel of the whole life around us—you've got to have some revolutionary ground on which to stand." But Dos Passos and Lawson were moving at a rapid clip in not only opposite but opposing directions, though neither seemed to realize it at the time.[35] As Lawson deepened his commitment to the Party and sharpened his critical acuity by theorizing about drama and critiquing critics, it was bound to have impact on his personal relations—with the increasingly crusty Dos Passos in the first place.

Yet amid the writing of plays, screenplays, books, and think pieces for newspapers and organizing the SWG and critiques of colleagues, somehow Lawson found time to be a leading organizer of radical film projects,[36] then the League of American Writers (LAW), thought by many to be a "Communist front." It was during this time, he recalled later, when there was

> the first strike of publishing house office workers in New York in the middle thirties. I went at the appointed time. One lonely figure was walking up and down—a tall, aristocratic individual wearing spats and twirling a cane in his gloved hands. His name was Dashiell Hammett. And I fell in behind him. The next day many writers answered the call. I happened to be late arriving just as the literary crowd was being hustled into patrol wagons. I tried to join them but a cop pushed me away. On our arrival at the police station I was again refused admission to the company of the jailed elect.[37]

It was these "jailed elect," including Hammett, who formed the core of the LAW. Late 1936 found Lawson in Manhattan, joining with Malcolm Cowley, Joseph Freeman, Granville Hicks, Albert Maltz, Philip Rahv, and other writers who sought an organized expression of their abhorrence of fascism and war. Lawson chaired a critical evening session "devoted to the first formulation of plans for a national congress of writers in the spring."[38]

He was elected to the Executive Council of the LAW, and one of his plays received one of the organization's top awards.[39]

The League of American Writers was a rather amorphous group that sought to bind together famously atomized writers around a progressive platform targeting the global shift to the right and its domestic concomitants of antiunionism and lynching. A tightrope had to be walked, since Lawson was loath to dilute standards to expand the organization. LAW, on the other hand, had focused on "creative writers"—even "newspapermen were not included"—and Lawson thought this should change.[40] Lawson's ideas tended to carry the day, as he jousted with other well-known writers, including Dreiser, Marc Connolly, Archibald MacLeish, Heywood Broun, Langston Hughes, and his old friend Dawn Powell. The LAW was not a "trade union," he said—"we believe in trade unions; but that is different from entering into [the] trade union field"—but "such things as cheap books" and "contraction of markets" should be its métier.[41]

Yet the LAW seemed to promise more than it could deliver. Shortly after its inception, it was reported that "Hollywood seemed to be doing nothing in the way of chapter activity."[42] Despite the growing number of left-wing screenwriters, there remained a need for "enlivening the League within that industry."[43] Even Lawson was not able to take up the slack. Nonetheless, there were advantages to the LAW, for it allowed him to get to know better other talented scribes, such as Langston Hughes.[44]

Still, Lawson had a good excuse for not being more active in LAW as he continued to churn out plays and screenplays in profusion, in addition to helping other writers. The eminent drama critic Brooks Atkinson was taken by Lawson's latest offering, the pro-labor *Marching Song*.[45] The renowned black actor Rex Ingram played the key role of Lucky Johnson in this play that challenges the idea of Negro scabs. "Don't call me that," said one Negro character referring to the term "scab," since "you been scabbin' on the black man the whole o' your life." Reflecting Lawson's unhappy sojourn south of the Mason-Dixon Line, Johnson says, "If this was the South, I'd get killed for saying this ain't the south."[46] This was one of Lawson's more militant, more committed plays, reflecting his recently cemented political engagements, though it did not impress Harold Clurman, who found it "cold, artificial, a creature of the author's will—lacking spontaneity."[47]

Clurman's scolding notwithstanding—seemingly—the mere fact of Lawson's Party membership had not eliminated the accolades accorded his writing. Like many on the left, Lawson had developed a deeply personal and emotional tie to the Spanish civil war. He served as secretary—alongside Waldo Frank—of the "American Society for Technical Aid [to] Spanish

Democracy," which sought to dispatch U.S. nationals with technical skills to this battle-torn nation so that their Spanish counterparts could be released for frontline combat.[48] Though to modern eyes his epic film *Blockade,* starring Henry Fonda, suffers from its paltry and pitiful sets and less than convincing cinematography, it still packs a powerful emotive punch in its call for defense of the fledgling Spanish Republic. As one study has noted, it was "the most politically controversial film of the decade," with "Hollywood's nearest approach to the 'mass' scenes of Sergei Eisenstein and Vsevolod Pudovkin until the 1940s war films." *Blockade* "approached *Battleship Potemkin,* at least in certain spectacular scenes."[49]

It was his old colleague Harold Clurman who brought Lawson to the attention of the producer Walter Wanger. Wanger asked Clurman "to recommend a writer who would revamp the script," and he suggested Lawson, "who was having a hard time, financially speaking," not least because of his tiffs with moguls over organizing the SWG.[50] Indeed, Lawson freely acknowledged that he was able to secure a contract to write this film—despite his open, unabashed radicalism—"due to the courage, really, of one man," that is, the prolific producer Walter Wanger. Later he conceded that "as for the aesthetics of the picture, it is not a fine picture in many ways. I wouldn't say it's a bad picture, because it's touched by the greatness of the subject. There are moments in 'Blockade' however, when you can see a definite conflict between the documentary aspect—the faces of the Spanish people, peasants, city people in the little town, . . . and the second-hand spy story which is the central story." The problem was, he confessed, "you just cannot fit them together." He owned up to the defect: "That is my fault, no one else's fault but mine. I never could find a way of dealing with this material that would give it its full weight and strength in relation to the tremendous historic issues that were raised." The external pressure on the production was no small factor either, as Wanger was "forced to send copies of the script not only to Washington but also to Paris and London for advice as to changes that would be made."[51]

The political pressure inexorably impinged on Lawson's creativity as a screenwriter. The film, said Lawson, "certainly didn't turn out the way I wanted it," since it "was written carefully so the two factions were never identified and then rewritten along melodramatic lines."[52] The playwright Lillian Hellman was perplexed after seeing the film. When asked how she liked it, she responded, "Fine," though she had "one question. Which side was it on?"[53] Ruefully Lawson noted later, "It was obvious that the food ship which saved the people from starvation was sent by the Soviet Union, but there was to be no hint of its nationality in the film. Compromises of this sort were less troublesome than the problems of structure and content which arose from the attempt to combine a realistic portrayal of mass activity with an artificial spy story." As it turned out, "the discrepancy between the two styles is startling." "I must confess," Lawson acknowledged, "that I bear the main responsibility for failure to create an organic relationship between the story of the woman trapped into spying for the fascists and the desperate reality of the people's struggle." There was blame to spread, however—once more, to the actors. "The difficulty related to the performers," Lawson said, "and especially to Madeleine Carroll's personality and manner as an actress," since "it was hard for her to express the woman's feelings." Lawson discussed a key "scene with her at length and the speech in which she confesses her guilt was rewritten a dozen times," but "it remained acting with glycerine tears." On the other hand, "The power of the mass scenes in 'Blockade' is largely the work of the director, William Dieterle, who consciously followed Soviet examples in his portrayal of the crowd, cutting to give a constant sense of movement and rhythm achieving painful intimacy in close-ups."[54]

It was not as if industry censors were asleep at the switch when Lawson's screenplay emerged. Joseph Breen, the reactionary anti-Semite who monitored movie messages on behalf of the industry, instructed Wanger before the film was produced that "any material involved with, or played against, the background of the present civil war in Spain, is, in our judgment, highly dangerous, at the present time, from a practical standpoint, as well as distribution in Europe." There was a "great danger involved," he warned, and "from reading these first thirty pages," it was clear "that you have an enormous amount of slaughter and the suggestion of dead bodies, horribly mutilated"—that is, akin to the war itself. Breen found this script "not acceptable."[55]

He was gracious enough, however, to propose changes that would make the production acceptable. "In shooting this picture," he commanded, do not "definitely identify any of the combatants with either faction of the Spanish Civil War." Wanger was also told to "delete" from a random scene "the title of the book 'Madam Bovary.' Censor boards in various parts of this country are of the opinion that there is no need at any time to emphasize books which in their judgment border on the pornographic."[56]

In short, it was not as if there was a smooth path for the production of antifascist films in the 1930s, contrary to HUAC in 1947. *Blockade* was assailed by the Knights of Columbus—a Catholic grouping—as a "polemic for 'the Marxist controlled cause in Spain . . . a red trial balloon . . . historically false and intellectually dishonest.'"[57] Those involved with this film said the Knights were "well-known leftists." These Catholics found the movie "insulting to the truth and to the Catholic people"; the film was "stupid, the plot weak" and "confused." The "acting" was "only mediocre," yet the picture was "considered an opening wedge for all who have a cause." "Blockade 'Blockade'" was one considered opinion.[58] This was attempted. Yes, said Breen, "some attempts have been made—not always successfully—to prevent the showing of the picture, 'Blockade.'"[59]

No doubt this uproar prompted prime film censor Will Hays to ponder the "perplexing question" of "how far Communistic ideas were finding their way into our own entertainment pictures." For as early as 1937 "Archbishop John Timothy McNicholas of Cincinnati made the statement that Communism was using the screen, and he instructed his pastors to deliver sermons to that effect." The pope himself showed Hays in Rome only three months before McNicholas's démarche "copies of orders sent out from Moscow to 'capture the cinema of the world.'"[60] That the Vatican itself would become exercised about Hollywood confections was suggestive of the high stakes involved. Says one close student of the era, while *Blockade* was "breaking box-office records in London, it opened in New York at Radio City Music Hall and was picketed by Catholic clergy and laymen. John Howard Lawson had become Hollywood's bete rouge and the producers who hated his union organizing and political activism as well as the IATSE [union], which despised his watchfulness and his alliance with radical labor, . . . were ready to attack anything he was associated with."[61]

Blockade was seen as celluloid dynamite by its more unforgiving critics. The "powerful Fox–West Coast theater chain . . . refused to take 'Blockade' as a regular first feature." Will Hays was away when the script of this picture "was submitted for approval in accordance with standard practice," and Breen, no less reactionary, was viewed by some as being insufficiently rigorous in blocking production. Yet the producer, Wanger, was buckling and reconsidering release when "three 'sneak' previews showed an unusual degree of audience enthusiasm," which led to "record breaking attendance" in England. "Britishers" were among those "cheering," as the film did "a whirlwind business in both England and France," though back in the United States the projectionists' union threatened not to show the film.[62] In Boston the "City Council endeavored to ban 'Blockade' without even bothering to see it."[63] A theater in Omaha canceled *Blockade* after the Knights of Columbus denounced it as "leftist propaganda."[64] In Flint, Michigan, the newly minted Congress of Industrial Organizations—joined by the United Auto Workers Union—organized showings after the "film had been withdrawn" in the face of pressure. As elsewhere, Catholic group-

FIGURE 2. In *Blockade,* Lawson created scenes that dramatized mass heroism in a manner rarely attempted by Hollywood to that point. (Courtesy of the Academy of Motion Picture Arts and Sciences)

ings were in the vanguard of opposition.[65] *Blockade* was something of a breakthrough and was viewed as such by all sides. As *Variety* put it, "Upon its success financially revolve the plans of several of the major studios heretofore hesitant about tackling stories which treat with subjects of international economic and political controversy."[66]

As Lawson recalled, Wanger "intended to follow" *Blockade* "with a picture dealing with Nazi Germany" that he, Lawson, would write and "guided by the same director. The script was completed, the sets were built, the cast selected, when the pressure from the banks forced the cancellation of the projects."[67] The dynamic duo, writer and producer, planned "a blistering indictment of fascism," but "two days before the start of production," Wanger beckoned Lawson "and announced that the whole thing must be abandoned. The bank had informed him that he would never receive another loan if he proceeded."[68] Associated Film Audiences, a laudable attempt to organize movie audiences as a pressure group, lamented that Wanger was "forced by pressure from his bankers to give up temporarily plans for the production of 'Personal History.' This film using the

FIGURE 3. *Blockade* was one of the few films to address the Spanish civil war. Lawson's screenplay also provided a breakthrough role for Henry Fonda. (Courtesy of the Academy of Motion Picture Arts and Sciences)

title of Vincent Sheean's famous book, was to picture the reactions of a young American to the brutal happenings in Germany," with Lawson and Budd Schulberg to write the screenplay.[69]

Later Lawson came to realize that the pressure exerted on *Blockade* "marks the beginning of the drive against meaningful content in motion pictures"—a process "which culminated" in the 1947 congressional hearings. Strikingly, it was after *Blockade* that an "anti-trust suit against the major motion picture companies [was] instituted on July 20, 1938." Indeed, as Lawson observed, "On the same day that the government anti-trust action was reported, Wanger stated that the campaign against 'Blockade' was intended 'to frighten the exhibitor, distributor and producer.'"[70] That it did. The studios' supposed reluctance to allow diverse voices—as evidenced by the allegedly one-sided *Blockade*—demonstrated that Hollywood was an illegal monopoly in violation of antitrust laws.[71]

Lawson had arrived at a critical crossroads—and, by implication, so had Red Hollywood as a whole. The experience with *Blockade* had taught him that expecting to produce radicalism on celluloid consistently was wildly naive. But if the screen seemed unpromising, the stage appeared likewise unappetizing. Writing for the stage increasingly meant writing for the more well-heeled, who were about the only group who could afford the price of the ticket. In addition to the mass audience that flocked to cinema, Lawson's "trouble in the theatre" was that he had "never been willing to work with that kind of [affluent] audience" that Broadway attracted. "I dislike them," he said with some intensity. "I have no respect for them and it's hard to write plays for people for whom you have no respect. I'm not saying this to excuse the great weaknesses in my own work," he added self-critically years later, "because I don't consider that I've achieved any satisfactory success as a playwright. I've never found a style or technique of the theatre that would enable me to express what I want to express." Lawson thought a "play is as detailed and as complex in its construction as is any symphony," but somehow he had never found his métier on stage. "I must say frankly," he confessed, "that I failed to achieve my purpose in the theatre. I failed almost totally to realize my potentialities. This was due in part to the fact [that] times were out of joint for almost all of us." "My personal reason for working in films," he admitted in 1961, "was largely my inability to find satisfactory expression and achievement in the theatre. I am still facing the same problem today."[72]

Moreover, it was becoming increasingly dangerous to put on theatrical productions even if Broadway were to be circumvented. Lawson, no stranger to this phenomenon, spoke dramatically of how producing a simple play could mean "police terrorism: nightsticks, tear-gas, riot calls and jails. Municipal persecution: violation of non-existent fire regulations, condemnation of theatres used for years, trumped-up charges of 'blasphemy' or 'obscenity,' the threat of losing your regular job if you appear in an amateur production of a play of social protest. And the kidnapping and beating of and robbing of actors and directors—such are the dangers that confront the vital, sincere theatres in America today! Free speech and free stage become a mockery! The soil becomes ripe for the foul seed of fascism." Like the movie "blacklist" years later, this throttling censorship was warping the kind of themes that theaters deemed worthy of projecting.[73] Lawson was not deterred, however. Like Karl Marx, Lawson too agreed that "the writer must, naturally, make a living in order to exist and write, but he must not exist and write in order to make a living."[74]

Helpful to his earning a living was that Lawson did not exalt the lucrative screen over the penurious stage—or vice versa. Instead, Lawson opined, "The fact that the motion picture has a far greater sweep and more varied contact with reality than is possible on the stage may lead enthusiasts to conclude somewhat prematurely that the film is, at least potentially, a 'greater art' than the theatre." This was not accurate, for the "assumption can only be attributed to a misunderstanding of the relationship between a work of art and the reality that it mirrors." The stage, too, could reflect truths and realities no less powerful than the screen. "A play may have a great many changes of scene," he said, "but the driving force of the play is found in the inner content of the scenes and only to a minor degree in the contrast and linkage between them." "In the motion picture," by way of contrast, "the inner content of the scenes is continually transformed, given new meaning, driven forward by the movement between the scenes." In cinema, "montage is as much an accepted convention [as] the imaginary fourth wall in the theatre." In cinema, unlike theater, "the close-up is the key to the film structure. It provides the emotional insight, the pattern of will and purpose that bind the action together in a rational design." The close-up was abused in cinema, of course, in "an empty and repetitious manner"; for example, "kisses, parted lips and heaving bosoms" were "more common than the study of less obvious reactions."

Lawson agreed with his fellow screenwriter Dudley Nichols that "the truth is that the stage is the medium of action while the screen is the medium of reaction. It is through identification with the person *acted upon* on the screen, and not with the person acting, that the film builds up oscillating power with an audience." Like Nichols, he too saw the close-up "as the key to the human root and meaning of the action" in cinema— a simple reality often lost on too many cinematographers. Like other screenwriters—and consonant with *Blockade* and *Sahara*—Lawson felt that "the most creative artists of the cinema have shown a preference for historical subjects." For "history" was "people in motion." Yet Lawson the film theorist felt that the young art of motion pictures had hardly explored its potential. "There has been so little experimentation," he lamented, "with sounds as an active dramatic agent that any assertions regarding its use must be tentative and based more upon speculation than experience." The influence of "business" on this "art" of moviemaking "explains the partial neglect of the camera's potentialities and the far more complete neglect of the microphone." Poorly schooled cineastes were another reason for this deficiency, for "in most cases the screenwriter has no knowledge of the camera. The cameramen knows nothing about story values, except what he has picked up in the course of his work on the set. The editor is given strips of film without any previous consultation concerning the script or the problem that it involves. The composer is given his assignment belatedly after most of the photographic work has been completed. The director, who in many cases, does not participate in the preparation of the script and who may or may not know anything about the camera, is given the impossible task of unifying these separate and discordant elements."

What was to be done? On this, Lawson was clear: "The structural unity of the film must originate in the screenplay," but this was made difficult by the producers' fear of the power of writers and the latter's own weaknesses. Yet Lawson continued to insist that "there can be no unity unless the screenplay is actually a screen invention, fully realized in film terms, with genuine understanding of the function of the camera and the microphone and the free creative use of these marvelous instruments."[75]

Yet Lawson's ambitious words about filmmaking could hardly be implemented unilaterally—he was a simple writer, after all. Nevertheless, after *Blockade*, Lawson would attempt to implement his ambitious cinematic vision, but his equally and fiercely held political commitments would complicate enormously his creative compulsions.

7 Struggle

The explosive debut of *Blockade* had cemented further Lawson's eminence, and at this juncture, the fact that he was a Communist did not erase this grand status. His financial problems seemed to be over, as he resided in a prosperous, sun-dappled neighborhood in Southern California with his wife and children and hobnobbed with the Hollywood elite. His life was not as luxurious as that of his future cellmate, Dalton Trumbo, but it was not far behind.[1]

Yet there were not too distant roars and rumbles that carried the potential to disrupt this pleasant reverie that had enveloped Red Hollywood. The Communist Party, of which Lawson was a preeminent member, had endured a semilegal existence during its early years and after escaping from this rockiness had to navigate through the choppy shoals of intense surveillance. The notorious Los Angeles Police Department contained a hyperactive "Red Squad" that whiled away hours monitoring Communists.[2] The mogul Louis B. Mayer—"like his friend and hero, J. Edgar Hoover, whose photograph was on prominent display in his office"—"insisted on knowing everything about everybody," and this most definitely included Reds, like Lawson, who had supped at his table.[3] Cecil B. DeMille, with whom Lawson had collaborated upon arriving in Hollywood in the 1920s, one-upped Mayer, having "started the Hollywood chapter" of the "American Protective League," a "civilian secret service operating as an auxiliary of the Department of Justice's Bureau of Investigation." At its "peak the APL had between 200,000 to 250,000 members organized with military-style ranks in 1200 different divisions."[4]

It was said that there were "approximately 1550 members of the Communist Party in Los Angeles" and that "there were many Communist sympathizers in other organizations and that the total number of such sympathizers might reach as high as 25,000." In 1934 a horrified police agent attended a Red rally and was stunned to see that "the speakers were of all races and nationalities, including several Negroes and a Japanese."[5]

It seemed—or so the authorities believed—that a good number of the comrades subjected to surveillance were Jewish, and this could only mean ill for Lawson. One late 1937 intelligence report that focused on the "Hollywood Section" of the party found it worthy of note that "there were 29 members present, 28 of whom were Jews."[6] By then it was reported that "the CP now has more than 2300 members in Los Angeles, and when it is taken into consideration that the Party really started with only 19 in the year 1920, one must agree that the Party is making headway."[7]

In 1938 Culbert Olson was elected governor as the "state overthrew forty-four years of Republican rule. At the same time Los Angeles progressives won a fight to recall the corrupt Republican Mayor Shaw."[8] The screenwriter Philip Dunne alleged that the Olson campaign was the first major instance of the politicizing of the artist. "Hollywood won that election," he concluded. "They saw how you got headlines."[9] The nervous HUAC in turn had reason to believe that Olson "'fraternizes with and accepts the program of the strategy committee of the Communist Party.'"[10]

The Communist Party grew accordingly as its main conservative predators were knocked back on their heels. John Weber, a Party organizer, recalled later that "there were never more than 300 members in the Hollywood Communist Party. Not quite half of them were writers and the rest were actors, directors, various white collar workers and even some backlot workers." Weber, who also had served as an agent for the powerful William Morris Agency and as a producer in France and Italy, had touched on one of the weaknesses of the Party apparatus in the film colony. For its Marxist theory would have suggested that "backlot workers"—the carpenters, painters, the veritable "proletarians"—should have been better represented in the ranks of the party that described itself as the tribune of the downtrodden working class. That writers were overrepresented was anomalous though rarely articulated. Instead, the Hollywood party was walled off—presumably for reasons of security—from the rest of the party in the region, which may have deprived it of a kind of ideological ballast that could have kept it afloat when storms loomed. As a result, Lawson—who quickly became the most visible spokesman and leader of the Hollywood party—dealt directly with the party center in Manhattan, more specifically with headquarters' "cultural designee, V. J. Jerome," described by the acidulous Weber as a "feckless pedant who simply parroted the Party line."[11]

Jerome became a boon companion of Lawson, but Weber's sour recollection of him has been echoed by others. The Communist tandem—Lawson and Jerome—both have been described as unsmiling, dogmatic, unimaginative hacks, the epitome of all that was wrong about the Party.[12] Lawson, like his comrade, had a decided dearth of empathy for writers who were writhing in the kind of confusions that had entangled him before he found the Party. Neither reacted as badly to criticism as many others; they seemed like leaders of the brusque brigade. Party leader Dorothy Healey "felt that Lawson and V. J. Jerome bore the responsibility for the sort of cultural sectarianism that hurt the Party."[13]

One reason that criticisms from Lawson were taken so seriously by Budd Schulberg and others was because of his prominence, both as a writer and as a radical. He had been a prominent leader of the avant-garde, a pillar of Broadway and a principal organizationally and creatively in Hollywood. He was now thought to be the most radical of the radical, the leader of Red Hollywood. "Running through all the Hollywood Communist fronts," claimed one dour critic, was "the name" Lawson, "active in at least forty" of these suspect groupings.[14] The screenwriter Michael Blankfort "commented that he once saw Lawson coming out the dentist's office when he was going in. 'I was shocked,' he said, 'that Jack would have trouble with his teeth. He seemed to be beyond the frailties of humankind. It was like seeing Lenin going to the can." But he also added tellingly, "'Jack was so rigid, so didactic, it ended up making a lot of people resent him.'"[15] When Lawson "addressed a meeting," notes one historian, "he had a way of laying out a policy with the cool, imperturbable logic of a general explaining a stratagem. One writer compared him to Lenin."[16]

Yet it seemed that after Lawson had stumbled his way through the darkness of his own confusion to the light represented to him by the Party, he had difficulty in accepting the perplexities and bewilderments of others. Perhaps this was fueled in part by Lawson's temperament having been slightly warped because he was sprinkled with the powerful pixie dust of celebrity, which gave his words—and aura—more sheen.[17] He did not consort directly just with Communist leaders but with Hedy Lamarr, Henry Fonda, and Charles Boyer. As Jeffrey Lawson recalls, "There were many people of his generation who not only admired but worshipped my father."[18] Lawson not only wrote movies but also was characterized in them. The high-flying screenwriters Ben Hecht and Charles MacArthur responsible for the crackling, quick-fire dialogue of *The Front Page*, among other chartbusters, also wrote the aptly named *Soak the Rich*, which concerns a "rich young college girl . . . who falls in love with a student radical played by John Howard, hired by Hecht and MacArthur partly because of the similarity of his name to that of the Communist screenwriter and organizer, John Howard Lawson."[19] Later, Lawson's erstwhile friend John Dos Passos wrote a roman à clef about theater and film featuring a character who resembled Lawson.[20]

Like some other celebrities, Lawson also became a lightning rod, a tendency exacerbated by his controversial political stances. "There are people whose sheer existence causes a vibration in the surrounding air," said one critic. "They are slated to disturb the world and create unrest wherever they move." Lawson was "such a stormy petrel." His work was not "merely reviewed; it has either been raved about or fumed at or violently discussed."[21] This drug of "hero worship"—even its apparent opposite of mindless detraction—could contribute easily to brusqueness.

It could also contribute to distortion, even false memory. It is striking— even given the white-hot heat created by the anticommunist crusade— how swollen and irritated and unlikely recollections of Lawson have become. Jack Tenney was a former leader of the musicians' union—he wrote *Mexicali Rose*—who became a famed right-wing legislator in California and a backer of domestic fascists. A portly, balding man of six feet, he was pasty faced and uncomfortable to be around.[22] But, as so often happens, his past dalliance with the left had been transformed powerfully into a rancorous antagonism.

In 1969 Tenney recounted the time when he, a union leader, would meet "'the most important man in Hollywood'"—Lawson. Now Lawson was prominent, but certainly Harry Cohn, Jack Warner, Will Hays, Daryl Zanuck, and a passel of others could rightly object to this title going to a mere screenwriter, albeit a Communist leader. Thus, Tenney's colleague Mischa Altman met Tenney "at seven o'clock in the evening of the appointed day. . . . We drove out through Hollywood and into the hills around Beverly Hills." It was like a bad film noir—which might not be coincidental. Altman "parked the car, led me up a series of stone steps, along a narrow foot-path that led to the rear of a rather pretentious home into a small patio. The man who opened the door in response to Altman's knock" was the "most important man in Hollywood"—Lawson. Tenney and Altman "were immediately invited into what appeared to be a well-stocked and luxuriously appointed library. Lawson, obviously Jewish, was quite gruff, if informal. I had never heard of him. . . . I was also mildly surprised at the change that came over Altman as soon as he found himself face to face with royalty. His air of arrogance and self-assurance slipped away as soon as Lawson opened the door, and he sat through our interviews as an adoring disciple sits before the master." The regal Lawson "lost no time in small talk," then "unceremoniously dismissed" the two awestruck visitors "after fifteen or twenty minutes."[23]

George Campbell, also a musician, alleged that Lawson also "directed" the "Communist bloc" among musicians. During their conversation, it was said, Lawson "questioned him on his social and economic beliefs and generally indulged in considerable double-talk which was then incomprehensible" to him. There was a "shroud of secrecy and permeating conspiracy" to the events that seemed straight out of a film thriller.[24]

Now neither Tenney nor Campbell is the most reliable witness, and their recollections should not be accepted unreservedly. But what is striking is the ominous atmosphere said to surround Lawson, as if he were some kind of evil force of nature. Such constructions stuck to Lawson, however, and also helped to shape the demonic image of the Party, with him as its celebrity-in-chief personifying this satanic representation.

Lawson had already attained a certain celebrity, but the relative success of *Blockade* helped to make him tabloid fodder. Thus it was that in mid-1938 the *New York Post* invited him for a luncheon interview in Manhattan. Readers were told chattily that he had arrived from "way out on Long Island, where he's burying himself in a new play," and were briefed on details of questionable relevance intended to situate him within celebrity culture— "he looks amazingly like Spencer Tracy." He then went on to engage in idle chitchat about his latest script, which he discussed in "even happier tones."[25]

There was one point in this idle, celebrity-drenched chatter on which Lawson was not mistaken, however: his latest script, *Algiers*, was a success. "A certain hit before any audience," said the *Hollywood Reporter*, "and, released immediately, will keep a lot of those theatres that are now threatening to close, open, and prosperously so."[26] The story of the beautiful Gaby and her encounter with a jewel thief in the mysterious Casbah also became something of a cultural touchstone, featuring as it did Charles Boyer and Hedy Lamarr, with cinematography by the eminent James Wong Howe. This film bequeathed to the culture timeless lines about "'the Casbah,'" still being riffed on by Las Vegas comedians and late-night talk show hosts. Even after he had been "blacklisted," Lawson was still being queried by curious reporters about his memories of Lamarr—she "looked too 'cold,'" he said, though she was "very beautiful"; but she "'lacked expression' for the role she was playing." He told Walter Wanger "he thought she was wrong for the part" but was waved away indifferently—so much for the "most important man in Hollywood" grilled in 1947 for forcibly smuggling radicalism into cinema.[27]

FIGURE 4. *Algiers* brought an Academy Award nomination for Charles Boyer (left). (Courtesy of the Academy of Motion Picture Arts and Sciences)

Here again, however, Lawson was highly critical of the actors on whom he depended to translate his vision faithfully. Watching Lamarr as production proceeded, he noticed that she "never changed her facial expression. Watching her on the set, I was alarmed by her lack of feeling. She seemed like a wax figure and at times one could only tell by her breathing and the slight movement of glittering jewels on her flesh that she was alive."[28]

According to the *New York Times*, this movie was "clearly one of the most interesting and absorbing dramas of the season."[29] *Variety* described the first- week gross of $85,000 as "plenty potent."[30] This classic garnered four Academy Award nominations, including one each for Charles Boyer and James Wong Howe.

This film was not as politically pointed as *Blockade*, but that did not spare it political protest. France's consul in Los Angeles represented the colonial power in the nation, Algeria, that was to detonate soon in a bitter conflict. Thus, he was sensitive to any cinematic portrayal of any city there—least of all Algiers—no matter how seemingly fluffy. "This title has already been the object of several protests to my Government by French official touristic [*sic*] and artistic organizations," snapped Gerard Raoul-

FIGURE 5. In *Algiers,* Lawson wrote descriptions of the "Casbah" that entered the popular lexicon. (Courtesy of the Academy of Motion Picture Arts and Sciences)

Duval.[31] Wanger drolly informed him that "as remarkable as it may seem, I assure you the majority of Americans do not know where Algiers is."[32]

Perhaps that explains why Lawson's handiwork, with its veiled women—an indigenous woman betrays the film's hero—and men in fezzes, exudes the kind of exotic "Orientalism" that subsequent generations would find repulsive. Still, at times it tends to invert the pervasive stereotypes in a judo-like fashion, deploying the audience's often ignorant preconceptions about an Arab nation for contrary perceptions. This is done through Lawson's staple—class conflict expressed in the context of romance. Hence, the corpulent and affluent male tourists—one of whom competes with the jewel thief played by Charles Boyer for the affections of Hedy Lamarr—are not portrayed sympathetically, and they are the ones often prating ignorantly about "natives." Moreover, the deft use of light and shadow and music helps to create a seductive atmosphere that contemporary filmmakers could study profitably. In fact, *Algiers* holds up better today than most Lawson films.

With *Blockade* and then *Algiers,* Lawson had demonstrated that—despite his Party membership—he could tap profitably into the consciousness of a mass audience and this struck a number of powerful forces as being extremely dangerous. *Blockade,* released in June 1938, made a nifty profit that was exceeded by *Algiers,* released shortly thereafter. (Lawson received an Oscar nomination for *Blockade,* a sign of critical success.)[33] *Algiers* rivaled another Wanger classic—*Stagecoach*—in profitability. [34]

However, Wanger himself was heavily dependent on banks—actually, the conservative Bank of America, which financed both *Blockade* and *Algiers*—and it was unclear how long they would countenance making films, even profitable films, with a Communist at the helm.[35] Initiated by Italian émigrés known not to be unfriendly to Mussolini, "from 1936 to 1952" this bank "financed upward of five hundred feature pictures and more than half as many shorts, representing an outlay (by the bank) of nearly half a billion dollars."[36]

In 1939 Wanger was granted "extension of time of borrowing," a necessity despite the successes of *Blockade* and *Algiers.*[37] Not only that, but Wanger was also seeking to distribute films in the lucrative market that was Germany[38]—not to mention a China under siege by Japan[39]—whose ultraconservative rulers were not pleased with the antifascist politics of *Blockade,* no matter how vaguely stated. Likewise, the negative portrayals of corpulent capitalists in *Algiers* were not altogether consistent with the ideals of another profitable market—South Africa.[40] Lawson was writing movies for a global audience, and those who contracted for his services were not simply seeking to make an aesthetic or political statement. They were trying, above all, to make a profit, and it was unclear how nations with less than progressive regimes would react to his visions—or his politics.[41]

This list decidedly included the United States. Martin Quigley was highly influential and a direct influence on Joseph Breen, the film industry's censor. He was a boon companion of Joseph Kennedy, father of the future U.S. president, whom he credited for having "launched me successfully on the waves of the film industry."[42] To say that Quigley was extremely disturbed by this turn of events involving Lawson is understatement.[43]

There was rampant and internecine conflict within the censor's office and with the moguls railing against the latter, uniting against communism—and Jews and Jewish Communists like Lawson—was a way to escape otherwise coruscating contradictions that could derail them all.[44] The censors were "receiving enormous protests day after day because of what is termed 'excessive drinking in pictures' and the so-called 'left-handed gangster pictures.'"[45] This was causing all manner of ills,[46] and diverting the brewing anticinema energy toward "Communist pictures" no doubt seemed like a neat idea.

By now Lawson may not have been the "most important man in Holly-wood," but he was a force to be reckoned with; he may have been the "most important man" or at least the most influential in the Communist Party and, perhaps, the most affluent besides. Yet his increased celebrity was seemingly complicating his relationship with old friends, particularly John Dos Passos, a man who benefited directly from Lawson's improved income because of his penchant for borrowing. But as Dos Passos's profile—and income—improved, unlike Lawson, he seemed to be moving not left but right and steadily away besides from his most reliable source of funds. Out-siders may have seen the two prolific writers as being in accord politically and artistically, but the reality was quite different.[47]

The now famous Hollywood screenwriter did not approve of his friend's latest work, which he took to task with hammer and tongs. Writing from the comfort of his fashionable abode at 4542 Coldwater Canyon Boulevard in North Hollywood, Lawson admitted that "frankly I was so upset (and shocked, if you'll pardon the expression!) by your last book that I haven't recovered. This is the chief reason I haven't written you." Lawson con-tended, "I insist on the ascertainability of facts," while Dos Passos, he sug-gested, "repeatedly violated known and available truth." Lawson was so in-censed that what he wanted to say "could really only be said properly in a careful criticism running to a minimum of forty thousand words," a small book in other words. "It's a writer's job," he reminded a man soon to be a sworn ideological foe, "to show people battling with a recognizable envi-ronment, in which events and forces correspond to what people know." Yet Dos Passos had "written a subjective book about objective reality." The book made Lawson "angry." In fact, he argued, "I doubt if there's any common ground on which we can talk about these things. I think that's tragic and I assure you [I] don't take it lightly." Who was the cause of this rift? "You're to blame," charged Lawson, "for turning so far away from the sort of agreed fundamentals of feeling and purpose, the groundwork for common thought—which is also common action—that we started with. That's not a nice thing to say—and it probably won't have any effect—but there it is."[48]

What was roiling relations between the two erstwhile friends? Certainly Lawson was displeased with Dos Passos's literary turn in *The Adventures of a Young Man,* as unfriendly to the Republican cause in Spain as Lawson was friendly, and as critical of the Communists as Lawson was infatuated. Put simply, Dos Passos was not as taken with the Communist Party and the Soviet Union as was Lawson. As Dos Passos recalled it later, his own "con-fidence in Marxism and the CP fluctuated wildly from the time of the first excitement of the news of the Russian Revolution" to the 1930s; "at the beginning of that period," he says, Lawson was "further from the CP" than he was—but that changed spectacularly.[49] Moscow became the dividing line between these two men.[50]

Now Lawson was determined that "we *must* get somewhere by continuing to talk it out." However, he said, "where my goat is gotten, and starts not only to bleat but to neigh like a horse, is that, starting from a disagreement about certain facts (what is happening in the Soviet Union, the actual functioning of the Soviets, the Russian foreign policy, etc.) you jump in (in my opinion in the most inexcusable and wildest manner) to the *realm of theory*." "If you believe," he said, "that people should not be imprisoned or executed for their beliefs, unless they commit to overt acts, I entirely agree with you, and my impression of facts is that there is no case, in the Soviet Union or in Spain, of people being imprisoned or executed for their beliefs." Later Lawson was to agree that these monstrous illegalities did occur in Moscow. "I may be wrong about the facts in these countries," he said, referring to the Soviet Union and Spain, "but at least I'm less likely to be wrong about activity of which I'm a part and in which I know what I'm doing and what I'm doing it for." "You," he said derisively about Dos Passos, "stay outside of this (which is certainly your right) but you ought to go easy at jumping at conclusions, because you don't know what you're missing—and what you're missing is a first-rate education in actually working democratically, by democratic means, for democratic means."[51]

With the fervency of a true believer, Lawson had leapt to the front of the crowd hailing Moscow and, in the process, was discarding furiously doubts and friends alike. Lest one think that some other subtle underlying issue was driving this conflict with Dos Passos, it seemed that Moscow was also complicating his ties to others less smitten with socialism. He denounced the prominent liberal publisher Oswald Garrison Villard for his "inexcusable withdrawal" from a "debate" on Moscow. Lawson felt that "the Russian situation is being seriously misrepresented," particularly allegations regarding "Soviet executions." In "attacking the working class government of Russia," he bellowed, "you are also directly attacking the working class of your own and other countries, aiding fascist reaction." Thus, Lawson demanded, "I therefore request you herewith to debate with me on the question: 'the Soviet executions—are they justified?' under any auspices, at any time, and under any conditions which you select." In this macho hand-to-hand combat, it was "understood that you and myself shall be the only speakers."[52]

Moscow also was the source of the conflict between Lawson and the "National Committee for the Defence of Political Prisoners"—"the organization in which I was most active," he said. The "Kirov affair . . . almost destroyed" this grouping and certainly made more knotty Lawson's ties with Edmund Wilson, Clifton Fadiman, and other intellectuals with whom he worked.[53] This lengthening list included the writer Sidney Howard. Lawson "very urgently" asked him to "reconsider your resignation" from this body. He hoped his departure was not "motivated by any feelings in regard to protesting the recent Russian executions,"[54] an event that Lawson was then unwilling to denounce.[55]

"I hungered for the truth," Lawson said longingly years later about this tempestuous era, though his contemporaneous comments did not necessarily reflect this desire. "I have never been more conscious of the limitations of my knowledge [than] I was in that year" of 1937, he said. He admitted belatedly, "If I had known of the crimes committed by Stalin I would have acknowledged the facts."[56] Maybe so. But at the time Lawson expressed few doubts, regrets, or reservations about Moscow's policies. Subsequently, Lawson was a harsh critic of this Soviet era, asserting, "The Stalin period limited creative effort and imposed a distorted concept of 'socialist realism' on the arts."[57] Still, even after he had become more critical of the Georgian leader, he contended, "My strongest reasons for opposing the Trotsky position came from Trotsky himself. I had read all his works and found him dull, and irrational and self-centered."[58]

Unfortunately, the flap about Stalin effectively separated Lawson from allies who felt no urge to rush to his defense when he came under attack in 1947; in fact, it gave some reason to revel in his being pulverized. Still, as the screenwriter and director Abraham Polonsky once put it, "The Soviet Union doesn't always act well," but "does that mean we have the right to persecute the free speech of Communists in this country?"[59] Many of Lawson's most resolute detractors answered this question affirmatively.[60]

Lawson, a romantic rebel of sorts, did not use Polonsky's persuasive arguments with his partner in hurly-burly, Dos Passos, but he certainly used a number of others. Lawson had made the difficult journey from confusion to commitment, and he was convinced more than ever about the rightness of his views. "I've drifted in various mystical and revolutionary directions," which was "more or less a reflection of the whole mess of the liberal mind during the past ten years"—liberals who now refused to line up behind Moscow. Lawson was now "quite willing to agree with the Communists that the liberals are the greatest enemies of the working class" and willing to believe the worst about those whose ranks he had only so recently departed. "You and myself and all the people we know," he told Dos Passos, "people like ourselves, are individualists, and we're soft and we're not particularly given to accepting any kind of discipline." The immensely self-critical Lawson crossed the eminently perilous line from self-flagellation to self-abnegation as he felt that "the Communists have the fullest justification for their distrust of the intellectual." As at times happened with intellectuals who joined a party that glorified proletarians, Lawson felt the need to thump vigorously those of his own stratum to prove his class mettle. Lawson knew where he stood, and it was not with "the Dreisers and Sherwood Andersons and Bunny Wilsons and Archibald MacLeishes and Hemingways and Menckens and Nathans and Heywood Brouns and Calvertons and Eugene O'Neills and Roger Baldwins and Sidney Howards—the whole caboodle of 'em are lining up exactly where they belong—in the name of their artistic integrity, they're serving fascism and war and Jew-baiting and Negro-baiting." In one fell swoop, Lawson had isolated himself from those whose aid he would need so desperately a few years hence.[61]

Subsequently Lawson tried to rescue his floundering relationship with "Dos." "I don't see why we should break our friendship because we disagree about the policies of the Soviet Union," he purred; nor should Dos Passos's "plain ornery red-baiting" be an obstacle to camaraderie of a sort. Friendship, said Lawson, "is not just a matter of 'gratuitous illogical and purposeless bonds'"; it was a "rather serious business and is based on a good deal of understanding." And though he did not agree with Dos Passos "about the movies—nor about religion or politics—for that matter!" friendship was still not out of the question, in his opinion. But Moscow had created a schism too deep and profound to bridge.[62] An immediate casualty of the purges in Moscow was the tattered friendship of Lawson and a man to be hailed as a major twentieth-century novelist: John Dos Passos.

What was driving Lawson so relentlessly to the point where he would skewer longtime friends and choose to ignore stories flowing from Moscow? Like another renowned intellectual—W. E. B. Du Bois—who also was loath to accept the grim realities of Stalin's rule, Lawson found it hard to accept that a bourgeois press that routinely distorted the truth about, say, Blacks, would all of a sudden become a beacon of enlightenment about Reds.[63] More to the point, some who were demanding that he denounce Stalin often were insensitive in ascribing the real and imagined flaws of Communists to those, like Lawson, who were Jewish. This is the now forgotten flip side of the discourse about Stalin. "You talk about cultural New Yorkers being Jewish in mentality," Lawson told Dos Passos remonstratively, to which he replied furiously, "*NUTS.*" "I'm sorry to get so excited about this," he said none too sorrowfully, "but it's a terribly serious question—and *you*, who have never been the nearest thing this country has had to a Proletarian writer, are desperately needed right now." How could Dos Passos, an otherwise intelligent man, "lump all cultured Jewish New Yorkers" in a "damned generalization." Dos Passos's persuasiveness pushed Lawson to say "of course, there's a small element of truth in psychologizing about Jewish mentality, but like all half-truths [it is] deeply dangerous." And "when you talk about the CP New York Jewish leadership, it's far from true," since "as a matter of fact most of the leaders are people like [Clarence] Hathaway and [Earl] Browder. The majority of the leaders of the party are *not* Jewish. And what's more, they [do not have] a Jewish mentality. Anyway, that's not the point either. I wouldn't care if everybody in the party—if the whole twenty five thousand members were all Jewish, the racial question would still be a piece of absurd confusion." Why ascribe Red flaws to ethnoreligious factors anyway, he asked. "Mike Gold is a rather bombastic simpleton who happens to be a very able writer. I'm sorry to get into so much detail on this," he added with a scant apologia, since "the Jewish psychology seems to me to be an idiotic issue to even raise, but *you* raised it" and the "first duty of any revolutionist is to fight nationalistic and racial ideas."[64]

In the 1930s Lawson felt under assault as a Jew. As he scanned the horizon in search of allies to combat the pestilence of prejudice, he alighted on Communists—who happened to be then assailed for providing too wide a berth for those who were Jewish. This made them all the more attractive to him.

If anti-Semitism were limited only to the overheated imagination of Dos Passos, it could have been possible to overlook it. But that was not the case. Hollywood, an industry said to be dominated by Jews—and where some thought Lawson, a Communist Jew, was the "most important man" in town—had attracted the vilest anti-Semites.[65]

The moguls were not as circumspect about fighting anti-Semitism as some have thought,[66] though they had reason to be wary when Major General Smedley Butler "revealed" that he had been "asked by a group of wealthy New York bankers to lead a Fascist movement to set up a dictatorship in the United States" and "organized 500,000 veterans into a Fascist army."[67] The message was received and heeded. For "throughout most of the 1930s, Hollywood showed a remarkable reluctance to produce films about the political situation in Europe, especially Adolf Hitler's rise [to] power," and "in addition to avoiding controversial subject matter, American producers also complied with certain Nazi regulations, such as dismissing their 'non-Aryan' employees in 1933. Only Warner Bros. refused, choosing instead to close its German operations," though "only one prominent actor—the silent film star Lillian Gish—publicly supported" the isolationist America First Committee.[68]

F. Scott Fitzgerald, then in close touch with Lawson, had an experience in writing *Three Comrades* that echoed these currents, for "as the screenplay evolved, its political content became more pointedly anti-Nazi, although the Nazis were not identified. A private screening was arranged for the German Consul in Los Angeles who naturally objected to the anti-Nazi material." Then Joseph Breen "suggested . . . that the movie could be altered to show that it was about the Communists—not the Nazis." The film's producer, Joseph Mankiewicz, refused, and the next day when he showed up at the MGM commissary, Fitzgerald "ran up, threw his arms around [him]," and "kissed [him]." This was the "only [film] credit Fitzgerald received."[69]

Thus, from Lawson's viewpoint, the rising tide of fascism that he could espy from his comfortable doorstep had to be confronted by a force of formidable potency. This created another dilemma, however. Lawson's disdain for the liberalism from which he had only recently escaped was palpable, not least since he was unhappy with how this force confronted the fascist beast, but this disdain made it difficult for these very same liberals to rally to his cause when he came under siege: he was trapped in a circle hard to square.

Yet this development also contained a related dilemma for those who saw Communist cells as little more than updated covens for witches. Marginalizing Communists was heavily dependent on demonstrating their "un-American"—indeed odd—nature, but how could this be done when a member in good standing of the glamour industry not only was a Red but also was responsible for creating prototypical cultural lodestones?

Lawson in turn—in between writing screenplays, studying history, and tending to a family—threw himself frantically into a wide range of antifascist and radical activity. He assisted materially "anti-Nazi German seamen" and Spanish Republicans; he assisted the Australian émigré stevedore Harry Bridges, under fire after spearheading a general strike in San Francisco. He helped to organize Frontier Films, an alternative and radical maker of movies. He was leading the Communist Party in Hollywood.[70] And he was embroiled in a range of anti-Nazi activity as the rise of Hitler stirred the planet.

Lawson joined his friends and comrades Donald Ogden Stewart, Frederic March, Dorothy Parker, and others in the Hollywood Anti-Nazi League.[71] The radical Stewart was the leader of this group,[72] though they were joined by many others.[73] In short, Lawson was not simply a lone "Hollywood Red"; the dangers he witnessed were viewed similarly by a growing cohort of "Red Hollywood," and he would not have been as effective as he was but for the protective coloration provided by colleagues.

With their star wattage, it was not long before "seven thousand persons, a large number of them standees jammed the Shrine Auditorium," and "two thousand more were turned away. It was the first large demonstration arranged by the Hollywood Anti-Nazi League." The mayor of L.A., Frank Shaw, spoke, and there was a "large attendance of famous screen personalities"—and "ample police protection," since the fascists were known to disrupt gatherings of this kind.[74] Of course, Hollywood was not uniformly of one view. Sam Marx, for example, "was opposed to the Anti-Nazi League because they weren't opposed to Stalin." "I remember," he recalled years later, "they were condemning Hitler and I raised my hand and said, 'do you include Stalin' and they hissed and booed and my wife and I had to leave the meetings."[75]

Still, Lawson's preconception appeared to be largely accurate: the menacing specter of rising fascism *was* confronted with a growing Red movement and bore the brunt of defeating Hitlerism on the plains of Russia. Meanwhile, back in the United States, the Communist-influenced journal *New Masses* saw its circulation gyrate from a mere four thousand to a respectable twenty-five thousand over a matter of months during this era.[76]

This growth in turn stirred the powerful to action. The Catholic prelate Francis Talbot was quite "concerned about" the "activities of Communists or communistic adherents" and found it curious that the "magazine" of the Federal Theatre Project—which was known to be infested with Reds—"was for sale in Los Angeles nowhere except" at a Communist bookstore. This "federal publication was on display there yesterday amidst copies of Moscow, Soviet and other publications of the sort"; it was "very convenient to be able to buy the 'New Masses' and the 'Daily Worker' and the latest from Moscow" and the Federal Theatre Project journal at the same time. "But then," Talbot said in a swipe at a key New Deal operative deemed responsible for this assumed outrage, "Harry Hopkins was ever thoughtful."[77]

A good deal of this anticommunism—which was tinged with anti-Semitism[78]—was propelled by conservative Catholics like Talbot. They were especially active in Southern California, where Jewish Communists, like Lawson, were thought to be influential. The high-ranking journalist William Wilkerson scoffed at this idea, writing with emphasis that *"there is no closed fist of Communism gripping Hollywood."*[79] Yet one self-described "American" writing anonymously from Hollywood asserted that the "Communist group in Hollywood is active but completely unimportant—both numerically and financially. They do not, for an instant, threaten the complete Catholic dominance of the American screen which now exists and which is so ably administered by Mr. Joseph Breen. I hope it not blasphemous," he added puckishly, "to believe that Our Lord (who is not without a sense of humor) is laughing today at the ease with which was duped the poor dumb Protestants into aiding the Legion of Decency by which we gained complete control of this vital American agency of opinion. When He contemplates the vast amounts of deft Fascist propaganda which we turn out daily (in the Jews' studios and financed with the Jews' money), He must laugh merrily." The Red Scare was simply a convenient smoke-screen to deflect attention from actual conservative Catholic influence, he suggested. "Our Holy Cause is winning Spain," he exclaimed, so "be of good cheer—we are more than holding our own in Hollywood," since "Catholic domination of the screen is much more complete than is our domination of the press and the stage. But this will come. What has been done in Holly-wood can be done throughout America."[80]

Father Talbot dissented, averring, "I am not yet convinced that Holly-wood is as free of communism as you assert," and he only needed to point to Lawson for evidence to sustain his demurral.[81]

8 Fighting—and Writing

As the hoofbeats of war began to sound ever louder in Europe, the reverberations were felt intensely in Hollywood. As the face of Red Hollywood, John Howard Lawson was positioned strategically to be either bathed in warm sunlight or drenched in a cold rain as the political climate changed. His reasserted commitments both personally and politically had provided him with a comforting cocoon of a Communist collective—and a stabilized marriage—that could serve as shelter in the fiercest storm. It was hard to foresee, however, that brutally cyclonic winds would come sweeping through Hollywood that would disrupt his carefully constructed existence.

The personal example of Lawson—and a number of other writers who would come to constitute the "Hollywood Ten"—would inspire other writers to move to the left, to the point where one scholar has claimed that "in the early 1940s, 25 to 30 percent of the most regularly employed members of the Screen Writers Guild were members of the CPUSA." Some of the most brilliant stars in Hollywood's galaxy were said to be glowing as red as Mars as well. One informant maintained that Charles Chaplin was a "devoted and loyal member of the Party, but that to protect him and to protect the best interests of the Party, he should remain a member at large and not be affiliated with the Party units being set up in Hollywood."[1]

There was a Communist-influenced left that encompassed the Anti-Nazi League and, particularly, the committee to free Tom Mooney, jailed during World War I due to accusations of his participation in a bombing. The screenwriter Dudley Nichols chaired his Hollywood committee, but joining him were James Cagney, Melvyn Douglas, Lillian Hellman, Boris Karloff, Frederic March, Groucho Marx, Robert Montgomery, Paul Muni, Dashiell Hammett, and others.[2] Given this leftward tilt, Lawson and his comrades could hardly envision during their heyday in Hollywood that doom would be their destiny.[3]

The composer and conductor Albert Glasser was among those who did not have warm feelings toward Lawson. He was king of the B-movie music men, with work that included *Confessions of an Opium Eater, Varan the Unbelievable, Monster from Green Hell, Oriental Evil, The Gay Amigo,* and other films of little redeeming value. When HUAC brought its road show to L.A. in 1956, however, the congressmen present hung on Glasser's every word, as if he were the Coltrane of witnesses: he was loquacious in his indictment of Lawson and this earlier era. "We went," he said, "up to a home on Sunset Plaza Drive. Whose home I wasn't aware at the time and never have been. But when we came to this big, very fine home, there were about 40 or 50 people sitting around in the living room. And after a few minutes a gentleman came to the front and said, 'ladies and gentlemen, welcome to the Communist Party.'" It was all "very friendly, very jovial, a lot of fun," and very suspicious, too, since all present were "total strangers to me." Then a "gentleman began to speak"—this was Lawson. "He was a very bright man, a very intelligent man," Glasser said, making a seeming compliment sound ominous. "But as far as I am concerned, his political thinking was way off the beam, completely confused." The garrulous Lawson spoke "for an hour or two—I forget how long—just going along" about "how they hoped to bring about certain changes in the Government through normal legal processes, through the ballot, through the vote of the American people"—"and he talked and talked and talked. And at times he would go off on tangents, which at times sounded like double talk. And toward the end he kept building up toward the fact that we have to do this through normal legal processes, due process of law. He pounded his fist and would get very dynamic because he is a very dynamic man."

When Lawson finished, Glasser's spouse—"a very spunky little woman"—"raised her hand to ask a question. And he said, 'yes,' and pointed to her. And she said," with mock innocence, "'Mr. Lawson, what is the ultimate goal of the Communist Party?'" As Glasser recalled it, Lawson "immediately went into a long series of double talk, divergence, tangents, all over the place. He didn't answer her question one iota. When he finally got through with the story," Mrs. Glasser said, "'I still ask the same question. What is the ultimate goal? What happens if we can't accomplish this through legal processes, through the ballot box?'" And "again he went off on a long-winded story, evading the issue. Three or four times she kept after him. And I almost started to poke her," said Glasser, "and say 'cut it out.' I didn't realize what she was after. She kept needling him," like an expert lawyer seeking to goad a hostile witness into revealing his true persona to the jury. She "was insisting he answer the question," and then the Perry Mason moment arrived. "He finally got so angry, and his face flushed up—I shouldn't use the word 'red,'" said the avuncular storyteller. "But his face came red, and he just blurted out with vehemence," forcing it out against his own will, like the right-wing presidential adviser played by Peter Sellers in *Dr. Strangelove*, "'Revolution'"! "[I] think he forgot himself," said the self-satisfied witness, "because there was a general murmur of dissatisfaction in the group. They felt this wasn't necessary." But the wiser Glassers "knew right then and there, oh, oh, something is wrong."[4]

This targeting of Lawson reached a raucous crescendo when the writer and then Communist Budd Schulberg submitted to his comrades his manuscript for the novel that was to become *What Makes Sammy Run?*

Now Lawson was not alien to criticism or the swapping of manuscripts. The left-wing writer Franklin Folsom observed that "exchange of criticisms [and] of manuscripts was very much a part of literary life at that time— certainly of literary life on the Left. John Howard Lawson and Dalton Trumbo engaged in vigorous analysis of one another's work. 'Your comments, received this morning, were *exactly* the kind of thing I was looking for. No, Jack, you do not lose *this* friend because of criticism. I wasn't looking for 'it's wonderful!'—I was looking for 'it's wrong here, and this is why.'"[5] One reason Communists came to wield such strong influence among screenplay writers was that they offered a collective to a profession that was enmeshed in tremendous isolation at the typewriter. Their "Writers' Clinic" had "an informal 'board' of respected screenwriters"—for example, Lawson and Ring Lardner Jr.—"who read and commented upon any screenplay submitted to them. Although their criticism could be plentiful, stinging and (sometimes) politically dogmatic, the author was entirely free to accept or reject it as he or she pleased without incurring the slightest 'consequence' or sanction."[6] The League of American Writers, in which Lawson also played a leading role, also sponsored a "writer's clinic," which was "very successful"—so successful that the "chapter's financial status was better than before because of the successes of the school."[7]

Carl Foreman, the Communist who wrote the screenplays for *High Noon* and *Champion*, found Lawson's insights and these clinics generally invaluable. "The party was helpful in organizing my mind," he recalled later. "I don't know if it was the LAW schools or in the party discussions, but I was learning about form and content. Somewhere I learned there was always a theme or a premise and that unquestionabl[y] made me a better writer. The biggest thing it helped me with was organizing my mind."[8]

The budding feminist historian Gerda Lerner also "joined a newly formed writers' workshop" that combined literary criticism and activist commitment. Lawson was central to these efforts. Indeed, the class sponsored by the LAW "had a far greater impact on me than I realized at the time," Lerner recalled later; this was the class in "American history given by John Howard Lawson. It was, in fact, my first ever course in American history." Though Lawson was "pilloried in the press and media as the 'Communist cultural czar' of Hollywood," she "knew him as a brilliant lecturer, a fine teacher, a man of broad learning. His course was a combination of what now would be called American studies—intellectual and social history, literature and film. It was lively, informative and judging from my class notes and syllabus, which I still have, offered a traditionally Progressive interpretation of history. Its most radical aspect was a heavy emphasis on the role of race and racism in U.S. history. What seems quite remarkable to me now was Lawson's matter-of-fact inclusion of sources by women and material about women." On the other hand, the generally laudatory Lerner adds tellingly that the "only tendentious aspect of the course was Lawson's approach to creative writing. Here he followed the traditional Marxist line of his day—he downgraded any work he considered 'formalistic' or 'mystical' (Emily Dickinson, T. S. Eliot) and upgraded any work with easily accessible social significance (Whitman, Carl Sandburg). The style he favored was realism."[9]

Yet Schulberg's reaction to criticism of his novel—and the subsequent construction of this episode—was vituperative and not as sunny as Lerner's assessment. This scion of a Hollywood family was one of the "crowned princes" of the industry. He had visited the Soviet Union in 1934 and was "ravished by the hopeful new spirit of Russia." Like Ring Lardner Jr., who traveled with him, "they saw in Russia the only true attempt to rebuild a new world."[10]

This was to change. For before a rapt congressional committee and a curious television audience in 1951, his words pouring forth slowly like cold molasses, Schulberg repented and sought expiation. With a high forehead and a complexion often reddened by the sun, Schulberg possessed dark blue eyes, a large, flattish nose, and teeth that were surprisingly bad for a man of his class.[11] The broad-shouldered witness told of how, in 1939, he "went to see Lawson" about this work after being advised to do so, though he was reluctant to show him his words.[12] Schulberg had given Ring Lardner Jr. his manuscript; the latter did not find it anti-Jewish but decided to "discuss the matter with two of the more notable ideologues of the Hollywood branch of the party, [Lawson] and V. J. Jerome, from whom he got a harsher reaction."[13]

"The first pressure upon [Schulberg] to write under guidance was exerted" by Lawson.[14] The pudgy, pasty-faced writer complained that after reviewing his novel, "John Howard Lawson and other Communists called a meeting at the Hollywood-Roosevelt Hotel and asked him if he wanted to come and defend himself. He reflected that, 'if I were Russian, I wouldn't be invited to the Hollywood-Roosevelt: I might be on my way to the camps.'"[15] The idea was hammered home relentlessly that Communists in the shape of Lawson were ruthless in suppressing creativity and artistic freedom; they were truly "Stalin's stars."

But it was not just Lawson who was critical of Schulberg's work. The contemporary writer Neal Gabler finds the novel "coarsely written and quaintly primitive." "People . . . hated my book," Schulberg admitted. "Some said it was the most disgraceful, vulgar, callow novel they had ever read." Schulberg compared his travail to "the attack on Richard Wright's hero-villain-victim, Bigger Thomas, in 'Native Son,'" which was "strikingly parallel" to his own situation.[16]

Lawson later appeared confounded by the controversy over his sharp criticism of this work. He recalled a time in 1939 when *Processional* was revived and was "violently attacked by the Communist papers as an example of Dada and surrealism. 'I can't recall that that had any devastating effect on me.' He got a frantic telegram from V. J. Jerome saying the play went against all principles of socialist realism. Lawson replied, 'Sorry, I disagree.' Besides forty people's jobs depended on it, so [he] let it run." Lawson also remembered the time that Mike Gold castigated him as a "bourgeois hamlet." "'I didn't like it but it wasn't the end of the world,'" he said.[17]

Put candidly, Lawson disapproved of Schulberg's novel. Though his own *Success Story* and his own character Sol Ginsberg could be profitably compared to Sammy Glick, even the passage of time had not altered appreciably his lack of enthusiasm for this novel.[18] Repeatedly, Lawson excoriated Schulberg's book. "I've never questioned a writer's right to write what he pleases," he told the *New York Times* in 1973. "But I also have the right to say what I think about it, and I thought 'What Makes Sammy Run?' was not a great Hollywood novel, not a great proletarian novel and not a great novel. In fact, I thought it was a piece of junk. I thought that then, and I think that now, and I think history has proven me correct."[19]

Schulberg should not have taken it so personally. Lawson generally had a dyspeptic outlook on the Hollywood novel—and Schulberg's novel, too, he thought, hardly captured the richness and contradiction of this endlessly fascinating industry.[20]

In retrospect, Lawson's overreaction to this still illuminating novel was off base—just as Schulberg overreacted similarly to his misguided criticism. The nature of the times, the onset of war, and the signs of impending genocide led to frazzled nerves and heated debates. For Al Mannheim, a hero of Schulberg's book, is a "blacklist" victim portrayed sympathetically. There is a contempt for red-baiting—"Sammy came into my office to save California from annexing itself to Russia." There was an attempt to argue that Glick's venality was intimately connected to the bigotry to which he had been subjected; going to school in New York, he would often hear, "'kill the dirty sheeny. . . . [S]end him back to Palestine.'" Readers were taught that "people . . . aren't just results. They're a process. And to really give them a break we have to judge the process through which they become the result we see when we say so-and-so is a heel." Glick's "childhood environment was the breeding ground for the predatory germ that thrived in Sammy's blood, leaving him one of the most severe cases of the epidemic." He spelled it out for the denser reader: "What makes Sammy run? The childhood, Kit had said, look into the childhood."[21]

Yet lost in these charges and countercharges about this book is the question—as then Communist Richard Maibum put it—was it proper for Schulberg to create an offensive Jewish character, Sammy Glick, at a time of rising anti-Semitism? Timing is what may separate Glick from his putative brother-in-law, Sol Ginsberg. Moreover, the attack on Schulberg may have been compensatory, blunting the allegation that the Party was soft on anti-Semitism, which was alleged in the aftermath of the nonaggression pact between Berlin and Moscow.[22]

L'affaire Schulberg paved the way for a dour view of Reds—and Lawson specifically—as the thought police, even though Lawson's opinion of this book was apparently not shared by all Reds.[23] Hence, the image of Red Hollywood, a community that centered heavily on writers, is recalled as doctrinaire and dogmatic, serious and censorious—the popular image of Lawson, in other words.[24]

Hence, when one comrade decided that he wanted to exit the Party, a "committee of the so-called Disciplinary Commission called on him at his home and brutally warned him that 'something could happen' to his children if he defied the Party"—or so it was said. "Shortly thereafter one of his children was almost run down by an automobile."[25]

Rigidity was said to be one of Lawson's attributes.[26] This did not win him many friends, particularly when the Party was under siege and comrades were scurrying. He "had many enemies within the party," according to the writer Nancy Schwartz. "He was a superb leader but he [provoked] a great deal of resentment."[27]

Actually, this unpleasant image of Lawson and Jerome captures only a small portion of a community that, in some ways, was defined more by dissolution and debauchery than by demonizing.[28] This environment was not conducive to a healthy family life either.[29]

Lawson was known to take a drink or two occasionally, though he hardly rose—or descended—to the level of some of his comrades. What was impelling this abandoned inebriation? Besides fretting about the fate of the planet, these writers were also being pressured by the competitive nature of screenplay writing, where their income and lifestyles turned heavily upon their ability to make magic on blank sheets of paper.[30]

Dependence on controlled substances was often the lubricating "magic" that created screenplays—or so it was thought.[31] This dissolution may have contributed to an unhealthy atmosphere in Red Hollywood. Yet the fact that this trend was not unique to the left suggests that it may have been a constituent element of Hollywood itself.[32]

There was a general pressure faced by all writers in Hollywood and a special pressure faced by Communist writers. This atmosphere contributed to substance abuse and unfair assailing of writers like Schulberg, but it also created conditions for the growth of radicalism and the Screen Writers Guild, in which Lawson played the leading role. For it was the much beleaguered screenwriter who carried the burden of a multi-million-dollar industry on his back while being accorded utter disrespect: this in itself was enough to drive a person to the nearest bottle of spirits or the most destructive of criticisms.

For Cecil B. DeMille was among those who felt that "writers were more important than stars, producers, cameramen, or directors," including himself. Yet despite this presumed preeminence, writers—even after, particularly after, the formation of the guild—hardly received the respect they were due. Jack Warner insisted that "writers keep a nine-to-five-thirty schedule, take only half an hour for lunch, and wear their pencils down to a certain length by the end of the day. Warners' writers used to put their pencils into a sharpener to grind them down to half an inch." "Nunnally Johnson, one of old Hollywood's top screenwriters, . . . spent at least a portion of every day at the typewriter"—"even on his honeymoon."[33]

Red Hollywood in particular blanched at this speedup—which was to bring them all grief later.[34] Yet despite—or perhaps because of—their clear preeminence in moviemaking,[35] writers were abused routinely—and not just by moguls.[36]

The ultimate expression of this "resentment" was the compensation writers received for their labor. According to one authoritative study, "As late as 1939, the median weekly wage for screenwriters was only $120. As a group, screenwriters did not earn anything like what their counterparts in directing, producing, or lead acting made. In 1931, for example, screenwriter salaries accounted for only 1.5 per cent of the total payroll of the motion picture industry."[37]

The SWG had sought to halt these abuses, though before it secured a contract, this group was still semilegal—and semieffective; "it was being kept alive through secret meetings at various homes. 'After the Guild fell apart,' remembered [Lawson], 'it was sustained underground, which was something unusual and dangerous for writers, the fact that they stayed together without industry support.'"[38]

Budd Schulberg could continue to write in 1941 in his novel about Hollywood that "the producer encourages as many as a dozen aspiring writers to work on his idea. They knock themselves out over his story for two or three weeks in return for nothing but the vaguest of promises. Then the producer comes out of it with enough free ideas to nourish the one writer he finally hires." This was the "the ten-man-for-every job side [of Hollywood], the seasonal unemployment, the call-again-next-month side. The factory side."[39]

Fiddling with the creation of the screenplay writer was a specialty of producers, which was understandable, since a movie required such a significant level of investment, but this obvious fact at once undermined the post-1947 notion that these same writers were forcefully and unilaterally smuggling subversion onto the silver screen. In *The Grapes of Wrath*, Fox was pressured to "take out any references to Communist influences in the American labor movement or, worse still, to demonize organize labor as pawns of the wily Reds."[40] The diminutive Daryl Zanuck—"Twentieth Century's Fox"—had capacious ideas about movies. According to the screenwriter-director Robert Pirosh, "he would wind up dictating the rearrangement of your material. He had a secretary taking down everything he said," and the writer would receive later "about a thirty-page memo taking out material and adding much of his."[41]

Zanuck, with whom Lawson collaborated on *Four Sons*, was not shy about giving him instructions for alterations.[42] Lawson was told bluntly, "Mr. Zanuck wants all the American stuff dropped. He does not like a story of foreigners turning into Americans. . . . ours is not that kind of story."[43] The boss found his worker's labor "commendable," but "several major changes had to be made." For example, "Mr. Zanuck would like to see sprinkled throughout the script a few phrases in German, like Guten Abend,

Guten Morgen, Auf Wiedersehen . . . etc., so that the Heil Hitlers do not hit us in the face."[44]

On *Earthbound*, Lawson was informed that "generally speaking, Mr. Zanuck likes very much the way Mr. Lawson has handled the story"— except that "our personal story has been submerged to give prominence to the March of Events. It must be the other way around. . . . the people seem to be of secondary importance. Handling it like this causes us to lose fifty percent of the story's value as *entertainment*. The political, historical situations should serve only as a *background*. . . . [T]he most important change you make is to *transpose the emphasis from the events to the characters and their personal story*. Milk the personal story for all its values and bring in the events as it affects them." Lawson was told that "Hitler's name should be mentioned only once—in the early part of the story"—so much for an anti-Nazi screed. "Mr. Lawson is to write a first draft continuity incorporating these changes"—the writer, per usual, followed the lead of the producer.[45] Unlike many writers, Lawson was philosophical about this process, asserting that "it is simply absurd for a writer to say his lines cannot be changed. . . . I can say with some pride that I am one of the few . . . who has always accepted criticism and learned from it. I have always been willing to change lines or scenes."[46]

Hence, Lawson later could argue credibly that he was "definitely blacklisted in the industry, as were many other people too because of their known record as supporters and activists" in the SWG before being rescued by Wanger—and not because he was a devious writer seeking to smuggle subversive lines into scripts.[47] It was in August 1939 that RKO executive B. B. Kahane snarled at the SWG delegation, "You fellows talk about blacklist. If this thing [i.e., SWG] goes through, I will show you a blacklist that will blast you out of business."[48]

Some of the writers' wounds were self-inflicted, boozing and savage disputes aside. They were not without weapons, but this was not always evident—least of all to the writers themselves. One reason was because there were so many categories of writers. As Schulberg put it,

> The low-paid writers wanted the Guild to be a real bread-and-butter union, and the congenial five-hundred-dollar-a-week guys thought what writers needed most was a communal hangout like the old Writers' Club where they could sit around and get to know each other. The twenty-five-hundred-dollar-a-week writers with famous names seemed to be most interested in increasing their influence in picture productions and spoke fine, brave abstract words about the scope of the medium and dignifying the position of the screen writer. . . . [W]e have some of the most unique union members in the history of organized labor.[49]

"I used to think that Negroes lacked organized-labor consciousness more than did any other group," mused the Jamaican-born writer Claude McKay. "But it was much worse on the movie lot. I saw the worst sort of sycophancy in the world."[50]

There were other problems. Writers, specialists in crafting dialogue, loved talking. Lester Cole, the Communist screenwriter who was to write *Born Free*, was also a former actor and was not averse to drama at meetings.[51] There were arguments about everything at meetings, often sparked by a *Hollywood Reporter* article—an organ of the opposition—that would foment round-robin discussions and interminable debate, perhaps intentionally. Given that all those sitting around the roundtable lived and died by the word, verbosity was the coin of the realm. Further, some of the writers (e.g., Paul Jarrico and Emmett Lavery) were lawyers, and all, not just Lawson, thought of themselves as brilliant tacticians. Hence, meetings often bogged down in the mud of verbiage.[52]

Nevertheless, despite the debilitation wrought by alcohol and the anomie brought by moguls taking cleavers to their prose, Lawson and his comrades in Red Hollywood were not without influence in the era before 1947, most of all in the SWG they had built in the teeth of opposition. Philip Barber, one of Lawson's tennis partners in Hollywood, spoke disagreeably about him when asked. "In the thirties," he recalled, "there was a complete Communist control and blacklist. So that if you weren't favored by the Communist Party, you'd have trouble working in the theatre or in Hollywood." It was not quite as brutal as the post-1947 "blacklist," since "it never had the same economic power but it worked in exactly the same way."[53] This is a slight exaggeration: producers, not writers, provided jobs. Yet with their writing clinic overseen by Lawson, Red Hollywood was sited propitiously to take advantage of available opportunities.

The relatively meager fruits reaped from the labor of the writer's imagination helped to spur the SWG—just as the New Deal taking root and the Olson gubernatorial victory in 1938 helped to propel California Communists, it also gave a boost to the guild.[54] Though certainly the writer did not reap the full fruit produced by his imagination, certainly writers were—or at least those who could snag work—not doing badly, which meant that the SWG had the sustenance to withstand the hammer blows of the studios. An "analysis of working conditions and salary status of screenwriters in Hollywood" in 1940 involved 1,000 questionnaires and 520 replies, 330 of which were from active guild members. The "highest salary reported was $3750 a week; the lowest $27.50 a week," while "50% of the screenwriters actively engaged in Hollywood in 1939 earned less than $120.00 per week"—respectable, but hardly a fortune.[55]

Still, friction between writers and studios contributed to F. Scott Fitzgerald's depiction of the fictional mogul, Monroe Stahr, and Brimmer, the Red, who pummeled him.[56] The stiff opposition from the economic royalists had the perverse effect of rallying a number of decidedly non-Communist writers around Lawson's banner. Yet there were ill-omened signs. As Robert Rossen noted at the time, in the fall of 1941, at an "open meeting of the nominating committee" of the guild, when the names of Lawson and his comrade "Lester Cole were proposed for re-nomination, the five members who voted against their re-nomination were unanimous on two points. The first was that these two members had served the Guild well and faithfully. The second was, because of the political opinions held by these two members, they were not fit to hold office in the Guild. To further augment that argument, they stated that a certain percentage of the membership felt the same way, and that, therefore, they were justified [in] removing these two names for consideration for re-nomination."[57] If this was the view on the cusp of the SWG's triumph, how would fellow writers react when the SWG was under fire?

There were also tensions among the producers. David O. Selznick, an independent producer, was successful creatively and financially but did not have the wherewithal or the margin for error of a studio. The "minimum wage" for writers was "outrageous," and the "producers will be a laughing-stock of America if they accede to it"—"why not $1500 a week instead of $150 a week," Selznick guffawed. The "vacation clause for writers" was "also absurd since they take vacations whenever the mood strikes them, sleeping in the office three-quarters of the time and playing tennis most of the other quarter." Besides, he said scornfully, "they have loads of time off between assignments and if the time they loafed were stretched end to end, it would take nine months out of every year. It's a bit like asking for a vacation for a Senator." A "united front should be maintained by the independent producers," he warned, "preserving anonymity as to the source of individual opinion so that no one producer is the goat on holding out on any one point." He wanted "immediate notification . . . that the independent producers will not be bound [by] what the large studios do." "I have always been very pro-Guild," he said to some skepticism, "but I don't want us to be chumps as the producers have been in the other Guild agreements." He demanded that the SWG "penalize through expulsion or through fine any writers who are deliberately dishonest through such practices as not working, when they are supposed to be working; working on their own material on salaried time; working for other producers and directions on the side; taking credit for work they did not do; etc."

But in his militancy—which ultimately proved unavailing—Selznick also signaled why Lawson had placed such a high priority on organizing all writers as a matter of self-defense for the SWG. For Selznick already had his eye on "important foreign writers" who "don't want" or "don't have the time to, or cannot afford, to join the Guild." Besides, there were "thousands of young writers dying to get to Hollywood who would give their eye-teeth for a chance to write."[58]

．　　．　　．

Lawson also had a starring role in the League of American Writers, which saw as a prime function helping to assist the organizing of *all* writers—be they employed by magazines, newspapers, technical journals, or whatever. This not only could boost the overall wage level for writers generally—including those in Hollywood—but also could hamper the ability of the moguls to recruit elsewhere if screenwriters chose to continue their course of militancy, not to mention hampering Selznick's more ambitious plans.[59]

But the LAW had its own problems. The organization included Communists but a smattering of liberals as well, and the two often clashed on basic matters of foreign policy, which hampered their ability to unite against their common adversary. Thus, "When the Left refused to support the British during the period of 'the phony war,'" Ella Winter "was out of sympathy." She detected "a vast difference between Nazi Germany and 'Imperial Britain' but to my amusement," she recalled later, "my arguments made [me] suspect to former friends."[60] The backdrop to tension was the Soviet-German nonaggression pact, which many Communists felt bound to defend and many liberals were determined to denounce. It had a "tremendous impact" said Carey McWilliams, a writer and lawyer. It "ruptured friendships. People weren't speaking to other people, the Left was in the doghouse, and [it was a] very bad time, very, very bad time." In fact, he declares, "I think the foundations were laid then for the subsequent witch-hunting that came along later. It was a very, very bleak period." McWilliams was "in the middle of this because," he asserts, "my position was that I could understand why the Soviet Union had done what it did from the point of view of national self-interest," and he understood why liberals felt it opened the door to further aggression by Berlin.[61]

In a better world, a liberal like Philip Dunne should have been allied closely with those of Lawson's persuasion. But in 1940 he was embroiled in a public debate with McWilliams, Dalton Trumbo, and Dreiser in a forum sponsored by the LAW on whether the United States should enter the war.

He remained stunned by "the savagery that characterized the schism on the left which resulted from the Communists' abrupt reversal of position" after the treaty was inked.[62]

Moreover, the fissures were renting the fabric of the Party itself. In late 1939 at a Communist meeting in L.A., Pettis Perry acknowledged that "it seems that the Russian-Finnish war is causing some of the Party members to express themselves as opposed to the Soviets. Some of them cannot withhold their true feelings in the matter." "One thing is very apparent," he concluded sadly, "and that is that there is a great deal of suspicion between EVERY member and his fellow Comrade."[63]

If such issues were roiling the Party, one can easily imagine how it was riling the LAW. As early as mid-1938, concern was expressed that "League members are completely free to state, when occasion arises, their belief that the building of the Popular Front is the best means to preserve Democracy, as long as League members are not asked to take part in programs which include red-baiting."[64] When confronted with one finely wrought, excruciatingly worked-out statement, Upton Sinclair remarked, "I can see that somebody must have sweated blood trying to prepare a statement which everybody could accept."[65]

The disruptions caused by foreign policy were a change from past practice. In 1938 Lawson faced little opposition when he blasted Washington, which "through its shameful 'neutrality' legislation has given direct aid to the German and Italian assault." William Faulkner agreed, declaring that he was "unalterably opposed to Franco and Fascism." Fannie Hurst embroidered this simple point, seemingly sarcastically, by adding, "I am against smallpox, murder, race prejudice, war, injustice, diluted milk, fascism, stealing pennies off dead men's eyes and shell-shocked Chinese babies." John Steinbeck, Felix Frankfurter, Richard Wright, James Weldon Johnson, Alain Locke, I. F. Stone, Nelson Algren, Dashiell Hammett, and Josephine Herbst were equally pointed though less colorful.[66]

But this was to change. "Should America go to war on the side of Great Britain?" And who is responsible? This was the "debate" held in the fall of 1940 featuring Hemingway, Richard Wright, Archibald MacLeish, Albert Maltz, and others.[67] When the board of the LAW met just before then, it debated whether the LAW should oppose the fascist powers more definitively.[68] The writer Oliver La Farge crossed swords with Lawson on this issue—and resigned.[69] As was his wont, Lawson was not just the most outspoken advocate for his fiercely held viewpoint; he was also the most searing in his analysis. Repeatedly before June 1941—when Berlin attacked

Moscow and he and other Communists flip-flopped—Lawson was the most vigorous in asserting an antiwar position, though he also attacked the "Lindbergh 'peace movement'" of the right.[70]

The Hollywood chapter of the LAW often was stirred by angry debates over foreign policy that then carried over to the SWG—thereby making more difficult the unity of writers. Thus, in January 1940 Lawson and his comrades—for example, Donald Ogden Stewart, Robert Rossen (author of such screenplays as *All the King's Men* and *The Roaring Twenties*)—jousted with Irving Stone (author of the screenplay for *The Agony and the Ecstasy*). The exhausted group of LAW members adjourned at 1:30 A.M. after a lengthy meeting at the home of Sheridan Gibney, author of screenplays for *I Am a Fugitive from a Chain Gang* and *Anthony Adverse*—who must have felt like one of his characters.[71]

Stone had demanded that the board "refrain from taking any stand on questions relating to the international situation," and "John Lawson" was the most adamant in opposing Stone's view that "the war is one of 'democracy vs. nazism' and that we should cooperate with the Allies to the utmost."[72] These fierce battles were creeping from meetings to movie sets. The left-wing actor Lionel Stander "got in a fight with [Adolph] Menjou on the set of . . . 'A Star Is Born.' I was playing the press agent. He was playing a director. He had gone to the 1936 Olympics as a guest of Hitler. He was a goddamn Nazi," Stander roared years later. "I got into a fight with him on the set."[73]

The battles did not stop there. Subsequently Gibney requested that the LAW condemn the "Russian aggression against Finland" but "after much discussion it was unanimously voted down." Nevertheless, a Lawson resolve that members vote for "desiring free and continuous discussion" and "active participation with . . . the peace movement" was "unanimously carried."[74] These were not just Communist versus non-Communist battles. Carey McWilliams, no Party member, also was hotly "opposed to American participation" in the war.[75]

Yet the broader left was split by these conflicts, which did not augur well for the SWG—or Lawson. The novelist James T. Farrell, known to be a devotee of Leon Trotsky, was irked by LAW viewpoints on foreign policy, terming them "shameless,"[76] and his vehemence was widely shared. When on 14 June 1941—days before the German invasion of the Soviet Union—the *Motion Picture Herald* blared the headline "Stalin Cheered, Roosevelt Booed, Writers See 'Cultural Emergency,'" it was evident that the "emergency" that would soon arise would entrap the LAW itself and its leaders like Lawson.[77]

Lawson sailed on nonplussed. In a lengthy interview with the *Daily Worker* in mid-1940 on his first trip to New York in a year, Lawson declared confidently, "I'm thoroughly convinced . . . that the people of our country are wholeheartedly against involvement in the war." He was exhibiting a "sun tan acquired on an auto trip from the West Coast," and "on that journey he talked to people of all types in many states. 'I didn't run into a single ordinary American soul who favored entry into the war in Europe.'" Lawson "was particularly enthusiastic about a tremendous peace demonstration held two weeks ago on the steps of City Hall" in L.A. "'It was one of the most alive gatherings I have ever witnessed in my life,'" he exulted. He spoke glowingly of the "Hollywood Peace Council . . . comprised of nine organizations" and "sponsors a weekly forum that is literally the 'talk of the town. . . . [It] regularly attracts 700 people each week.'" Asked "what he thought of Noel Coward and other representatives of Britain who are conducting war-making activities in this country under the guise of culture, [Lawson] answered tersely, 'I think they are vile. We have a number of Mr. Coward's twin brothers out in Hollywood.'"[78]

Soon the LAW was to dissolve, which was a tragedy for writers—Lawson not least, because he was now more isolated and ripe for the plucking—and a setback for antifascism. For before its demise the LAW had done good work, on behalf of exiled writers, for example, who were being imported by Hollywood in large numbers.[79] LAW, true to its mission, sought to improve the status—particularly the economic status—of all writers.[80] The League gave an early boost to the soon-to-be influential journal *Partisan Review*, which sooner still was to turn on writers like Lawson with a vengeance,[81] though it initially considered "affiliating with the League."[82] Richard Wright, Ralph Ellison, Grace Lumpkin, Meridel LeSueur, and Dawn Powell were active participants in the LAW, providing a premature diversity.[83] Above all, the league was a bulwark against fascism, particularly before 1939. It was under the aegis of the LAW that Ernest Hemingway mounted the platform at Carnegie Hall on a warm June day in 1937. "Fascism is a lie," he cried, "told by bullets. A writer who will not lie cannot live nor work under fascism." Because fascism is a lie, said the writer who incorporated vivid antifascist themes into his most compelling novels, "it is condemned to literary sterility."[84]

Besides aiding writers exiled from Europe as the pestilence of fascism spread, the "700 members" of the LAW made "contributions of four ambulances to Spain" and published numerous pamphlets chastising the ultraright. In one stirring publication, the LAW gathered statements on anti-Semitism by fifty-four leading writers, statesmen, educators, clergymen, and trade unionists and donated the "proceeds from the sale of this pamphlet" to "exiled anti-fascist writers." Lawson, who had a hand in this project, proclaimed, "As a Jew, I am proud of the historic role of the Jewish people."[85] This antifascist crusade took some courage in light of the effort by Senator Gerald Nye and others to investigate Hollywood for its supposed anti-Nazi bias and its concomitant scrutiny of those with "non-Nordic names."[86]

Yet the experience with the LAW showed that there were ominous storm signals that Lawson could ignore only at his peril. The inability of Communists and liberals to unite—even in the face of a monstrous fascist threat—did not bode well, least of all for a Communist screenwriter with an elevated profile.

For amid the interminable meetings and debates about foreign policy and passionate protests about anti-Semitism, Lawson was managing to find the time to write a number of screenplays. Lawson, it was said, "never managed to make himself into a Communist screenwriter; he was, and remained, the screenwriter *and* the Communist *par excellence,*" as "his gifts as radical activist far outshone his modest endowment as a creative writer."[87] Yes, Lawson was an outstanding radical activist, towering above his counterparts. Yet even a cursory glance at some of his more neglected screenplays bespeaks a talent that is more than "modest" and is certainly fertile in its diverse themes. Moreover, one strains in vain to locate the subversion that he was accused of—unless simple and decent human values were thought to be antithetical to the dominant culture.

Party Wire again represents class conflict in the guise of a romance, with the added bonus of providing one of cinema's more adroit analyses of the phenomenon of gossip. *They Shall Have Music,* featuring the extraordinary violinist Jascha Heifetz in one of his few starring roles, presents family fare in a way that Disney could well emulate in its story about a boy running away from home and winding up at a music school for poor children. Heifetz's artistry, said the *New York Times,* "create[s] an effect of transcendent beauty which is close to unique in this medium."[88] William Wyler was certainly ecstatic about this film—as were the critics.[89] It was an "exciting, impressive picture," said *Variety.*[90]

Then there are the "curiously spiritual *Earthbound*" and Lawson's *Four Sons,* a "remake of a 1928 silent film (now anti-Nazi rather than antiwar) has a Czech family divided over the German takeover. Son Don Ameche and his mother finally resolve to save Jews—and save themselves as moral beings—by resisting the supposedly friendly invaders."[91] *Earthbound* was "excellent," gushed the *Hollywood Reporter.*[92] *Four Sons* was "the most powerful picture yet introduced concerning events in Middle Europe," said the *Los Angles Times*.[93] It was "deeply moving," enthused the *Los Angeles Examiner*.[94] Strikingly, the sharpest dissent to this enthusiasm was registered by the *Moscow News*,[95] yet soon it became conventional wisdom that Lawson and his comrades were little more than the tool of Moscow, a view that elided a more complex reality.

9   Writing—and Fighting

The African soldier chased the escaping German prisoner across the hot sands of the fictional North African desert. He caught him, and a fierce struggle ensued. The African pummeled the German vigorously, then began to strangle him. Finally he choked the last breath out of the man's body, just as white supremacy itself was being suffocated as a by-product of the antifascist war that had led to this startling cinematic chase scene. Such was the celluloid progressivism crafted by John Howard Lawson in his wartime epic *Sahara*. Helen Slote Levitt, one of Hollywood's leading women writers,[1] and Julian Mayfield, a leading black writer, were among the legions inspired by this still-stirring movie.[2]

· · ·

World War II and the resultant alliance between Moscow and Washington eroded the difficulties brought to Lawson and his Party by the 1939 nonaggression pact between Germany and the Soviet Union. Simultaneously, anticommunism itself was placed on the defensive, which allowed Lawson to flourish in Hollywood in a way that was unlikely before this war—and virtually impossible afterward.

It was his wartime movies, as well, that burnished Lawson's reputation as a filmmaker—particularly *Sahara*. Made with the cooperation of the U.S. Army, it portrays an intensely homosocial environment, with men making constant references to "dames" and at times treating their valuable tanks like lovers. Humphrey Bogart stars in this tale of Allied soldiers battling their German counterparts in the desert. There are references to the Spanish civil war and other progressive touches, such as when the German prisoner does not want to be searched—for "racial" reasons—by an African

149

FIGURE 6. Lawson's *Sahara* was hailed as an antiracist and antifascist classic. It also brought him into closer contact with Humphrey Bogart. (Courtesy of the Academy of Motion Picture Arts and Sciences)

soldier; Bogart threatens to punch the prisoner after he utters a racial epithet. The Negro soldier is portrayed heroically; it is he who finds the life-saving well in the desert. There is bonhomie shown between the African and a "white" Texan; they share cigarettes, and the former, a Muslim, tells the Texan, "We both have much to learn from each other." A good deal of this film concerns the necessity of those from different backgrounds getting along—not a minor lesson to be imparted by a nation with an official policy of bigotry, then struggling to conduct a war against a foe that had proclaimed "race war."[3] On the other hand, there were no negative comments made about a white South African, and the insulting term "Jap" was used frequently. The penultimate scene—and a still reigning classic of cinema—occurs when the German prisoner seeks to escape and is chased down by the African. The African then is shot down by the enemy, but he gives a thumbs-up before collapsing.

Lawson acknowledged that this movie was "patterned on a similar situation in *The Thirteen*, made by Mikhail Romm," the Soviet screenwriter and director, in 1937. Modestly, he added, "the Negro soldier" was "an unusual figure in American films, . . . played with great warmth by Rex Ingram."[4] There was an enduring humanity to this film that time could not erode. A half century later the cable television service Showtime produced another version with the actor Jim Belushi in Bogart's role.[5]

As with other wartime films in particular, the script for *Sahara* was scrutinized by U.S. government authorities. "This script offers the basis for a picture which will be a real contribution to the war information program," gushed one bureaucrat in a "confidential" report. There were problems, however: "The British government might feel that not sufficient credit is given to the achievements and heroism of the British forces in this story," and "with the possibility of release of this picture in North Africa, care in the presentation of the Sudanese Negro, Tambul, a Mohammedan, is essential." Moreover, "The presentation in the script might in certain respects be resented by other Africans." The penultimate scene was questioned, since it "could possibly have an effect the opposite to that intended, and might be better omitted."[6] This scene also left Hollywood's chief censor, Joseph Breen, a bit queasy. He instructed, "Please take care to avoid undue gruesomeness in this scene where Tambul strangles the German officer."[7]

The critic James Agee was impressed by *Sahara*,[8] though he was not alone in his effusion.[9] It was "one of the best of all the desert-set war movies," proclaimed one critic.[10]

Lawson knew that "*Sahara* could not convey its message without the [Sudanese] soldier." Yet this had to be conveyed against the backdrop of the "virtual exclusion of the Negro" from Hollywood, which was "part of a code that prohibits the presentation of wide areas of American life: poverty cannot be shown, because it is 'depressing.' Workers cannot be portrayed in terms of jobs or trade union activity, because these things suggest criticism of the *status quo*. Women are derided, to prove that their place is in the kitchen, or the bedroom."[11]

Yet, with all these elisions, it was the depiction of the Negro that was the central transgression committed by Lawson. This was an era, as one popular front grouping put it, when "the only Negroes we see" in films "are the maids and butlers who represent one segment of Negro life. Similar distortions are evident in the portrayal of other minorities—for example, the stereotype of the lazy Mexican, the shuffling Chinese laundrymen or cook, the shrewd or sentimental Jew."[12]

In his other wartime epic, *Action in the North Atlantic* (1943), Lawson sought to grapple with the issue of the warped image of the working class. Lawson knew that traditionally in U.S. cinema "working life" was something to be "despised and that workers who seek to protect their class interests are stupid, malicious or even treasonable."[13] *Action in the North Atlantic,* which also starred Bogart, contravened this traditional image. Based loosely on the exploits of the Communist-led National Maritime Union (NMU), it concerned the union's heroic attempt to deliver desperately needed supplies to the Soviet ally in Murmansk. Breen objected sharply to this script, too.[14] Since the Soviets were allies to the United States, the irredeemably anticommunist Breen was not officially hostile to the idea of aid to Moscow, though he did find other problems with this script, particularly prudish concerns about Bogart's character and his relationship to a woman.[15] Stern objection was taken to the "reference to Hitler as a 'louse' by the young sailor," since "this word is on the list of banned expressions of the Association."[16]

A more important critic, the FBI, was not antagonistic. Contrary to Red Scare critics of the future, this eagle-eyed analyst found "no Communist ideology expressed openly or directly," though Lawson "took advantage of the opportunity to glorify" the NMU, this after he "spent much time in [its] headquarters at San Pedro," California.[17]

The FBI critic must have been reading the *Daily Worker,* which reported enthusiastically that Lawson "spent many hours at the [NMU] hall in San Pedro" and "made friends with the seamen, listened to their tales of the fighting fronts, made sure of every detail on board ship and in the union." The "result," enthused this Communist paper, "is a powerful movie and one of [the] finest screenplays of the war."[18]

Still, while making this highly praised work, Lawson was becoming increasingly exasperated with the obstacles strewn in his path. "Even the wearing of union buttons," he groaned, "was a matter of concern and some soul-searching by studio officials, who finally agreed that the buttons must be visible." Moreover, the "story could not be built around the lives and feelings of the [ordinary] seamen, because it was necessary to give major attention to the parts played by the two leading actors: Raymond Massey [and] Humphrey Bogart."[19]

As often happened with Lawson's ambitious screenplays,[20] this one was whittled down by studio executives, film censors, and the presumed dictates of the box office. Thus, the production values were so chintzy as to undermine the film's authenticity. "The fleet of ships that made up the convoy," as Lawson noted, "consisted of miniature vessels manipulated on a small bay at Santa Barbara."[21]

As in all his films, Lawson did not have carte blanche regarding its content. The Office of War Information had "considerable input," and the "Bu-

FIGURE 7. Lawson's World War II epic *Action in the North Atlantic* also happened to provide a heroic portrait of sailors. (Courtesy of the Academy of Motion Picture Arts and Sciences)

reau of Motion Pictures objected to several things" in Lawson's "first script, including a black pantry man who asks why he should fight." Lawson's "symbolic solution was to have a white sailor save the mess steward's life but that didn't solve the BMP's problem with the character. He was still unequal." The studio "satisfied the Bureau by writing the characters out, leaving one less role for black actors"—and one less victory for Lawson. Retained were the "combat scenes," which remain "gripping" and help to explain why this movie "was successful at the box office" and almost broke "'Yankee Doodle Dandy's' opening day record in New York."[22] Exposing the frailties of film criticism, one writer—though giving the film a "21 gun salute"—chided it and added, "Next time, by the way, let's see a couple of Negro seamen in the crew."[23] Other reviews were less equivocal. For "forthright thrills," said *Variety*, "the film stands in the annals of adventure picture-making."[24]

What remained after moguls and censors had gnawed on Lawson's script was still a keen example of popular front filmmaking, from the voice-over by Roosevelt to such lines translated from Russian as "that means 'comrade,' that's good." There are scenes of wild joy as Soviet planes greet U.S. ships as they approach Murmansk and similar expressions of elation by Soviet citizens greeting U.S. sailors. There are references to "Jesus Christ" and a character who expresses faith in "God, President Roosevelt and the Brooklyn Dodgers." Gender attitudes, sadly, are unenlightened by contemporary standards. Still, the director "followed Lawson's suggestions" concerning "Soviet-style montage, with a virtual absence of mise-en-scene" accompanied by a "narrow-focused cutting and tonal montage, light and shadow, for its effects," creating—according to one analysis—a feast for the eyes.[25]

Not only the studio executives were peering nervously over the right shoulder of Communist screenwriters. Washington's "Co-ordinator of Government Films" wanted writers to "become sensitized and very aware" of the nation's problems—there was little room for anything beyond that when the nation was in the vise of a life-and-death struggle. The movies, he thought, were essential to "the ideology of the war, the intangibles," and "our ideal medium of explaining . . . these intangibles [is] the basis of the war effort. If they are not adequately explained, then this war doesn't make sense." Meeting with writers, he "dwelt at some length with the 'danger signals' in popular opinion today," such as "suspicions that Britain and Russia are fighting solely in self-defense." Echoing Lawson's approach to film, he stressed, "We cannot win this war without the Negroes, not only the Negro in this country, it is a matter of the colored peoples of the world."[26]

Why would the Bank of America, not to mention a film studio, turn over its precious investment to a Communist screenwriter or insufficiently monitor the scripts it commissioned? Why would a wartime government ignore the powerful medium that was film? "There was little danger of Communist ideas being slipped into wartime movies undetected," concluded one accurate analysis.[27] As Gerda Lerner, who was in Hollywood at the time, put it, "To anyone knowing how the industry operated and how little control the individual screenwriter had over his or her product, the question is ludicrous."[28]

When the budding Red writer Alvah Bessie arrived in Hollywood in 1943, he discovered that "Jack's attitude" was "optimism personified. . . . he told me at lunch that first week that I would have an opportunity to do my best work and that, despite the monopolistic character of 'The Industry' and the total control that the producers exercised over the content of film, any decent writer could develop honest characters and situations in the work he had to do and could contribute to the stature of a medium whose potential could be seen by anyone who looked at the screen."[29]

The Communist screenwriter Michael Wilson, who wrote *Planet of the Apes, Lawrence of Arabia,* and *Friendly Persuasion,* among other award-winning scripts, was of a similar opinion about Lawson. "I was impressed from the start with John Howard Lawson, who was the leading Marxist scholar," he said. "It was Lawson, I suppose, who was mainly instrumental in altering some of my views about film as an art form at that time. Because he spoke often of the struggle for content in motion pictures, by which he meant that although it was extremely difficult to do a truly progressive and honest film in Hollywood, we, as radicals and Marxists, had an obligation to try our damndest to do so; and that one could accomplish certain things, even in the pictures which thematically seemed silly or vapid."[30]

When the young Red Helen Slote Levitt came to Hollywood to be a "reader" of materials for studios, determining what might be transformed into scripts, by her own admission, she was a "theater snob in the worst sense of New York theater snobbery." Like many on the left, she "looked down my nose at motion pictures." But one thing she has "never forgotten . . . about Jack [Lawson]" was "that he was open-minded, that he would listen to me from my really very junior position and be convinced." She knew that "that's not people's impression of Jack." In those rarefied circles, "Stanislavsky was the party line!"—"not because he was Russian but because the Group Theatre felt that that was the way." In other words, Lawson was not the locus—as she saw it—of a theoretical rigidity and ossification that existed in Red Hollywood.[31]

Nonetheless, the FBI—one of the more important film critics—thought it had reason to believe that Reds were manipulating scripts for devious ideological purposes, whatever the opinions of Red L.A. "It has not been a function of this Bureau," it was said too modestly, "to review motion picture productions for political content for it was not believed that the Bureau's representatives are experts in this field nor was it believed that censorship of motion pictures was within the purview of the activities of the Bureau." Yet Communists were taking advantage of their lassitude, it was thought. They "are now content to insert a line, a sentence or a situation carrying the Communist Party line into an otherwise non-political picture," and this was "not restricted to war-type pictures or serious drama." No, this was even done in "the so-called 'musicals.'" The Reds "also prevent all material that the Party might consider objectionable" and "actually prevented the making of certain pictures. Among the pictures of this type [was] 'Uncle Tom's Cabin'. . . . production of this picture was particularly attacked by elements of the Communist Party due to the fact it was felt that the picture did not reflect a proper attitude on the part of the Negroes. As a result of this pressure, this picture was withdrawn."[32]

Who was spearheading this conniving scheme? Lawson was targeted.[33] It was as if the FBI—and its version of Lawson—seemed to think that actors and writers could operate autonomously and that directors were ciphers who hardly paid attention to an actor's rendition of a role. Of course, in this scenario, producers did not exist. If the FBI had simply perused the files of other government agencies[34]—agencies that were aggressive in shaping film content—it might have been disabused of these ideas.[35]

Still, this misleading idea of Communist subversion of movies dogged Red Hollywood—where writers were central—after 1947. An amnesiac seizure had overtaken the wartime reality of Washington routinely submitting scripts to the Soviet embassy for its imprimatur;[36] substituted was the notion that Lawson and Red Hollywood submitted these screenplays. In this topsy-turvy wartime environment, movies hailing Great Britain were subjected to searching scrutiny,[37] films that were contrary to Lawson's pro-Negro depictions were scorned,[38] and Lawson's view of the Spanish civil war was vindicated.[39] In short, the U.S. authorities monitored Hollywood assiduously, and given such strict filters, it would be virtually impossible for images and ideas to emerge that they found repellent.[40] Of course, careful inspection of scripts and the movies by the powerful was not just a wartime phenomenon;[41] indeed, it would be astonishing malfeasance on the part of any ruling elite to be indifferent to the production of such potentially powerful propaganda tools.

Yet Lawson knew intuitively what an authoritative study showed subsequently: yes, his films often echoed a "Party line," but they also reflected a "point of view expressed . . . by large and identifiable non-Communist groups in the United States." In his films, said the Fund for the Republic, which was tasked by major foundations to examine this critical question, there was nothing "even remotely suggestive of the *positive* impact of Communist propaganda of that day," for example, "the demand for revolution, for violent overthrow of existing agencies of government," or "for support of defense of the Union of Socialist Soviet Republics." The "most controversial of all films credited to the Hollywood Ten during the Popular Front period," it was said, were *Blockade* and *Four Sons,* and these "warranted especially careful study." The first draft of *Four Sons* was written before the nonaggression treaty of 1939 between Germany and the Soviet Union and was released afterward, so the Fund for the Republic was keen to ascertain if this intervening event caused a change in Lawson's formulations.

Hence, "The film was screened twice and all story materials from the original script . . . to the treatment . . . and the final script . . . were studied and compared [and] noted in great detail, and in turn compared to the cutting continuity of the film." It was true that this movie provided a "cold and grim picture of aims, ideology and tactics of Nazi Germany, at that time an ally of the Soviet Union"; it was "definitely an anti-Nazi film. Indeed, when viewed today in retrospect," said the Fund for the Republic's 1956 analysis, "the portrayal given to the Nazis in 'Four Sons' rings more true and is far more believable than [do] many Nazi screen portrayals of that day." Thus, "The anti-Nazism implicit in this film obviously was not . . . in keeping with the party line of the Pact Period." Changes in the script were prompted by Daryl Zanuck, "who produced this picture" and "wanted to play up the personal story, rather than the political aspects of the picture." Even *Block-ade*, it was said, "cannot legitimately be labeled 'leftist propaganda,'" though it was true "the picture was utilized as the focal point for a campaign of 'leftist propaganda' once it was released." On the other hand, this was not unique, since it was "well-known that *Ninotchka* (at the behest of the United States State Department) was credited with helping to swing an election in Italy after the war when the Communists were in danger of seizing control."[42] None of Lawson's cinematic creations had such compelling impact.

But if the idea of Red subversion of scripts was ludicrous, then what was at issue?[43] The primary issue was the strength of writers in Red Hollywood, where radicals were deeply embedded. Lawson and his comrades had built the Screen Writers Guild, which inspired actors, and had built the League of American Writers, which sought audaciously to influence, if not organize, writers across the board. Then they had intervened in statewide politics in 1938, helping to elect Governor Olson—a staggering blow to the GOP—"thus ending approximately [44] years of reactionary Republican administration in California."[44] Out of this fierce struggle grew the Hollywood Democratic Committee (HDC), perhaps the most influential popular front entity of all, and again Lawson and Red Hollywood were at the center of this effort.

The problem for Lawson was that in 1947 his antagonists were after larger game than a mere affluent screenwriter—ultimately they were after the organized left, notably the Communist Party, and its alternative view of how society should be administered. This was why even when the Soviet Union was being viewed through rose-tinted glasses in Washington, Lawson and his Party continued to receive searching inspection. Given all this, how could Lawson do anything but conclude that his 1947 interrogation was a blatant ruse, designed to oust him from the industry under the guise of rooting out Red subversion? If so, then why not challenge the committee frontally and angrily?

Above all, the authorities were concerned with the relationship between the Party and Hollywood unions—such as the SWG—perceived to be within its ambit, which were the locomotive for the HDC and the popular front in the West. "Almost half of the unions," said one FBI report in 1943, "appear to be controlled by the Communists or follow the Communist Party line for business reasons." It was hard to trace these serpentine connections, however, since "prominent actors, actresses, writers, directors and executives" shrouded their membership; "directives were issued that all party membership books were to be destroyed and all documentary evidence of every kind was also to be destroyed," and "all units to which personages were made 'closed units.' A 'closed unit' is one which retains the same membership continuously, taking in no new members thus preventing a leak. Members of these units, when paying their dues to the party, merely bought the required dues stamp and then destroyed them." Lawson, it was reported, was the "dominant Communist in [the] Los Angeles area," while "the Communist domination of the Screen Writers Guild has been so continuously obvious that in 1936 a small group of writers revolted against this domination and attempted to oust the Communists from control." Their slogan was "'Writers of Hollywood unite! You have nothing to lose but your brains!'"[45]

Lawson's League of American Writers was deemed "one of the most influential and far-reaching Communist front organizations ever sent up in this country"; it was essential to the "Hollywood 'cultural' division and the feeder for all Communist activities in the top structure of the motion picture industry." The "Hollywood chapter" was "particularly of extreme importance because, operating through its members who are firmly entrenched in the motion picture industry, it can and does exercise a most insidious influence over the type of picture produced." This was alarming, since the "motion picture is now considered necessary to national defense." It was curious, it was thought, that "in almost every case where a picture is being made dealing with the war situation as it affects the [Soviet Union] the writer or writers, and in many cases directors, are persons who have been identified as members of [LAW]." This had given the Party an enormous boost, since "attracted by the huge salaries paid by the motion picture industry and the glamour attached, many persons will adopt any means to gain access to that favored institution." The LAW's Hollywood School for Writers, in which Lawson played the preeminent role, was little more than a "transmission belt" moving naive recruits smoothly into the Party. Viewed with suspicion was this school's slogan, "'Words are your weapon—you must learn to use them.'"[46]

Collaboration between the LAW and the Party, thought the authorities, "has resulted in the building up in the Hollywood motion picture industry of a machine which is well-nigh impregnable under present war conditions."[47] Though Red L.A. was "weak in steel and maritime" and "strong in longshoremen and electrical workers," it was most formidable in Hollywood, notably among writers—and no small reason was the personal and political role of Lawson.[48] Inevitably this influence among writers—the fulcrum upon which the entire industry rested—sent ripples coursing through Hollywood; actors, for example, who desired certain roles often found themselves catering to the whims of Red writers, as did directors lusting after important assignments. The entire "entertainment world" was "linked to Communism," concluded one official government report in the spring of 1944. "At the current [Party] convention there were over 70 invited guests who in some manner belonged" to Red Hollywood. "Hollywood is full of Reds up to its eyebrows, and this is no joke," it was warned gravely.[49]

What was striking was the intense focus on actors who had performed in Lawson's movies, including Humphrey Bogart, who was "well-liked in Communist circles."[50] Rex Ingram, who starred in *Sahara*, was—according to an official report—"reportedly recruited into the Los Angeles County Communist Party in March 1944, was issued 1944 Communist Party Membership Book No. 84702. . . . subject's Communist activities began about 1938 in which year he was active in the Hollywood Committee for Federal Theatres."[51] Then there was Jack Moscowitz, "alias: Moss, Jack," an "independent movie producer" who was "stated to [be] a close friend" of Lawson's and "has attended Communist meetings at Lawson's home." The portly entrepreneur had blue eyes, brown hair, and Red affiliations—or so it was thought. Moscowitz—or Moss—was "employed from 1932 to 1938 as manager for Gary Cooper" and was "producer and director for Paramount Studios, Orson Welles' Mercury Theater and Columbia Studios."[52]

But the problem always came back to writers.[53]

Though the Party was painted as shrouded in deviousness and mystique, the liberal writer and lawyer Carey McWilliams disagreed. It was "one of the least conspiratorial organizations that I ever observed," he said. "It had an obsession for mimeograph machines! They had publications at every level: propaganda, organizational, ideological, theoretical, and they would spell the whole thing out week after week, month after month, year after year. Anyone that could read could see what the line was and what was going on. It was far less conspiratorial, for example, than the kind of meetings in both major parties that go on in smoke-filled rooms. And that it was ever a menace I could never for a second believe!"[54]

The FBI vehemently disagreed. Yet if the FBI had been able to read the reports of its sister agency, the Office of War Information, with its passing on scripts to the Soviet Embassy for approval, it might have placed their officials under arrest—or at least accorded them the same level of surveillance accorded the Party. The point was that the FBI—and those who backed it—had an unremitting right-wing agenda that would not be detained simply because Communists and the United States were on the same antifascist side.

Lawson's Communist comrade V. J. Jerome was given credit for the Party's revival—it was he who "reorganized the Hollywood branch of the Communist Party separating top ranking stars and big name personalities"—though Lawson's role was crucial, since following his "arrival in Hollywood almost any Communist who could write would be sent by the National Office to be put under Lawson's wing." Among these were "Albert Maltz, Alvah Bessie, Dalton Trumbo, Michael Blankfort and others."[55]

The bureau had a hard time discerning who was more disreputable—Lawson or Jerome. The latter was a "highly secretive man"; thus, "when he made calls to the members he always did it from telephone booths. He arranged to meet a member on street corners . . . being about as conspiratorial in his movements as Molotov's bodyguards." In fact, he was "so overly secret that he ran the risk of drawing attention to himself." He helped to bring into being a system whereby Communist writers—Lawson, Jarrico, Lester Cole, Richard Collins, and others—"each . . . would bring along to the meeting the particular movie script he was working on at that time." The "purpose of such discussions was not necessarily to put in Communist propaganda"—contrary to what was thought at the highest levels of the bureau—"but rather to try sincerely to make the scripts better." Thus, Lawson brought his script for *Action in the North Atlantic* to one of these gatherings. Lawson was depicted as some sort of superman, "who would put in as much as eighteen hours a day for the Communist Party when necessary" and who intimidated almost all his comrades into toeing the line, except Abraham Polonsky, "probably the only man who ever chose to challenge the position of [Lawson] on any particular issue."[56]

It was almost as if the FBI considered Lawson sufficiently powerful that he could not only mandate the content of the movies but also order cowering moguls to hire his cronies and comrades. John Charles Moffitt, the screenplay writer responsible for *The House on 92nd Street*, helped to confirm the bureau's darkest suspicions. Lawson was reputed to have said, "If you can make the message come from the mouth of Gary Cooper or some other important star who is unaware of what he is saying, by the time it is discovered he is in New York and a great deal of expense will be involved to bring him back and reshoot the scene." Lawson's sheer lack of scruple, it was said, knew no bounds.[57]

Ultimately, Lawson's prodigious organizing attracted the attention of the California legislature. On a bright fall day in October 1944, he was invited by the state's Committee on Un-American Activities to be interrogated, arriving in grimy downtown L.A. from his comfortable abode in Coldwater Canyon. Preceding him to the witness chair was the state's Party leader, William Schneiderman—whose birth in Russia in 1905 caught the eye of his interlocutors—who revealed that his organization had "probably between five and six thousand" members statewide. Pettis Perry, a Negro from the rural South, was titular leader of the Party in L.A., earning the princely sum of twenty-five dollars weekly.[58]

The presiding legislator, state senator Jack Tenney, claimed to have met Lawson when he was a leader of the musicians' union. Tenney, who "recognized him at once as he approached the witness stand," immediately pounced and asked him about his surname. "There was a moment's pause not indicated in the record," said Tenney. "He looked sharply at me, a glow of momentary hatred flashing in his eyes, and snarled 'anti-Semitic, eh!' Although a court reporter evidently did not hear it," it was "clearly audible," as "obvious" as "Lawson's anger."[59]

After an exchange of innocuous pleasantries—his interrogator termed *Action in the North Atlantic* a "good picture"—Lawson was asked gruffly, "Isn't it a fact that you drove" your "blue Buick" to "Wilshire and La Brea" in L.A. "and went to lunch at Melody Lane Café there" on 7 February 1943? Blandly, the rumpled Lawson replied, "I have had lunch with Mr. Maltz a hundred times . . . there and other places." Yes, he had known Red leader Carl Winter, "slightly, yes" for at least a "year or two." What about the advice he had given on "The Sun Rises in the West"? "I have advised people on many, many plays and productions," Lawson replied accurately.

All right, said his interrogator, switching gears, did you know John Steinbeck? Lawson confided that he had not had the pleasure and had never read *The Grapes of Wrath*. Well, what about V. J. Jerome—surely, he must have known this Communist eminence grise? Vaguely, Lawson responded, "Several years ago. . . . I think I met him somewhere at a party in New York when I was there, probably four years ago but I couldn't recall." So, "Did you ever see him in Hollywood?" "No," responded Lawson flatly—

no doubt relying on the reality that technically Hollywood was simply another L.A. neighborhood and had not been an actual center of movie production for years.

Then what about the Hollywood Writers Mobilization? Certainly he must know something about a grouping he helped to bring into being. Again, Lawson was direct though evasive. But all this was just a prelude to the broaching of the central question: "Mr. Lawson," said his interrogator, "have you ever affiliated with the Communist Party of the United States in any way?" Now no matter how one parses the verb in that sentence, it was hard to see how Lawson could avoid answering affirmatively. But he did not. "No," he replied. "Never have," was the response. "No," he said, even more firmly. Then "did you ever hear of Group 3, Branch 'A' of the Northwestern Section of the Communist Political Association?" Lawson: "I never did, no."

Why avoid answering truthfully, particularly since Communists were now presumably no longer in bad odor in light of the antifascist war? Even then, Lawson had reason to believe that this question was a prelude to demands that he also name the names of others who were in the Party, who might be compromised as a result—in other words, Lawson thought his questioners were not operating in good faith.

However, Lawson did not hesitate to answer forthrightly another controversial question. "Do you subscribe in theory or support their activities," referring to the Reds, "in their endeavor to bring about social functions, mingling of black and white together, such as dances of both sexes?" he was asked with a whiff of salaciousness. "I can tell you unhesitatingly," he replied, "I support the complete equality of the Negro people of this country and I feel passionately about it. I think the safety of the whole country depends upon the equal rights of the minorities." That is why he was arrested in Birmingham. "I was profoundly aroused," he said, "as I am always, about civil rights." Thus, Lawson did not hesitate to associate himself with ideas traditionally linked with the organized left as he disdained professing his formal membership in their ranks.

Then Senator Tenney, who claimed to have met Lawson in his capacity as a leader of Red Hollywood, probed what he thought was a vulnerable point—"intermarriage of Negroes and whites." Again, Lawson did not flinch. "It is a question of absolute individual preference, and it is one of those things that is completely misleading in relation to this investigation. It is your business, not mine," he said becoming more irritated. Sensing the undertone of his questioner's tone, he turned in a parallel direction. "I am advocating the complete political, economic social equality of the Negro and white, and also the Jewish people. I am of Jewish ancestry, and I am very happy to make this comment. I believe in full equality of all races, creeds and colors."

Tenney would not back down. "You are aware," he said, "of what your statement would include, I take it, the repeal of our miscegenation laws in this State?" Did Lawson not know that this "law prohibits the intermarriage of whites and Negroes and other races?" Lawson, who would not publicly claim a still unpopular Party membership, did publicly claim a then unpopular viewpoint: "My opinion would be, it is a bad law; but I wish to qualify that formally: it is improper procedure to ask a citizen regarding a law he hasn't read or studied. I know nothing about the law beyond what you tell me." At that juncture, Tenney shifted to the underlying gravamen of the interrogation: "Mr. Lawson," he intoned, "I want to ask you if your family had been O'Brien, would you have had the same feeling about the minority Irish you apparently have toward the Jewish group?" Lawson, a bit stunned by the blunt intemperance of the inquiry, responded, "I should say I would." He then added heatedly, "My whole opinion of your procedure is that it is grossly improper."[60]

One of Lawson's comrades, the Communist screenwriter Albert Maltz, author of *The Naked City*, echoed this opinion, though the committee was more interested in his opinion of Red Hollywood. But he, too, denied Party membership and pooh-poohed the effectiveness of the LAW. What about his subscription to the Communist Party newspaper? he was asked suspiciously. "I like to read one paper," replied Maltz, "which regularly supports the war and the Commander-in-Chief without nagging him, and there aren't many in this country." Of course, this did not mean at all that he was a Communist—no, no, he suggested.

The Communist screenwriter Waldo Salt, author of *Midnight Cowboy* and *Coming Home*, was not as congenial as Maltz but bristled at the questions to which he was subjected. This mauling, he said, had everything to do with Senator Tenney's "recent switch-over as a Republican" and the resultant newly discovered passion of a true believer. He, too, denied his Party membership and was reluctant to acknowledge his membership in the Hollywood Democratic Committee, responding, when asked, that he did not find the question "pertinent," adding that "it may be prompted by the fact that we are in an election year with three weeks to go."

Like Maltz, he also was queried closely about his relationship with Lawson, perceived as the "key man" in Hollywood. Sure, Lawson "has a swimming pool I like to use," but otherwise Salt disclaimed any particular intimacy.[61]

These L.A. hearings were a rehearsal for their Washington counterpart of 1947. Tenney was physically similar to Senator Joseph McCarthy, beefy though not terribly obese. As in Washington, there was an "'undertone of anti-Semitism,'" as when Lawson was asked about his father changing his name. As in Washington, here too writers flatly denied Party membership whereas a few years later they sought to avoid answering. In both cases they felt they were up against a suspect fishing expedition that meant them ill, with cooperation viewed as collaboration in executing their own demise. Though the Communist Party was the ostensible target, it was not lost on some legislators that "for several years" Lawson "had written parts of the Democratic [Party] platform . . . approved by the state Democratic Central Committee."[62] This had happened "for several years," according to former leading Democrat Robert Kenny.[63]

The prominent L.A.-based African American publisher Charlotta Bass was not seduced by these hearings. "Every now and then," she commented, "a gust from one of the Sacramento investigating gentry would lift the Tenney Committee's skirts and reveal the dainty Fascist pantaloons underneath." It appeared, she argued passionately, "that the Committee was in search of people who fought discrimination and segregation. . . . and that was about all the Committee accomplished—the persecution of those who believed that all men were created equal."[64]

For Lawson this was a notably painful dilemma. His son Jeffrey—no huge fan—still termed him "probably the single most law-abiding human being I ever saw"; "During the second World War," he said, "all the good patriotic types here on the home front bought black market gas ration stamps. Everyone did it. I did it." But not John Howard Lawson. He "turned down a job as a producer because he was afraid it would [lead] to his having to compromise himself politically, ethically."[65] The war allowed Lawson's rectitude to merge seamlessly with his political outlook and ignite a kind of patriotism, which as a Communist he welcomed as a refuge from his normalized marginal status. Of course, it was dangerous for a radical to be in bed with economic royalists whom he normally opposed—even if it was for the good cause of antifascism.

Such tensions were to erupt within the Party shortly after the war concluded, as Lawson was charged with being a lamb much too anxious to recline beside lions. For during the war the affluent Lawson backed his government with a full-throated fervor. "I keep giving out so much," he said at that time, "to the Democratic campaign, to War Chest, bonds and charities," to the point where he could not "seem to get much ahead." He was "spending most" of his "time on the political campaign" and had come to "shudder to think what would happen to the country—and war—if Dewey should win."[66]

He was not alone. Richard Collins, the prolific screenwriter, recalled that during this era he "attended, speaking of all meetings, not only meetings of the party, which were maybe once or twice a week, but meetings of whatever organizations I believe to—I attended 4 or 5 a weeks for 3 years, then about 3 a week. I figure it comes close to 5000 hours." That, he concluded, was "enough for a lifetime." The Hollywood Party "met every 2 weeks and [I] think during the war once every 2 weeks."[67] Screenwriter Albert Maltz could "remember periods at certain times in the thirties when I might have only fifteen hours a week for writing; the rest of the time was doing other things," for example, politicking: "I regret it," he moaned, speaking of the time expended, if not the "4 percent of the $300 a week salary he made."[68] But Lawson, as the leader, was exceeding them all.

Lawson would have to pay a heavy price, heavier than most, as a result. Actually, the obdurate right wing which the FBI represented had reason to believe that the growth of Red Hollywood would reduce the bureau's own oxygen supply—and responded accordingly.[69]

10 Red Scare Rising

The camera zoomed in lovingly on tall glasses of alcohol, as Susan Hayward, the beauty with flaming auburn hair, prepared to appear before a crowd of celebrants at a smoky nightclub. Wearing a dress that clung to her every curve, she rapidly downed one of these beverages, then ambled to the microphone, confidence bolstered, and belted out a popular tune.

So began Lawson's "premature pro-feminist" film, *Smash-Up, the Story of a Woman,* one of the last films he was able to write under his own name before the clampdown of the "blacklist." It is a remarkable story that focuses on a subject Lawson knew well—the intersection of substance abuse and show business—which was a recurrent real-life theme of Red Hollywood. It explores romance and class conflict once more, his "root idea," his mannequin on which he draped an extensive wardrobe of themes. The film is a psychological exploration that suggests that pervasive feelings of insecurity and inadequacy lead to this kind of abuse. It also is a critique of capitalism, suggesting that this system brings an emptiness, a void, even to those who reside in comfortable surroundings, encircled by a panoply of servants. "I've lost my self-respect," cries the Hayward character at one point—reentering the labor force is the remedy, suggests Lawson. In this Lawson anticipates the plaint and plight of the middle-class woman to be sketched by Betty Friedan years later.[1]

Hayward's costar Marsha Hunt did not think much of the movie. As she later commented, "It's the story of a weak, self-pitying woman who acquires a serious drinking problem because her husband isn't paying attention to her. . . . I don't understand why it is so popular"—but her opinion was not widely shared.[2]

Though Lawson's women characters, for example, in *Action in the North Atlantic* or *Blockade,* are hardly memorable, the Hollywood writer

FIGURE 8. In one of his last screenplays—the feminist classic *Smash-Up*—Lawson created a memorable role for Susan Hayward. (Courtesy of the Academy of Motion Picture Arts and Sciences)

Norma Barzman was "surprised" when visiting Vienna years after *Smash-Up*'s release, to see a film of the 1940s written by the "rigid" Lawson. Referring to Hayward's breakthrough performance and her depiction of a woman on the edge, Barzman exulted, "I felt it could have been written by a young feminist woman writer today!"[3]

Like many Lawson projects, a convoluted road led to this production. The raconteur Dorothy Parker had developed this project—then termed *Angelica*—and by August 1945 was at work;[4] but by January 1946 she was "off" the script, her "employment" was "terminated,"[5] and Lawson was hired in her stead.

This film, according to Hayward's biographers, at last catapulted her "to the brink of stardom." Her acting was one reason, for "during dramatic moments" in the film she "imitated what could only be described as 'a . . . girl having an orgasm.' She takes a deep breath, heaves her bosom, crosses her arms and pulls away from something which is causing her both pain and ecstasy in the central part of her body. Female flamenco dancers perform the same gestures all the time [*sic*]. Clearly symbolic of the female orgasm, they produced for Susan some fairly amazing results."[6] Indeed. "Full-fledged stardom eluded her until her appearance" in this "bleak pre-feminist cry for freedom." Strikingly, male costar Lee Bowman "would go on to become a TV adviser to Republican politicians."[7]

Per usual, the industry censor, Joseph Breen, monitored this screenplay like an intelligence agent—an irony considering that shortly after its release, Lawson would be hauled before a congressional committee and face accusations that somehow he had bamboozled moguls, Breen and all the rest, in sneaking subversion onto the screen.[8] Lawson's revisions left the demanding Breen dissatisfied. "Please omit all prolonged, lustful or open-mouthed kissing," and definitely delete that "affectionate pinch," which "should not be on the posterior." And the "kiss [with] the couple on the bed" and "any sex suggestive inference" in the bedroom? Forget about it. And that "man in scene 22," he "should not be naked to the waist but should be wearing an undershirt."[9] And "Scene 140C"? It "should not be played with the couple in bed."[10]

It was not only producers and censors who had to be placated; other lobbyists and special interests had to be handled gingerly, particularly when the topic at hand was something as sensitive as alcoholism. When temperance advocates got hold of the script, they suggested alterations; the alterations were accepted, which the advocates graciously thought did "improve the picture." They wondered, would Hayward—whose frequent portrayals of temperamental women were deemed to be not just acting—consent to do a tour for the Women's Christian Temperance Union?[11]

Academics were not disinterested either. Dr. E. M. Jellinek of Yale wangled a visit to the set, "and his professional advice was solicited"; he "expressed professional enthusiasm for the treatment given alcoholism in our film. He regarded 'Smash-Up' as a positive contribution to the problem of alcoholism. . . . [He] drew several comparisons between 'Smash-Up' and 'The Lost Weekend' to the credit of our film," since the Lawson picture "makes an intelligent study of the emotional complications and frustrations that induce acute alcoholism rather than merely presenting the Fait Accompli as in 'The Lost Weekend.'"[12]

The film was far from being a runaway hit, though it received respectful consideration. The reviews were "extraordinarily good," according to Hayward's biographers,[13] a point perhaps confirmed when she received an Oscar nomination.[14] Agreeing with Dr. Jellinek, the *Los Angeles Herald-Express* hailed the film as a "feminine version of 'The Lost Weekend'" and a "powerful love story" that was a "hit besides."[15] It was "prematurely feminist," said Bernard Dick, as *Blockade* was "prematurely antifascist." It "dramatizes the effect of a husband's success on both his wife and their marriage within a show business context"; "one of Lawson's least political films, it is blatantly critical of a society that allows the affluent to pursue a life of leisure devoid of meaningful activity."[16]

In contrast, *Counter-Attack*, produced as the war was expiring, was in tune with the then prevailing ethos. It is another wartime epic—this one starring Paul Muni and Larry Parks, directed by Zoltan Korda with cinematography by James Wong Howe—detailing the military conflict between the Soviet Union and its German counterparts.[17] Again, James Agee was quite taken with this movie.[18] Audiences agreed. "The first two day gross," said the Columbia studio, "was bigger than any picture we played in theatre[,] exceeding opening days [of] 'Commandos' [and] 'Impatient Years.'"[19]

The critics agreed, too. "It simply tells a good story with dramatic clarity and suspense," said the reviewer for the *New York Times*.[20] "Thrilling melodramatic action," said the *New York Daily News*.[21] "Absorbing and notable," said *Time* magazine.[22] "Tense and gripping," said the *Hollywood Reporter*, finding it akin to Lawson's *Sahara*, which was "one of the finer war pictures to issue from Hollywood." It was "cannily constructed," with an "excellent knit screenplay."[23] "Clever writing," agreed *Variety*.[24] But as the political climate shifted, such favorable notices became meaningless; instead, the consensus became almost instantly and magically that the film was "essentially a very heavy dose of Soviet propaganda."[25]

Typically, Lawson worked "closely" with the U.S. government's Office of War Information on this production; he changed several points when the OWI feared a shift in audience sympathy if the Russians appeared to be too willing to "'sacrifice lives for objectives.'"[26]

Of course, though his banning was ostensibly the result of the celluloid subversion he supposedly crafted (allegedly subverting the very government he collaborated with closely), in truth it was his activities off screen—and how he leveraged his healthy income and celebrity to this end—that generated such a furor. For example, Lawson was the locomotive of the Hollywood Democratic Committee (HDC), which grew out of the successful campaign to elect Culbert Olson as governor in 1938.[27] He was the dynamo driving the Hollywood Writers Mobilization (HWM), which was initiated at a massive confab at UCLA during the war and attracted Wanger, Jack Warner, Zanuck, Chet Huntley, Ira Gershwin, James Wong Howe, Thomas Mann, Hanns Eisler, Walter White of the National Association for the Advancement of Colored People (NAACP), and many guilds, including the SWG.[28] The HDC and HWM were the heart of the popular front in Hollywood[29]—a development that was then congruent with White House objectives.[30] Yet a telling signal occurred when the anticommunist philosopher Sidney Hook rebuked FDR after the president had consented to become an honorary member of another constituent element of the popular front—the League of American Writers—which Hook deemed to be "one of the chief front organizations of the Communist Party." Conveniently, he fingered those within the LAW he deemed to be Reds.[31]

The HWM grew out of an important though submerged reality of the war—the proliferation of writers. In terms of the "training, educational, scientific and industrial film," there were "well over a thousand [writers]" alone.[32] Out of that "first writers congress" at UCLA "came the first collaboration between working people in the media—film, radio and later television—with academic people. I can say with pride and without any hesitation," said Lawson "that I was largely responsible for this first collaboration." He was one of the editors of the *Hollywood Quarterly,* one of the first journals devoted to the serious study of cinema, and he was "largely active in determining policy" for it—until "the day when [he] was called into the office of Clarence Dykstra," the UCLA provost, "and with great regret and with apologies he told me that he had been told that he had to either drop" the journal "to sever all relations between it and the university or else I had to resign as one of the editors."[33] This was a loss, as the actor John Houseman—who for years had been "dealing personally and collectively with members of the party" and "never felt 'manipulated'"[34]—was not alone in asserting that this journal "remains the first serious cultural publication in which members of the motion picture industry were collectively involved."[35] The journal was "denounced by Senator Tenney as a Communist project," though Houseman felt that a "glance at its contents during its brief life will show the absurdity of the charge."[36]

Tenney's viewpoint emerged triumphant, however, as his denunciation carried the day.[37] The California legislature was contemptuous of Lawson, deriding him as a class traitor "presently eking out a miserable proletarian existence as a screenwriter at a fabulous salary in Hollywood." It had protested from time to time the University of California's role in "printing of a quarterly magazine, edited, among others," by Lawson. "As far as the committee has been able to learn the University has done nothing about these protests," though the solons were convinced there needed to be "immediate steps to rid the University of its Moscow devotees and sever relations with such outstanding Communists as John Howard Lawson and his Communist front group, the Hollywood Writers' Mobilization."[38]

But it was the HDC whose impact was probably more significant. Its personnel came to include Duke Ellington, Ronald Reagan, Groucho Marx, Billy Wilder, and a bevy of the industry's brightest stars. The presence of outstanding Negro artists was no accident. At its June 1944 gathering "it was also suggested that the following prominent Negroes be invited to join the Board," including "Lena Horne, William Grant Still, Rex Ingram, and Hattie McDaniel." The HDC was not just interested in ornamentation either. The festooning of its board with Negroes was followed quickly by aggressive action against the "Hollywood Roosevelt bar" after it was "reported that Rex Ingram was refused service."[39] Augustus Hawkins, who was to become one of the most powerful African Americans in Congress, representing South Los Angeles, expressed "appreciation" for the HDC's labors.[40]

Lawson often chaired the committee's meetings, and when nominations were made to the executive board, he came in ahead of Trumbo and Wanger—and just behind James Roosevelt—in getting votes.[41] Serving with him in 1946 at the highest levels of the organization were Bogart, John Garfield, Sterling Hayden, Rex Ingram, Gene Kelly, Groucho Marx, Gregory Peck, Edward G. Robinson—and Ronald Wilson Reagan.[42]

If the organization had a leader who was a reputed Communist, didn't that mean that the HDC was little more than a "Communist front," and in the rapidly changing political environment wasn't such a characterization suicidal? When the HDC changed its name to the more awkward Hollywood Independent Citizens Council of Arts, Sciences and Professions (HICCASP), that did not fool the bloodhounds now trailing it. At one notable meeting in June 1946, Lawson sat alongside Edward G. Robinson and Ring Lardner Jr. as it was reported that "the broad coalition that elected Roosevelt no longer existed."[43] Thereafter there was "presented for open discussion the matter of allegations that HICCASP is being 'controlled by the left,' which allegations were apparently causing difference of opinion within the organization." Lawson was present at this meeting in posh Beverly Hills, alongside Linus Pauling and Artie Shaw, as these bombshells were detonated.[44]

Ronald Reagan was becoming increasingly skeptical of this group. At one meeting, as he recalled, "Jimmy Roosevelt" asked that it issue a statement that repudiated Communism. "It sounded good to me," thought the soon-to-be conservative thespian. But he was "amazed at the reaction." Linus Pauling, "the scientist, who was there, was very quiet. Dalton Trumbo, the writer, was very vociferous. Most vehement of all, however, was John Howard Lawson."[45] These clashes were "dynamite," thought Reagan; "it proved strong enough" to "blow the whole organization sky-high." Reagan was outraged by Lawson's deportment. "'The membership isn't politically sophisticated enough to make this decision,' I was blandly informed by Lawson. It was the first time I had ever heard that phrase," Reagan recalled. "It was a goodie. I still hear it used and like Pavlov's dog I react, particularly when innocents use it defending the idea of government by an intellectual elite." Reagan was disgusted, and his encounter with Lawson had helped to push him further to the right. They "didn't get to the membership—we didn't even get back to the board. It seems that HICCASP had an even more exclusive intellectual elite—an executive committee—and somehow it was decided to settle the issue in this rarified atmosphere."[46] This was a turning point in Reagan's evolution.

Soon the group was wracked with bitter "open discussions" on the "matter of allegations that HICCASP is being 'controlled by the left,' which allegations were apparently causing difference of opinion within the organization." There was "frank discussion" about this—a gross understatement.[47]

And as these liberal and left forces fragmented, perhaps unsurprisingly, the items discussed by HICCASP became more morbid. Lawson was present with producer Dore Schary, Lardner, and Trumbo as they "discussed dramatically the recent lynchings of Negroes in Georgia and other outrageous violations of civil liberties as evidence of [the] growth of Fascism." Lawson, a frequent contributor to the group's coffers, joined in when these well-heeled individuals voted "to offer [a] $1000.00 reward for capture of those responsible"; in addition, they placed "ads in trade and Negro papers announcing" their "activities" and sent urgent "wires of protest to President Truman."[48] To improve "race relations," they decided that "CBS would be contacted for the purpose of producing a show something of the same nature as was produced during the Detroit riots."[49] Before that, leading Negro actor Canada Lee joined Groucho and Harpo Marx, Edward G. Robinson, and George Burns in backing repeal of the poll tax.[50]

But there were nonmembers who hardly appreciated the efforts of this group, now increasingly viewed as a damned "Communist front." They were sent Japanese currency with a note attached, instructing them to use it "for the protection of the niggas [*sic*] for just what its worth."[51]

The center would not hold. By the summer of 1946, HICCASP was reluctantly accepting the resignations of the influential sisterly combo of Olivia de Havilland and Joan Fontaine.[52] Members were jumping ship in all directions in the run-up to the crucial November 1946 elections, in which the left suffered punishing losses, notably in California.[53]

The authorities monitored this group ceaselessly. In June 1945 an agent of the U.S. Senate was present at a mass gathering of 725 at the American Legion Club. Somehow the agent was able to ascertain that the crowd was "predominately Jewish." Lawson, "a known Red, . . . as usual dominated this meeting by his presence on the floor at various times answering questions." It was Lawson, it was said, who had recommended that the HDC change its name to the more cumbersome HICCASP; he "again took the floor as he did at least half a dozen times during the evening when the arguments got to waxing hot." The agent seemed almost disappointed that procedures were "very democratic," though subject to manipulation, it was noted with consuming and salivating interest: "All [that] was necessary to get a new ballot was to show a blue card they had sent you in the mail."[54] They also maintained a hungry interest in the role of Reds in the ranks. The U.S. Senate was told that "Communists and fellow travelers are revealed to hold seven out of twenty positions on the newly elected Executive Board of the Los Angeles chapter of the [NAACP]."[55]

The "threat" from HICCASP had become so powerful that U.S. Army intelligence, headquartered in downtown L.A., began to monitor the group's activities. The agent viewed this group with extreme skepticism, agreeing with the actor Robert Young, who had "recently berated 'black tie liberals'" who "while eating rich food, smoking big black Havanas, drinking rare beverages, and living in splendor" somehow "profess an inordinate interest in what they call the little man." Lawson became such a lightning rod for an almost free-floating hostility not only because he was a Red—or that he was Jewish—but also because he was relatively affluent and therefore seemed to be a class traitor. He was considered ungrateful, betraying a system that supposedly had served him well.[56]

Even the fabled Oscars were being affected, it was thought. Congress was informed that "the Academy Awards for 1945 were made to many persons, who, if not members of the CP, have engaged in various Communist and Communist-front activities in the past."[57] This supposed capture of the desirable Oscar was an accusation made repeatedly against members of Red Hollywood—ironic, since the Academy had been established precisely to blunt their specialty: labor organizing.

The authorities were under the delusion that the connective tissue between the Party and Hollywood consisted of Jewish Americans—like Lawson. The "motion picture industry and stage industry, which is practically controlled by the Jewish race," was reputedly "one of the finest outlets for propaganda they [Reds] have." For "out in Hollywood, Communism and the Jewish group seem to play hand in hand. It is simply stupid on the part of many people to claim there are very few Communists in Hollywood. There are hundreds of them and a great many of the leaders are Jews."[58] Repeatedly government operatives somehow managed to ascertain who was and who was not Jewish within the ranks of progressives. At one meeting of the HDC during the war, it was said that there were "approximately 250 people in the hall. Nine of every ten person were Jews."[59]

The response was not long in coming. Postwar L.A. was rocked by an astounding series of anti-Jewish incidents, though it was not as if wartime had been paradise.[60] Tellingly, Sam Goldwyn told Jack Warner that he thought postwar anti-Semitism "'was worse than it has been in years.'"[61] Thus, in June 1946 there was the "desecration of Temple Israel, Los Angeles . . . at 1704 North Ivor Street" in Hollywood, which was "laid at the door of the Ku Klux Klan." The perpetrators "wrote on the wall downstairs in German, 'Die Juden Parasite. They also drew swastikas." The rabbi "stated that the only person who might be looked upon with some suspicion who was in the [temple] that day while the janitor was gone was a man in the uniform of a captain of the U.S. Army."[62]

Even before the war had concluded, the neofascist Gerald L. K. Smith had decamped to L.A., where he made Jewish Communists—for example, Lawson—his favorite whipping boy. Smith was not marginal, referring to Lawson's nemesis—state senator Jack Tenney—as "'my good friend'" who "'would vouch'" for his character.[63] Weeks before the bombing of Hiroshima, he was addressing a crowd at 1204 South Hill Street downtown, where he hacked away at the "Jews in Hollywood" who were "bringing immigrants from Mexico to Hollywood to take the place of Christians in the studios." Even the government informant, who descended into anti-Jewish stereotypes regularly, was a bit frightened by this spectacle: "Something should be done to counteract movements of this nature. If meetings of this nature continue, something serious is going to happen."[64]

But Smith was not finished. He recognized that by linking Jews and Communists and Hollywood, he had scored the trifecta of hate politics. Days later he was back in downtown L.A., at Ninth and Grand, at a larger facility with a larger crowd—almost eighteen hundred screaming bigots. Again, he chose to "take out after the Jews in a more or less rabid manner"; amid "cheering and applause," he "cut loose on the Jews and he delivered a tirade against them that would make Adolf Hitler blush." Again he assailed "'alien minded Russian Jews in Hollywood'"; at "every meeting," it was said with some trepidation, Smith was becoming "more violent than he was in his previous meeting." If this trend continued, "bloodshed in this town thru [sic] a race riot will be the eventual outcome in the writer's opinion."[65]

But Smith was far from finished. Days later he had moved up to the spacious Shrine Auditorium for his mass rally. He "started off by reading a long letter which he had sent to Congressman [John] Rankin," the notorious Mississippi xenophobe, "commending his coming investigation of the Communists in Hollywood"—which was to bring Lawson before the klieg lights two years later. He "mentioned" Lawson specifically before he "slammed the lesbians of Hollywood," another of his targets.[66]

The conclusion of the war had erased whatever circumspection had engendered restraint in confronting Communists. Soon the FBI was circulating increasingly hysterical reports about "Communist Infiltration" of the "Motion Picture Industry." As of "June 1944" there were "nine known Communist Party members and fifteen members of one or more Communist Party front groups" among "directors and producers." There were only "five actors and actresses" who were Reds—but that was five too many—and "twenty four others" in so-called fronts, including Ida Lupino, James Cagney, John Garfield, Walter Huston, and Franchot Tone. Writers seemed to be a lost cause, from the FBI's viewpoint; within their ranks there were "56 known Communist Party members," with the "outstanding figure" being Lawson. There was an apparent tremendous inflation rate among Reds within the SWG, for by the time the FBI reached the end of its report, it was said that there were "approximately 1300 members" in the guild, "of which about 100 are reported to be members of the Communist Party." Of these guild members, the FBI found that 972 were "active"; of these, "only 366 are presently employed in eight major studios." MGM led the pack with 116, followed by Paramount with 50, Fox with 44, Warner's with 41, Columbia with 36, Universal with 32, RKO with 27, and Republic with 20.[67]

Why did scrutiny of writers increase after the war's end? Of course, the easy answer is that some among the powerful in Hollywood and Washington felt the pendulum had swung too far during the wartime alliance with Moscow and a course correction was required—desperately, immediately. In that sense the presence of well-paid, influential writers—and suspected Reds—like Lawson was a target too fat to ignore. Yet this broad point was intimately tied to another: moguls were not the only ones who thought a correction was needed. Many writers, emboldened by the advance of the SWG, thought they should be appropriating a larger share of the fruits of their labor, and left-wingers were in the vanguard of this trend. A rising Red Scare placed them on the defensive.

Much of the initial furor centered around the idea of the writer James Cain to establish the American Authors' Authority (AAA) to garner a larger share of the wealth generated by writers. He thought it was "about as Communistic" as the National Association of Manufacturers. "I am a registered Democrat but worked for T. E. Dewey," Cain insisted, but his critics thought his AAA was little more than just another "Communist front."[68]

The FBI was unusually concerned about the mundane matter of how much writers would be paid. Through "technical surveillance" on Lawson, it discovered that the SWG had "opened discussions among its members whether to ban the sale of material to the motion picture industry and adopt the procedure of licensing of all material." Moreover, the FBI was deeply concerned with the SWG's support for the Fair Employment Practices Commission, designed to eliminate job bias, particularly against African Americans.

As Communists pressed for change in France, Italy, China, and elsewhere, the FBI came to believe that it had its own homegrown Red Menace to confront. "Through a technical surveillance maintained on John Howard Lawson," it "was learned that Lawson while discussing the best way [to] 'communize' the United States stated 'the best part is by communizing the writers and producers of Hollywood, and eventually controlling every picture and fiction story produced in Hollywood and perhaps one day controlling every news article in the U.S. that the people read."[69] Then the *Hollywood Reporter* began echoing the FBI.[70]

Their concern skyrocketed when workers in the studios went on strike as the war was winding down, and writers led by Lawson were among the first to lend support. It was at the 20 August 1945 SWG executive board meeting that Lawson "suggested that the actors and directors be asked to set up a Joint Committee with the SWG to discuss the strike situation and to see what might be done."[71] Weeks later, when picketers were met with violence at the hands of police and plug-uglies at Warner's, "it was moved by Jack Lawson . . . that we notify the membership by telegram that we are holding a meeting to discuss the strike." Tempers in the executive suites were not eased when this "motion"—backed by stalwarts of Red Hollywood, including Lardner, Harold Buchman, Richard Collins, and Howard Koch—was "denied." Likewise rejected was their motion calling on SWG to "give legal aid" to those arrested.[72] The SWG was split hopelessly over whether its fellow laborers should be backed in their confrontation with the common foe—the moguls. The list of defeats included a Cole-Lawson motion that the SWG donate $10,000 to the strikers.[73]

More controversy erupted when SWG involved itself in film trade agreements, a lucrative area jealously guarded by the moguls. "'Another vote for Stalin,'" harrumphed the *Hollywood Reporter*. Why would the SWG take a stance akin to Moscow's and object to pacts that would increase Hollywood exports? it asked with some exasperation. The finger of accusation was waved first at the Communist Party, then its most visible representative—Lawson.[74]

The moguls' representative, Eric Johnston, was incredulous. "I am profoundly disturbed by the implication" of the SWG's action.[75] Ominously, he took his grievance directly before the notorious House Un-American Activities Committee, which subsequently was to hound Lawson and Red Hollywood mercilessly. "In most countries which are Communist dominated," fumed Johnston, "there is virtually a ban on American films. In other countries, our pictures are under attack by vigorous Communist minorities. . . . French Communists made a bitter attack against the accord and they have waged a constant campaign of vituperation against American pictures ever since. In countries behind the Iron Curtain, Communists resist the showing of American films and use every bait possible to lure the people into houses showing Soviet films. In some cases, they even offer free tickets and free transportation."[76] According to the *Hollywood Reporter*, the guild's views on global trade agreements in movies demonstrated that this group "continues to take its orders from Moscow!"[77] Even the state legislature in sleepy Sacramento got involved.[78] Sergei Eisenstein had demonstrated that Soviet films could be globally competitive. Would this Communist competitor—with the aid of Red Hollywood—pose a direct threat to Hollywood's unchallenged postwar hegemony?

This was not just an abstract question in postwar Hollywood. As the pivotal year of 1947 was winding down, Johnston told the mogul—and former Lawson employer—Cecil B. DeMille that "the year behind us has been a tough one." Nevertheless, the U.S. ambassador in Moscow, W. B. Smith, hailed the chief of the industry trade association for the "correctness of your stand in opposition to exporting certain films like 'Grapes of Wrath' and 'Tobacco Road' to the Soviet Union unless an equal number of films showing more favorable aspects of life in the United States are also exported."[79]

Lawson's affiliations were coming to be viewed with growing anxiety. He was on the executive board of the National Negro Congress—a so-called Communist front; he was a leader of the Committee for Motion Picture Strikers, which beginning in 1945 had brought the industry to a grinding halt as a result of its militancy. The Northwest section of the Communist Party had 545 members, thought the FBI, the "largest in Los Angeles county and contains approximately 1/5 of the total [Party] membership"; again, Lawson was the leader of this branch of mostly film workers.[80] One of the FBI files on Marlene Dietrich relates how she, along with

Gerhart Eisler, Odets, and Lawson, was "instrumental" in forging in "Hollywood a circle which secured thousands of dollars for the financing of the European Communist parties."[81] Matthew Woll, a vice president of the American Federation of Labor, weighed in, griping about the "many high salaried stars and script writers who are part of the Communist Fifth Column in America." Hollywood, he said, was "the third largest Communist center in the United States," but it loomed even larger in terms of contributions to Red coffers; this "playing at revolution," he barked, "seems to justify the possession of a swimming pool and improves the taste of astrakhan, caviar and the feel of Russian sables."[82]

The *Hollywood Reporter* summed up many of the postwar reservations about Red Hollywood, then cited comments that revealed the moguls' dilemma: "We need writers, good writers," said one, and "I don't care if the fellow is a 'Commie' or not; if he can write, if he can do the job, I'll hire him."[83] Harry Cohn of Columbia routinely employed Lawson and, says his biographer, was "oblivious to political matters"; he "gave no consideration to the inadvisability of hiring suspected Communists or supporters of Communist causes. His criterion was talent and a man's political views were of no concern to him."[84]

The moguls had been working with the likes of Lawson for years, and they knew that he was no more than a bird dog who retrieved the pheasant that they consumed; they could live quite well with this system, thank you very much.[85] But other voices, strong and resolute, insisted this simply would not do. Of course, many among these did not recognize that writers—Communist or no—could not simply impose any vision they so desired on screen, ignoring censors, moguls, and banks alike.

But the point was Red Hollywood itself. According to the FBI, by the fall of 1947 there were "six hundred Communists employed in the motion picture and radio industries in Hollywood," with only 127 being writers, alongside 92 actors, 15 directors, 42 musicians, and a mere 12 technicians.[86] As the moguls saw it, these Reds—no matter how talented—were becoming more trouble than they were worth. They opposed lucrative trade agreements, backed strikers seeking to take money out of their pockets, and brought uncomfortable scrutiny of their Jewishness. On that latter point, the moguls' failure to oust them was leading to ever louder whispers about how their supposed ethnoreligious loyalties were stronger than their class loyalties. This was not true—obviously.

There was a reserve army of writers just waiting for their shot in Hollywood, and purging Reds would provide just that. Lester Cole, a preeminent Hollywood Red, summed up the postwar dilemma of writers generally. "We are faced then," he said in a report to the SWG, "with the existence of a large pool of writers available for a greatly fewer number of jobs open at any given time." Though working writers desired more for their labor, the fact was that "1% of what American movie-goers pay for their entertainment is allocated to the writing of screenplays." The "average screenwriter [has] only a fairly modest income and no security at all against illness and unproductive, arid periods common to us all." What to do? "Secure more money for writers," was the answer; "impose a minimum royalty on the total industry gross to be distributed by the Guild to its active members . . . in somewhat the same way as ASCAP does in the songwriting field."[87] As the moguls saw it, this proposed redistribution of wealth downward was the worst kind of communism.

There were many targets to select when defenestrating Communists—and their radical proposals—but Lawson's was the face of Red Hollywood. There was much hand-wringing in the FBI about Lawson. A detailed analysis reported that he had a "salary of $1000 a week"; "his wife" was a Party member, while "his daughter, Mandy," was enmeshed in similar circles. Lawson himself seemed to be "very interested in the establishment of [a] Russian library in the Los Angeles area" and had "connections with Soviet officials in Los Angeles," including "Mikhail Kalatozov, Russian film representative in the United States." Fortunately, it was thought, "there is no evidence available that he has been engaged in propaganda dissemination at the behest of Russia."[88]

The FBI was not totally off base, at least regarding Lawson's income—which was stratospheric, given the times and his politics. After he settled more or less permanently in Hollywood in 1938, his "salary was $750 per week, then $1000 per week." In 1942 he had garnered $6,500 from Paramount, $17,500 from Warner's, and $15,000 from Columbia. Generally, at the zenith of his popularity, he was earning more than $50,000 annually. Suggestive of the point that Lawson may have been taken unawares by the changing political climate, it was in 1946 that he chose to "devote all my time to writing [a] book on American history." He "refused all assignments, except a one-week rewrite." Thus, moviegoers were spared his adaptations of *Look Homeward, Angel* and *The Foxes of Harrow.*[89] The problem for Lawson and his fellow Red screenwriters was that the studios were downsizing: in a move that was to be common in many industries in the twenty-first century, Hollywood was moving away from maintaining writers on the payroll as workers and, instead, was contracting with them on a "job-to-job" basis, developing what might well be termed the "Hollywood mode of production."[90]

This conversion from workers to contractors had implications for the political consciousness of writers, their ability to maintain solidarity in the wake of the new "every man for himself" mentality that inexorably characterizes contractors. Thus, in March 1947, MGM employed the most writers—83; Republic the fewest—23. This was out of a total of employed writers of 331. Yet in March 1946 the same eight major studios employed 434 writers, with MGM then employing 132 and "independent" studios employing 168.[91]

Beyond the FBI, Lawson was faced with another pressing problem after the war came to a close. During the war, the Communist Party became the Communist Political Association (CPA), a signal that a new approach was needed. This was a direct product of the unprecedented alliance between Moscow and Washington, which U.S. Communists thought could be extended domestically—an idea of which they were disabused after the war ended and a Red Scare emerged. According to his comrade Lester Cole, Lawson—a "brilliant intellect and fearless activist"—"seemed to me to go overboard in what I considered his dogmatic projection" of the CPA "line." He was not "merely 100 percent" for this line but "120 percent for it." This led to "sharp, at times bitter, conflict. It was something less than a harmonious period."[92] Edward Dmytryk, a former Communist and a director, concurred,[93] as did Richard Collins.[94] Even Lawson's personal magnetism could not deflect a Party crisis of this magnitude. Jean Butler, spouse of the writer Hugo Butler, recalls that during that this time she fell asleep and awoke at 2:00 A.M. hearing Trumbo stating that either Lenin was right and the CPA was wrong, or the CPA was right and Lenin was wrong—and the mustachioed writer preferred to think that the Russian revolutionary was correct.[95]

Thus, as the FBI and others began nibbling at the flanks of Red Hollywood, Communists became consumed by a debilitating internal struggle. As one Red recalled it, "If Lester Cole wasn't constantly trying to tear Lawson apart, Alvah Bessie was morosely clawing away at Cole."[96]

This vicious backbiting and infighting were not alienating to all. It was in the immediate aftermath of this rotten atmosphere that the soon-to-be-famed director Joseph Losey joined the Party.[97] But the clashes between Cole and Lawson—confrontations that challenged the idea of "monolithic Communists"—were not helpful in creating an environment conducive to Party recruiting, or survival for that matter.[98] Worse, thought John Weber, another Party leader, "even leading Hollywood Party people had a poor grasp of Marxism—Jack Lawson, Lester Cole, almost all of them."[99]

The authorities may not have created internal Party problems, though certainly they were in an advantageous position to exploit these rifts.[100] It was not long after this that the authorities were sniggering that the "top split between Soviet Russia and her allies has penetrated Communist circles in California and Los Angeles." It was reported that a "Soviet agent" addressed the comrades about the worsening fissure between the United States and the Soviet Union and its implications for L.A. Reds. He "spoke grimly and ominously, and his listeners were too astonished to even smoke or look at each other; all stared at the speaker and several trembled with the portent [of] his talk, and they separated silently when permitted to do so after he was gone."[101]

The internal flux, combined with the worsening relations between Moscow and Washington, destabilized Red Hollywood and Red L.A. alike. Military intelligence reported almost giddily in mid-1946 that there was a "great deal of discussion in high circles regarding the security of the party, particularly regarding the use of names and addresses, telephone conversations and mail"; one novel tack was to "assign the responsibility to one member to memorize party names and corresponding true names of the entire membership of each club."[102]

Besieged, Lawson's Party started purging, at times arbitrarily, in one case the talent-starved organization asserting, "We must understand that it is not enough for a comrade to be an able speaker, writer, journalist, etc."[103] At this juncture, the Party in L.A. still had a hefty 3,770 members, 45 percent men, 55 percent women—with 1 percent Mexican, 8 percent Negro, and 45 percent trade union membership.[104]

But who would want to join an organization that was under military surveillance and beginning to cannibalize itself? Lawson, a true believer, had nowhere to go unless he renounced his bedrock beliefs, which this man of "commitment" steadfastly refused to do. Meanwhile, the authorities were continuing to squeeze the Party's "Hollywood section, which is the largest in terms of membership within the County Organization." Happily, it was reported that "during recent months more and more emphasis is being placed on security measures" within the ranks; Reds were "so security conscious that any activity out of the ordinary places even a heretofore responsible person under investigation." It was as if an overly melodramatic screenplay writer was describing the realities of what was occurring. "All trash from the [Party] office is taken home each evening by one of the office workers for burning," while "if any writing is to be done a piece of paper is torn off the pad and placed on a hard substance such as a desk before the message is written. . . . Locks on the doors to the office at the [Party's] headquarters are changed periodically." But why this intense focus on Southern California, which in turn generated these extraordinary security measures? Well, said the authorities, they could not be indifferent when "out of 239 World War II veterans recruited" by the Party "in the state of California, 195 were recruited in Los Angeles."[105]

Still, it was not surreptitious surveillance alone that was dogging the heels of Red Hollywood. In the fall of 1946, not coincidentally just before important midterm elections, downtown L.A. was the scene of state legislative hearings sponsored by Sacramento's Un-American Activities Committee. Settling down in the witness chair was SWG leader Emmett Lavery. The "difference between me and other people in Hollywood," he said, "is that I oppose Communism in another way. I think the answer to the Communist and Marxian philosophy is to live a better philosophy." He then explained his far-reaching Catholic beliefs and his Irish background— a trait he shared with a number of those questioning him. Still, one could almost hear the legislators sigh and see them roll their eyes as they rushed to return to their key topic. State senator Tenney inquired, "Do you know John Howard Lawson is considered one of the outstanding Marxian Communists on the Pacific Coast?" Lavery slid over to what he thought was underlying this interrogation, observing that "the guilds and unions do not employ people who work in the motion picture industry. . . . I have not yet in my ten years experience in Hollywood found a man who can finance what you would call a Communist picture through Louis B. Mayer or Mr. Sam Katz at Metro."

But these inquisitors were seeking not commonsense thinking about moviemaking but confirmation of their fervent desire to rid the industry of Lawson and Red Hollywood. Undaunted, Lavery plodded on, patiently seeking to explain how movies were made and how it would be virtually impossible for a Red writer to sneak subversion past the sentries of executives and censors alike. "It goes on like the 40 mule team on the Borax ad," he said, groping for the popular touch. "They think the more people who work on it, the better. So in Metro you can find scripts where as many as fifteen different writers have gone to work on a script, each rewriting what the last man left before him has written." The committee was not buying it, however. Again and again, it returned to the presumed toxicity of allowing Reds to exist in Hollywood. With exasperation, Lavery blurted out, "Shall we be only for those things the Communists oppose?" If the Party "says two and two are four, and know it to be so, shall we oppose it?" He received no direct reply and perhaps realized that such questions were futile for a body that had made up its mind.

Lawson's good friend Paul Robeson was also called to testify. The Negro artist and activist was handled with kid gloves, not least since he refused to cut his comments to meet the current fashion. "In the state of California,"

he said in his booming bass voice, "there are big interests, big powerful interests, oil and fruit interests, for example," and they "might be forced to
do exactly what happened in the South, of what happened in Germany, if
they were challenged by people who wanted a decent wage." Robeson's interlocutors thought they knew why he was making such statements. He
was asked, "Are you a member of the Communist Party?" Robeson said
no—not avoiding a direct answer as he was to do frequently later—but the
suspicion lingered that he, like Lawson, was dissembling.[106]

Pressure was building on the state—then federal—legislature to do
something, anything, about the Communists, particularly in Hollywood,
where their influence was thought to be most significant. Robeson thought
that it was Lawson's activism with the SWG, LAW, and HDC—not simply
his screenplays—that had led to the anticommunist persecutions. Some of
the mail that the GOP governor, Earl Warren, was receiving bolstered this
suspicion. "At the Uptown Theatre in [San Francisco]," he was informed,
"there has been a group of Negroes, urged on by Communists, picketing the
theatre. They march back and forth about three apart with banners." California "got rid of the IWW," the anarcho-syndicalist unionists, "now it is up
to someone to outlaw the Communists. They are getting too strong. . . . get
busy with the legislators and pass a law outlawing Communists. If you do,
it will make you, with a little publicity, a solid contender for the GOP nomination" for the White House "in '48."[107]

This was a message that the GOP itself decided not to ignore.

11 Inquisition

John Howard Lawson was dragged forcibly from the witness chair during his stormy testimony in Washington during the fall of 1947.[1] It was a huge room from which he was shanghaied, perhaps a hundred feet long and fifty feet wide. There were three large French crystal chandeliers, each containing perhaps a hundred lightbulbs, and affixed to the chandeliers were "six baby spots some directed at the audience," giving the scene the appearance of being—appropriately—a movie set.[2] Capturing this tempestuous moment for eternity were "at least four newsreel cameras"; "six or more still photographers—often as many as 10" crouched near his chair before he was snatched, "popping up from time to time to take a flashlight picture." A "candid specialist" held "first one exposure meter and then another a few feet from each witness' nose" as klieg lights and "other floodlamps" gave the otherwise stuffy congressional room the glamour of a Hollywood set.[3]

In a real sense this was a staged performance no less intentional than some of Lawson's own masterworks. "Four major radio networks" were "cranking." There were "press arrangements [for] 125." This "newspaper sensation" and "capital attraction" was to "outrank the year's previous colossal," that is, the "debate on the Taft-Hartley law and the Howard Hughes investigation."[4] A central purpose of this burlesque was to discredit Lawson and the rest of Red Hollywood as agents of an increasingly discredited foreign power, the Soviet Union, and their presumed domestic puppet: the Communist Party. As during state legislative hearings, Lawson denied his Party membership, but he had hardly been evacuated from the busy sanctum on Capitol Hill when a congressional investigator unveiled a "registration card No. 47275 made out in the name" of Lawson.[5] Lawson's travail brought back memories of the screenwriter Nunnally Johnson, who when asked by Daryl Zanuck if he were a Communist, reputedly replied, "'We're not allowed to tell.'"[6]

What about the charge that had brought Lawson to Washington, that he and his comrades had deliberately inserted "allegedly 'subversive' lines or scenes in motion pictures"? Lawson was dumbfounded. This was a "fantasy out of Arabian nights," he said. "When I am employed to write a motion picture, my whole purpose is to make it a vital, entertaining creative portrayal of the segment of life with which it deals." Did these people have no clue about the filmmaking process? "I never write a line or develop a situation," he insisted, "without discussing its implications, its meaning, its tendency, with the man in charge of production. Where a line might relate to controversial issues, I am particularly insistent on full discussion, because issues affect studio policy, critical response and popularity of the picture." "I don't 'sneak' ideas into pictures," he said exasperatedly.[7] Most likely the authorities were not surprised by Lawson's words, since when he and his subpoenaed comrades met at the Shoreham Hotel in Washington to plot strategy, they "were fairly sure" that the rooms were "bugged"; hence, they trooped "into [the] garden" for privacy, though it was not clear if the bushes were bugged as well.[8]

Though "controlling the content of motion pictures" was ostensibly a major reason for the congressional investigation, when Dalton Trumbo told HUAC, "I have 20 scripts which I propose and wish to introduce into the record," he was turned down. The committee members displayed an odd dearth of curiosity about these writers' supposed cinematic intentions. Instead, they were bent on determining who was or was not a Red, and the writers were just as intent on avoiding a direct response.[9]

I. F. Stone, the investigative journalist with the contrasting qualities of poor eyesight and grand vision, was "convinced that a committee of Congress has no more right to question an American citizen about his political beliefs than it has to question him about his religious beliefs." Worse, "the striking aspect of the Hollywood inquiry was the complete absence of any evidence that one of the many films written and directed by the men under investigation contained anything which could reasonably be described as Communist propaganda."[10] Seeing further, the perspicacious journalist asked with mock innocence, "If a committee of Congress assumes the right to investigate the movie business on the theory that the movie business is being used to spread 'Un-American' ideas, can't that committee—on the same grounds—assume the right to investigate the newspaper business?"[11] Yet Congress had bedazzled its audience with allusions about Red perfidy in Hollywood but could not point to one millimeter of celluloid to substantiate this fantasy—even though those who were grilled under klieg lights included some of Lawson's closest comrades in the industry, who came to be known as the "Hollywood Ten."[12]

The screenwriter Philip Dunne was among those who flocked to Washington to object to the hearings but like others left disturbed that some of those writers subpoenaed "had made the incredible blunder of lying to their own lawyers" about their Party membership.[13] Later the Communist screenwriter Lester Cole was to maintain that only three of the nineteen subpoenaed writers were not Communists.[14]

Even this omission could not halt the flux of piercing headlines: "Communist Issue Splits SWG" was a typical caption that blared on the heels of this congressional inquisition.[15] Shortly thereafter there was an updated report: "Anti-Red candidates make a clean sweep of top offices" in the SWG; "more than 600 writers jammed the California Room of the Roosevelt Hotel, many standing . . . . due to steaming debate on most of the issues, the meeting recessed at 12:10 [A.M.]."[16] "It was remarkable," said one commentator, that "in the New York meetings" of the SWG "there was not *one* dissenting voice among the 50 or more who were in attendance." A consensus had arisen, he argued, that "any Communist is a traitor and is conspiring against the peace and happiness of this nation and each is an agent of a foreign government." If any screenwriters avoided answering—as Lawson sought to do—the sixty-four-dollar question of whether they were party members, well, "those refusing should be jailed or taken to the Russian border."[17] With raging emphasis, the *Hollywood Reporter* shouted, "SOMETHING MUST BE DONE ABOUT THESE PEOPLE! IT MUST BE DONE IMMEDIATELY!"[18]

Lost in the red sauce of allegations of communism was the SWG's ardent desire to reap a greater percentage of the wealth created by its members' agile imaginations via the American Authors Authority or similar devices. Later the SWG acknowledged that in the early postwar era, the AAA "brought left, middle [and] right together . . . . never before or since has [there] been such unanimity in SWG on any one issue"[19]—a promising trend disrupted by the 1947 hearings, which pitted the left against the "middle" and right. Submerged and overwhelmed, as a result, was the front-page headline—days before Lawson's aborted testimony—that spoke of how the SWG "seeks 1 [percent] of film take," which "would slice off $18,000,000" more in revenue for the writers on the basis of 1946 computations. Such an arrangement would have meant comparatively less for the moguls and those who backed them.[20]

Instead, the SWG was consumed with determining who was Red and who was not. The liberal screenwriter Philip Dunne had once said that "the great fear of studios and producers is that the writer will some day want control of the script in movies as he does on Broadway."[21] That fear increased exponentially in 1947.[22]

The mogul Cecil B. DeMille did little to discourage this opinion when he preceded Lawson to Capitol Hill. He launched into a blistering tirade against unions as the real "monopoly" of the industry. The congressmen present pledged to heed his impassioned words.[23] Such cupidity maddened the quintessential L.A. writer Raymond Chandler, whose novels *The Big Sleep, The Long Goodbye,* and *Farewell, My Lovely* all captured the rapt attention of moviemakers.[24] Hollywood produced a "class of kept writers without initiative, independence or fighting spirit; they exist only by conforming to Hollywood standards, but they can produce art only by defying them." It was the "only industry in the world that pays its workers," meaning writers, "the kind of money only capitalists and big executives make in other industries."[25] But Chandler, a writer positioned to benefit from this state of affairs, was hardly overjoyed. "I reserve my real contempt," he proclaimed, "for the movie moguls who in conference decided to expel" Lawson and his now "blacklisted" comrades "from the industry."[26]

Ultimately, it was not the viewpoint of Chandler that prevailed after 1947—and the gathering consensus was not pretty. "I hate Communists," exhorted the conservative columnist Westbrook Pegler. "I wish it were possible to round up all those who are reasonably known to be Communists, including all who have invoked the Fifth and put them into concentration camps as austere as the Arizona State Prison, where relatively harmless & morally stupid criminals of the common sort must dip water from the john if they get thirsty in the dead of summer nights in the desert."[27]

J. Parnell Thomas, the chairman of HUAC and no stranger to baiting Reds, was exultant about the reaction to his hearings. Echoing Pegler, he was elated that he was "deluged with friendly mail." "They wanted us to keep at it. They approved what we were doing. They knew we had a lion by the tail," he said, mixing his metaphors liberally, "but they also knew that we were striking pay dirt." He had received a "tip off" about the industry's intention to "blacklist" Red Hollywood from an aide to Eric Johnston, head of filmdom's trade association. "Mr. [Edward] Cheyfitz . . . oddly enough had the seat right next to mine in the Pullman car in which I was traveling to New Jersey. Of course, it was only a coincidence that Cheyfitz had that seat, but the more I heard him talk the more suspicious I became about the coincidence."[28]

. . .

Not only Red Hollywood but also Liberal Hollywood initially viewed these congressional hearings as a clear and present danger. Stars of dazzling wattage signed up with the Committee for the First Amendment. Henry Fonda, Ava Gardner, Benny Goodman, Gregory Peck, and Billy Wilder were among those who took out a full-page ad denouncing the HUAC hearings as "morally wrong."[29] Another ad was joined by Leonard Bernstein, Kirk Douglas, Rita Hayworth, Van Heflin, Canada Lee, and Burt Lancaster.[30]

The stars had "decided to ask Howard Hughes" for a plane so they could make the long trip eastward. CBS, through William Paley, chief stockholder of the self-proclaimed "Tiffany" network, "was approached for free time to answer news commentators and other speakers who all along had given only a one-sided picture of the Washington hearings. Paley offered a half hour, provided it was a forum and that both sides could speak."

But at that precise moment, pressures were rising. Thus, at the last minute Eddie Cantor, Ava Gardner, Ethel Barrymore, Katherine Hepburn, Joan Bennett, and others also withdrew. Sounding a good deal like one of his characters, Jimmy Stewart said, "'Gosh, I don't know anything about politics. I've never even voted.'" He lent his name to CFA—"and later denied he had, as did John Payne and a couple of others." Sticking to their guns—at least at first—were John Huston, Evelyn Keyes, Gene Kelly, Paul Henried, Danny Kaye, Sterling Hayden, Ira Gershwin, Jane Wyatt, Philip Dunne, and others.

As they boarded the plane in L.A. for their rendezvous with destiny in Washington, it was a "beautiful day" and "high spirits" reigned. "No one in this group had ever been active on any committee before," and though they lived or died by their ability to speak, "no one was politically articulate in short sentences." As they sped eastward, the "co-pilot tuned in our radio show," and they "took turns sitting in the cockpit listening on headphones to the radio show that stirred up tens of thousands of letters and telegrams, topping the number of letters ever received for any program" and "which during the following five days was rebroadcast nine times in different localities."

They stopped in Kansas City, and the impressed crowd stared agape at the stars among them as the press took pictures. The "best way to be invisible," said one nonstar present, "is to stand next to Bacall" and "Bogart." The stars, not viewing this mixing with the hoi polloi as a pleasure, signed autographs "without smiles, without the attempts at pleasantry"—not exactly the approach to be recommended when one is crusading for a cause that was not universally popular. However, there was no set policy on whether their crusade was on behalf of Lawson and company or the abstract principle of freedom of speech. Marsha Hunt, for whom Lawson had crafted a career-defining role in *Smash-Up*, was the vocal leader of the crew, but it was evident that she could not speak unchallenged on behalf of all assembled.

On the flight across Missouri the group's members decided that the line should be that the CFA was "not acting specifically in the defense" of Lawson and the others but of "American civil rights." They "preferred to lay off the Communist question entirely for fear of misquotes and misrepresentation. John Huston became the spokesman and he was to answer for the group on tricky questions." When they landed in St. Louis, the crowd was "twice the size of Kansas City's," and there were "mounted police," too. Pittsburgh brought "the largest crowd yet," and they arrived in Washington "around nine-thirty at night."

Later, the group met with the press in a comfortable suite of the plush Statler Hotel. Paul Henreid, arms folded, lounged against a wall. Bogart, chain-smoking as usual, sat on the floor. The carrot-topped comic Danny Kaye sat by his side, gnawing on his fingernails. Next to him was John Garfield. Strangely, the windows remained shut as heat and cigarette smoke added to the suffocation of a room that was not stifling tempers, already inflamed by the tenseness of the moment. Gene Kelly called the treatment of Lawson a denial of free speech and asked what difference would it make if Lawson were a Red. Bacall asked a reporter how would he like it if Congress investigated the press. Undaunted, the reporter for the *New York Times* provided a presentiment of doom when, after a Huston response, he said, "'I don't get the dialectics of that' and this use of the word 'dialectics' was a deliberate innuendo that we were all Marxists." Still, the CFA was not displeased with the initial press coverage—something that was to change soon.

After the tumultuous hearing, June Havoc, Jane Wyatt, and Marsha Hunt "were taken to the Senate restaurant by the New York Times man," who "then lectured us as fools, babes in the woods." A harbinger occurred during the hearing when "at one point there was spontaneous applause for Lawson," and some of the stars "joined it for about three claps, and then remembered" that they were supposedly neutral, at least on Lawson. Another telltale sign occurred when after the press conference, supposedly the "biggest reporter turn-out since Roosevelt died," a man "got drunk and betrayed an anti-Semitism that was fairly foamy. He wanted to hit Danny Kaye and he said we were Communists."

That was only the beginning. The powerful gossip columnist Hedda Hopper began to berate the CFA, then printed letters "purportedly from her followers agreeing with her. She printed one letter disagreeing with her and that letter was the only one she printed the name of the letter with. He was a Jew. A local [progressive] meeting was broken up by the American Legion." A local theater in L.A. showing *Forever Amber*, cowritten by Communist Ring Lardner Jr., was picketed by a priest "standing outside taking down names of any of this flock he saw buy tickets. The *fear* is here." Hollywood was "split," with "liberals going to cover." The "Communists [are] fighting for rights, the confused are more confused, and the Right is arrogant, stupid and terribly ugly. You can almost hear the cry, 'lynch the bastards . . . cut their balls off'!?"[31]

Philip Dunne denied that the CFA was in full flight from the right after its bracing experience on Capitol Hill.[32] Maybe so. But after the fall of 1947 Hollywood liberals were hardly to be found declaiming from mountaintops in defense of civil liberties.

Understandably, Lawson and his comrades thought they had a sound case, since being a Communist theretofore had not been embraced warmly but certainly had not been used as a predicate for imprisonment. They thought that the idea that being a Red meant one could sneak propaganda onto the silver screen was utterly risible—the problem for them was that this became the excuse for their persecution.

David O. Selznick was among the many who was calling for the scalps of Reds. "[I want] no part," he spat out, "of any group that did not openly, and as part of its platform, condemn treacherous attacks of foreign Communism and at the same time express its abhorrence of any form of Communism for America."[33]

Thus, HUAC, which was deluged with press coverage, proceeded in its crusade to discredit Red Hollywood. The film critic for *Esquire* magazine, John Charles Moffitt, pointed to Lawson's influence in charging that not only Hollywood but Broadway too was "'practically dominated by Communists'. . . . [H]e asserted that forty-four plays out of 100 produced on Broadway between 1936 and 1948 furthered the Communist Party line and thirty-two others favored that line." The debonair actor Adolphe Menjou termed Hollywood "'one of the main centers of Communist activity in Hollywood in America'" that was manipulated by the "'masters of Moscow'" under a "blaze of klieg lights and the admiring glances of most of a larger audience." The reporter present at this congressional testimony found it had "the elements of a lively Hollywood script. It had humor, anger, glamour, climactic action and cheers for the star as well as his supporting cast."[34]

Jack Warner brought gravitas to Washington; he told the attentive solons of his experience with Lawson's *Action in the North Atlantic*. He accused Lawson of trying to "swing a lot of things in there, but to my knowledge there wasn't anything." His interrogator pounced, asking if Lawson tried "to put stuff [in the script]." Warner answered, "Yes, I would say he did in [one] form or another," though he did not bother with specifying what he meant, and incurious congressmen did not follow up.[35]

MGM executive James McGuiness, a "husky man with gray hair and a small moustache," said Lawson was seeking to give the SWG the "'power to destroy' any screenwriter economically." This mini-mogul also said that Lawson "over objections from some writers supported a strike at the North American Aircraft factory at Inglewood, although it had been condemned by President Roosevelt"—which was suspicious at best given wartime urgencies.[36]

Professional stool pigeon Howard Rushmore attached to Lawson a term redolent with Soviet meaning that the screenwriter was to take to his grave: he was Hollywood's "'Commissar.'"[37] Rushmore, a former Red, said that Lawson had told him that the Party "had been successful in getting producers to plan some films supporting Loyalist Spain."[38] Lawson, he said, was leader of the "Red Fascists," "one of Hollywood's capitalists" and "virtual dictator of Communist policy in Hollywood."[39] It was Rushmore who claimed that Reds received "scripts for early preview," then launched protests against those disfavored. This assertion was a "stick of dynamite" that implicated the "names of alleged Hollywood Communists" and "exploded like popcorn all over the landscape."[40] Yes, agreed one columnist, "this royal palm treed, warm weather corner of the country" known as Hollywood "is the last frontier for the Communist Party."[41]

Writers were fleeing in fear—at times being chased by other writers.[42] Arthur Koestler charged that Lawson and his cronies "should 'shut up'" and "'remember the Moscow purge—Russian style—extinguished more than 200,000 lives. I have yet to see any blood on Santa Monica Boulevard,'" at which point "the audience laughed."[43] Reds "don't make any more 'Songs of Russia' or 'Missions to Moscow,'" the *Los Angeles Times* editorialized grudgingly, "but where they can get in a lick at the unwary, [they are] always in wait for the target of opportunity. They are proving that the pen is mighty. They work among the Hollywood writers. They can't write a whole picture, but every now and then they can throw in a line or two for the Party."[44]

But how could Red writers sneak their propaganda past a legion of censors and moguls? Cecil B. DeMille, part of this legion, thought he knew the answer. Hollywood Reds were "dangerous because they're brainy."[45]

Ronald Reagan told HUAC, "I would hesitate, or not like, to see any political party outlawed on the basis of its political ideology," but the militant Lela Rogers—mother of Ginger—adamantly disagreed. Walt Disney waffled on this fundamental point.[46]

Yet at the end of the day, Jack Warner may have been the most effective witness before HUAC, from Nixon's viewpoint, since—like Reagan—he was seen as a liberal but was rapidly moving to the right. His words dripped with the pain of feeling that he had been betrayed by those like Lawson. This process began with the contentious Hollywood strike of 1945, where his studio was targeted and Lawson avidly backed the picketers.[47] Perhaps the last straw for Warner was when Lawson—who had been paid handsomely for scripts—joined Rex Ingram, Artie Shaw, Trumbo, Howard Koch, Albert Maltz, Hanns Eisler, and others in signing a telegram to Warner that vowed to continue to back "the picketing at your studio . . . in order to do our utmost to prevent violence of any kind."[48]

The bewildered Warner asked John Cromwell, president of the Screen Directors Guild, if he really signed what Warner deemed an insulting telegram "accusing us of engaging thugs to combat the picketers at our studio." "The wire was uncalled for, untrue and unjust," Warner fumed, "and I personally will demand an apology in the public press."[49] The animator Sidney Sutherland, responsible for *The Wacky Wabbit* and *Wabbit Trouble*, among other films, was not wacky but articulate when he reassured the mogul of his undying support.[50]

Hence, by the time Warner settled into the witness chair in Washington, he was in no mood for compromise, and the same held true for millions of others. These witnesses were reflecting a growing trend. Dore Schary was told by one movie fan that she had taken note of "your announcement that you will continue to hire writers & actors & actresses who are Communists or followers of the party line. I have an announcement to make too—I shall from this time forth boycott all of your pictures—& moreover will influence everyone I can to refrain from going."[51] Schary was coming under special attack as a Jewish producer who was not conservative. One journal charged that "Schary's 'red record' is typical of the Jewish part in Communism since its beginning."[52] Later he was referred to, bizarrely, as a "Jewish Black Muslim," evidently intended as the ultimate epithet.[53] In a trend that was becoming common, his health was affected adversely as a result of the pressure. The leftist producer Adrian Scott bumped into Schary and found him "miserable about the outcome of the hearings"; he "expressed himself violently on the personal attack on him by the Hearst Press" because of his declaration that "he would not fire a Communist or an alleged Communist." Schary felt he was "being singled out, that he was being made the patsy . . . that the position he had taken in Washington was the position that all producers were to take and which he alone took. He resented the sell out of Jack L. Warner and L. B. Mayer." Scott was now worried that *The Boy with Green Hair,* which he had developed, based on the experiences of his son, might be jeopardized because it could be deemed "subversive." He was right—in a sense. Shortly thereafter, Scott and director Edward Dmytryk were called in by RKO "and handed two typewritten sheets and a place for our signatures on the bottom." They were suspended and later discharged.[54] Another man who developed "stomach pains" was the director Joseph Losey, who joined the Party in the inopportune year of 1946,[55] but soon found that he could not "contemplate with any heart or less than active sickness at stomach the idea of returning to Hollywood at all."[56] He went into exile in Europe. In a show of support, even Elia Kazan, who was to become notorious for "naming names," told "Dear Adrian" of his offer of support.[57] This was all heartening, but this apparent rock-solid support was to dissolve like snow in a Congo summer.

Schary was not the only man with "stomach pains." MGM executive Bernard Fein, in commiserating with Scott, also spoke of how "muscles are knotted in stomachs—the well-fed ones as well as our friends of the ulcer set. There is only one subject of conversation, no matter the setting or the occasion—and that's you and the guys with you," referring to the "Ten."[58] Hysteria gripped Hollywood. A system of federal censorship was the remedy proposed by one local newspaper, apparently unaware of the existence of Joseph Breen.[59] Jack Moffitt, who was reviving his otherwise moribund profile by denouncing Red Hollywood, gleefully reported in 1947 that "the [FBI] is said to have so many agents planted in the Actors' Laboratory that audiences aren't quite sure whether they're applauding J. Edgar Hoover or J. Edward Bromberg," referring to the actor suspected of leftist tendencies; even "Communists are writing anti-Communist pictures," he reported. Jack Warner has "forbidden the reissue of 'The Public Enemy' and all other Warner pictures that could be used as propaganda to circumvent the foreign policy of the United States. 'Little Caesar' and 'I Am a Fugitive' are among those withdrawn from circulation. . . . [U]nfortunately, prints of

'The Grapes of Wrath' already are being circulated in a number of the countries we hope to save. It is impossible to recall all of them." There were an amazing number of "American motion pictures containing concealed propaganda for the class war" penned by writers like Lawson skilled in "doctoring movie scripts to carry out the plans of Mr. Stalin," but now "the dramatic muse no longer will be a saleslady for a secret bill of goods."[60]

Moffitt's opinions were bolstered by a remarkable series of articles appearing in daily newspapers detailing an alleged Red takeover of Hollywood. Headlines focused on Lawson and "3 Russian Born 'First Families'" [that] "Rule Moviedom," referring to Warner, Mayer, and Schenck, who were all said to be soft on Reds.[61]

Soon another type of full-page ad was replacing the brave ones once placed by the CFA. One, entitled "A Memo to a Bunch of Suckers," argued that "we are threatened with disgrace, loss of revenue and censorship because some of our workers are Communists or party-liners."[62] All they had to do was throw overboard these ingrates, and the rest could live comfortably. This fierce assault was not without effect. In late 1947, days after Lawson was collared, Earl Warren, making his "first public address since becoming a candidate for President[,] endorsed the efforts to expose and nullify Communistic infiltration in the motion picture industry."[63]

Lawson had written some of Bogart's most memorable roles, which is why the chain-smoking actor was to be found on Capitol Hill on that fateful day in October 1947. "This has nothing to do with Communism," Bogart said of his politicking. "It's none of my business who's a Communist and who isn't. . . . I am an outraged and angry citizen."[64] But days after this hearing, he had been transformed from a snarling bulldog into a toothless terrier, as he was groveling before Hedda Hopper, apologizing for the "confused and erroneous interpretations" of his "recent trip to Washington." "I am not a Communist. I am not a Communist sympathizer. I detest Communism," he declared. Besides, his Washington "trip was ill-advised, even foolish."[65] It was Lawson's alleged misbehavior in Washington that "disgusted" the actor and the other stars who dissolved the CFA. Almost magically the organization with so much promise had disappeared "within a few weeks." According to his biographer, "Bogart and other prominent figures came under public and private pressure from journalists, gossip columnists, studio executives, financial backers, managers, agents, family and friends. To save their careers, they had to withdraw their opposition to HUAC and obtain a clearance from the FBI—as if acting were equivalent to working for the State Department or doing atomic research."[66] Just as worrying for Lawson was Hopper's close relationship with the producer who had rescued him from the penury of Broadway—Walter Wanger. Wanger cultivated ties assiduously with Hopper, and she reciprocated warmly.[67] Despite his liberalism, he would be loath to rescue Lawson—again.

For at this point, Lawson needed lawyers—good ones—and he was fortunate to have one of the best: Ben Margolis, a left-wing L.A. practitioner. He "continued to work without any pay for years" for Lawson and was "very optimistic that we could go right up and win that case." Lawson had to deal with the less cheerful question of how to avoid prison for contempt of Congress in light of his not answering directly inquiries about his Party ties.

Desperately seeking support, Margolis traveled to Communist Party headquarters in Manhattan and went straight to the "'ninth floor,'" the seat of power there. Margolis cautioned, however, that, contrary to popular opinion, decisions in this pivotal case were made by the defendants themselves. He said, "No one, absolutely *no one* decided what they would do for them." "There weren't very many Communist Party members that made $2500 a week or $5000 or $10,000. Not very many. And these people were generous and did give to the Party," Lawson especially, so if anything, the Party leadership was beholden to them, not the reverse. Lawson "was very modest in his [income]. For one thing, Jack didn't want to work all of the time. He was so busy politically and he gave away, you know, so much of his money. So John, Jack, was a man who had . . . a very modest home— lived very modestly." Chaplin, on the other hand, was a "very, very, very rich man—and I mean he was *very* rich," he said with added emphasis. Unlike Lawson, however, Chaplin was "very tight with his bucks," which only increased the importance of Lawson to the coffers of Red Hollywood. "So they were important to the Party but not from the standpoint of controlling the content of motion pictures" on the leadership's behalf.[68]

It seemed that Lawson and company could rely on a modicum of favorable and/or neutral public opinion, which no doubt influenced the CP response, as well as that of the "unfriendly witnesses." Lawson's consul, Robert Kenny, had met with the industry's chief representative, Eric Johnston, who told him, "'You know that I would never sponsor anything so Un-American as a blacklist.'" So bolstered, Kenny spent a good deal of time during the hearings—in the words of novelist Allen Drury—"'smoking cigars and cigarettes in indiscriminate profusion and uttering exasperated wisecracks in a belligerent murmur.'" "Fireworks" were this lawyer's specialty, but they hardly seemed necessary. "At the end of the week" of hearings, he thought that "it seemed to most observers that the Hollywood people had the best of" HUAC.[69]

Others agreed. George Gallup found that those queried about Communists placing "their ideas into movies" named "chiefly pictures about Russia such as *Mission to Moscow, Ninotchka, Song of Russia*," though all these films were either inspired by or vetted carefully by the U.S. government they were supposedly undermining—and if *Ninotchka* was pro-Soviet, then Stalin was an agent of the GOP. "When asked to *name* the ten 'unfriendly witnesses,'" only 12 percent of respondents could name one or more, and over half were unable to "name anyone."[70] Similarly, early on, editorial opinion was quite hostile to the congressional inquisition. A typical judgment was that of the *Atlanta Journal,* which concluded that "whether Mr. Lawson is or is not a Red does not affect the main point at issue. He is an American citizen, and, as such, enjoys the rights and privileges guaranteed under the Bill of Rights. His political beliefs, so long as they are not actionable under the laws affecting treason, are his own business."[71] The *Denver Post* felt that the "committee needs some deodorization."[72] The *Tampa Morning Tribune* argued that "the assertion by some witnesses that leftist writers control filmland or its output is sheer nonsense." Forced to assert the obvious, the paper alleged, "Movie producers are not Communists."[73]

But even the good news was bad, for it does not augur well when the palpably observable is at issue and has to be argued. Yet this editorial opinion reflected the optimism felt by Red Hollywood as the political climate became more frigid. "I really didn't feel any fear in 1946," said Sylvia Jarrico, then married to Paul Jarrico, "so I guess I underestimated the dangers." She was not alone—then again, the initial excessive optimism then led to an overcorrection. "But I remember later on," she said, "reaching the panic stage, as I was reaching that advanced state of despair, I realized this is why people commit suicide. We (on the left) really began to love each other when things got tough. Friendships were formed from '47 on that lasted for life."[74]

Dramatic experience was the furnace in which these bonds were forged. "I don't have any statistical tables on the subject," said Ring Lardner Jr., "but I think it is safe to say that more writers have been sent to jail than members of any other normally respectable profession."[75] This was suggestive of the uphill climb encountered at Lawson's 1948 trial for contempt of Congress. Lawson himself was dumbfounded. On 21 May 1948, "I stood in a Washington courtroom," he cried, "and heard myself marked as a common criminal and sentenced to spend one year in jail. A man's experience is wounded by such an experience," particularly when he feels he has done no wrong; it was "as humiliating as the physical indignities of a term in prison." He was to feel a "deep sense of pride and responsibility" for his troubles, though it was "not pleasant to live in a cell." "But," he added rebelliously, "it is better than living with a guilty conscience."[76]

He would have plenty of time to contemplate the gravity of this high-flown view. He got a glimmer of what was to come when he was booked in a common Washington, D.C., jail. His codefendant Alvah Bessie was repulsed by it all. The "bullpen was filthy and crowded with men. . . . the paint was peeling off the walls, the open latrine in the corner stank; the men—mostly Negroes—sat on battered wooden benches around the walls, for the most part apathetic, depressed and disinclined even to ask each other, 'What you in for?'"[77]

This is where Lawson was brought on a wintry day in January 1948. The scene was a cramped, tiny courtroom of the Criminal Division of the U.S. District Court for the District of Columbia. On the bench was Judge Raymond B. Keech, a mild-mannered, scholarly-looking man who had toiled as a prosecutor for years and had a reputation for kindliness and scrupulous fairness. Alongside Lawson, dressed for the occasion in a tie with a coat and jacket, were assorted purse snatchers, check forgers, numbers racketeers, burglars, and failed bank robbers. Gone were the klieg lights, the batteries of motion picture cameras, the long rows of press tables, the shouting. Here everything was antiseptic, orderly, quiet. No voices were raised, no flashbulbs popped. The clerk broke the monotony of it all when he called Lawson's name. Flanked by his counsel, Robert Kenny of L.A. and Martin Popper of New York and Washington, Lawson—now on a fast track to oblivion—pleaded not guilty.[78] "I would rather be convicted by the cynical politicians who are appointed as judges in our courts," Lawson argued defiantly, "than be convicted before the bar of history for sharing in the betrayal of my country's honor and tradition. I would rather bear the physical indignity of imprisonment than the sacrifice of my right to think and write as I please."[79]

His chief lawyer, Ben Margolis, argued vehemently that the "alleged investigation of the motion picture industry turned out to be . . . a virtual trial of the issue as to whether or not" his clients were "members of a trade union," that is, the SWG and "members of a specified political party," that is, the Communist Party. This was improper, he said. Further, the statute authorizing HUAC was "invalid on its face" due to the "First Amendment." HUAC sought to "pressure" Hollywood to "make anti-Communist films," which was a violation of basic free speech protections. HUAC argued that "no *material of any Communists should be used*" in Hollywood "regardless of its content." HUAC also "attacked as un-American" such notions as "absolute racial and social equality," "opposition to the Franco government of Spain," and "advocacy of the dissolution of the British Empire," while "urging unity of all writers within the [SWG]" was derided as a "Communist tactic."[80]

Philip Dunne testified on behalf of the defendants and sought to show that screenwriters cannot insert propaganda into movies, but the judge continued to sustain objections to this line of questioning. Finally, the defendants' attorney made an offer of proof to the effect, adding, "After each day's shooting, the producer and director review the scenes upon the screen in a projection room and then exercise the right to change lines, motivation, scenes. . . . the finished film, before being finally scored and edited, is reviewed time and time again by the executive heads of the studio, who make such changes therein as they alone determine."[81] The judge remained obstinate.

The corridor outside the cramped courtroom was piled with prints and scripts on which Lawson worked, supposedly the "smoking guns" that would display his sneakiness in smuggling Red propaganda into movies, though the judge was startlingly incurious about their content. Ben Caplon, a short, round, red-faced man, strolled to the witness stand with film cans containing a print of *Counter-Attack* and a fat wad of scripts. Lawson's lawyer asked that this movie be screened for the jury. The prosecution objected and was sustained. Caplon carefully hauled his material out of the chamber, making two laborious trips to cart it away from the witness stand. Then Dore Schary came to testify but added little to what was already known.[82]

Margolis sought to develop a "gimmick" in the face of a legal situation that seemed hopeless. He told jurors that when his clients responded to the question of whether or not they were Reds, they "did not refuse to answer. They answered by saying that under the Constitution they were not obligated to answer and that this was the only kind of answer that was required." The problem, recalled Margolis, was that "it didn't work." The "reason it didn't work is that the judge gave instructions to the effect that the only issue [was] whether or not there had been a deliberate failure to answer," and "that an answer which explained the reason for not answering responsibly was not a defense." With such an instruction, "the only way that the jury could acquit was by going contrary to the judge." The jury "had no choice"—it "did convict." Lawson had a speedy trial; "from the time of the impaneling of the jury through the jury verdicts took two days." "It was a canned verdict," Margolis recalled. "We had decided in advance that, as a practical matter, the case was going to be decided on appeal."

One reason for this approach was that the defendants "did not have the kind of jury that would be very likely to acquit under any circumstances. In the city of Washington," where the case was tried, "it was impossible to get a jury the great majority of whom were not either themselves in the government employ or didn't have a member of their family, or very close friend, that was in the government employ." The lawyers "wanted to put in evidence that there was a tremendous amount of fear and intimidation," but they "lost on that one too." They had "little hope of winning the case in the Court of Appeals," which was "very conservative," but a "great deal of hope" in the Supreme Court; that, too, proved unavailing.[83]

Still, the lawyer and writer-activist Carey McWilliams rose to the defense of Lawson. As he saw it, there was "no effort" by HUAC "to determine the extent to which the Communist Party, its affiliates, or its members had infiltrated or controlled the management end of the industry. Nor was any such inquiry directed to the ultimate financial controls of the industry." That is, would the banks so easily allow Reds to shape their multi-million-dollar investments and loans? Further, said McWilliams, "no effort was made to show that these unions," such as the SWG, "were in a position to control the industry or to influence its policies or management." Further, "the Committee did not use content-analysis as a means of determining the stated purposes of the investigation, namely 'the extent of Communist infiltration and influence in the motion picture industry.'"[84]

For example, an authoritative study found that the Hollywood Ten received credits on a "total of 159 Hollywood films" over the period stretching from 1929 to 1949. Of these, 17.15 percent were "murder-mystery, mystery, spy, espionage"—the leading category—and 16.3 percent were "social themes," for example, prison dramas. There were "very few westerns, period pictures, horror films or musicals credited" to these writers. Unsurprisingly, the defendants were "most active in film creating during the two periods when the Communist Party line was in many respects running parallel with the general policies being followed by the United States government." If the Office of War Information were to draw up a "list of the top ten war films," "at least four" from the Hollywood Ten would be included: Lawson's *Sahara, Action in the North Atlantic, Thirty Seconds over Tokyo,* and *Pride of the Marines.*[85]

Hence, what HUAC did amounted to a bill of attainder, an unconstitutional targeting of one recognizable group—Communists. Moreover, McWilliams's analysis revealed that Lawson and his colleagues were being punished for doing too good a job at what moguls and the government alike had requested. "Almost no one wrote more passionately patriotic movies than American Communists did in wartime,"[86] said one critic—and their reward was to be prison time. It would be as if the screenwriters who wrote anti-Soviet movies were to be sent to jail in the twenty-first century for adhering to prevailing political winds in the twentieth century—for example, segments of the *Rambo* series—for hailing those who would later be denounced as Afghan terrorists. Lawson and Red Hollywood were in a vise, with the walls of misery closing in on them rapidly. For if they simply asserted their Party membership in the atmosphere then prevailing, they may have been asked to discuss meetings, "name names" of others, and place them in jeopardy too. Instead, they all fell on their swords—though they did not necessarily realize they were disemboweling themselves at the time.[87]

Lawson and company were back on their heels, in any case, in the wake of the internecine conflict that gripped the Party simultaneously. And not only Communists were splitting; liberals, under siege from the right, were yearning to break their relationship with the Reds. The 1948 presidential campaign of former secretary of agriculture—and vice president—Henry A. Wallace provided an opportunity for this rupture to be cemented. When the split occurred, the possibility vanished of united support for Lawson and his comrades.

Like the early post-1947 editorial opinion backing Lawson, it seemed at first that the Wallace campaign was an unstoppable juggernaut, destined to transform the nation. Charlotta Bass, an African American, found that "the enthusiasm for Wallace for President almost bubbled over on Central Avenue" in the heart of her neighborhood in Black L.A. In May 1948 the ruddy-faced, smiling candidate visited the City of Angels and "spoke to an enthusiastic crowd of 31,000"—a remarkable figure from any angle—"that jammed Gilmore Stadium to more than capacity."[88]

These huge crowds were evidence of the tireless organizing of the Progressive Citizens of America (PCA), which included in its Southern California leadership Bass—and Lawson.[89] The PCA's first item of business in the spring of 1947 was swinging "into action behind Henry Wallace's foreign policy," which was prematurely pro-détente.[90]

There was a de facto merger between those defending Lawson and those advocating for Wallace; the campaigns were seen as two wings of the same bird. This was exemplified when the PCA in late 1947 held a rally for Lawson and his cohorts; at this optimistic moment, this joint effort was supported by a bevy of stars, including Eddie Cantor, Henry Fonda, Ava Gardner, Van Heflin, Katharine Hepburn, and Myrna Loy.[91] This glittery alliance was to last—for a while. Burt Lancaster, Howard Duff, Arthur Miller, and

Waldo Salt—Bogart and Bacall were conspicuous in their absence—joined "over two hundred Hollywood professionals and almost as many luminaries" from "'other arts and sciences'" in an amicus defense of Lawson and his colleagues.[92]

William Wyler was again a mover and shaker behind the scenes, hosting gleaming receptions at his tastefully decorated home in Benedict Canyon for the Wallace campaign.[93] In the spring of 1948 the list of acceptances included Chaplin, Lancaster, Jules Dassin, and Thomas Mann. Tellingly, however, among those who turned down his invitation were Bogart, now in full retreat, and Lucille Ball.[94]

Soon some stars were seized with fear about the otherwise mundane. Katharine Hepburn was panic-stricken after speaking at a PCA rally, exclaiming, "I wore pink. Pink! How could I have been so dumb!"[95] A similar anxiety overtook Lauren Bacall. When she noticed belatedly that the "name of the plane" that ferried the CFA delegation to Washington was the "'Red Star,'" she worried whether it was "coincidence or design."[96]

Soon Dore Schary, the respected producer, was equally in panic mode, unveiling arguments that were to be deployed deftly against third-party challengers into the twenty-first century. "Henry Wallace cannot be elected President," he argued, "but if the Liberals get their signals crossed, he can take California out of the Democratic column. And he can put a Republican in the White House"—the "same strategy the Communists used when Hitler came to power in Germany," he added forebodingly.[97]

A truer sign emerged in the early fall of 1947 when Roger Baldwin of the ACLU was told by his Southern California affiliate "the truth is that after all these months we have said nothing that has effectively challenged the Un-Americanism of the present witch-hunt. . . . just as in the case of the Japanese evacuation orders we are thrashing around with academic questions instead of hitting an essential and recognizable wrong in a way that really counts for democracy."[98] Later, leading civil libertarians like Baldwin and Arthur Garfield Hays were, according to Baldwin, "disturbed by the recent action of the motion picture producers" in imposing a "blacklist"; "it is only a short step from this employment policy to depriving the public of that independence in the production of films which our democracy has a right to demand."[99]

12   Jailed for Ideas

The roasting encounter endured by Lawson in Washington in the fall of 1947 was a turning point for this writer, now well into his fifties. Since his romantic diversions some years back, his marriage to Sue Lawson had stabilized; yet this ordeal, combined with his "blacklisting" from Hollywood, placed added pressures on his family. She found these unfortunate occurrences "simply terrible." As with so many others compelled to undergo this vale of misery, her "stomach" was feeling "entirely ulcerated." Thus "I know," she told her spouse, "what yours must feel."[1]

Sue Lawson's response to the congressional inquisition was not unique. The actor Mary Davenport was a Communist like her husband, the screenwriter Waldo Salt, whom she had married in 1942. When the "blacklist" hit them and the Party was scattered, it was "emotionally, personally," devastating: "It was like the family that I lost. And this was a much more brilliant and meaningful family, because it was a set of values that seemed so generous. . . . Nobody other than our own dearest friends and comrades would have [anything] to do with us, nobody would speak to us. Nobody would have dinner with us. I couldn't even buy meat from the local butcher. I had to change where I bought—I would go to different supermarkets or butchers. I couldn't be seen there. My neighbors didn't want anything to do with me." Her children may have been affected even more, since the turbulence "created a need to belong, a feeling that they didn't belong."[2] They were not alone.[3]

When Sue Lawson was brought before HUAC and questioned about her "connections with the organization called the Southern California Peace Crusade," she "declined to answer," but "because of her extreme nervous condition, the Committee dismissed her without further questioning."[4] There was a brutal physical and psychological toll exerted on Red

FIGURE 9. Lawson (his photo is at the far right of the speaker, Jeanne Prior Cole, wife of the screenwriter Lester Cole) was the most notorious member of the Hollywood Ten, the "blacklisted" writers and directors. This was one of many rallies held on their behalf. (Courtesy of Southern California Library for Social Studies and Research)

Hollywood—and liberals, too, as the plight of Dore Schary suggested—that was little recognized, then or now.[5]

Red Hollywood was disintegrating; as early as 1949 the L.A. writer Carey McWilliams had detected a "great decrease of political interest and political activity in Hollywood." It was not just the congressional inquisition, either. The strike, then lockout, of production workers in the industry, had taken a severe toll. Even Lawson had not realized altogether how progressives in Hollywood were ultimately dependent on the existence of a solid corps of left-leaning production workers. Once they were wiped out, undermining the writers became virtually foreordained.

Hollywood could hardly be allowed to avoid the heightened anticommunism that was becoming de rigueur when other institutions were moving to embrace it. But the impact of Lawson and his comrades was not entirely eviscerated even after they had been ousted from the scene. For

McWilliams correctly noted that "racial tolerance is apparently the one controversial theme that may be presented from the liberal or progressive point of view," as *Pinky, Intruder in the Dust,* and a number of other films then in production or debuting exemplified.[6]

The larger point, however, was that the crackdown on Lawson and his comrades simply presaged a wider purge in Hollywood that drew into its ambit anyone to the left of conservatism. This purge took many in Hollywood by surprise, perhaps understandably, since the moguls had been hiring Reds for some time. After Lawson was dragged away from his congressional testimony, Eric Johnston, head of the industry's trade association, strolled to the witness chair.[7] He was expected to reaffirm, even in the vaguest terms, the typical feel-good rhetoric about freedom of expression and association. He did not. He was asked bluntly, "If all of the evidence which was submitted was proved to your satisfaction to be true, would you say Mr. Lawson had any place in the motion picture industry as a picture writer?" Without skipping a beat, Johnston replied just as bluntly, "If all of the evidence there is proved to be true, I would not employ Mr. Lawson because I would not employ any proven or admitted Communist because they are just a disruptive force and I don't want them around."[8]

A man of his word, Johnston carried this message to the now infamous meeting at the Waldorf-Astoria Hotel in Manhattan a few weeks later, where the "blacklist" was launched.[9] This meeting sounded the tocsin for the decline of Red Hollywood—and Lawson. But they were not alone. Right behind them on the road to decline was Liberal Hollywood, as even those who were mildly progressive[10] were compelled to backpedal, repent, and write lengthy apologies disclaiming their pasts,[11] and promising not to veer in that direction in the future.[12]

Canada Lee tried to resist. He had acted in Lawson's script written via a "front," *Cry, the Beloved Country,* filmed in newly apartheid South Africa, and then returned to Hollywood fired up by the inhumanity he had just witnessed and eager to do something about it. Walter Winchell, a columnist skilled in gossip-mongering, was informed that Lee "feels rather strongly about the USA"—and its own peculiar institutions of "race" since "being exposed to conditions in Jo'burg." Lee was outraged by the "police state" that was Johannesburg—a then radical opinion that may have contributed to his "blacklisting."[13] Walter White of the NAACP complained bitterly about the "iron curtain of suspicion and fear which was damning [Lee's] career" and "how desperate his financial situation had become"—to no avail.[14]

FIGURE 10. Members of the Hollywood Ten and supporters gather. The persecution of Red Hollywood, of which Lawson was the reigning symbol, also inflicted significant collateral damage on Liberal Hollywood.

Given the dire situation faced by the likes of Lee and Lawson, it was easy to understand why few wanted to emulate them. "Anybody who sat through the weary hours" of the Lawson trial, said the Communist writer Joseph North wearily, "had no illusions the jury would bring in any other verdict than 'guilty.'" One did not need a "crystal ball, somebody at the press-table suggested, to discover what it was all about." The jury was "permitted to hear only scattered bits and pieces of testimony in the six week long trial. If they heard six hours worth, they heard a lot. Most of the time they lounged outside the courtroom while Lawson's consul desperately argued" that the judge should allow "testimony to prove" the HUAC hearings to be a "monstrous, illegal hoax from its inception." The "proceedings," said North sadly, "shocked even the hard-boiled reporters at the press-table." Said one wag, "'It's a Hollywood inquisition without klieg lights.'"[15] One of the attorneys for the Ten realized the overwhelming problem they faced after Trumbo was convicted. "We left the courtroom," he recalled, "and as we descended the steps we spied, further down the steps, three black girls who had been jurors. We wanted to talk to them, to find out why. . . . [A]nd when they saw us coming they started to run, those girls, and [we] ran after them. It was a bizarre episode, frightening to see the fear [in] them. It was a testimonial, to them, we were devils."[16]

Still, it was remarkable that so many signed on to an appellate brief in support of Lawson and his comrades. Chaplin, Losey, Du Bois, Hellman, Hammett, Mailer, Robeson, even Schulberg, did so, noting that "motion pictures [are] a composite form in which all the free arts find expression: dance, drama, painting, sculpture, opera, pageant; the plastic and the graphic as well as the verbal and literary arts. As a complete form, the making of motion pictures has an influence on the other arts and is in turn influenced by developments in these related arts"—hence, a "blacklist" here was bound to have maximum ripple effect, not least since movies were the most popular of the arts. "Weekly world wide attendance at motion pictures is estimated at 235,000,000," while the "weekly attendance in the United States has exceeded 85,000,000." Thus, HUAC's actions were bound to have an extreme chilling effect. "The industry was severely criticized—and more important, *publicly* criticized—for having made certain motion pictures which were discussed, by name, at considerable length. . . . references, for example, were made to films depicting evil bankers and corrupt Congressmen." Combine this with the "committee's preoccupation with the role of the writer in the motion picture industry," and its idea that "the writers should [be] dismissed" was a recipe for creative gridlock in Hollywood.[17]

Who would want to run the risk of following in Lawson's footsteps? Certainly not Albert Lewin, who had been in and out of Lawson's home— and vice versa—in the 1930s but now deserted him.[18]

"One of the things I resented most in the House Committee attack on me," Lawson countered angrily "was the charge that I did or would have violated my understanding with my employers. There was never any social or economic issue in any film written by me [in] which I advanced any view that was not satisfactory to the studio that employed me and discussed honestly with the producers."[19] Lawson's concrete experience with moviemaking was contrary to the "conspiracy theories" that were used to assassinate his character. Ordinarily, he observed, "the writer discusses his task with the producer and presents his ideas at 'story conferences,'" and "at a certain stage of the story's development, the director is assigned to the project." "Close collaboration between writer and director . . . is the most fruitful method of work." "Film is not merely words," he contended, "it is a succession of photographic images, which derive their impact from their form and interrelationship as well as by the words and gestures of the performers," and "the finished motion picture is properly the result of their joint creative effort. Some of my best films were the result of such a collaboration from the start of the screenplay to the end of production—for example, I did *Blockade* with William Dieterle, and *Sahara* and *Counterattack* with Zoltan Korda."[20]

Lawson had a point. Things were not that simple. Otherwise how to explain why so many liberals suffered as a result of the "blacklist"?[21] As the witty Charles Chaplin put it, "These days if you step off the curb with your left foot they accuse you of being a Communist."[22] The ultimate loser was art and culture, as many of the most creative minds were shunned. The celebrated playwright Sean O'Casey was no liberal, being closer to Lawson on the ideological spectrum, yet he believed that Hollywood was "'not a place for a conscientious artist.'"[23] "Anyone with a first-class respect for art of any kind," he added, "would keep a helluva way from Hollywood."[24] His colleague Eugene O'Neill concurred, since it was a "fantastically impossible notion" for Hollywood to "treat a subject of depth and integrity with depth and integrity."[25] O'Casey demonstrated that he was not merely popping off when he turned down a hefty $75,000 to write a screenplay for Thomas Wolfe's *Look Homeward, Angel*.[26] He did not "revere Hollywood," as did many well-paid writers, but he recognized that, "like us all," Hollywood "must, sooner or later, change with the changing world."[27]

Perhaps so. But advocates of "blacklisting" would have disagreed heartily, along with Lawson's more hard-hearted critics. He was deluged with scurrilous mail in the aftermath of his brush with Congress. "You despicable cur," was one of the kinder descriptions.[28] A "soldier" asked Lawson, "'Where did you get that name with that nose? You should have 'ski on it,'" a scurrilous reference not to Alpine slopes but to Lawson's ethnoreligious heritage. A copy of one of his books in the L.A. Public Library was marked throughout with anti-Semitic annotations.[29] Congressman Rankin "left no doubt, " replied Lawson, when "he made fun of the names of the Hollywood people who came to Washington to protest, and made an especially unpleasant reference to Melvyn Douglas." This "anti-Semitic reference was greeted with laughter and applause," while "Adrian Scott and Edward Dmytryk" were "called to Washington solely because they had made *Crossfire*," a classic attack on anti-Semitism.[30]

"Louzinski, you are a bright looking 'kike' parading as an American," countered one less than admiring writer to Lawson. "Your face, nose, ears and eyes give you away as to what your race is. A shame and a disgrace to the boys who gave their lives to salvage your kin over the sea." Lawson, said another detractor, was "the rat of Russia, a Jew"—and a "louse" besides. Lawson and his comrades' class betrayal was also a note frequently sounded. One cartoon featured the "Hollywood proletariat," in the form of a man with a large, protruding nose, large glasses, and unkempt hair dining with a starlet; a waiter passes by carrying a steaming tray of food, and in the background are starving masses in rags carrying "cabbage soup" and "black bread." The caption reads: "Maybe some of you Hollywood Red squirts want to trade places with us?"[31]

It is difficult to separate a troubling rise of anti-Semitism in the postwar era from the crackdown on Jewish writers like Lawson,[32] who were represented disproportionately in the Hollywood Ten.[33] The scholar Andrea Most is not alone in suggesting that "much of the anti-Communist activity of the early Cold War years was tinged with anti-Semitism."[34] When Lawson's tormentor state senator Tenney, accepted the 1952 vice presidential nomination of the Christian Nationalist Party on a ticket with the rabidly anti-Jewish Gerald L. K. Smith and then began to "publish attacks upon Jewish organizations," this cemented some of Lawson's worst fears about the ties between bigotry and the coarsest anticommunism.[35]

Since Lawson was on the fast track to a tiny, cramped, and dank prison cell, his fate seemed decidedly undesirable. Knowing that the door of doom was about to snap shut behind him, and well aware that his most fecund period of script writing was in his past, Lawson turned abruptly toward the writing of history. Interviewed in the summer of 1948 in the offices of one of his publishers, Boni and Gaer, he appeared to be gushing with enthusiasm for a man who was now a convicted criminal. But it was the subject that was animating him, his latest project, a sweeping cultural history, published as *The Hidden Heritage.* He had begun research a decade earlier, but now, given his sharply altered circumstances, found himself with more time to complete it. The reporter found his "manner" to be "warm and friendly, his speech sure." As had many others, his interlocutor was struck by Lawson's disregard of sartorial flair: "His coat was about a sixth cousin to his trousers and both looked as though they could use a pressing"— "apparently clothes mean[t] little," it was thought, to the "fairly short, about five feet seven," Lawson, who was "very broad, especially across the chest and shoulders." But Lawson was not interested in discussing fashion or appearance; he was consumed with his current research, which provided comfort for him as he grappled with his own plight. "'Calling people whom one doesn't like foreign agents is such an old story,'" he sighed. "'It was used at the end of the 18th century against the Jeffersonian movement.'"[36]

The manuscript, which incorporated this and other themes, was completed under the duress of an awaiting jail cell. A war in Korea loomed that was to accelerate already existing anticommunist trends. It was a "curious sensation," said Lawson, "to work with feverish concentration on the revision" of this book "with the knowledge that I cannot read the proofs or perform the usual tasks connected with publication. I have thought of Roger Williams and his denunciation of 'the bloody tenet of persecution for cause of conscience.'" He hoped that "if some voices are temporarily silenced, others must speak more boldly and clearly."[37]

It was not just his forced separation from screenwriting that drove him to the writing of history. He also was concerned about what he saw as a widespread cultural ignorance. As early as 1941 he remarked, "There is no field which has been so neglected as the theater. I recently urged a young playwright to study the origins of American drama. 'I'm sure there's nothing worth studying before O'Neill,' he replied, 'because if there were I should have heard of it.'"[38] Such replies led to the writing of *The Hidden Heritage*.

The manuscript was completed under adverse conditions. On "entering prison in June 1950," he recounted, "I left the manuscript with Dr. Philip Foner. I was not permitted to correspond with him." Thus, "editorial decisions" were made "without consulting" the author. Racism was a major theme of this text illuminated by Lawson. It is "built into the structure; our culture is not accidentally or occasionally racist; prejudice against the Negro is part of an overall pattern of myth and misrepresentation." He continued, "The essential characteristic of the first decades of slavery is the intensity of the struggle initiated by the Negroes. It was a far more unequal struggle than that introduced by the Indians; since the slave was a commodity, wholly owned by his master, it involved a more irreconcilable clash of interests and more intimate relationships of persons and property."[39]

Doxey Wilkerson—then a leading Black Communist—termed this book a "mature and careful work of Marxist scholarship" that was "comprehensive in scope" and "theoretically sound." It was "only an able Marxist" like Lawson who "could have written—or even conceived—this book." Wilkerson was notably "impressed" with the "substantial and continuing attention given to the woman question; with the major emphasis on the Negro question; with the primary force throughout on the struggles of the peoples of many lands against oppression."[40] Others were not as enthusiastic.[41]

The message of his book was also reflected in the unyielding, unapologetic message Lawson took to the streets as the cause of the Hollywood Ten became a cause célèbre of the domestic and global left during the early cold war. The beaming Red journalist Joseph North chortled that "the 'Hollywood 10' has become a household phrase displacing the Lion of [MGM] as the symbol of the American movie industry."[42] But as evidenced by the retreat of progressives such as John Houseman and John Huston, fewer and fewer ears were willing to listen to what Lawson was saying. Typical was a late 1947 rally in Philadelphia to protest against HUAC. There "in the shadow of Independence Hall" there were fiery speeches—"punctuated by scuffling, booing, stench bombs and shouts of 'send them back to Russia.' More than 30 policemen paraded through the milling throng of 2000 gathered to cheer and heckle" Lawson's allies in the Progressive Citizens of America. The latter had arranged for Lawson and company to come to the City of Brotherly Love, where they were compelled to experience a modicum of hate.[43]

This rally was part of a national tour that burned the cause of the Hollywood Ten into the annals of cultural and political history. At Harvard law school, the FBI captured Lawson's words, including his "two hour speech before" the left-leaning Lawyers Guild chapter; his "presence had created a considerable 'fuss'" as the "chairman of the Guild had resigned rather than preside at a meeting addressed by him." Nevertheless, it was noted that "the students had voted overwhelmingly to hear Lawson."[44] A similar rapturous welcome greeted him at another local college in the Bay State.[45] With African American publisher Carlton Goodlett and folksinger Josh White, he spoke in Berkeley decrying the "fascist" HUAC.[46] In Oregon he told the 150 assembled that HUAC was "trying to steal the torch from the Statue of Liberty to light the fire of a new war."[47] More than eight hundred people heard his words at Seattle's "New Field Artillery Armory."[48]

As time passed, Lawson expanded his critique to encompass the entire apparatus of the cold war. Early on he joined the nascent "ban-the-bomb" movement. He was a sponsor of a massive peace congress in Paris in the spring of 1949 and addressed a similar meeting at the Waldorf, where months earlier the "blacklist" was ratified. There he marked the decline of U.S. cinema from that moment, lamenting the rise of "the present cult of sex and violence."[49]

As if facing down hostile mobs were not enough, Lawson and his codefendants also had to contend with contradictions among themselves. Though yoked together as avatars of a supposed "monolithic communism," the Hollywood Ten quarreled and wrangled incessantly.

Apparently, their lawyers had given them confidence that the approach they had taken in the hearings would be vindicated by the U.S. Supreme

Court. The problem was that in the interregnum, the composition of the court, as it tends to do, changed, bringing on less forgiving judges. In a typically verbose riposte—forty-one pages in all, two decades after being convicted—Trumbo curtly informed Albert Maltz that "there were some among" the Ten "who were positive they would *not* be blacklisted; and a very substantial body of informed and sophisticated legal opinion throughout the country that they would *not* go to jail."[50] Maltz was apoplectic about his comrade's opinion.[51]

Actually, such vitriolic exchanges were par for the course for these Red writers. Though they were thought to be part of a tightly bound and colossal conspiracy, rarely has the planet seen such a bunch of contentious, contrary naysayers. Lester Cole, no fervent admirer of Lawson, also recognized that "Trumbo disliked me—I didn't feed his insatiable ego."[52] Trumbo and Cole actually were at odds over many things, not least since the latter "once threw us out of his house for having the good taste to admire his wife."[53] Brecht, the German émigré, had a "lasting quarrel with John Howard Lawson."[54] He "resented Lawson's ideology and aesthetics," terming his writings on playwriting "'reactionary stuff.'" He was not that fond of Maltz's ideas either.[55] There was no love lost between Lester Cole and Maltz.[56] To Alvah Bessie, Cole was a "no-talent sourpuss. . . . we do not speak to each other if we can help it."[57] Edward Dmytryk quickly emerged as the object of discontent of many of his codefendants after he became the first to become an apostate.[58] Maltz deemed him either a "perjurer" or "self-confessedly . . . a citizen without principle, honor or sense of public duty," not to mention a "scoundrel" and a "commodity for hire."[59] And Maltz and Trumbo often were at odds, as their exchange over legal strategy demonstrated.[60]

Maltz's recollection of the legal situation differed from Trumbo's. Lawson, as noted earlier, did not answer directly the query about his Party membership, instead launching into an interrupted soliloquy about the nature of civic participation. The Ten, according to Maltz, stood on the First Amendment, their right to freedom of association and speech. Sure, there was a meeting where it was "suggested that we consider the possibility of taking *both* the First and Fifth Amendments. When we asked whether this would result in our getting the Committee into the courts, he told us it would not. Thereupon all of us rejected the idea. We had decided to destroy the Committee if we could, and we would not retreat." That is, their approach was designed to create a legal dispute based on the First Amendment that the high court could resolve by ruling that HUAC was unconstitutional. No, replied Trumbo. "I carefully refrained from even mentioning the First Amendment in my testimony and so did you and so did all but one of the other ten witnesses."[61]

That otherwise intelligent men could not agree on the nature of their legal strategy—albeit two decades after the fact—is indicative of the tumult that encased the Hollywood Ten at the time. "Immaculate recollection is as impossible to achieve as immaculate conception," quipped Charles Katz, one of the Ten's attorneys. "Man recalls history—as he recollects making loving—but always in his own fashion." "Who indeed can be sure?" he concluded.[62] Ben Margolis avowed that strategically there were two major considerations—keeping the men out of jail and defeating HUAC—and the First Amendment was seen as the surest route, that is, not literally stating a refusal to answer queries about Party membership, then depending on a constitutional argument in court to vindicate this approach.[63] In any event, the lawyers were confident about prevailing—until Justices Murphy, Stone, and Rutledge passed away in quick succession, altering the nature of the court. Katz concluded, "Perhaps in the tragic deaths of these three . . . tomorrow's historians may find the key to the tragedy of the Hollywood Ten."[64]

Figuratively throwing up his hands, the sardonic Alvah Bessie recalled later that the lawyers "assured us from the start that we would win the case & cited precedents as long as your arm (or mine). We went to prison, all of us."[65]

Margolis felt that "what is most important about the Hollywood Ten is that even though they lost in the courts and they all went to jail they held back the on-rush of the Committee for several years (and I think helped greatly to defeat at that time an American brand of fascism)."[66] Maybe. But the underlying story about the Ten was an ultimate lack of concord, not least about legal strategy.

It is not as if a clearer legal strategy would have made that much difference, since powerful forces were determined that having pro-Soviet writers in a position to write scripts—even those that simply radiated liberalism— was incompatible with the new political dispensation. HUAC itself, as the New York Times pointed out, was "unique in the history of Congress." It had "no legal counsel"—understandable if one understood its flouting of due process. That the unscrupulous knife fighter Richard M. Nixon was viewed widely as being the most evenhanded member of the panel—he had a "reputation for fairness to witnesses," said the paper of record—was indicative of the uphill climb faced by the defendants.[67]

What about the refusal of Lawson and his comrades to acknowledge their Party membership? Was that not disingenuous at best?[68] Maltz disagreed with many Reds about fundamental matters, yet he too agreed with Lawson's viewpoint on the matter of not testifying about one's political affiliation. "You could not declare yourself a Communist, he says, without risking your job and in some situations, your physical safety. He compares the Communists' predicament with that of the Abolitionists in the South. . . . Hollywood, adds Maltz, was even less tolerant than other communities." "'Announce it in Hollywood?'" asked Maltz rhetorically and amazingly, "'not a chance. You'd never work again.'"[69] Ring Lardner Jr. took a slightly different tack. "I didn't consider my political beliefs anything to hide; [but] I objected to being made to reveal them under threat of compulsion."[70]

On the other hand, Red Hollywood may not have taken sufficiently into account how jolted Liberal Hollywood would be once Lawson and others were accused of being Communists. When Lawson was unveiled as a Red, an unidentified FBI informant reported, "They nailed Lawson. . . . [T]he town is shocked. People didn't believe that Lawson was a Communist."[71]

Still, as some would have it, Maltz was not the best spokesman to defend Communist Party membership, since he had been subjected—with Lawson playing a critical role—to one of the more fabled episodes that exemplified what some saw as the Party's perfidious approach to writers. It had all begun before the fateful congressional inquisition, though in retrospect, the "Maltz affair" lubricated the path for this event and the subsequent pillorying of the Party. Maltz had argued that a writer did not have to be progressive in order to be appreciated, citing the well-known case of the respect for the work of Balzac, a feudalist, by Marx and Engels. As the then Communist writer Walter Bernstein recalled, this was "criticizing the concept of 'art as a weapon'" and was akin to "heresy." "He might as well have attacked Stalin. The Party fell on him like the wolf on the [flock]," and instead of gearing up to meet the challenge from the right, the Party was consumed otherwise.[72] The "Maltz affair"—like the earlier contretemps over Schulberg's novel—was essential in the construction of Communists and Lawson most notably as crushers of civil liberties, which obscured the real point of how the Red Scare was doing precisely that.[73]

What befell Maltz, in short, was not terribly unique. It was part of a contentious culture in the Party that coexisted oddly with the popular idea that members were mindless automatons.[74] Alice McGrath, married to the Communist writer Tom McGrath, had a similar dispute with Lawson, for he "criticized Tom for not being a truly proletarian or revolutionary poet." Yet when the now elderly screenwriter was "asked what were his specific criticisms, he kind of mumbled about it, and [said that] it didn't follow the

Party line." "But," she added bitterly, "they couldn't articulate what the Party line was because there really wasn't any Party line."[75] The screenwriter John Bright also was the target of Lawson's wrath in an incident not unlike Maltz's. As with the Maltz episode, an "incident of censorship that was arbitrary" was laid at the door of Lawson. "I was offered [Norman] Mailer's novel, 'The Naked and the Dead,' for review," evidently by *Masses & Mainstream*, the "Party-controlled monthly." Bright "wrote a review praising the book," with a qualifier—but "the key paragraph of qualification was taken out arbitrarily, because it was pessimistic and a prediction of McCarthyism," and this occurred "without consulting me at all." So when Maltz came under fire, Bright "was on the side of Maltz" and was disappointed when Maltz "recanted," since "his capitulation to the Party was a little short of disgraceful."[76]

Lawson was not on the side of Maltz. In fact, according to some, he was leading the charge against him, burnishing his reputation as the Party's ideological enforcer. Maltz's argument, said Lawson, was "an extreme example of the tendency to deal with art (and the desires and illusions of the artist) subjectively, without reference to the external events and forces." He accused Maltz of paraphrasing Engels "inaccurately."[77]

Strikingly, outsiders seemed to be more upset with the treatment of Maltz than the able screenwriter himself.[78] Given an opportunity to take a potshot at Lawson years after the controversy, when he had repudiated some of his previous political associations, Maltz demurred.[79]

The Party, in any case, welcomed Maltz back to the fold after his apologia for his presumed misfeasance; the occasion was a rally in L.A. featuring remarks by Lawson and Trumbo, among others. Maltz himself did not feel his apologia was an error, though liberals—most effectively Arthur M. Schlesinger Jr.—passionately argued otherwise, characterizing the dispute as an example of "Stalinism's" impact on the arts.[80]

Others were equally ungenerous. That list decidedly included the director Edward Dmytryk, the member of the Ten who strayed farthest to the right after their tribulations. Lawson, he told HUAC, was "the 'high lama' of the Communist Party at that time." He "settled all questions. If there was a switch in the Party line, he explained it. If there were any decisions to be made, they went to John Howard Lawson. If there was any conflict within the Communist Party, he was the one who settled it." Thus, after the incident with Maltz, as Dmytryk recalled, "Adrian Scott was also concerned and he thought we should have a meeting with John Howard Lawson." They had a luncheon with him at the "Gotham Café in Hollywood. It was a very unsatisfactory meeting. [Lawson] was very uncommunicative; he would not explain his actions, would give no reason for them. He said we obviously showed we could not accept party discipline." After that, the alienated director "never attended any other meeting" of the Party.[81]

According to the FBI, Lawson had raised probing questions about the Scott-Dmytryk film *Cornered*, and—said the agency—the Party sought to "force" the moviemakers to "alter a film already produced to make it conform to the Party line."[82] The result, though, said the FBI, "was that the film *Cornered* remained as [written] and filmed at that time."[83]

Dmytryk termed Lawson the "Gauleiter of the Hollywood section of the Communist Party" and suggested that this nickname was no more appropriate than when it came to *Cornered*. The conversation with Lawson was "cold, unpleasant and unsatisfactory." Lawson was "unfriendly and uncommunicative. . . . his final words were: 'for the time being consider yourselves out of the Party. When you decide you can accept Party discipline, we'll explore the situation further.' Wearing his usual mirthless smile, he left us." Later Dmytryk charged that Lawson had upbraided Robert Rossen, who "had just written, produced and directed *All the King's Men*, the acclaimed Oscar winner of 1950. And he was being called on the carpet by [Lawson]. *Censure* is too flabby a word. Rossen's *excoriation* took place during a meeting of the Ten at Maltz's home. Thoroughly bewildered, he was, for the better part of the evening pilloried by Lawson and those two acid-tongued specialists in the Party's disciplinary procedures, Biberman and Bessie." "I was dumbfounded," claimed Dmytryk. "It was *Cornered* all over again." Rossen was "really getting hell for exposing the evils of dictatorship, the rock on which the Communist Party was founded." Enraged, Rossen shouted, "'Stick the whole Party up your ass!'" and stormed out. "And out of the Party."[84] Lawson had a sharply different view of this encounter, scoffing that "Dmytryk claimed that discussions with fellow-craftsmen were an attempt to 'intimidate' him."[85]

Yet there were too many witnesses coming forward to dismiss out of hand their testimony. This list included Lawson's former protégé Clifford Odets, who rebuked his former mentor before HUAC.[86] Howard Fast, the prolific Red novelist who wrote the book on which the popular film *Spartacus* was based, expressed "unhappiness" about Lawson's critique of his book.[87]

Fast was not off the mark.[88] Lawson acknowledged his tendency to be brusque and overly blunt. He also seemed to think that the ability of confident writers like himself and Trumbo to absorb criticism—at times welcome it—was universal among creative writers, who in fact were often notoriously sensitive. This was not the ideal approach for a leader in the creative community. Yet it is hard to dismiss Lawson's subsequent recollection in 1973, toward the end of his life, that "there was a minimum of interference with members of the Communist Party, and a great deal of emphasis on creative *problems* rather than solutions. The Maltz discussion in my opinion has been totally misunderstood because it has been regarded as a dispute about freedom of expression solely, whereas what was involved was the whole question of artistic integrity. I was concerned with a deeper understanding of the nature of the artistic experience."[89] In sum, the "Maltz affair" and similar incidents probably said more about Lawson's personality than they did about Party praxis—though, inevitably, it was the reputation of both that suffered grievously as a result.[90]

Still, despite being ostracized at home, Lawson and the Hollywood Ten fared appreciably better abroad[91]—and ultimately this global pressure was to prove important in helping to erode the "blacklist," especially after Hollywood grew increasingly dependent on foreign markets as its product, now bleached ideologically, gained fewer and fewer adherents. One Londoner told Adrian Scott that it was a "hilarious joke that your country—which is the first to publicize an alleged lack of freedom of expression among artists in the Soviet Union—should so humiliate themselves in the eyes of the world."[92]

Closer to home, the playwright Arthur Miller proposed to the director William Wyler that a full-page advertisement be taken in the leading New York newspapers to protest what had befallen his fellow artists.[93] Apparently Albert Einstein "had agreed to be on a [radio] hookup" for the Ten, and Thomas "Mann had made a recording for it;" it was "suggested" that the defense committee "get Lena Horne and Al Capp *in addition* to Einstein and Mann" for this effort.[94] Though Pearl Buck[95] and Oscar Hammerstein II[96] could not find the time to lend support, Gladys MacDonald of the Association for the Study of Negro Life and History considered the "invitation to be an honor." "His fight [is] the fight of all of us, but as a Negro," she maintained, "I feel and have felt for a long time the need and the deep appreciation for all of the John Lawsons everywhere."[97] A black pastor from L.A., the Reverend Fred Mitchell, agreed. The Ten were persecuted, he thought, "for the purpose of striking terror into the hearts of the Negro people" and their supporters—by the likes of Congressman Rankin—"so that they will not fight for their rights." Capturing his impassioned words, the FBI reported that "he pointed out" that the Ten "were similarly prosecuted to frighten other people," notably those who sought to reform Hollywood a "Jim Crow town, the worst in America."[98]

Mitchell and MacDonald reflected a support among African Americans who found it hard to forget that Lawson was one of the few screenwriters who portrayed them fairly—and now he was under siege, not coincidentally perhaps. And as the United States was compelled to retreat from the anti–civil libertarian Jim Crow, the enhanced power and influence of Negroes improved the atmosphere for civil liberties generally to the benefit of the Ten. This was a note frequently sounded by the defendants,[99] as well as by their supporters.[100] And this was so for good reason: one report claimed that "less than .001 percent of 15,000 weekly film workers in Hollywood are Negro employees. Almost all of them are employed in menial or janitorial positions. There are more Negro women judges in America," it was stated with amazement, "in proportion to the white population, than there are Negroes working in films!"[101] This was a "blacklist" perhaps more thoroughgoing than what Reds were enduring.

Still, there was an obvious downside to aligning with Lawson that only the brave—or foolhardy—could ignore. When a "three inch thick" stack of letters backing the Hollywood Ten was "left at the Northwest gate" of the White House shortly after Lawson had been jailed, "they were turned over to the Secret Service for analysis of the names"—with the distinct possibility of signatories winding up on a "blacklist" all their own.[102] This was one of many setbacks endured by the Ten.[103]

Thus, when Lawson trooped off to prison in Ashland, Kentucky, neither his morale nor that of his comrades was very high. He had been convicted for contempt of Congress, having been "found guilty on one count of refusing to answer the question, 'Are you now or have you ever been a member of the Communist Party.'" He received a one-year term and a $1,000 fine.[104]

The night Lawson and Trumbo left New York for Washington—and prison—they arrived at the train station in Manhattan and were greeted by a bevy of supporters. The line of backers extended as far as the eye could see—and beyond. Paul Robeson had led a thousand people from a peace meeting to join those already waiting to say good-bye, and their cheers echoed throughout the vast building. Two young men hoisted Lawson and Trumbo to their shoulders and carried them into the crowd, where their voices were carried by portable loudspeakers. Lawson's voice was virtually drowned out by the announcements of all the stops the train would make once it got under way. Taking this cue like a trained performer, Lawson announced defiantly, "'Our voices will not be silenced,'"[105] and the estimated two thousand present cheered in response.[106]

FIGURE 11. Lawson and his comrade and fellow celebrated screenwriter Dalton Trumbo are cheered by supporters at the train station in Manhattan in 1950 as they are about to depart for prison. (Courtesy of Library of Congress)

Years later, Lawson's memory of this incident had not dimmed. "A great shout went up," he recalled of his "most vivid memory of Paul," when the actor-activist "moved through the dense crowd, striding tall above the heads. He spoke there and a small group of us retired to some corner in the station for a last affectionate conversation."[107]

This defiance notwithstanding, incarceration proved to be dismal. After Lawson arrived in the nation's capital, he was led in handcuffs through the crowd, then taken temporarily to a local jail. His son Jeffrey came to visit. Lawson's son "rang the bell and a paunchy stereotype of a jailer appeared" and "entered a medicinal waiting room with a set of metal benches." He talked to his father through a telephone. It was late June 1950 and sweltering hot, so beads of sweat rolled down both of their faces as they talked, sweat that could be easily and understandably mistaken for tears. The "other prisoners were very friendly," said Lawson, "and seemed to understand very well the significance of his kind of jailing."[108] The guards went through Lawson's belongings "with a fine comb to make sure that he was not taking" to his cell "'subversive' literature. They deprived him of a large tin of toothpaste because they feared that it might be used as a hiding place for written material. They even took the built-up shoe that he wears on his lame leg completely apart, examining every bit of it for secret compartments and hidden literature."[109]

Later Lawson was placed in a cramped compartment on a train to Kentucky. Four armed deputies accompanied him, confirming how dangerous this elderly, out-of-shape man with fading vision was considered. They surrounded him, one occupying the compartment to his right, one to his left, while the remaining two put him in an upper berth where they shackled his ankles. Taken to prison, he was stripped and examined in every orifice, then photographed, numbered, clothed in prison garb, quarantined, and finally, thirty days later, assigned to a cot, adjacent to Trumbo.

The men in this prison were mainly from the South—for example, bank tellers who had been unable to support families on salaries of $200 a month and, thus, succumbed to temptation. Every night while Lawson was in prison his cot was surrounded by his fellow inmates. They felt in him, according to Trumbo, a sympathy that compelled them endlessly to tell of their troubles, themselves, their families, and their hopes. Lawson would write letters for prisoners and read letters they had received. As Trumbo recalled it, in composing these letters, Lawson transformed mundane news from prison "into a full page of simple and interesting news." He was "an artist and he was using his art in behalf of [inmates]," and "by his art he had changed a broken, humiliated convict into a youthful lover; he had transformed a tired, toothless, middle-aged mother of seven into a youthful bride, beautiful forever in the eyes of her beloved."[110]

Lawson followed an "artificial routine . . . hermetically sealed off from the outside world. You read the newspapers, you hear the frantic voices of radio commentators; but the lack of contact or participation is so complete that the sound and fury seem muted, imminent and yet unreal: you are like a fish in an aquarium looking at the stir and movement of dim figures in the world of air and light beyond the sealed glass." The "time behind bars," Lawson said forlornly, "is like suspended animation, a trance, a temporary death."[111] His codefendant Herbert Biberman felt similarly,[112] though he was "knocked off [his] feet" when he was given a shorter sentence than Lawson—six months versus a year. He "literally was so shocked-and-embarrassed" that he "had to grab tight hold of a chair in order not to fall." This was early evidence for something that became clearer as the "blacklist" unfolded—Lawson was to be punished more heavily than others, perhaps as a reflection of his role as Party leader and his reputation for being the "hardest of the hard-liners."[113] Lawson's cellmate, Trumbo, was of a different though parallel view.[114]

Lawson was as guilty as his codefendants in seeking to use incarceration as an extended study period. "I ought to be glad to be getting such a large amount of relaxation here," he said two months into his jailing, "but, oddly enough, I manage to keep busy and never seem to have time to get everything done." Lawson was "occupied with all the reading material [he could] handle. We now get a regular avalanche of reading matter, newspapers and magazines."[115] Unfortunately, the poor lighting in his cell, combined with his excessive reading, worsened his already deteriorating eyesight.[116] His now strained vision was also used to view the movies that were exhibited behind bars. *Rachel and the Stranger* was "atrociously bad, morally and artistically."[117] He had a viscerally hostile reaction to *White Heat*.[118]

Though Lawson was "profoundly optimistic about the future," he ruefully conceded that his being behind bars was a "fantastic low comedy situation." Now he had to be more sensitive to financial matters, advising his wife hopefully that "there is likely to be a big jump in real estate," which could aid their diminishing fortunes. "I am told," he also said, again optimistically, that "our old cars are becoming valuable again."[119] He had bonds stashed away "valued at $7000. . . . when cashed, they are really worth maybe $5000" that could be used in a pinch. He had a "signed will, giving everything to you, for you and kids," he told Sue, "except a small amount for Alan," his son by his first marriage. He had $1,000 in various accounts, and "the life insurance amounts to $30,000."[120] Thus, unlike many of his fellow prisoners, his family was not on the verge of starvation.

His lawyers counseled "extreme circumspection in letter-writing" to the point where his spouse was advised to "write direct to Jack."[121] She decided to do so but soon found that some of her letters—which were opened and read by the authorities—were returned to her as being improper.[122]

The left-wing writer and documentary filmmaker Carl Marzani, who was also a Williams graduate, also did a stint in federal prison. His experience, not surprisingly, mirrors Lawson's. "In jail," he remarked, "one builds time. Building time is an art, a ceaseless process of prudent socializing and wary introspection—like one's sense of political freedom or personal integrity. It is the result of many small acts, harmonized. A certain degree of channeled routine helps, making for 'easy time'; but be careful: if the routine becomes monotonous it's 'bad time,' leading to 'stir trouble'—that is, melancholia, depression and despair. Sleeping is 'building time,' the best there is." There was a deadening routine: the "whistle blows at six, you get up. Whistle blows at seven, you go to breakfast. Whistle blows at eight, you go to work. Once at work there is no moving around without a pass. Whistles at eleven-thirty, knock off work; whistles at twelve, lunch; whistles at one, work; and so on."[123]

Ironically, J. Parnell Thomas, the man chiefly responsible for placing Lawson behind bars, also wound up jailed—in the company of Lester Cole and Ring Lardner Jr.—in Danbury, Connecticut, because of various peculations, though this was hardly redeeming for the Ten.[124] It was "very mean to put you in jail," said the future scholar Laura Foner, then a child, to "Dear Jack Lawson." "I hope you get out soon," she added hopefully.[125] He did, soon enough, but that did not end his travails.

13   "Blacklisted"

Rain was pouring down relentlessly at one minute after midnight on 9 April 1951, as John Howard Lawson ambled to an automobile that was to whisk him away from his home of recent months—federal prison in Ashland, Kentucky. But he "hardly knew" he was being drenched, so ecstatic was he about leaving.[1]

Lawson's fellow left-winger and Williams alumnus, Carl Marzani, captured what this veteran screenwriter may have been feeling as he embraced lustily a new birth of freedom. "A man out of prison," he says, "feels like a convalescent out of doors after a long illness. Sensations are heightened; the very air feels different. Prison air is brackish, tinged with yellow stone and black iron bars, laden with overtones of jangling key rings and arbitrary boss voices. It is a heavy ozone. The outside air," he enthused expansively, "stretched illimitable, scrubbed by winds from the Hudson Bay and the Gulf of Mexico, from Aden, Suez, Spitzbergen and Kamchatka, from Cape Hatteras and Luang Prabang."[2]

But this freedom had a price. As a result of the Waldorf meeting of moguls in late 1947, hard on the heels of Lawson's tumultuous testimony in Washington, he and virtually all of Red Hollywood were now "blacklisted," barred from the industry they had helped to construct. Unlike a director, such as Edward Dmytryk—and this may shed light on why he was one of the few of the Ten to renounce totally his previous beliefs—Lawson as a writer could continue trying to ply his trade, albeit being paid considerably less, hiding his light under a bushel of a "front."[3]

Still, Lawson entered the netherworld of the "blacklist," where credit could not be taken, though responsibility had to be shared, an experience he endured with perhaps his most powerful film, one that created a genre—the antiapartheid drama *Cry, the Beloved Country*, based on the novel by

FIGURE 12. Carrying placard, John Howard Lawson protests his "blacklisting." (Courtesy of Southern Illinois University)

South African writer Alan Paton. Filmed on location in South Africa, it exposed audiences to the grimiest of ghettos, which made Harlem and Watts pale in comparison. It featured a narrative device familiar to Lawson's movies—a voice-over narration that allowed for clearer explication for the audience's sake and a more cogent flow to the narrative. A critical scene occurs as a train—another Lawson favorite—rattles through a barren moonscape as African workers explain in simple though profound terms the process of gold mining and its value to capitalism. Religion is portrayed positively—another Lawson staple, and ironic given that one strains to find similar positive portrayals of socialism in his movies, the "offense" for which he was pilloried—and a cleric, an admirable figure, is a leading character. But these elements are accompanied by a devastating portrait of apartheid and the slum conditions that were its handmaiden. Moreover, the church is critiqued for its weakness in dealing with temporal realities, though the movie is replete with liberal and Christian pieties.[4]

The heart of the plot concerns a young African leaving the countryside for the ugliness of the city and his brutal encounter with a white liberal. It is more compelling dramatically than the second version of this classic, produced as apartheid was crumbling—which is a compliment to Lawson's skills as a dramatist in that the later screenwriter obviously had more to draw from in sketching his plot and limning his characters. It is a film that made the reputation of one black actor—Sidney Poitier—as it destabilized another: Canada Lee.

"I wrote the screenplay anonymously for my old friend, Zoltan Korda," said Lawson. "Paton came to Hollywood and we discussed it in great detail." His "final payment"—a hefty $12,500—arrived in April 1951, a handsome gift that greeted him as he walked out of prison.[5] This was audacious, for an angry controversy would have erupted if it had been known that a "hard-line" Red had written this movie. Lawson's agent, George Willner, told Sue Lawson in early 1951 that "the picture turned out great" and "there should be some monies coming thru" soon. But "naturally," he warned, Lawson "is more frightened today than ever before and has urged extreme caution so no one should be told about your visit to him or about my conversations either."[6]

The apartheid rulers—whose hatred of communism was exceeded only by their disgust at the idea of racial equality—little knew as they swept into the gala premiere in South Africa that the film they were celebrating was written by a Red jailbird. Alan Paton was there to accept the praise heaped on the film, which was not viewed as threatening to the existing order; "side by side" with him and his wife was "the Prime Minister, Dr. Malan, a principal engineer of apartheid," and a man with a fond fascination with fascism. "There was not a single black person to be seen, not even an actor from the film." In the United States the film "received very poor distribution," perhaps because the geniuses that controlled Hollywood undermined the fact that the movie was based on a popular novel by "changing the name of the film to the inappropriate 'African Fury,'" a maneuver that "infuriated Korda."[7]

Despite the snafus, the film received admiring reviews. The progressive *Daily Compass* called it a "movie of enormous dramatic stature and human fervor."[8] The famously anticommunist *New York World Telegram* called it "passionately eloquent"[9]—though it is doubtful if such praise would have been forthcoming if the critic knew who actually wrote the movie, exposing the abject fraudulence of the "blacklist." The influential Bosley Crowther of the *New York Times* was effusive, calling it a "motion picture of comparable beauty and power" to the novel.[10] The *New York Daily News* said the film was "powerful" and "dramatic."[11] The *New York Journal American* termed it a "document of powerful realism."[12] However, the *New York*

FIGURE 13. *Cry, the Beloved Country,* which Lawson wrote with a front, was one of the first movies to address South African apartheid. It also brought Sidney Poitier to the attention of a wider audience. (Courtesy of the Academy of Motion Picture Arts and Sciences)

Herald Tribune had reservations.[13] Across the Atlantic in South Africa, the *Sunday Tribune* acknowledged that "few could have failed to be moved by the utter poignancy of the story of Kumalo's search for his son and its tragic end."[14]

Lawson may have been barred officially from filmdom, but he remained a vocal and active presence in cinema, not least in commenting on Hollywood trends.[15] At the epochal peace conference at the Waldorf in 1949, he took off in a direction contrary to those who had postulated the "blacklist" months earlier at the same site. "The quality of American films has declined during the past two years," he moaned.[16] Yet Lawson sought to take a balanced view toward movies, even hailing *Intolerance* by the repellent D. W. Griffith—he of *Birth of a Nation* infamy—since "it establishes all the essential elements of the form" in cinema. He deemed *The Informer* "the greatest work of this period" and *Grapes of Wrath* "the great film of this period." *All Quiet on the Western Front* "touches greatness," he thought, whereas *Stagecoach* was "greatly overrated." Sadly, he could not "think of any really outstanding American film which probes a woman's psychology," dismissing his own *Smash-Up*. Though *Scarface* and *Little Caesar* were acclaimed, Lawson thought that they "would seem pretty silly on the printed page." He also bemoaned "the lack of comedy," despite the "marvelous antics of the Marx Brothers"; the "great comedy films, with the exception of Chaplin would probably not read too well" either.[17]

Lawson also was self-critical, understandable for a man who had fallen so precipitously from the heights of Hollywood. Thus, he found his previous analyses of the "study of the American film and the issues arising out of [HUAC's] attack fail to recognize the class forces that have controlled American production from its small beginnings to its present world influence." He had insufficiently examined "the film and all forms of art and communication as class weapons, serving a specific purpose in the cultural superstructure of capitalism."[18]

It seemed that the stiffer resistance became to lifting the "blacklist" against him, the more time he found to comment—often acerbically, as if he were exerting revenge on the industry that had rejected him—on movies and imaginary casting decisions. He had studied acting and, according to the actor Lee J. Cobb, had little good to say about the renowned Stanislavski method.[19] He was similarly unimpressed with the Schulberg–Elia Kazan collaboration, *On the Waterfront*.[20] After he left prison, Lawson continued to denounce *White Heat* in similar terms.[21] Lawson's bitterness perhaps reflected the fact that he no longer could write films under his own name, effectively barred, shut out, cast into the wilderness.[22]

It was a time of terror for Red Hollywood, a reversal of the applause it once enjoyed.[23] Those who formulated the "blacklist" were hoping that it would drive Lawson over the cliff into bankruptcy—with a resultant decline in influence—and, minimally, obscurity. Lawson was no pauper. But, he bewailed, since the tempestuous 1947 hearings, his agent, George Willner, had "made repeated efforts to sell" his client's "services to Hollywood" and had "uniformly been greeted either with outright laughter, or the comment, 'are you kidding?' or the observation 'don't you know what the score is on Lawson yet?'" Not a single offer was made to Lawson in the aftermath of the "producers' adoption of their 'blacklist' policy."[24]

Lawson refused to accept the post-1947 "blacklist" as a final judgment, however. Covertly, he sought to set up "an independent commercial film company, controlled jointly" by a colleague, Mitchell Lindemann, "and myself and backed by two different people." One of the properties they sought wound up as the critically applauded film *Inherit the Wind*.[25] Another failed project with which Lawson collaborated with the black moviemaker Carleton Moss was a script about Frederick Douglass, just as he provided a deft "critique" of the monumental independent left-wing film *Salt of the Earth,* and the "filmmakers labored mightily to strengthen the film in response."[26] Also—unfortunately—falling victim to the times was a Lawson script on the South American liberator Simon Bolívar.[27]

The FBI heard that "Lawson has consulted several times with Zoltan Korda, brother of Mr. Alexander Korda, regarding the possibility of working on a script of a picture called 'Magic Mountain' to be made in Africa."[28] This ubiquitous agency also got wind of an "extremely confidential" plan by Lawson to "work on a picture for the Montecello Film Corporation," which "planned to do a picture" involving "'Crime on the Waterfront.'"[29] Interestingly, after this, the Schulberg-Kazan film with somewhat similar subject matter was produced.

There was nothing glamorous about the "blacklist." It was profitable—to the producers, since it allowed them to hire first-rate talent at bargain basement prices. The civil lawsuit brought by the Hollywood Ten charged that studios "make undercover deals with blacklisted writers for one-tenth, or one-fiftieth of the salaries these same authors would command under fair bargaining for their work or services."[30]

Generally a "front"—or a poser who acted as if he or she had written a screenplay—was paid 10 percent of the money received for the work. "But when his name appears on the screen," said one investigative journalist, "he is likely to demand 50 percent of the next check. The blacklisted writer is in no position to refuse, since he is in danger of being exposed. However, the front also fears exposure and his head is often turned by his new-found glory. He is praised by his friends and begins to feel that he is really a writer and can make deals of his own"[31]—not unlike the Woody Allen character in the Walter Bernstein film *The Front.*

In a sense, the "blacklist" contradicted the fabled Hollywood notion that the industry was concerned only with box office, for if that were the case, would "blacklistees" have had so much difficulty in getting work? The box office was only one god to which Hollywood prayed; the other was politics, which at times, took precedence.[32]

But it was not easy to fight against—or even sue—litigants with pockets as deep as the studios and their friends in banking who were behind the "blacklist." The well-heeled attorney Thurman Arnold said that the SWG simply "could not afford to engage in a contest with the motion picture companies to see which could obtain the most cumulative evidence."[33]

Certainly the then senator—and soon to be vice president—Richard M. Nixon was not unhappy with this development. Indeed, he thought Howard Hughes deserved commendation, since he "refused to compromise" with

Reds. When a person was asked about his Communist ties, that person had "three choices": yes, no, or the Fifth Amendment—and "only if the answer [was] 'yes' would there be a chance of incrimination." Nixon thought that "if there were only one" Red in Hollywood, "that would be too many."[34]

These were questions that had to be answered not only by eminent writers and directors. HUAC had a list of "324 writers, producers, directors, actors, miscellaneous craftsmen and many wives" of the foregoing who had been tabbed as Reds and "blacklisted." Then there were those who had been "graylisted," barred "though no public charge [had] been made against them." All were subject to being extorted by those who had to be paid in order for them to be "cleared,"[35] as inevitably a profitable industry developed in response to this ban.[36]

Ring Lardner Jr. suffered "a large reduction" in his income as a "blacklistee", then had "to open a bank account under an alias," then "go to Social Security and register this name as . . . a pseudonym." Like others of his ilk, he wound up writing for television, in his case for the series *Robin Hood*, to scrape by during the fifteen-year period—from 1947 to 1962—he was banned.[37] This reduction in income was not unusual and was part of the punishment inflicted on those perceived to have been misguided politically.[38] After leaving prison, Lawson was in "desperate need of money," which led him, he commented humbly, to "write advertising copy . . . used by some company to promote a new product in the medical field. I was not well paid, and some of the money due me was never collected."[39]

The "blacklisting" process was designed to thwart the best efforts of those—like Lawson—most determined to subvert this banning method and crafted to drive those affected to the depths of despondency. Lawson, for example, craved collaboration, particularly with the director and the producer; it was such collaboration, he thought, that led to the creation of his best work. But "the writer in the black market cannot function in these accustomed ways," since "he cannot enter a studio." "I have written and sold only seven stories or screenplays in the black market," he reported in 1961, "(as well as doing a number of television scripts) and I have never been inside the doors of a studio during this time." His relationship with his front, Edward Lewis, "led to a tangle of misunderstandings and disputes," which was not unusual.[40] Then there was the flip side, where a writer could not receive the psychic benefit of congratulations for having written a celebrated film.[41]

It was not as if the FBI was resting, as Red writers scrambled to keep in business. "FBI Builds Case on Red Ghost Scribes," the headline in the *Hollywood Reporter* screamed in the spring of 1956.[42] The actor Ward Bond apparently had grown suspicious about some of the lines he was reciting and hearing and went straight to his comrades in the FBI. This put producers on notice that retribution would swiftly follow for the sin of hiring the "blacklisted." Not even Walter Wanger, who had given Lawson his first big break, would hire him now, not least since the famed producer himself was under siege. "Walter Wanger has been responsible for bringing a number of 'weird and radical people' from New York to Hollywood," reported the FBI, and if pressed for evidence it could just point at Lawson.[43] The notorious Red-baiting leader of Hollywood production workers, Roy Brewer, also pressured Wanger.[44] Backtracking furiously, fearing that his career and affluent lifestyle were at stake, the remorseful Wanger apologized for his statement in 1944 when he criticized the very idea of Communist infiltration in Hollywood.[45]

Brewer was now at the controls. Having been a central force in the ouster of the Reds, he was now on a path that would lead to his being helpful in assisting his comrade, Ronald Reagan, become the U.S. president. He was working closely with the ideologically compatible Jay Lovestone in pairing "stars" with "labor delegations" to the benefit—or detriment—of both.[46] A major goal was developing films "with anti-Commie themes," which appeared in profusion in the era of the "blacklist."[47] Soon one producer was happily informing Richard M. and Pat Nixon, "I can now release an anti-communist movie, which nobody would distribute for me while the Democrats had power."[48]

Nixon of Southern California was adroitly attentive to the local industry—witness his starring role in the 1947 HUAC hearings—and counted film criticism among his many talents. He took to the floor of Congress to praise the movie *Walk East on Beacon,* "which dramatically portrays the FBI's never ending battle against the intrigue of Soviet espionage." Graciously he introduced into the *Congressional Record* glowing reviews of this film.[49] FBI director J. Edgar Hoover congratulated him for his "remarks pertaining to our [*sic*] new picture 'Walk East on Beacon'"—he received a story credit.[50]

Where was the Screen Writers Guild when its members were being "blacklisted"? One SWG insider, Adele Buffington, worked directly with HUAC in persecuting members. It was HUAC's John Wood who was informed by her of the "time, effort and personal risks which I assumed by opening my All-Guild records to your investigators and my subsequent volunteered and complete cooperation in keeping your committee informed"; she pledged—and did not renege—"to keep you informed and up-to-date on my anti-communist fight" in the SWG.[51]

Among other things, the "blacklist" was the inevitable outcome of a left-right battle in the SWG that culminated in the defeat of the former. As noted earlier, the effort to form the guild had not gone unchallenged. Screenwriter Rupert Hughes—uncle of the better-known Howard—led the charge internally, claiming Lawson and company were "trying to build a 'Soviet' for writers." Questioning at the storm-tossed 1947 hearing focused not only on the Party but also on the guild. With the left in retreat, the SWG lost sight of the basic issue of a union as a device to defend the interests of the membership and instead leapt with both feet into the fray of the Red Scare—against the interests of a significant portion of its members. Thus, in the wake of the dispute between Jarrico and Hughes over credit for *The Las Vegas Story*, "it revised its agreement with the producers granting them the right to deny credit to writers" on the basis of Party membership. "After heated discussion at a membership meeting," this proviso "passed by a vote of 242 to 61 and," argues journalist Elizabeth Poe, "the Guild placed itself in the position of permitting political considerations to affect a union member's right to work." If, she concludes, "a union submits to McCarthyism under any guise, can it be expected to resist other pressures affecting the job security of its members"?[52]

Apparently not. The guild "sat silent" as "picket lines appeared at *David & Bathsheba* demanding" that icons of Liberal Hollywood—Gregory Peck and Phillip Dunne—be "blacklisted."[53] Yet even when screenwriters tried to engage this important matter, they encountered stiff opposition. Ray Bradbury, the author of *Fahrenheit 451*—adapted marvelously for the silver screen—and other science fiction classics was also a guild member. He recalled poignantly in 1965, "I myself have stood up on the floor of the Writers Guild on more than one occasion during the last eight or nine years and screamed my lungs out about giving the studios the right to blacklist"—but with little evident effect.[54]

For his part, Emmett Lavery, who headed the SWG as the assault began in 1947, found that before this turning point, "we had no difficulty working together as Board members"—referring to Lawson, Trumbo, and Lardner. He thought that a central aspect of the "blacklist" was a simple vendetta against the guild and its militancy, as well as "just a way of pruning away the competition," increasing the value of those writers remaining. "There never was" a majority of Reds on the board of the SWG, and unlike others in Liberal Hollywood, Lavery "never had that feeling of being used by the Party."[55]

Whatever the case, the fact is that the SWG was historically something of a left outlier politically, especially when compared with its counterparts among actors and directors. [56] So, when the writers were purged, it became easier for conservative trends to assert themselves profoundly in the other "talent" guilds. [57]

More than this, the high profile of Hollywood, the wealth it generated, its location in Southern California, and the exaggerated impact of HUAC's investigation of the industry all combined to create enormous movement toward conservatism. As more stars flocked to this placard, it created a self-perpetuating momentum toward the right that eventually came to dominate the White House and, in fact, all branches of government. Indicative was a 1951 meeting of the San Diego County Central Committee at the elite La Jolla Tennis Club, attended by 665 paid dinner guests at $100 per plate. Bill Knowland, a powerful politician, was "the principal speaker," but he had no "showmanship" and had "gone Washington"; ditto for "Goody Knight," another traditional politician who "was not in his best form either," telling "corny stories." But the actor Adolph Menjou "stole the show with the 7 minutes allotted to him—he received the most enthusiastic applause." [58] He had the dazzling star power and had been featured in the now legendary HUAC hearings that had attracted outsized attention. A new era in California, and then in national, politics had been inaugurated—movie stars transferring their fungible skills in dramatization and articulation from stage and screen to political rallies and electioneering.

"Hollywood's the only city I know," said one stupefied commentator, "where many of the energetic labor leaders are Republicans," [59] referring to George Murphy, Robert Montgomery, and—ultimately—Ronald Reagan. They became a bulwark for Nixon, who then relied on them as he was settling scores with those not so inclined. Thus the powerful Nixon was informed in 1952 that the GOP should "pay tribute to Irene Dunne, June Allyson, Dick Powell, Arlene Dahl, Barbara Stanwyck, Robert Taylor, Charlie [sic] Coburn, John Wayne, Daryl Zanuck and all those wonderful and highly respected movie stars who went on the radio and TV in yours and Ike's behalf." But Nixon—he of the elephantine memory—was also told that he should "try to remember" those like "Lauren Bacall and Humphrey Bogart," who "on radio and tv declared they were against *EVERYTHING* that Dick Nixon was for." Added ominously was the comment, "I'm not forgetting how friendly they were toward those unfriendly witnesses when they went to Washington. When you and Ike entertain stars in Washington, please omit Bacall and Bogart and Shelley Winters." [60] Humphrey Bogart was designated for special scrutiny. [61]

The pleasing winds were not blowing in Lawson's direction: the right wing had more to offer. Soon actors like James Stewart were rubbing shoulders at intimate dinners with Nixon, Leonard Firestone, and bank executives.[62] Looming above them all, Louis B. Mayer reiterated to Nixon, "Of course I sing your praises" and said he was "even prouder that we are friends."[63]

On the other hand, those performers not so inclined to swim with this tide received differing treatment. When the FBI heard that Marilyn Monroe had "drifted into the Communist orbit," it seemed extraordinary given where Hollywood itself was heading.[64] Since, however, this same FBI thought that another glamorous actress, Paulette Goddard, "was connected with the group that arranged [the] assassination [of Leon] Trotsky," its reports must be read cautiously.[65]

Still, in the eyes of certain authorities, this question of communism was inseparable from the question of Jewishness, an equation that met neatly in the person of Lawson. This, too, was intimidating, particularly to stars, a number of whom were Jewish and many of whom were notoriously insecure with famously fragile egos and notional concepts of self-worth.

Variety reported nervously that several "close associates of Communist Party members" in the United States "had become interested in establishing the 'Israeli Film Studio'" in the newly established state "with a capital[ization] of $600,000"—a report that only increased paranoia about the alleged subversive tendencies of those who happened to be Jewish.[66] As a result, intelligence agencies monitored Red Hollywood as if they were engaged in surveillance targeting Jewish Hollywood. In the crucial year of 1947, agents of the Internal Security Subcommittee of the U.S. Senate reported that there were five thousand Reds in Los Angeles County alone—probably an overestimate—but what they found striking was that the "percentage of Jewish people far outweighed that of Gentiles," just as the "percentage of women . . . outweighed that of men." Moreover, a "great many Gentile women are marrying Jewish men"—and it was "astonishing and somewhat frightening to see and feel the atmosphere of 'do or die' and 'we are the chosen few' that these people have."[67]

When a conference on "thought control" was held at the refined Beverly Hills Hotel, sponsored by the left, the Senate agent present was haughtily dismissive; it was the "same old crowd, about 95% Hollywood Jews of the 'commie' type . . . from John Howard Lawson on down."[68]

When Lawson received his L.A. farewell, the agent present was spitting mad. It was a "rabble rousing affair from start to finish," and there were "approximately 3000 in the crowd and it was SOME crowd. About 90% Hollywood Jews and that is speaking conservatively and advisedly; about 5% Negroes and the other 5% were renegard [sic] whites." While the "national anthem was being sung, many of the spew from the gutters of Hollywood did not even remove their hats. It would be impossible for many of them to sing the song because some spoke very poor English and the rest cackled like geese in Yiddish."

Inflamed virulence was directed at Lawson's son, who "read a nasty, scurrilous article that he had written" about how his father was being treated; "this boy is just as vicious as any of them," it was said, as he "verified the biological theory that 'nits will be lice.'" The agent suspected that Lester Cole was Jewish too—"where he ever got the name of 'Cole' I do not know but [I] have a hunch that is not his real name." That was not all: "After the crowd left one felt like he needed a bath, morally, mentally and physically, because after rubbing shoulders with these immigrants and sons and daughters of immigrants, you felt unclean. They seemed of another world, had different ideologies than Americans, different customs and languages. It is difficult to make people believe that the Los Angeles Communist movement is about 90% Jews."[69]

In report after report these agents focused almost maniacally on the alleged connection between Communism and Jewishness, with Lawson as the focus. "The writer," said the agent, speaking of himself, "has recently placed two undercover operators in this organization as members"—speaking of the successor to HICCASP—"so reports and literature will be forthcoming." At the meeting in question there were "80" present, with "Jewish predominating" and "about eight Negroes." "One white woman," it was deemed worthy of mention, "came with a Negro man and [they] sat together."[70]

The reasons for this obsession with Jewish Americans no doubt can be found in the depths of a cesspool, but the FBI thought that a "considerable amount of influential persons are of Jewish extraction and they will occasionally promote a person of the same race [*sic*], thus facilitating that individual's [rise] in the theater and subsequently in Hollywood."[71] In other words, there was something akin to a "Jewish cabal" that transcended ideology and class. How else to explain, it was thought, the meteoric rise of the likes of Lawson, the flaming Red?[72]

Yet this agent did capture one central reality: the attempt by the Party and Lawson after his departure from prison to revive HICCASP—now simply the ASP or the Council of Arts, Sciences and Professions—was proceeding fitfully. There were bright moments, such as the spring 1951 rally at the Embassy Auditorium in downtown L.A., which attracted a stomping, cheering crowd of fifteen hundred paying a fee of "seventy cents each." Even the agent present worried that "if they are not stopped they will continue to grow as big as they were before." And, yes, it was noted that there were about "fifty Negroes" present, "about 100 Gentiles and the rest the typical Boyle Heights and Hollywood Jewish Reds."[73]

Once Lawson returned from prison, forces on all sides expected the ASP to flourish. Thus it was in August 1951 that the organization returned to the Embassy Auditorium "to welcome back to Los Angeles" Lawson himself. This time seventeen hundred showed up—"90%" were "Jews, about 2% Negroes and the balance, the usual white trash." When Lawson "came out on the stage," the "crowd went wild, they all stood up and cheered. 'Commissar' Lawson stated he was deeply moved by this great ovation," as "he spoke in a low tone of voice for a couple of moments and seemed to be sort of overwhelmed with humility by the great ovation." Only months out of prison, Lawson—it was reported—"has been more or less of a 'psycho' and has kept in the background and manipulated the strings of the Party in speaking to small selective groups." But "the way he cut loose at this meeting you would have thought he was 'stir crazy' after being in jail for ten months. He has always in the writer's opinion had more or less of an inferiority complex. Now he seems to have a persecution complex. He was vicious, vindictive and his descriptions of the people he talked about whom he figures are his enemies, was absolutely venomous." Particularly worrisome was Lawson's vow to conduct a "concerted drive made from 'today on' on studios and television" to "insist" on the "hiring of Negroes in jobs such as writers, actors, etc."[74]

Yet the ASP's membership "has steadily decreased," the FBI reported merrily, with "only 270 members . . . currently paid up in dues." As of mid-1953, though, the group "remained the predominantly active Communist-controlled organization in the Los Angeles area." Lawson was the "dominant force in this organization," as his "comments and analyses . . . are invariably considered with considerable attention and respect." Such was the case at their "all day conference" on increasing Negro influence in Hollywood when "between four and five hundred" attended. The whole while Lawson was "sitting in the rear of the room" until the end, when he moved forward and articulated an "'action program'" that, according to the FBI, was "accepted without question with no argument from anyone."[75]

Michael Wilson, a luminary of Red Hollywood who went on to write screenplays for *Lawrence of Arabia* and *Bridge on the River Kwai*, echoed the widespread sentiments of his comrades when he argued that the "key approach to bringing the progressive movement into [the] film industry" was targeting "'Jim Crow.'"[76] But, symptomatic of the era, the few African

Americans who were then employed in Hollywood took out a full-page advertisement in a trade newspaper that "repudiated the conference."[77]

In 1953 the FBI reported that the "local ASP organization is in dire financial condition but [Lawson] and its executive board have decided to keep it going." Seeking new and fresh blood, Lawson reportedly "included in future ASP activity . . . plans for young people 10–14 years old." He even "offered to breach the [financial] gap himself by advancing funds to the organization."[78]

Thus by 1955—ironically as Jim Crow was beginning to come under withering assault,[79] thereby eroding a central predicate of the conservatism that had buoyed the "blacklist"—the ASP was holding its "last function of any importance." According to Lawson, "federal action" that was "pending" was the reason; certainly it was not lack of interest, for even though those in attendance knew that they would be subject to a "blacklist"—if they were not already—five hundred attended.[80] By then Lawson was "without any question the most effective influence in keeping the organization going"; he "guides the affairs of the organization," it was said. The FBI knew this, since for some time it had engaged in "technical surveillance" of Lawson,[81] including his residence. In fact, the surveillance of Lawson was so comprehensive that the authorities should have known that their contention that he was a Moscow dupe smuggling subversion into movies was absurd.[82]

The swan song for the ASP occurred in November 1955; by January it was no more. Appropriately, it was a testimonial for Lawson at a restaurant in L.A. with more than five hundred in attendance and his comrade-cum-nemesis Paul Jarrico presiding. By then Lawson, now in his sixties, was facing deteriorating health, not least failing eyesight. With the ASP dissolving and the Party falling on tough times, there was little joy in Red Hollywood. Yet this did not still the passions that poured forth in honors for the beleaguered Lawson. The prominent African American psychiatrist Dr. Price Cobbs chaired, and tributes were read from Chaplin, film workers from China, the Mexican painter David Siqueiros, and the Spanish writer Rafael Alberti. Other accolades came from virtually every continent. Extolling Lawson rapturously were the likes of Maltz, Robeson, and Du Bois.[83] Harry Hay, the founder of the modern gay rights movement in the United States, spoke of a "material measure of my own debt, as a progressive, to Mr. Lawson's cultural leadership."[84] Walter Lowenfels noted Lawson's generosity to fellow writers, including himself and others, for example, the "Negro poets, Lucy Smith and Sarah Wright"; "many of his admirers, as well as his opponents, do not know how much he gives to younger writers," he said.[85]

Actors Jeff Corey and Gale Sondergaard performed, and stellar fellow writers Michael Wilson and Dalton Trumbo were among those singing his praises. FBI spirits were soaring high, too. The agency was exultant precisely because this event marked the end of the road for the ASP, which had left Lawson slightly depressed. Though Lawson's "draft of the dissolution statement indicated that 'many aspects of our program have today been taken over by large professional organizations with thousands of members,' he personally admitted in private that actually no parallel organizations are successfully accomplishing much at the present time."[86] With the demise of the ASP, one espies the decline of Red Hollywood, a falloff that was mirrored in a concomitant decline of the Hollywood Party. The FBI reported happily in 1957 that "for the first time in 20 years, Hollywood film industry is without an active front [sic] organization."[87]

The next year it was reported that the Hollywood Communist Party "had by far the worst record of accomplishment during the drive in behalf of the [Party newspaper,] recording only 3.7 percent of its $1000 quota and failing to obtain one new subscription to the Party's press." Part of the problem was that, as in 1945, the Party was undergoing one of its periodic bloodlettings, this time in the wake of the 1956 announcement in Moscow that Soviet leader Joseph Stalin had committed grave and serious crimes— a declaration that took by surprise those comrades who had denounced routinely such charges as witless propaganda. This controversy had "served to divide the membership into warring splinter groups with [the] result that new lows in demoralization had been reached along with big losses of membership." Evidently there was an internal ruckus about whether the "cultural worker" was a "second class citizen in the [Party]"—thus, "the word culture did not even appear in the draft resolutions of Party policy in 1948, 1952 and 1956."[88]

Thus, L.A. Party leader Ben Dobbs reported in late 1957 that "our membership in January of 1956 totaled 1970. In July of 1957 we estimated," he reported forlornly, "a 25 to 30% drop. Since then more have left our ranks," though the Communist Party still maintained "about 75 clubs in Southern California."[89] In 1956 the Party in Los Angeles County "registered a total of 35 members in its cultural section," according to the FBI. "By comparison," in 1944 the agency reported contentedly, there were "100 writers alone in three Writers Branches with an estimated total in all cultural categories of 500."[90] By the mid-1950s, the Party in Hollywood— again, according to the FBI—had 35 members; 9 were reputedly in the Actors Guild, and 10 in the SWG.[91]

California historically had been a rebel in conflict with the Party's Manhattan-based leadership, and this time was no exception. Yet now the Party did not split. "It decomposed. It disintegrated. The faith and morale of thousands were shot," said John Gates, who left the Communist Party in the wake of the Soviet intervention in Hungary in 1956. A "most shocking example of this is the story of how a proposed letter from the American Party to the Soviet Central Committee—on the Jewish Question—has been allowed to gather dust"; this "letter called for an official Soviet statement on what happened to Yiddish-language writers and culture between 1948 and 1952"—but "the document lies in a desk drawer."[92] This alone caused many Jewish Reds to bolt—but not Lawson. During this time of turmoil, the Southern California Party challenged repeatedly the top leadership, but Lawson's name was nowhere to be found on these letters.[93]

Certainly the accusation of neglecting cultural matters—one of the other points of contention internally in the Party, supposedly contributing to its decline in the budding cultural capital that was L.A.—could not be laid at Lawson's doorstep. The collapse of the ASP and the decline of the Party provided him with more time, which he filled by giving lectures. According to the FBI, he held "weekly study or lecture groups with an average audience of about 40. At these study groups Lawson discusses various cultural subjects dealing principally with the writing field. A fee is charged [which] provides a source of income for Lawson."[94] One that caught the eye of the FBI "discussed at some length" the Russian writer Boris Pasternak and his then ballyhooed novel _Doctor Zhivago_, which Lawson "characterized" as "horrible"; the "book's main figure" was "an idiot rather than a hero,"[95] not a remark designed to curry favor in liberal and centrist circles. Lawson did not stop there. "There certainly is as much freedom for writers in Russia as in the United States," said this leading "blacklistee," citing his "own case as an example of writing freedom in this country."[96] This was not the first time that Lawson had waded chest-deep into the rough waters of Eastern European affairs. Earlier an FBI agent listened agape as Lawson proclaimed that "the press in the United States reported news concerning Russia inaccurately and unfairly and stated that his son and daughter had traveled in Czechoslovakia during the past summer and had noted complete freedom of speech and action. He said there was no persecution in those countries"[97]—an opinion he was to revise after living in that region.

From Lawson's viewpoint at that juncture, these nations were coming to his aid and merited consideration—a point not lost on the authorities. For the "Motion Picture Association of America, U.S. State Department and other groups concerned with . . . U.S. public relations abroad, reportedly are agitated over [ASP's] plan to give the film [on the Ten] wide distribution overseas." The film had "already played the Czecho-Slovak Film Festival where it reportedly won high praise," and "another print is already in France." Naturally, "theatrical showings" would be "few" in the United States, despite the fact that, "being a documentary," it fell "into [the] newsreel category, requiring neither a production code seal nor censorship certificate."[98]

Lawson may have been wrong on some matters, but he was rarely in doubt, an approach viewed as arrogant by some of his comrades, among them Paul Jarrico, who must have gritted his teeth in hosting the ASP's tribute to Lawson. As Jarrico remarked years later, this "theoretical fight"—or, more precisely, fight over theory—"continued and came to a head, as I recall, as late as 1954, when we had some very, very serious seminars, discussions, in an attempt to come to grips with the theoretical rather than simply the tactical essence of this question." "There," he asserted sarcastically, "I continued my 'right opportunist' line. Jack Lawson, who had sort of switched back and forth several times, was then the leader, the absolute leader, of what was the National Cultural Commission line [of the Party], which reflected very directly the line of [Andrei] Zhdanov in the Soviet Union and that was about as intense a disagreement as we ever came to grips with." The question was not new; it pivoted on to what extent one could inject progressive or even humane content into films and to what extent this was next to impossible. Jarrico's faction distributed a leaflet saying, "'These are pictures that were written by people who are now being blacklisted.' It was a list of about a hundred pictures and they were good pictures," for example, *Tom, Dick and Harry*, which Jarrico was proud to have written. But as he recalled it, "Lawson said, 'Tom, Dick and Harry,' a progressive picture?'" "Well," chuckled Jarrico ironically, "here you have the leftism versus rightism within the Party illustrated. We said, 'yes. In terms of this fight, yes. It's good for people to know that the people who were being blacklisted wrote a lot of pictures they liked.'" Now, he said, these were not "knock-down-drag-out fights. They were just differences in line."

Like many conflicts in the Party and among Red screenwriters generally, this one was more bitter and disruptive than it should have been, as if they were taking out their frustrations on each other since they could not effectively challenge the moguls. "The Party was essentially falling apart," said Jarrico. "Its chief activity after '51, after the spring of '51 was to defend people against the committee," meaning the fearsome, take-no-prisoners HUAC. "People were quitting," leaving in droves in response. "Even good people, they were scattering, they were leaving town, they were certainly leaving activity." Amid the ruins, Jarrico and Lawson still found time to squabble, like two bald men quarreling over a comb. Lawson, thought his adversary, "wanted, understandably, to regain the leadership he had more or less naturally assumed before he went to jail. Some of us who had perforce emerged as the leaders during his absence didn't want to give the leadership back to him because we disagreed with him about the line." So, "some of us refused to give the leadership back to Lawson." But, he concluded, not altogether wrongly, "these fights within the Party were, in a sense, meaningless, because the context was we were in full retreat," particularly in 1956, when "the bottom just fell out of the Party."

Jarrico himself "quit, early in '58," and followed others to Europe, where he worked on "films in English meant for the international market, very often financed by American companies," and wrote for a "TV show called 'The Defenders' which was quite a prestigious show."[99]

In the event, the Red Hollywood Jarrico left behind was a mere shadow of what it once was; HUAC and all the rest had taken a toll. Yet the demise of the ASP and the drop in Party activity freed Lawson to devote more time to Negro affairs; this was propitious at a moment when the Negro struggle was blooming and bidding fair to erode the encrusted conservatism that had given rise to the "blacklist." *Sahara* had earned Lawson a certain cachet among Negroes, particularly Negro writers, such as the leading Negro playwright Theodore Ward.[100] Charlotta Bass, publisher of the leading black newspaper in L.A., was among those who sought his counsel about writing.[101] Julian Mayfield sought his help as he was seeking to "round off my first novel"—though he found it typically curious that "the envelope came open" and was "resealed somewhere in transit."[102]

Thus, after being barred from screenwriting—except through cumbersome fronts—Lawson not only turned to history and film criticism but returned to playwriting, although his experience here was frustrating. He poured hours on end into his play *Thunder Morning*, which featured leading Negro characters, and, as a result, turned anxiously to some of the best Negro minds for their unvarnished comments. Though he was bashed repeatedly for his own rapier thrusts at the works of others, Lawson welcomed "criticism," deeming it "an invaluable instrument in the creative process." "To reject criticism," he argued "is to my way of thinking, a lack of creative responsibility and it also, in many cases," constituted a "lack of ordinary good sense." Perhaps, he ruminated, it was a "matter of self-confidence." "I have confidence in my ability," he said simply, and even unfair criticism could not shake it. But because he had "no roots, no intimate sense of the life pattern" of Negroes, this made writing this play "difficult," since "it is impossible to simulate cultural roots which are not there"[103]— which drove him even further to invite critique.

So he arranged readings in Manhattan, where invitees included Ewart Guinier, Langston Hughes, Lloyd Brown, Eslanda Robeson, and other members in good standing of the Black Left. "The letter of invitation was signed by Shirley Graham Du Bois," who "asked Sidney Poitier if he will read the play."[104]

Thunder Morning was a play about Negro heroism with a love story at its center that suggested Paul Robeson in the lead role.[105] In a broad sense it was analogous to an updated version of Howard Fast's *Freedom Road*, with a twist of betrayal,[106] though since Lawson was constantly revising this work—"I am now planning to have at least one, and possibly two more white characters,"[107] he said at one point—it remained a moving target of explication. However, Lawson rejected the idea that he was seeking "politicalization" through this work. He told Julian Mayfield, this was "nonsense. The only 'correctness' that I know is the urge to achieve the deepest truth of art and humanity," and if this goal were attained, he thought, the impact—including the political impact—would be desirable from any vantage point.[108]

Nonetheless, reactions to the play were mixed, and it never received a full-blown production.[109] There were, however, "public readings in one or more churches," with "cultural and political leaders of the Negro community" present—[110] featuring Frances Williams, the unsung radical black actress—that garnered a "wonderfully warm response."[111] But Lawson remained dissatisfied with this play about Negro heroism. "Perhaps this is because," he said later, "I have no roots in the kind of life about which I am writing." He commented, "One of the many weaknesses of Hemingway [for] whom I have very little respect is that he has no sense of place or of tradition," unlike Faulkner, for example.[112]

Lawson's dalliance with Negro theater was consistent with his Party's notion that African Americans constituted a formidable foe against the status quo. It was during this time that Lawson conceived of a "feature film about the life and achievement of W. E. B. Du Bois—a most intriguing and important idea"; per usual during this era, "the problem [was] raising funds for the project."[113] He discussed a "project to do a film about Ira Aldridge," the great Negro tragedian, but that too perished in stillbirth,[114] as did others, for the "blacklist" was formidably effective.[115]

14 The Fall of Red Hollywood

Hollywood's "blacklist" was simply the opening wedge in an all-sided assault against the now fading grandeur of Red Hollywood, a precinct once presided over by Lawson. Soon "mass meetings" were being held on "every major studio lot," during "which communism was assailed and patriotic speeches were made by film industry leaders."[1] Suggestive of the fall of the alliance between Red and Liberal Hollywood was that Walter Wanger "became one of a three man committee to enforce the blacklist."[2]

In the fall of 1961 these extravaganzas went from the studios to the city itself as the "world's largest anti-communist meeting" was "held in [the] Hollywood Bowl" with twelve thousand present. Naturally, there was a "television audience." The rising star of this movement, the soon-to-be senator George Murphy, was the host, and speakers included Jack Warner, Rock Hudson, Walt Disney, John Wayne, Robert Stack—and Ronald Reagan.[3]

But their impact was minor compared with what was becoming a ritual—HUAC hearings targeting Hollywood, a periodic ceremony that, at least, was off-putting to the mainstream journalist William Shannon. These sessions were "impossible to observe" in "any sustained mood of lighthearted cynicism," he said with disgust. In fact, the usually restrained Shannon had the "urge to go out and wash one's hands" at the end of the day. Why? "For what is going on here," he responded, "is one of the ugliest human spectacles this side of the Iron Curtain. What the spectators see each day is the degradation of a human spirit, groveling and abasing itself in a slough of guilt and self-denunciation before a little circle of cigar-chewing, bleak-eyed men." Despite the bright lights and the television cameras that now beamed these stylized performances into millions of living rooms, "the committee's hearings have so far turned up not a shred of new evidence on the long-dead Communist network in Hollywood." Instead, HUAC "acted as a tribunal, a panel of witch doctors to enforce American orthodoxy, as defined in the most narrow and conservative terms."[4]

Lawson and his comrades refused to accept meekly this newly installed status quo. When HUAC brought its traveling road show to L.A. in the 1950s, it was greeted routinely by an unwelcoming Party and those sufficiently brave—or foolish—to march alongside them. "Blatant, raucous and scornful," jeered one local newspaper; "the Commies marched this week— marched on the Federal Building with placards, sound trucks and songs." "They blocked the sidewalk," they "went upstairs to the hearing room" and "deliberately blocked the entrance" as they "crowded into choice seats."[5] But there were reasons why more did not join their picket lines, for on one violent occasion, their "placards" were "destroyed by U.S. sailors." Then the sailors, aided by some civilian bystanders, broke up the small demonstration, tore up the signs and threw them in the street.[6]

There was a reason for HUAC going to the expense of packing up and moving three thousand miles west to Southern California, for despite the repeated blows that it had absorbed, Red Hollywood—and, in fact, Red California—had yet to be subdued. When the Progressive Party obtained "464,000 signatures on petitions" to qualify for the 1948 ballot, one writer asserted that "the professional politicians were dumbfounded," as they were seemingly unaware that "class lines" were "sharply drawn" in the Golden State, "probably more so than in a state whose growth has been less rapid."[7] The authorities were staggered when the third-party ticket received a robust one hundred thousand votes in L.A. county alone, 5.77 percent of the presidential vote and 58.2 percent of the ticket's total statewide.[8]

They must have been flabbergasted when a few years later a Communist, Bernadette Doyle, garnered a hefty six hundred thousand votes in a statewide electoral contest.[9] Reds and their allies were still maintaining a boisterous presence on the streets, taking to Hollywood Boulevard "as far east as Western and extending to Highland Avenue," distributing "thousands of leaflets" about the Hollywood Ten.[10] Though an era that was "silent" was commencing, one would not know this from inspecting the Red beehive of activity. Thus, the hysteria was even more rabid: "Filmland Reds, Atom Bomb Spies? House Probers Say They'll Prove It,"[11] blared one headline, as an attempt quickly emerged to justify why the authorities were paying so much attention to studying scribblers of stories.

L.A. Communist Alice McGrath once recalled the statement of liberal opinion molder Carey McWilliams that "particularly in California, the progressive activity that took place" was "hardly imaginable without the activity of Communist Party members who got in and did all the donkey-work [*sic*] for everything."[12] Once this Party was destabilized, it facilitated the fall of Red Hollywood and, then, like dominos collapsing, the weakening of Liberal Hollywood, as there were fewer and fewer to do the "donkey-work."

From one vantage point, the lubricant that kept this Big Red Machine motoring was the cash supplied by Red Hollywood; it was alleged that Lawson himself "made reports boasting of raising $20,000 a week for the Red Fascist [*sic*] cause in Hollywood."[13] And note that these were not just any Reds generating these fabulous sums but disproportionately writers—a branch of the industry that Lawson had come to symbolize.[14]

So prompted, the U.S. authorities bolted into action. Soon it was jubilantly noted that "nearly all . . . top CP leaders are in hiding. . . . [A]ll section and club records now destroyed and no written records" were extant, as "strict security measures" were being taken amid charges of "factionalism.[15] *Variety* reported that a "wave of films depicting Communism as the villain" were placed in the pipeline.[16]

Thereafter the government indicted the top Party leadership in Southern California. It was a massive trial, said their attorney, Ben Margolis, with a gargantuan twelve thousand pages constituting the eventual record, with "over 600 exhibits," while "all of the mass media of communication, newspapers, the radio, the motion pictures, the television . . . hour after hour [were] conducting an attack upon people who are Communists or people who they label as Communists."[17] A good deal of the case would have been laughable if not for its utter seriousness, with the writings of Tom Paine, Abraham Lincoln, Thomas Jefferson, and Frederick Douglass introduced as exhibits to discredit the defendants and little evidence introduced about the actual workings of the Party.[18]

Seemingly beleaguered, sensing correctly the presence of enemies within the ranks, the Party members began to strike out—at each other.[19] The historian Gerda Lerner, then residing in the region, is largely correct in asserting that "there is no question in my mind but that the infiltration of FBI and police spies into the party apparatus tended to aggravate these destructive [internal] tendencies," and "in such an atmosphere it was difficult for trust and comradeship to flourish."[20]

Lawson was driven deeper into the "blacklist," scurrying to secure an undetectable front so that funds would continue streaming into his shriveling bank account. *Terror in a Texas Town* was most likely a film he was happy to avoid claiming openly. It originated as an adaptation of a Stephen Crane story, but "there was difficulty about the rights and eventually it turned into a conventional Western about a young immigrant from Sweden who comes to a Texas town."[21] Lawson received a paltry $5,000 for this B picture when "in ordinary times he might have gotten $100,000 to $150,000 for such a script," which underscored how the "blacklist" was a windfall for the producers.[22]

Then there was *Tales of the Vikings,* filmed in Germany and involving, as a producer, United Artists[23] and Kirk Douglas, a pioneer in breaking the "blacklist." It was filmed abroad, and Lawson complained at one point that "all of our German actors have great difficulty in speaking complex sentences and we should at all times avoid the use of the letters . . . g and w." Lawson had a hand in this series, targeted for television. Yet he found that the first thirteen segments "were among the worst scripts that we have ever read"; they were "photographed without taste, without tempo." He had "tied each story around an original notion that can be of interest to people of all ages," a smart commercial proposition, "for example, the Greek slave who knows the secret of making a diving bell." But his labor proved unavailing,[24] though this project provided a substantial portion of the $28,750 he had received in the immediate period leading up to mid-1959 for various scripts, treatments, and stories.[25]

But working long-distance with fronts, where he had to shroud his own participation, involved unique problems, not least Lawson's inability to go on location and provide pointers. Like many "blacklisted" writers, Lawson often squabbled with his front, Edward Lewis, which led ultimately to an acrimonious lawsuit.[26] For one project, the eminently forgettable *Careless Years,* Lawson protested that the "total apparently paid" himself was "$11,425." However, he had "no way of knowing whether this was the amount due under contract" signed by his front on Lawson's "behalf or whether it is the sum he received for the property." Lewis claimed this particular film "lost enormously and brought in a gross of $25,000," a measly sum, yet "people who know the business" told Lawson that "this figure is impossibly low for a film in major release throughout [the] U.S. and the world"; it "played everywhere, including . . . England and Canada" and other major markets.[27] Yet with all these difficulties, Lawson's labors were not entirely fruitless. One of his close collaborators during this era, Mitch Lindemann, went on to bigger and better things with "his sensational success" as producer of the award-winning *Cat Ballou,* which had "given him some influence."[28]

It was not coincidental that Lawson would mention foreign markets in detailing his complaint, for foreign revenues increasingly were becoming paramount in forming Hollywood's bottom line, and ultimately this proved decisive in eroding the "blacklist." For, as time passed, the industry was growing increasingly desperate, and it was apparent that sidelining some of the most talented writers—even if they were Reds—made little sense, particularly as foreign markets, where anticommunism was not as passionate a concern, increased in importance.

This was becoming evident to George Weltner, an executive at Paramount,[29] as early as the pivotal year of 1956.[30] Adrian Scott, still "blacklisted," noticed the same phenomenon in 1957, pointing to the "critical period through which the motion picture industry is now passing. The imminent closing down of 5000 theaters throwing out of work thousands of theater managers, projectionists and other personnel is a tragedy,"[31] though few wanted to hear then that banning the "blacklist" itself might pump new blood into a collapsing Hollywood.[32] Speaking in a "strictly confidential" tone, Weltner confessed to "sweating bullets because of the scarcity of important pictures during the first six months of 1958."[33] Things had gotten so bad for Paramount that it was beginning to invest in the oil business, which at least meant guaranteed returns.[34]

But amid the cascade of sobering news, one fact stood out: though the studio's domestic revenue in the late 1950s had "sunk back" to the levels of 1942, their foreign revenue had doubled since then; "the foreign market," Weltner concluded "is still a much greater field for expansion than the domestic."[35] In addition, unlike oil, there was an added advantage to investing in movies that could not be gainsaid. After meeting with State Department higher-ups in Washington, Weltner announced that "the greatest interest of our Government is in using the motion picture as the most potent existing force—the most successful form of propaganda—that is available." Even the most innocuous of Hollywood fare displayed a lifestyle and products that amounted to a lengthy commercial for the U.S. way of life. Thus, "the President, the Secretary of State," and other bigwigs "all share the opinion that a great deal of the winning of the Cold War can depend on the success of the motion picture program."[36]

Hence, Paramount pressed ahead aggressively on the foreign front.[37] The industry's chief spokesman, Eric Johnston, reminded the high-level diplomat Christian Herter that "we are a global industry," and London's push for "screen-time-quotas . . . which means that 30% of all screen time in Britain must be devoted to British films" was quite troubling. "If Great Britain should join the Common Market and their screen-time quota should be added to the quota of other countries in order to provide special treatment for films produced in other countries, it would have a drastic effect on us," since "approximately 52% of our total earnings are outside the United

States."[38] Moreover, to obtain a certain gritty realism—and, to a degree, reduced costs and scenes more pleasing to foreign audiences than backlots in Burbank—Hollywood was looking abroad for film locales, which also brought the industry into a tighter clinch with the State Department.[39] This was leading to a paradoxical result: the decline in the domestic box office and rise in foreign receipts, combined with a surge in antiracism that hindered conservatism, was helping to erode the "blacklist"—while an increased reliance on the State Department was having the opposite result.

One outgrowth of the changing nature of making movies was Paramount's effort—mirrored in similar efforts by other studios—to move out of making pictures directly on the industrial model and "concentrate on independent production of pictures at the Paramount Studio, financed and distributed by the company."[40] This would empower independent producers—for example, Kirk Douglas—and open the door for the crumbling of the "blacklist." There is some question regarding how wedded to the "blacklist" certain moguls were in any case.[41] Thus, when the industry suffered a downturn in the 1950s, pressure mounted once more to get rid of the "blacklist" and its suffocating accoutrements.[42] Bank of America alone reportedly had $53 million in movie loans outstanding by 1953,[43] an amount that could be jeopardized if the studios continued producing scripts full of puerile pap.

Shortly thereafter, Trumbo was contentedly telling fellow screenwriter Michael Wilson, "There is no longer a centralized control of industry tight enough to enforce the blacklist." Yet, he thought, "only the best blacklisted writers will profit from the end of the blacklist, while the rest will be confronted with a terrible competitive struggle for their existence." Trumbo, who was "receiving seventy-five thousand dollars and five percent of the picture" for writing the screenplay to *Spartacus*, cockily added, "Lou [sic] Wasserman, president of MCA and the most powerful single person in the business, knows that I have written the screenplay and actually has been negotiating for the moneys . . . which ultimately reached me." Trumbo also spoke of a "tri-partite alliance" of himself, Michael Wilson, and Maltz as the "best" who would profit from this new dispensation—a troika that pointedly excluded Lawson.[44]

It was true that Lawson, widely perceived as the most incorrigible Red, was left on the sidelines as his erstwhile comrades began to scoop up riches. Thus, in 1960 Frank Sinatra sought to hire Maltz to "write the screenplay of 'The Execution of Private Slovik'" before backing down.[45] The chagrined Maltz acknowledged that "certainly if Sinatra had remained firm, the blacklist really would have been on its way out."[46]

Yet Lawson would remain under wraps. Paul Jarrico, who was not the greatest admirer of Lawson, still conceded that the "blacklist" would not be over until Lawson could work openly in Hollywood; by that definition, when Lawson died in 1977, this bar had not ended.[47] But what "distressed" Lawson, as he said in 1967, was that this ban was "the main cause of the decline of the [film] industry," since "this climate of fear has discouraged experimentation, stifled initiatives and dulled moral sensibilities."[48]

Still, when an antitrust lawsuit was launched against this ban, Lawson was able to become a plaintiff with his Hollywood Ten cohorts.[49] They sued for $7.5 million,[50] settled for $80,000, and after the lawyers got their 30 percent,[51] Lawson took home a derisory $4,897.48 for his immense troubles.[52] "After seventeen years of blacklist," Maltz announced happily, "I signed my first film contract under my own name on January 15, 1964 with a film company financed by United Artists."[53] Ironically, this landmark in the struggle against the "blacklist" was marred by the gathering reality that the Hollywood Ten was becoming the "Hollywood One." As Lawson noted with some asperity, "I'm much more completely blacklisted than the others. . . . I'm much more notorious, and I'm very proud of that."[54]

Still, though the "blacklist" never plunged Lawson to the precipice of homelessness or bankruptcy, it took its toll. This settlement, no matter how meager, was welcome, although he received "no residuals on films under [his] own name, because the contract for residuals does not go back before 1947," a weakness of the SWG contract that benefited the producers and got lost in the brouhaha of the "blacklist."[55] This was no minor matter, since the Ten collectively spent a "quarter of a million dollars in their three years in the courts," then more in their subsequent antitrust lawsuit against the "blacklist."[56] When this ban was at its zenith, Lawson admitted that he was having a "rough time financially . . . although it has never been so serious as to be more than the kind of pressure which is so usual for most people." This pressure was not without consequence, since it "affects the time available for the work [that] is closest to my heart," continuing research in the vein of *The Hidden Heritage* and "revision of the play on Negro life" (i.e., *Thunder Morning*), which he "felt had to be withdrawn entirely for a very complete change in temper and theme." To supplement his dwindling income, he gave a "lecture every week to about forty or fifty people—an extraordinary attendance to maintain year-in and year-out."[57]

Yet, as Lawson's fortunes were sinking, that of his conservative counterparts was ascending correspondingly.[58] The leader of the Hollywood Republican Committee, George Murphy, was negotiating with Senator Richard M. Nixon to appear at the Beverly Hills Hotel at a fete "for about 400 people," with "proceeds of the dinner to keep us going for the next six or eight months." "We could get an excellent turnout representing not only the motion picture crowd but also the aircraft and oil interests, [and] newspapers," Murphy added brightly.[59] Gathering momentum, newly empowered Conservative Hollywood soon was backing then ex–Vice President Nixon for governor of California.[60] The beaming Nixon highlighted his role in sabotaging Red Hollywood as a rationale for his candidacy. "It was the insight into the Communist conspiracy to take over Hollywood," he declared, "and the militant action taken to expose the subversives by the leadership of the guilds and unions comprising the Hollywood film council—in conjunction with our congressional committee investigation—which brought defeat to well-laid Communist plans to take over the industry. Plans of the Kremlin [which] had stealthily and quietly wormed their way to power, masked as unionists and guildsmen, in this most important international medium, suddenly faced the full glare of public exposure."[61]

Nixon's rise signaled that Lawson was effectively barred from the industry to which he had contributed; so flummoxed he turned increasingly to film and literary criticism, which—surprisingly enough—had the added advantage of generating income.[62] He was receiving royalties from Moscow, for example, where his works were widely consulted.[63] He was also increasingly popular in Red China[64] and Japan.[65] The Japanese translation of *Film in the Battle of Ideas* sold "3000 copies (out of 4000 copies printed)," with a Chinese translation in the pipeline. As Lawson's publisher pointed out to him, "The message of your book is well received and largely enlightened the public."[66] He remained a celebrity abroad while "blacklisted" at home.[67]

The international left often flocked to Lawson's door, seeking consul on the nature of U.S. culture, what was worth studying and what should be ignored.[68] Yet in socialist Poland, there was a "negative reaction" of publishers to his book *Film: The Creative Process*. The "Polish intellectual community," he was told, "is extremely proud of its accomplishments, especially of its films," and Lawson's "strictures" of Polish films did "not go down well." There was "a certain touchiness" in Poland "about critical comments with respect to anything pertaining to the Soviet Union." Writing from Warsaw, Lawson's correspondent, Maxim Lieber, pointed him to a recent speech by Cuban leader Fidel Castro, in which he told fellow comrades, "'Stop washing . . . dirty linen in public,'"[69] which was becoming a Lawson specialty in his old age. Lawson was "not altogether surprised" that his book had "been declined by two publishers in Poland," since "its rather negative view of recent Polish films would not be too cordially welcomed," not to mention that his "view of modern Soviet film" was "quite critical."[70]

On the other hand, in revolutionary Cuba itself Lawson was venerated.[71] As in Asia, his books were being widely translated and studied—at a time when he was a pariah at home. "Your book 'Theory and Technique of Playwriting and Screenwriting,'" Lawson was told, "has come to be our textbook and [was] translated into Spanish by Tomas Gutierrrez Alea," one of Cuba's—and in fact one of the world's—leading moviemakers.[72] Consorting with Cuba was not designed to endear Lawson to Jack Warner, who complained that "Fidel Castro has [$]400,000 of our money in Cuba," while his patron in Moscow had "films . . . that were never paid for and we won't ever see again."[73] Both had expropriated sums and materials without compensation—a development that goes a long way toward explaining the ire directed at these nations and their domestic supporters, namely, Lawson.

But as he got older—by the time he won his lawsuit against the "blacklist" he was more than seventy years old—Lawson became even freer in dispensing his opinions, especially on literary and cinematic matters.[74] "I worry a bit about being so negative about American cinema," he said at one point, "but I don't know how it can be helped."[75] "Even the finest films of recent years," he told the moviemaker Abby Mann, "are flawed by failure to relate the large theme to the personal life of the characters. I find this true of such an admirable work as 'Judgment at Nuremberg' and it seems to me a crucial problem in 'After the Fall.'"[76] There were exceptions, he thought: *Dr. Strangelove* was "probably the most significant American work of the year," he announced; "it is interesting as a bitter satirical attack on the military-fascist [type]." But even here, Lawson retained his critical edge, asserting it was "not a great film," since "it lacks depth and vision."[77] Lawson was a pioneer in both film theory and screenplays featuring dialogue and thus was particularly suited to comment on cinematic developments.[78]

His insights, which deviated sharply from the presumed rudiments of Marxism, were increased after Lawson spent a good deal of the period from 1961 to 1963 in the Soviet Union. This eyewitness view of "presently existing socialism" was sobering, particularly for the infatuation of Lawson's life—film, aesthetics, and cultural matters.[79] He revised his view of Bertolt Brecht, for example, once a pillar of the theater in then socialist East Germany; he still maintained "enormous admiration" for the German "as a playwright, perhaps the greatest of our time, but his theory of the 'teaching' [of] drama seems to me wrong, because it makes a false separation of intellectual and emotional processes." The "concept of 'art as a weapon' was used mechanically and misleadingly in the thirties and there was a lot of loose talk (in which I participated)," he added sheepishly, "about 'proletarian art.'" Now he still contended that "'art is a weapon,'" but he felt this slogan had been invoked too crudely, not least by himself as a result of his own inadequate schooling, for "it was only in the thirties" that Lawson "began to make a thorough study of American history." Still, his "ideas about theatre [had] changed much less (although they have broadened and developed) than [his] ideas about film."

For Lawson "wrote about film at a period of personal and intellectual difficulty in 1949 and 1953," which led to a "defensive approach to Hollywood and [his] own role there." This was followed—in a manner he might have mocked as petit bourgeois vacillation if it had happened to another—by "a reaction in the opposite direction, a narrowly 'political' and mechanistic approach to film and especially American film in 1953." His thinking had "never been static" and this analysis had never been truer than in the aftermath of his journey to Moscow.[80]

"My life and work has been enriched by my sojourn there," he said, not least since "the issues which I regarded as having world significance seemed to them inconsequential or non-existent. They felt that the sole and all-embracing issue is 'the freedom of the artist.'" But Lawson, who had emerged from a land where that aphorism was forged, had a more constricted viewpoint of this notion. "While admitting that creative freedom is restricted under capitalism," his Soviet counterparts "saw no justification for imposing limitations on artistic expression in a capitalist society," whereas Lawson was much more sensitive to the propagation of anti-Semitic, racist, and sexist themes. Still, there was a persistent "view that Soviet culture exhibits a fixed opposition between state control and the 'independent' artist [that was] widely disseminated in the United States." It was often said during the cold war that African students who went to study in Moscow became critical of socialism, whereas those studying in Washington became critical of capitalism. Lawson seemed to be more "pro-socialist" than the Soviet artists he encountered—who he thought understandably had been profoundly influenced by the crimes of the Stalin era.[81]

Lawson found it "very puzzling that cultural people seem to freeze their attitudes in a fixed and (to me) abstract opposition between dogmatism on the one hand, and 'creative freedom' on the other. Of course, dogmatism is a real danger, and freedom is the deepest need of the creative spirit—but the frozen dichotomy forbids the exploration of the real problems of artistic values, cultural history, etc. In practice, I find that there [is] a cult of know-nothingism, which rejects the search for values and asserts that the artist can be free in a vacuum—which, unhappily, is where some of my cultural friends seem to be residing."[82] These meditations about cultural matters were of a piece with the crumbling of the "blacklist" and the general loosening of conservative restrictions, as exemplified by the rise of a freedom

FIGURE 14. Lawson was a leading Communist, but in the latter stage of his career he came to harbor deep-seated misgivings about the Soviet Union. (Courtesy of Southern Illinois University)

movement in the southern United States. Up to that point, for example, the idea of a Communist obtaining a passport to travel abroad was unlikely.

Despite the struggle that was required to deposit Lawson in the Soviet Union, a nation he had defended at the price of great detriment to his reputation in his homeland, it was a bittersweet experience he endured. "I hate Hollywood," he was quoted as telling the *Los Angeles Times,* "and I want no part of it. But I realized in the Soviet Union that I could never be comfortable in another country but this."[83] Lawson simply was not impressed with the thinking that he encountered in the Soviet Union—particularly on what was, to him, the fundamental issue of cultural matters. "It is my contention," he declared in early 1966, "that no adequate or defensible Marxist theory of culture . . . exists. This is true of the Socialist countries as well as among Marxists in the Capitalist World [and was] the result of systematic neglect of cultural problems in the main movements of Marxist thought for the past fifty years."[84]

Foretelling the crisis that gripped the Soviet Union, almost three decades after he had departed, Lawson "found it fascinating that bourgeois concepts still have such a hold on intellectuals in the Soviet Union."[85] Put crisply, Lawson was unimpressed with the quality of the intellectuals he encountered in Eastern Europe, though he confessed to having "many friends in the literary field in the GDR."[86] He retained and underlined a passage from the *New York Times* that noted, "The Polish government is somewhat at a loss when confronted by its creative artists—not only writers but painters, musicians, film makers, ingenious philosophers and inventive sociologists. Those who are responsible for dealing with this highly volatile, very talkative and generally competent group have devised an elaborate system of bribes and coercion in return for cooperation."[87]

Lawson did not find it easy to accept why Hemingway was "overpraised, especially in the Soviet Union." As he saw it and contrary to his harshest critics who accused him similarly, this was "really a 'political' approach to literature," in light of the Illinoisan's well-known stance in favor of the Spanish Republic, then the Cuban left. There was also in Moscow an "uncritical over-estimation of [Arthur] Miller's earlier plays," which "led inevitably to confusion and disappointment when the seeds of pessimism and psychoanalysis, etc. in the earlier plays began to sprout."[88] There was a "great honesty in [Arthur] Miller and this is the heart of both his failure and tragedy," Lawson declared.[89] He found "cultural theory" in the Soviet Union flawed. In his view, that "lack of cultural theory causes an enormous contradiction: on the one hand, they say the culture of capitalism is corrupt; on the other hand, they admire Hemingway and draw their main creative sustenance from Shakespeare, the old ballet, etc."[90]

Lawson thought it "'idiotic to talk about realism, for instance in the Soviet Union, where they make a whole issue of socialist realism yet the art they admire is the Russian ballet, which is not realistic at all and which is of an aristocratic origin.'" As he said repeatedly in words often ignored by his critics, Lawson "thought that more revolutionary movies"—and art—"would come from the interdependence of form and content and the deeper penetration of human character, especially in neglected sections of the population."[91] This trend would not emerge from Party diktats or stealthy screenwriters sneaking subversion into scripts.

Lawson was beginning to seem like a man without a country, uncomfortable in the United States and the Soviet Union alike. Like Karl Marx, who reputedly declared that he was not a "Marxist," Lawson stressed, "I do not emphasize Marxism in my critical writing because I do not think there is any such thing (as yet) as a Marxist approach to the arts."[92] This critique, however, meant no cease-fire in his conflict with capitalism: "'Western' art has in the main followed a course of decline, moral confusion, aesthetic triviality, in the past forty years. Everybody knows this."[93]

But Lawson was similarly critical of the Marxist tradition to which he had made a "commitment" decades earlier. "Marxism, to the best of my knowledge," he declared, "has done nothing to answer the complex problems of human personality raised by Freud and Sartre. . . . [T]he fact that a system of ideas is false does not mean that it does not open new possibilities to ask valid questions." "If you know the answer to that question," he told his frequent literary boxing partner Sidney Finkelstein, "you are a wise man. But if you say it is not a pertinent question (and it seems to me you infer that in your book), then I doubt your wisdom." He was "extremely critical" of the influential Eastern European Marxist philosopher George Lukacs, "finding him dogmatic" and "insensitive to cultural values." Lawson acknowledged his own "'existentialist,' 'metaphysical,' 'absurdist' convictions in the twenties" and, as a result, was hesitant to "dismiss philosophic systems such as pragmatism by saying 'philosophy of imperialism.'" Nor could one "dismiss psychoanalysis or existentialism in this way"—to do otherwise, he charged, was to apply a *political* yardstick to philosophic structures," which he deemed a grievous error.[94]

In the sunset of his life, what separated Lawson from his comrades was that he was moving beyond the consideration of *objective* and *structural* considerations in understanding society to the *subjective*. As he put it in his controversial 1967 book on film, "The most exciting contemporary development in cinema is the attempt to explore the inner life, to break through the barriers that obstruct psychological understanding"—a subject that any writer of fiction had to applaud, just as many of his comrades saw it as a diversion. "Alienation," he thought, was "not a subjective invention of troubled intellectuals. It is a real phenomenon of the present period, a reflection of the impoverishment of man's spirit in the era of declining capitalism."[95]

Moreover, unlike a number of his comrades, Lawson was not as hostile to trends that were given a boost by the tumult of the 1960s. Existentialism, for example, was "not a philosophy of fascism," as some doubters imagined. Yes, "it can do a great deal of harm but it also represents an anti-capitalist trend. Le Roi Jones, for example, has an existentialist view of Negro-white relationships (with undertones of Freud); I think it is a dangerous view, but it as foolish to associate him with the Establishment as to underrate his extraordinary talent and potential value as an artist." Lawson thought that too many Marxists were too rigid in their approach to middle-class intellectuals, whose rebellion against imperialism did not necessarily track the footsteps of the classic proletarian. "I knew Dreiser well," he said speaking of the novelist he brought into Red ranks, "and I have never known anyone more profoundly alienated, embittered, maladjusted. This is even more clearly true of O'Neill," who he also knew well. Should they be embraced by Communists or berated for their weaknesses?[96]

Unlike some who were slightly embarrassed about their class origins, not least because detractors treated them harshly as "class traitors," Lawson was rather unusual on the left in his failure to reject his background—and this made it easier for him to embrace other dissidents, rebels, and malcontents who did not emerge fully formed from the factory floor, as some of his comrades would have it. "I am also a bourgeois intellectual," he announced, "and much of my thinking is affected by the fact that this is my way of life and always has been."[97] For the longest time he did "struggle" with his "identity as a middle class person," and this "plunged" him "into metaphysics and furious questioning—then as a Jew, and finally as an American, not abstractly but class-consciously." Out of this troubled journey emerged "what is called commitment."[98] So why could other middle-class rebels not traverse this route?

This consideration of philosophy was part of a larger engagement with aesthetics that was to occupy Lawson's waning days. Here, too, he found "limitation in the development" of Marxism that shed light, he hypothesized, on why "so many writers and cultural people seem to have lost their enthusiasm and their sense of values." "I cannot quite agree with Mike Gold," he argued, "in denouncing their 'disillusionment' as simple weakness or venality."[99] This was all part of an effort by the elder Lawson to become more forthcoming toward those he may have clashed with earlier—

for example, Joseph Freeman, author of the novel *Never Call Retreat*—as if he were settling accounts before he passed on.[100]

It was ironic that Lawson, a man who at once had been persecuted for his beliefs and was sensitive to the horrors of the Stalin era—unlike some of his more obdurate comrades—was not moved by the cry for "freedom" of the Soviet artists he encountered, which convinced him that a life in exile in Moscow would only foist another kind of outlier status upon him. Certainly his "alienation" from his Soviet counterparts was not a by-product of the ill-treatment he received while visiting. Far from it. In early 1962 he and his wife were residing in a "huge suite at the Peking" hotel in Moscow, "where [they were] so comfortable that" they had reason to "wonder whether we should move again to the apartment which is still promised. In any case," thought Lawson, "this [was] ideal for work and rest. I am using it at the moment solely for resting—the clinic gave me some special medicine and instructions to do nothing but lie on my back for three days," said the elderly, now frail, writer.[101]

In fact, his presence in Russia was partially a product of his ill health and the desire to seek specialized health care that, at least, did not come with a fee. He happened to be there during the fall of 1962 as the so-called Cuban missile crisis brought the world to the brink of a nuclear holocaust,[102] though all he had to endure was "hospitalization" at "no cost" in a "magnificent hospital" in a "single room" with "nurses day and night for 8 weeks." The "film industry" there suggested that "we stay" and "asked me what I wished to do." Lawson appreciated some aspects of this society—"transportation, 5 cents. Telephone, 2 cents." But he was concerned about developments surrounding the "Jewish question"—there was "certainly no attempt to develop a broad culture in Jewish or Yiddish" matters, for example.[103]

Early 1963 found him in a city whose very name had become anathema in conservative circles. Yet he and his wife found Yalta in the Crimea just short of mesmerizing. "Now as I sit on a balcony watching the winter sunlight on the Black Sea," he rhapsodized, "with clouds piling up in the West, I review my experience during a year and a half in the Soviet Union." He was hypercritical of what he termed the "rule of barren formula imposed during the Stalin years" but still felt this nation contained a "dynamic society."[104] There were "snow splashed hills" that were "beautiful," though outside it was "so slippery under foot that we are told honestly that all the medical plaster was used up on broken bones." But now all was "clear and even sunshine" reigned. "What a relief" this was "from [the] Moscow winter which [was] a dilly . . . never over 10 below." Lawson, said his spouse, was "working like a yeast cake . . . much too hard of course," but his regimen was interrupted by a "darling man with only one leg from Kiev who took us all around," and there was a "charming couple from Georgia" who did the same. Neither Lawson nor his spouse could speak Russian—which also may have determined the kind of artists he would associate with and shape his thinking about Soviet artists generally—"Dumb, ain't we?" thought Sue Lawson.[105]

Lawson's lack of facility in the mother tongue did not prevent Soviet authorities from treating him royally. He was a "dissident" from the bowels of U.S. imperialism whose name could be invoked triumphantly to counter the pummeling Moscow had received over Boris Pasternak.[106] Although Lawson had difficulty getting plays mounted back home, his play *Parlor Magic* was "in rehearsal in two theatres in the Soviet Union—the theatre of Satire in Moscow and the Academy-Pushkin, said to be by far the best theatre in Leningrad," now St. Petersburg.[107]

As it turned out, the cultural crowd in Russia had as negative view of Lawson as he did of them. "Some Russian friends write quite negatively about it, as far as acting and production are concerned," he said, referring to the Moscow rendition of *Parlor Magic*, while in Leningrad, he found to his dismay, "there is no chance of doing the play."[108] On the other hand, those who were not part of these elite intellectual and artistic circles seemed to have a different opinion of his handiwork, or so suggested the *Daily Worker*. "Soviet audiences are enthusiastically welcoming a new play about American family life" by Lawson, readers were informed. "All scheduled performances were quickly sold out," as the audience—apparently—resonated with this play, which involved a "well-off American family from 1944 to 1957. It shows the corrupting and disrupting effects of war and McCarthyite persecution."[109]

The U.S. Communists Esther and Art Shields, then residing in Moscow, reported to the Lawsons that the sixteen hundred seats in the theater all "seemed full," though they said diplomatically that it "seemed to be a difficult play to stage." The "movie scenes of war were shown on a big picture window of upstairs," and, they added tactfully, choosing their words carefully, the audience "applauded more as the play progressed."[110] Lawson responded, somewhat apologetically, that "there is (and has always been) a weakness in the last act which lacks the emotional depth and clarity of the first and second acts."[111] He had written a play of the same name in 1938, then "used the title for an entirely different play, written in the Soviet Union in 1961." "I am dissatisfied with it," he admitted—and so were many in the audience.[112]

He remained "dissatisfied" with ongoing trends in that part of the world and thus was not taken aback with the turmoil that gripped Prague in 1968. It was "true that the capitalist press . . . and I suspect that the CIA has a hand in many of the struggles taking place in Czechoslovakia and Poland." "But these two countries," he thought, "represent quite different issues and situations. I don't know enough about the facts to make a judgment. Certainly we cannot deal abstractly with such concepts as 'pure artistic freedom' which is nonsense." Still, "enormous mistakes have been made in these countries," and blame began at the top with the Party. "I am shocked by the element of anti-Semitism in the treatment of difficulties with students in Poland," he said, a reflection of that nation's traditional Catholicism, which was to erupt in full force after 1989. Still, he remained ambivalent: "I don't know answers and I refuse to reach fixed conclusions without adequate information."[113]

And, yes, the Soviet Union also had "made grave mistakes in the whole period following World War II." However, Lawson had "no intention of aligning . . . with those left-wing people who join with Nixon and Reagan and all the most backward elements in this country in sweeping attacks on the Soviet Union, which take no account of the war danger." There was "room for a lot of legitimate difference of opinion regarding the Soviet handling of the Czech crisis," a position that put him at odds with some of his comrades, but he was not ready to abandon the socialist project altogether despite manifest flaws.

As for China, Lawson was less sympathetic. "I don't believe what I read in the commercial press," he said, this time commenting on upheaval in China. "I think there have been strange mistakes made in China—they go back to the views expressed by Mao Tse-tung during the Yenan period in 1943."[114] For it was there that Mao, in Lawson's opinion, made a grievous blunder; he "gave lectures on culture which propose that all the culture of the past (feudal or bourgeoisie) must be discarded to make way for revolutionary culture." This belief, he considered, was monumentally misguided and already had crossed the Pacific, where "the idea that people can get rid of the past (without understanding or using it) is common in the Black Liberation movement and the New Left." He rejected "Chinese charges of return to capitalism" in the Soviet Union—ironic in light of twenty-first-century developments in Beijing.[115]

Undeterred, Lawson returned to L.A.—to what a friend called "your wonderful hilltop home,"[116] "above (or almost above) the smog," said Lawson[117]—and in no time was pounding away musically on his trusty typewriter. "If Jack ever dies," said one admirer, "which, with his constitution, his will and his urgency to work, is a long way off, he will die with a typewriter on his lap!"[118] "Excuse my adopting such a literary tone to this letter," Lawson informed two friends. "But I've been sitting at this damn typewriter in this booklined study grappling with ideas for so long that the typewriter can't write in any other way. It just automatically starts to argue about 'alienation' and 'commitment' and the complex relationship of art and politics."[119]

There he sat and worked, hour on end, in his crowded study, surrounded by a library that filled three and a half walls of a room about fourteen by twenty-five feet in size. The books mainly concerned U.S. history and cultural matters, with a considerable section devoted to theater and cinema.[120] There were an estimated "3600" books in his formidable library,[121] and close by were piles of scholarly and popular journals. Now in his seventies and not as hale as he once had been, Lawson peered at the world from behind thick lenses and dark, ink-smudged eyes still weak from operations for cataracts, a condition worsened by unforgiving prison conditions. His limp, a product of injuries decades earlier, was more pronounced, his clothes more rumpled than usual, his shoulders more stooped. One journalist who met him then revealed that his "weathered face and sharp features give him the look of an ancient Indian medicine man. But there is no sourness of age, no taint of any pessimism. His thoughts sparkle and crackle as if high tension wires laced his skull."[122] "I am addicted," Lawson said at this juncture, "fatally perhaps, to analysis—not psycho but theatrical,"[123] and he could have added other categories besides.

He thought it "foolish to get so deep into any work that it occasions a sort of nervous exhaustion and/or concentration." "But," said the tireless writer, "I know from hard experience that this is the only way to get a good result," so there he was, "about to head down another long stretch."[124] He was off once more, well aware that "writing seems to get more and more difficult, probably because I grow wiser and less content with easy formulations."[125] When one interlocutor met him during this period, he "had the impression I was meeting a man in his early 30s so far as energy and purposefulness is concerned."[126]

This youthful mien was maintained in no small part because of Lawson's penchant in his latter years to spend considerable time on college campuses—though his reluctance to sign loyalty oaths hampered his ability to teach at some schools.[127] "I love teaching," he said at one point.[128] He appreciated the incipient rebelliousness of the 1960s and, in turn, learned as he was instructing.[129]

He found that the growing discontent on campuses translated into increased invitations to speak. "I was worried about my presentation and spent a good deal of time on it, feeling my views on existentialism, 'alienation' and the theatre of the absurd might run counter to the general trend," he said of one appearance. "But I need not have worried. The reception was heartening, with applause at moments and an ovation at the end"—though "most of the plays offered by various student groups were in direct contradiction to what I said."[130] Still, he was energized by the students and "very sympathetic to these youthful movements" they had spearheaded, and the "general ferment" they generated, which were to weaken the conservative hold on the nation that had brought the "blacklist" and so much misery to his doorstep.[131]

Though he still faced a deep and pervasive ostracizing, Lawson maintained stalwartly in 1966 that "with all the hardships we've had, my wife and I would both agree that we've probably been happier and more creative over these 10 or 15 years than any other parts of our live." Regrets? He had a few, one being "cut off from other intellectuals in Hollywood—many of them admire me," he contended, "but can't see me because it's dangerous."[132]

Now Lawson was rarely one to shrink from criticism. He no doubt agreed with what Trumbo once told him—"I have since learned that the mercy of friends can leave gaping holes in one's armor through which enemies may deliver the most telling and disastrous blows."[133] He probably also agreed as well with what the writer Joseph Freeman once told him: "Mark Twain was right: difference of opinion is a good thing, it makes for horse racing. Albert Camus was right, too: Politics divides, art unites."[134] Still, the enforced isolation he suffered and the slings and arrows launched at his integrity took their toll in his final years, especially on linked matters of art *and* politics, where he found that those who were not his friends had no mercy; this became clear when his book on film, which was critical of film in the socialist bloc, was reviewed as if he were an apologist for this same body of work. He "deeply resented Pauline Kael's 1965 review in the 'New York Times,'" which was most egregious in this regard. Yet, despite what he now wrote and thought, there was a "purely *political* attack on the book, which assumes that I am stupid, parroting a line and downright dishonest." He was treated as a Soviet parrot though his critiques of flaws in that society were more perceptive than most. For Lawson, this was all the more troubling because of "how deeply (and to my way of thinking) unfairly, I have been prosecuted and persecuted along these lines: my professional career has been wrecked, my creative opportunities limited." Yet somehow he was being written off as if he were the Grim Reaper, ready to exact fierce retribution on the straying. "I am emotional about this," he continued, "because I feel I have something to offer to the culture." The "fact that I have undergone brutal political persecution is one thing; the fact that people who call themselves intellectuals endorse this persecution and treat me as [if] I were an idiot supporter of dictatorship or even a traitor is another thing," he cried.[135]

But to Lawson's detriment, a nation that prided itself on its adoration of a "marketplace of ideas," "pluralism," and all the rest found it difficult to accept an unconventional Communist. Repeatedly he was described as dishing out apologias for policies he abhorred.[136] He thought he knew why. "I feel that I am one of the few left-wing people in the cultural field who can command some attention from at least a limited public," he explained at one point. "It seems to me," he said, "that this is the reason the book has been so savagely attacked."[137] Kael, undeterred, rebuked what she saw as the "displaced political fundamentalism" of this "tract of the thirties" by a "hack writer"[138]—remarks Alvah Bessie called "crap" and a "turd."[139] These denunciations were not assuaged by the fact that London's *Punch*— reflecting once more Lawson's more favorable treatment abroad, where the atmosphere was less conservative—found this book "authoritative, exhaustive and on the whole remarkably interesting."[140]

Lawson was sorely disappointed with the response to his book, "not because they find fault," he said, "but because they cannot seem to grasp the seriousness of the approach to the structure and organization of film as a new narrative form. In the history of film theory, there has been a split between aesthetic theory, which ignores story values and the story film, which is the commercial form and depends chiefly on theatrical and fictional values. I find it odd that no reviewer in the United States, or, as far as I know in England or France, has grasped this essential point."[141]

The burden of accumulated years and the insight it presumably brings—not to mention the need to go over the heads of critics to explain oneself—inexorably brings the writer to contemplate the memoir. And so it was that Lawson, who was motivated even more because of the felt need to explain himself and his times to those who "savagely attacked" him and to future generations, sat down to try to recount what had happened to him and his world. A man who valorized structure and form, he knew that "the autobiographical method involves many large difficulties, which are not by any means solved." So he sought to "develop an imaginative and vigorous presentation of the main cultural ideas and forces of each period, as they came to me personally, in my work and my contacts and my reading, etc." "It remains to be seen," he added self-critically, "whether I can get the right tone and structure for what I am seeking."[142] Lawson was "hampered," as he knew all too well, "by the fact that I take a very long time to prepare even a short article, and have never learned journalistic facility." Thus, his memoir remained unpublished at his passing,[143] not least since he had "nagging uncertainties about every page of it"; he freely acknowledged that it was the "most important work I have done."[144] Yet despite his writing skill and the immensely fascinating story he had to tell, he received repeated rejections from publishers for this work,[145] though he had more success in selling his vast archives on which he based this proposed book.[146]

This was so although he was focusing intensely on the project, at one point "[writing] every day for two months," though the "wolves are not too far from the door." He felt "intense personal emotion about this project: it means everything to me," to the point where he decided not to "take a commercial black market film job," which would mean "abandoning the whole thing for four to six months," something he desperately sought to avoid, despite his financial difficulties.[147]

But Lawson never published this book, which served to diminish understanding of the Red Hollywood he had done so much to construct—not to mention weaken comprehension of his own life and career.

Conclusion

By 1977 the once-energetic Lawson had slowed down considerably. Now well into his eighties, he had failing eyesight and was experiencing the onset of Parkinson's disease, a motor system disorder often characterized by tremors, stiffness of limbs, slowness of movement, and impaired balance and coordination. The cruelest aspect for Lawson, perhaps, was how this hindered his ability to write, to read, and to visit theaters to watch movies. This in itself was a death sentence.

His body, in short, had been "savagely attacked" by the ravages of time, which left him in ill humor. As early as January 1956, he had to spend two months in New York enduring "two operations for cataracts, which had rendered him partially blind"—a cruel penalty for an "omnivorous" reader.[1] "I had an exceptionally bad time," he acknowledged agonizingly "because the first operation (on one eye) seemed all right and then a film formed over it again." Then he "had a great deal of further trouble, because the attempt to cut through to open up the eye was bungled, and the eye was in danger." This led to the second operation, and "for a few days after," there was "bad pain and one must rest and be very careful of any strain for five or six weeks." After recovering, his eyesight was "perfect with glasses—indeed, it [is] actually twenty-twenty," he declared. But surgery is rarely cost-free, not least in the psychic realm.[2] It was not long before he was making a discreet "inquiry concerning" the "procedure necessary" for "an individual to will his body, following death."[3]

Soon he was putting his house on the market and moving north to San Francisco to be closer to his daughter.[4] "A buyer suddenly appeared," said a marveling Lawson, "and was crazy about the house—so crazy that he has agreed to take the dog as part of the deal."[5] Living among fellow senior citizens proved to be trying, however. It was a "curious experience" and "proved that we are not the types for Old People, gathered in homes and pretending that we are pleased." "We learned a lot and met some nice people," though the "communal meals" proved trying, and the "people (mostly women who dress carefully and want to pretend that they are busy and pleased with everything)" also tested his patience.[6] But age meant Lawson had fewer choices. He now walked with difficulty and was "considering getting small crutches, which only go to one's middle and are attached to the elbows."[7] He was suffering various illnesses. "The sturm und drang of moving was too much," he told Bessie, "for both Sue and me, and we have been on the edge of half or three-quarter sickness ever since."[8] Lawson came to realize that his Parkinson's disease was not abating.[9]

By August 1977, John Howard Lawson was dead, the commitment he had forged decades earlier was now interred. Appropriately, though, even in death he was stirring controversy. Setting the tone for future constructions of Lawson, his obituary in the *New York Times* repeated the canard that he "'used to give his colleagues tips on how to get the Party viewpoint across in their dialogue,'" and this supposedly contributed to his downfall. Ring Lardner Jr. quickly took up the cudgels for his erstwhile comrade. "Actually," he instructed the newspaper correctly, "he regarded anything of that sort as a puerile approach to the politicalization of screenwriting. More revolutionary movies, he said, would come from the interdependence of form and content and the deeper penetration of human character, especially in neglected sections of the population. To his younger, less philosophic disciples, his counseling sometimes seemed remote from the immediate struggle."[10]

Nor had other controversies that had touched him disappeared. In 1994 a hullabaloo erupted once more when a popular monthly magazine wondered if there were too many Jewish Americans in Hollywood.[11]

The posthumous assault on Lawson was of a piece with the continuing assault on writers—notably screenwriters—a process he had contributed exceedingly to combating. Just before the 1947 siege of Lawson, Sheridan Gibney, who wrote the screenplay for *Anthony Adverse*, among other movies, groused that "after fifty years of motion pictures, the words 'screenwriter' and 'screenwriting' do not appear in current dictionaries,"[12] and this kind of symbolic annihilation had not dissipated as a new century dawned.

In this regard, Britain in 2003 seemed similar to the United States. For there, said a London journalist, "the majority of writers live on less than the cleaners who mop the publishers' toilets. According to the most recent Society of Authors survey, two-thirds earned less than half the national average wage and half earned less than the minimum wage. Yet the creative industries of which they are the foundation—film, TV, theatre and publishing—generate some 60 [billion pounds] a year in revenue. So why is [it] that most authors, scriptwriters, and playwrights—apart from the rare few who break through the glass ceiling to become superwriters—remain so unloved and unrewarded?" Though Alfred Hitchcock had declared years earlier that "'the three most important elements in a film are the script, the script and the script,'" screenwriters in particular reaped only a tiny percentage of the wealth their fertile imaginations generated. Writers "may spend years attending meetings, pitching ideas and consider themselves lucky if they get paid peanuts. Even if the script gets made, their pay is a fraction of the producer's and director's cut," although "if it were not for the writers, none of them would have a job."

This crass exploitation had taken on weird psychological dimensions, it was thought. "Guilt," said this journalist, "is what we feel when we secretly rage against the thing we love because we also hate it. Producers, directors, editors, critics," in fact, "the entire culture business is stuffed with people who once cherished fantasies that one day they too would write that script/play/novel/autobiography, when they had the time/spark of divine inspiration/summer in a country cottage. Whatever their excuses, the time never came and they are angry with themselves for neglecting the writer they might have been"—and strangely envious of the writers that *be*. Writing is "an unbearably vulnerable activity," though as the screenwriters of Lawson's day often complained, too many feel duty-bound to make "suggestions" for pages of the script—after the page is no longer blank. Thus, if "producers and editors really want good writing it is time they stopped neglecting writers. Make sure they get fed; value and nurture their creativity."[13] Fat chance, Lawson would have advised from the grave, as long as writers were not organized sufficiently, which was the ultimate rationale for and lesson of his post-1947 troubles and, indeed, those of his fellow writers on both sides of the Atlantic.

"Screenplays are goddam difficult to write," said Frank Pierson, the author of *Cool Hand Luke*. "The ability to compress emotion and ideas into [a] concatenation of visual image is a rare talent."[14] Yet "even in movies about moviemaking, the writer is usually crowded out by the larger presences of directors, producers and actors," with the screenwriter—when depicted at all—often characterized as a feeble nebbish. It is "remarkable that writers have been so consistently incapable of imagining themselves sympathetically on the screen"—or, more accurately, perhaps, it is remarkable that producers and studios have been so consistently incapable of allowing writers to be portrayed sympathetically on screen. The "message" from Hollywood "is clear: screenwriters are pathetic" and "embodiments of impotence."[15]

It is not enough for producers to have hammered screenwriters into the background of their cinematic creations; now, in the penultimate turnabout, the cruelest cut of all, they were portrayed ridiculously on screen—when at all. Moreover, some producers of the twenty-first century developed the sweeping idea of ridding themselves of screenwriters altogether through the vehicle of "reality" productions, that is, simply turning the camera on "real" people and deftly editing the results into a "movie." This will probably prove to be a creation of limited shelf life if *The Real Cancun* is any indication. Said one critic in response, "For the screenwriters of America, here is the day's good news: your jobs appear safe," since "the ballyhooed so-called reality film" was proving to be a dud. "The need for writers who can create character and excitement remains unthreatened," it was reported confidently; "screenwriters can tonight sleep in peace."[16]

Maybe. For it remains true that "established film theory ignored cinematographers, composers, editors, sound and visual artists, inventors of innovations in cameras, lenses and film stocks and the rest of the army of technicians and staff whose role in the creation of the Hollywood style and message may have been slight as individuals, but whose participation was essential and something very new in dramatic art." But even this appropriate revision of the conventional wisdom also adds tellingly that "the category of screenwriter (or teleplay writer) is still, for the most part, the most misunderstood and underrated creative pursuit in American media culture."[17]

A major problem faced by screenwriters today is that the fighting union that Lawson had helped to build is today a shadow of its former self. To that extent, the 1947 inquisition and the "blacklist" "worked," that is, the once-roaring writers have been defanged. Eric Hughes, who in September 2003 lost his bid to head the organization now known as the Writers Guild—headquartered in Los Angeles—remarked after being defeated by a candidate who, as it turned out, was ineligible to run, that "this is a very, very corrupt guild. . . . it was stunning to find that the winner is designated. And then you discover that the president of the guild is not even a writer?"[18] Yes, the disrespect for writers' labors had come to this.

Actually, not all the news from Hollywood about screenwriters was unpleasant. In *The Majestic*, Jim Carrey—one of the industry's brightest stars—played the leading character, an about-to-be "blacklisted" screenwriter, who has an accident and a bout of amnesia and winds up somehow in "Lawson, California," where the name of the newspaper is the *Lawson Beacon*. The film concludes with the Carrey character providing Lawson-style combative testimony before a congressional committee, evoking riveting memories of the rank importance of 1947 as a dramatic turning point in film history and, indeed, the history of the nation—and, by inference, the planet as a whole.[19]

Meanwhile, the forbiddingly contentious screenwriter comrades continued bickering even after Lawson had descended into his grave. Cole, like Lawson, refused to abandon the Party and was contemptuous of those writers who did. He felt they had made deals with the devil to return to the luscious trough of Hollywood. To be sure, as early as 1960 the left-wing screenwriter Ben Barzman, responsible for the screenplay for *The Visit*, complained of "an enormous amount of various kinds of pressures" that "exerted" upon him and others similarly situated to disavow their politics. "I think it will be a long time," he announced regretfully, "before we will be able to work openly without such a minimum gesture"; it "will take at least a generation or so for the poison to be thrown off." "I wish it were true," he moaned with no small irony, "that the conspiracy with which we are charged, that is of having some kind of clandestine and mysterious liaison were true. Then it would certainly be possible to discuss this with all the interested people," writers who hardly were as closely bound as was suspected.[20] His correspondent, Adrian Scott, had "resolved not to give" a statement disavowing his "politics" as a "condition of employment" and had suffered as a result. "It is for me," Scott declared, "a toad meat for which my stomach is not conditioned."[21]

Certainly even a casual acquaintance with some of the films of Lawson's former comrades raised eyebrows. Thus, *Bridge on the River Kwai* helped to recuperate "white supremacy" in the face of a wartime challenge from Japan.[22] Trumbo's *Exodus*, a hymn of praise to Zionism, hardly acknowledged the plight of the Palestinians. *Lawrence of Arabia* glossed over the troubled history of British colonialism in Arab lands, a complication that continues to haunt the world to this day. Maltz, in response, blasted Cole for asserting that he and Lardner had decided to "purge themselves" to get work; "behind Cole's letter," he said publicly, "is personal rage that neither Lardner nor I are in accord with his political views." His was an "act of irrational animosity and quite pitiable."[23] Cole would not back down. Maltz had become critical of the Soviet Union—too critical, thought Cole—and the feisty writer, still a Red after all these years, tried to share his opinions with the *New York Times*, along with a swipe at Trumbo.[24] He reproved Lardner for abandoning the Party and threw a punch at his "not little pride" in his "background and antecedents" in the literary elite. Well, boasted Cole, playing the class card, "I speak with equal pride of mine, coming from the working class."[25] The best that could be said was that this was further evidence—if any were needed—that the idea of a monolithic approach in Red Hollywood, directed from headquarters in the Kremlin, was a fantasy not worthy of a screenplay, though this was precisely what had helped to sideline all the participants in this debate, including Lawson himself.

On the other hand, the demise of Red Hollywood meant that Liberal Hollywood had to take the uncomfortable position of being the prime target of conservatives. During the height of the "blacklist," the liberal publisher Bennett Cerf assailed Adrian Scott, asserting, "Communists, both declared and underground, have used Liberals shamelessly in the past—and laughed at them behind their backs while they were doing it. The time for that sort of thing has long gone by."[26] Yes, it had—but as one of the prime puppeteers of this compelled divorce, Richard M. Nixon, might have put it, "Liberals" no longer had "Communists" to kick around anymore, as they were busily defending themselves against boots in their own rear end propelled by conservatives. Television, argues the analyst Victor Navasky, "was born, and defined itself and its structure, amid blacklist assumptions"; the "impact of the blacklist on our culture," he says, "is, of course, impossible to measure."[27] The same can be said for the impact on politics generally.

.   .   .

At the end of his life, the "blacklisted" director Joseph Losey remarked, "I've been asked if I'm bitter. I'm not bitter at all. But I profoundly resent the lack of opportunity to comment on my own society, my own roots, my own country."[28] The tragedy of John Howard Lawson and Red Hollywood alike was not only what befell him and his comrades but what befell the nation in which he was born, when he was deprived of the opportunity to comment on—and influence—his society, his roots, his country.

Notes

1. *Los Angeles Examiner,* 31 December 1947.

2. See, e.g., Gerald Horne, *Class Struggle in Hollywood, 1930–1950: Moguls, Mobsters, Stars, Reds and Trade Unionists* (Austin: University of Texas Press, 2001). The apostate Communist film director Edward Dmytryk argued that Lawson and Hollywood were chosen for the spotlight, since their foes knew this would draw dramatic attention to the campaign to reverse the still-lingering pro-Moscow feelings from the war. See oral history, Edward Dmytryk, 1979, 193, Southern Methodist University, Dallas.

3. Clipping without source, 25 August 1938, Scrapbooks, V. 4:1, U.S. Congress, HUAC, 32 August 1937–10 November 1938, J. Parnell Thomas Collection, Richard Nixon Library, Yorba Linda, California.

4. Ibid., Scrapbooks, *Hudson News,* ca. June 1938.

5. J. Parnell Thomas, "The Price of Vigilance" [memoir], n.d., unclear pagination, J. Parnell Thomas Collection.

6. *Washington Star,* 26 October 1947.

7. Thomas memoir: "During the period from January 22, 1947 to December 21, 1948, accredited representatives of the Government made 5975 visits to the Committee file room to secure information." HUAC had "compiled lists alone of 363,119 signatures to Communist election petitions for various years in 20 states," allowing the committee to "afford an avenue of information not originally possessed by any other Government agency."

8. Ibid.

9. Ibid. He adds: "Our Negro staffer, Alvin Stokes was a sincere, extremely loyal, always fine worker. He was, however, never popular with the dyed-in-the-wool Southerners on the team." Investigator Robert Stripling had a "face and glassy eye" that "demoralized witnesses," along with a "photographic memory and total recall . . . a quick temper and a genius for work."

10. Quoted in Eric Bentley, *Bernard Shaw, 1856–1950* (New York: New Directions Books, 1959), 107.

11. A. M. Sperber and Eric Lux, *Bogart* (New York: Morrow, 1997), 376–77.

12. "Knute" to "Dear Thorg," 13 November 1947, Files on "The Hollywood Blacklist," Writers' Guild, Los Angeles.

13. Lauren Bacall, *By Myself* (New York: Knopf, 1979), 159.

14. U.S. Congress, House of Representatives, Committee on Un-American Activities, 80th Cong., 1st sess., 20–24, 27–28, 30 October 1947 (Washington, D.C.: Government Printing Office, 1947), 290, Reel 12, *Communist Activity in the Entertainment Industry: FBI Surveillance Files on Hollywood, 1942–1958,* ed. Daniel J. Leab (Bethesda, Md.: University Publications of America, c1991).

15. Thomas memoir.

16. *PM,* 28 October 1947.

17. *Daily Variety,* 28 October 1947.

18. Reel 12, *Communist Activity in the Entertainment Industry.*

19. Carey McWilliams, *The Education of Carey McWilliams* (New York: Simon and Schuster, 1978), 136. Ring Lardner Jr., one of the celebrated Hollywood Ten persecuted along with Lawson, remarked later that "by using the First Amendment" at the hearing, "we would be saying the whole investigation was unconstitutional—that where Congress was forbidden to legislate, Congress was forbidden to investigate. . . . all the relevant Supreme Court decisions up till that time gave us confidence that our position would be vindicated." See *New York Times,* 18 March 1978.

20. Paul Friedland, *Political Actors: Representative Bodies and Theatricality in the Age of the French Revolution* (Ithaca, N.Y.: Cornell University Press, 2002), 2, 3, 18, 167, 168, 181, 188, Reflecting on the role of actors in politics, Spencer Tracy once remarked, "'Remember who shot Lincoln.'" See Christopher Andersen, *An Affair to Remember: The Remarkable Love Story of Katharine Hepburn and Spencer Tracy* (New York: Morrow, 1997), 190. Note as well that Bobby Seale, one of the founders of the Black Panthers, wanted to become an actor. See Theodore Draper, "The Black Panthers," in Irving Howe, ed., *Beyond the New Left* (New York: McCall, 1970), 221.

21. Andrea Most, *Making Americans: Jews and the Broadway Musical* (Cambridge, Mass.: Harvard University Press, 2003), 14.

22. Lawson was not alone in facing bigotry of this sort. The activist actor Edward G. Robinson was singled out repeatedly for biased abuse. See, e.g., T. C. Condon to Edward G. Robinson, 12 December 1938, Box 30, Folder 14b, Edward G. Robinson Papers, University of Southern California, Los Angeles. Prompted by correspondence from Mary Pickford, Robinson had to remind the "nation's sweetheart" that "the charge that Jews in New York are going to vote for Roosevelt as a group, is wholly unjust and untrue." See Edward G. Robinson to Mary Pickford, 4 November 1940, Box 30, Folder 14b, Edward G. Robinson Papers. This tendency accelerated as the Red Scare dawned. See report by Arnold Forster on ultraconservative meeting held in L.A. on 9 June 1949, Box 30, Folder Misc., Edward G. Robinson Papers. Here Robinson was assailed as a Red; his "'real name,'" it was said, "'is Immanuel Goldenberg.'"

23. Edward S. Shapiro, *A Time for Healing: American Jewry since World War II* (Baltimore: Johns Hopkins University Press, 1992), 40, 35.

24. Thomas memoir.

25. Felicia Deborah Herman, "Views of Jews: Anti-Semitism, Hollywood and American Jews, 1913–1947" (Ph.D. diss., Brandeis University, 2002), 215, 216, 217, 174. A number of Lawson's comrades pioneered in raising the "Jewish Question" in their screenplays. Consider *Exodus*, written by Dalton Trumbo, and Trumbo's screenplay of Bernard Malamud's novel *The Fixer*. See Arnold Forster of the Anti-Defamation League (ADL) to Dore Schary, 5 September 1963, Box 156, Folder 1, Dore Schary Papers, State Historical Society of Wisconsin, Madison. With apparent satisfaction, Forster reported that the ADL "did not play any leadership role in the Washington March" featuring Martin Luther King in August 1963; "it had no delegation as such," suggesting how the targeting of Jewish Americans may have had impact on a broader liberalism: Arnold Forster to Ralph Lazarus, 9 September 1963, Box 156, Folder 1, Dore Schary Papers. Undaunted, right-wing bigots persistently raised this alleged tie between Jewish Americans and communism. See, e.g., George Van Horn Moseley to S. R. Rosenberg, 24 June 1939, Box 3, News Research Service Papers, Hoover Institute, Stanford University, Palo Alto, California: "The facts show that Communism is Jewish controlled." See also Gerald L. K. Smith, "Is Communism Jewish?" ca. 1946, Box 1, 73043–10, Glen A. Chandler Papers, Stanford University.

26. See, e.g., *Chicago Daily News*, 26 November 1955; *Washington Post*, 26 August 1960; *B'Nai B'rith Messenger*, 7 September 1956.

27. U.S. Congress, House of Representatives, Committee on Un-American Activities, 80th Cong., 1st sess., 20–24 October, 27–30 October 1947 (Washington, D.C.: Government Printing Office, 1947), Box 61, Folder 9, Jack Warner Collection, University of Southern California.

28. Leon Gordon of MGM to Richard M. Nixon, 6 August 1952, PPS 10.183, 8, Richard M. Nixon Papers, Richard M. Nixon Library.

29. Remarks of Ben Margolis, 8 September 1977, Memorial for John Howard Lawson, KZ0347a, Pacifica Radio Archives, North Hollywood, California.

30. Richard M. Nixon to H. L. Perry, 17 June 1947, PE 247, Richard M. Nixon Papers.

31. Richard M. Nixon on Ronald W. Reagan, 12 April 1961, Box 621, Richard M. Nixon Pre-presidential Papers, National Archives and Records Administration, Laguna Niguel, California.

32. Richard M. Nixon to "Dear Harry," 26 September 1957, Box 798, Richard M. Nixon Pre-presidential Papers.

33. "D" [Nixon] to "Dear Jack," 13 February 1962, Box 798, Richard M. Nixon Pre-presidential Papers.

34. Spyros Skouras to Richard M. Nixon, 8 October 1960, Box 698, Richard M. Nixon Pre-presidential Papers.

35. *New York Times*, 25 March 1973.

36. *Time*, 4 July 1949.

37. U.S. Congress, House of Representatives, Committee on Un-American Activities, 82nd Cong., 1st sess., 17, 23, 24, and 25 April and 16, 17, and 18 May 1951, Box 30, Folder 11, Edward G. Robinson Papers.

38. Ronald Reagan with Richard G. Hubler, *Where's the Rest of Me?* (New York: Duell, Sloane and Pearce, 1965), 161, 162, 166–67.

39. Edmund Morris, *Dutch: A Memoir of Ronald Reagan* (New York: Random House, 1999), 288.

40. Speech by Roy Brewer, 3 June 1953, Box 1146, Folder 5, Cecil B. DeMille Papers, Brigham Young University, Provo, Utah.

41. Raymond Chandler to James Sandoe, 17 January 1948, in Frank Mc-Shane, ed., *Selected Letters of Raymond Chandler* (New York: Columbia University Press, 1981), 106–8.

42. Interview, Dalton Trumbo, n.d., Box 1, Nancy Lynn Schwartz Papers, University of Wyoming, Laramie: "Every screenwriter wages guerilla warfare. . . . organized writers in Hollywood . . . contributed to [the] decline in use of reactionary themes in movies of [the] '30s."

43. John Howard Lawson, *Film: The Creative Process; The Search for an Audio-Visual Language and Structure* (New York: Hill and Wang, 1967), vii.

44. Quoted in *Chicago Tribune*, 11 November 1946.

45. Oral history, Edmund Hall North, 1986, 300/270, University of California–Los Angeles (UCLA).

46. Howard Koch, *As Time Goes By: Memoirs of a Writer* (New York: Harcourt Brace Jovanovich, 1979), 97.

47. Adrian Scott to "Dear Marian," 13 February 1949, Box 4, Folder 5, Adrian Scott Papers, University of Wyoming.

48. Interview, Emmett Lavery, n.d., Box 1, Nancy Lynn Schwartz Papers.

49. George Weltner to Barney Balaban, 5 November 1962, Box 1, George Weltner Papers, University of Wyoming.

50. See oral history, Alfred Lewis Levitt, 1991, 300/354, UCLA.

51. Quoted in Ronald L. Davis, *The Glamour Factory: Inside Hollywood's Big Studio System* (Dallas: Southern Methodist University Press, 1993), 350–51.

52. Quoted in Alvin Yudkoff, *Gene Kelly: A Life of Dances and Dreams* (New York: Backstage Books, 1999), 174.

53. Ronald Reagan to Hugh Hefner, 4 July 1960, in *Reagan: A Life in Letters*, ed. Kiron K. Skinner, Annelise Anderson, and Martin Anderson (New York: Free Press, 2003), 149.

54. Quoted in Martin Bauml Duberman, *Paul Robeson* (New York: Knopf, 1988), 527.

55. John Dos Passos, *The Best Times: An Informal Memoir* (New York: New American Library, 1966), 47. See also John Dos Passos, *Most Likely to Succeed* (Boston: Houghton Mifflin, 1966).

56. Roger Dooley, *From Scarface to Scarlett: American Films in the 1930s* (New York: Harcourt Brace Jovanovich, 1981), 598.

57. *New Yorker,* 21 January 1939, Box 7, Folder 3, John Howard Lawson Papers, Southern Illinois University–Carbondale.

58. John Howard Lawson, "Ten Days That Shook the World," Box 6, Folder 6, John Howard Lawson Papers.

59. Jeff Young, *Kazan: The Master Director Discusses His Films* (New York: Newmarket, 1999), 196. See also Albert Maltz to John Howard Lawson, 18 March 1959, Box 1, Folder 4, John Howard Lawson Papers.

60. Interview, Carl Foreman, n.d., Nancy Lynn Schwartz Papers.

61. Memorial for John Howard Lawson, 8 September 1977, KZ0347a, Pacifica Radio Archives. See also Jay Williams, *Stage Left* (New York: Scribner's, 1974), 205. Famed theater producer and Lawson intimate Harold Clurman declared that "'Odets knew very little of Chekhov's work at this time ... but quite a lot about Lawson's *Success Story,* in which he had served as Luther Adler's understudy. It was Lawson's play which brought Odets an awareness of a new kind of theatre dialogue. It was a compound of lofty moral feeling, anger and the feverish argot of the big city.'"

62. James Agee, *Agee on Film: Criticism and Comment on the Movies* (New York: Modern Library, 2000), 36.

63. Alan Pomerance, *Repeal of the Blues: How Black Entertainers Influenced Civil Rights* (New York: Citadel, 1991), 105.

64. See, e.g., Gerald Horne, *Race War! White Supremacy and the Japanese Attack on the British Empire* (New York: New York University Press, 2003).

65. Andres Soares, *Beyond Paradise: The Life of Ramon Navarro* (New York: St. Martin's, 2003), 142.

66. Manuscript of memoir of Charlotta Bass, Box 1, Folder 3, Charlotta Bass Papers, Southern California Library for Social Studies and Research, Los Angeles. See Angus Cameron to John Howard Lawson, 27 November 1953, Box 26, Carl Marzani Papers, New York University, New York City.

67. Interview with DeMille, 24 July 1957, Box 13, Folder 5, Cecil B. DeMille Papers.

68. Brenda Gayle Plummer, *Rising Wind: Black Americans and U.S. Foreign Affairs, 1935–1960* (Chapel Hill: University of North Carolina Press, 1996), 231.

69. Karol Kulik, *Alexander Korda: The Man Who Could Work Miracles* (New Rochelle, N.Y.: Arlington House, 1975), 314.

70. Aljean Harmetz, *The Making of Casablanca: Bogart, Bergman and World War II* (New York: Hyperion, 2002), 300.

71. Clayton R. Koppes and Gregory D. Black, *Hollywood Goes to War: How Politics, Profits and Propaganda Shaped World War II Movies* (New York: Free Press, 1987), 70.

72. Martin Berkeley, a harsh critic of Lawson, dismissed the idea that he or Communists generally could trick producers and executives and sneak propaganda onto the screen. See U.S. Congress, House of Representatives, Committee on Un-American Activities. 82nd Cong., 1st sess., 8 and 21 March; 10, 11, 12, and 13 April 1951, Testimony of Martin Berkeley (Washington, D.C.: Government Printing Office, 1951), 1590.

73. This group included, besides Lawson, Dalton Trumbo, Ring Lardner Jr., Lester Cole, Adrian Scott, Herbert Biberman, Samuel Ornitz, Edward Dmytryk, Alvah Bessie, and Albert Maltz.

74. See Maurice Rapf, *Back Lot: Growing Up with the Movies* (Lanham, Md.: Scarecrow Press, 1999), 88: "Being involved with the Party (politics) took a lot of time. I went to meetings two or three times a week and wrote articles, speeches, and reports when I was not at meetings. I had too little time to pursue my craft as a screenwriter."

75. Howard Fast, *Being Red: A Memoir* (Boston: Houghton Mifflin, 1990), 78–79.

76. Quoted in Natalie Robins, *Alien Ink: The FBI's War on Freedom of Expression* (New Brunswick, N.J.: Rutgers University Press, 1993), 426.

77. F. Scott Fitzgerald, *The Last Tycoon* (New York: Scribner's, 1941), 120, 126–27. One character is "thinking about Russia" and a film about it, "told in terms of the American thirteen states, . . . he considered he was very fair to Russia—he had no desire to make anything but a sympathetic picture." The protagonist, Monroe Stahr, a film mogul, "had the script department get him up a two-page 'treatment' of the *Communist Manifesto*." In the 1976 film version of this novel directed by Elia Kazan, Jack Nicholson—the Red—knocks out Stahr, played by Robert De Niro.

78. Quoted in Arthur Mizener, *The Far Side of Paradise: A Biography of F. Scott Fitzgerald* (Boston: Houghton Mifflin, 1951), 225. The Communist screenwriter Ring Lardner Jr., author of *M*A*S*H** and *The Cincinnati Kid,* said that Fitzgerald thought of himself during this time as a Communist, but the Party thought he was too unreliable to be admitted into its hallowed ranks. See interview, Ring Lardner Jr., n.d., Box 1, Nancy Lynn Schwartz Papers. See also Matthew Josephson, *Infidel in the Temple: A Memoir of the Nineteen-Thirties* (New York: Knopf, 1967), 449–50. The writer visited Fitzgerald. "I asked him if it were true that many Hollywood writers had gone left. He nodded, looked thoughtful, then ventured: 'I have been reading Marx too—very impressive.'"

79. Quoted in Norberto Fuentes, *Hemingway in Cuba* (Secaucus, N.J.: Lyle Stuart, 1984), 169, 189. See also Linda Patterson Miller, ed., *Letters from the Lost Generation: Gerald and Sarah Murphy and Friends* (Gainesville: University Press of Florida, 2002), 95, Ernest Hemingway to Gerald and Sarah Murphy, 7 November 1934: "All the Communists make a 'minimum of' a thousand dollars a week including Jack Lawson who says that no child has ever been born in one of my books because I am afraid to face the future." The FBI took note when Hemingway served as "vice-president and member of the Board of Directors of the League of American Writers, Inc., 'which is reportedly a Communist front organization.'" See Herbert Mitgang, *Dangerous Dossiers: Exposing the Secret War against America's Greatest Authors* (New York: Fine, 1988), 68.

80. See Barbara Leaming, *Orson Welles: A Biography* (New York: Viking, 1985), 88. See also Report, 24 October 1942, Record Group 46, R6157·, Box 46, Records of the United States Senate Internal Security Subcommittee, National Archives and Records Administration.

81. "Paul" to John Howard Lawson, 4 June 1953, Box 35, Folder 1, John Howard Lawson Papers.

82. Clifford Odets, "Looking Back," *Educational Theatre Journal* 28 (December 1976): 495–500; quotation on 495.

83. Helen Dreiser to John Howard Lawson, 31 December 1946, Box 10, Folder 5, John Howard Lawson Papers. See also Lawson's remarks in *Daily Worker*, 1 February 1946.

84. John Howard Lawson to W. A. Swanberg, 9 August 1963, W. A. Swanberg Papers, University of Pennsylvania, Philadelphia. See, e.g., John Howard Lawson to Bill Reuben, 11 February 1969, Box 45, Folder 1, John Howard Lawson Papers.

85. Charles Chaplin to "John," 9 September 1955, Box 1, Folder 1, John Howard Lawson Papers.

86. Eslanda Robeson to John Howard Lawson, 3 March 1965, Box 18, Folder 2, John Howard Lawson Papers. See also *Daily Worker*, 23 November 1964.

87. Jonathan Lee Chambers, "Artist-Rebel to Revolutionary: The Evolution of John Howard Lawson's Aesthetic Vision and Political Commitment, 1923–1937" (Ph.D. diss., Southern Illinois University, 1996), 30.

88. Edmund Wilson, *The Shores of Light: A Literary Chronicle of the Twenties and Thirties* (New York: Farrar, Straus and Young, 1952), 235, 371. Wilson added that Lawson "even more than his ally, [John] Dos Passos, . . . is given to adolescent grievances and adolescent enthusiasms." He also spoke of "Lawson's wit" and "technical inventions," along with his "bathos and bad rhetoric." See also Leon Edel, ed., *Edmund Wilson: The Thirties; From Notebooks and Diaries of the Period* (New York: Farrar, Straus and Giroux, 1980).

89. John Howard Lawson, "Ten Days That Shook the World," ca.1967, Box 6, Folder 6, John Howard Lawson Papers: "I spent a weekend with Edmund Wilson in January 1932. He was living near the ocean in Santa Barbara with his family. We argued earnestly about politics: he was involved in the struggle led by the Communist Party to organize workers and farmers to meet the ravages of the Depression. It was a time of suffering and anger. I admired Wilson, and was especially affected by his study of the romantic temper in literature from 1870 to 1930, 'Axel's Castle.'" Wilson was "sure that Marxism offered the answer to aesthetic as well as to social problems," though Lawson was not as certain—then; however, Wilson was "more familiar with Marxist thought than I was and he stimulated my curiosity." See also Harold Clurman, *All People Are Famous: Instead of an Autobiography* (New York: Harcourt Brace, 1974), 91: "I shall never forget—as a sign of [the] times—the evening . . . when [Edmund] Wilson attended the Group Theatre performance of [Lawson's] *Success Story*: on the line 'there's nothing in the world so rotten as business,' he applauded; someone else hissed."

90. Interview with John Howard Lawson, *Cineaste* 8, no. 2 (Fall 1977): 4–11, 58, 7, Clipping File: John Howard Lawson, Billy Rose Library, New York Public Library, New York City.

91. *Trumbo vs. U.S., Court of Appeals*, "Joint Appendix," ca. 1948, Box 20, Margolis-McTernan Collection, Southern California Library for Social Studies

and Research, Los Angeles: In 1920 writers attempted to form a loose affiliation with the Authors' League of America but met with stiff opposition from the studios. In May 1927, at the suggestion of the mogul Louis B. Mayer, the Academy of Motion Picture Arts and Sciences was formed to coordinate the various branches of the industry—a maneuver wisely viewed as a preemptive strike against further unionization.

92. Jorja Prover, *No One Knows Their Names: Screenwriters in Hollywood* (Bowling Green, Ohio: Bowling Green State University Press, 1994), 31–32, 13.

93. Paul Buhle and Dave Wagner, *A Very Dangerous Citizen: Abraham Lincoln Polonsky and the Hollywood Left* (Berkeley and Los Angeles: University of California Press, 2001), 92.

94. Adrian Scott to Dean Ward, 1 May 1970, Box 7, Folder 1, Adrian Scott Papers.

95. *New York Times,* 7 November 1976.

96. *New York Review of Books,* 20 September 2001.

97. The literature on these linked subjects is vast, but see, e.g., David Allan Mayers, *Cracking the Monolith: U.S. Policy against the Sino-Soviet Alliance, 1949–1955* (Baton Rouge: Louisiana State University Press, 1986); William Burr, ed., *The Kissinger Transcripts: The Top Secret Talks with Beijing and Moscow* (New York: New Press, 1998); Robert Dreyfuss, *Devil's Game: How the United States Helped Unleash Fundamentalist Islam* (New York: Henry Holt, 2005); Ted Fishman, *China, Inc.: How the Rise of the Next Superpower Challenges America and the World* (New York: Scribner's, 2005).

INTRODUCTION

1. *Los Angeles Times,* 21 August 1977.

2. *Daily Variety,* 20 September 1951.

3. *Daily Variety,* 24 May 1951.

4. Kenneth Lloyd Billingsley, *Hollywood Party: How Communism Seduced the American Film Industry in the 1930s and 1940s* (Rocklin, Calif.: Prima, 1998), 55, 48.

5. Edward Dmytryk, *Odd Man Out: A Memoir of the Hollywood Ten* (Carbondale: Southern Illinois University Press, 1996), 20.

6. Walter Bernstein, *Inside Out: A Memoir of the Blacklist* (New York: Knopf, 1996), 197.

7. *Los Angeles Times,* 24 December 2002.

8. Jeff Lawson, "An Ordinary Life," in Judy Kaplan and Linn Shapiro, eds., *Red Diapers: Growing Up in the Communist Left* (Urbana: University of Illinois Press, 1998), 59, 57.

9. Remarks of Jeffrey Lawson at Memorial Meeting for John Howard Lawson, 11 August 1977, *WGA News,* November 1977, Box 1, Edward Eliscu Papers, New York University.

10. Thesis by Leroy Robinson, Box 100, Folder 2, John Howard Lawson Papers.

11. John Howard Lawson to "Dear Ladle," 13 June 1973, Gaylor Wood Papers, Archives of American Art, Smithsonian Institute, Washington, D.C.

12. John Howard Lawson, "What Is Art? In the Soviet Union and Elsewhere," 12 August 1963, Box 5, Folder 92, V. J. Jerome Papers, Yale University, New Haven, Connecticut.

13. John Howard Lawson to Durand Van Doren, 24 December 1965, Box 24, Folder 2, John Howard Lawson Papers.

14. See Steinbeck to Mavis McIntosh, April 1935, in Elaine Steinbeck and Robert Wallsten, eds., *Steinbeck: A Life in Letters* (New York: Viking, 1985), 107–8.

15. John Howard Lawson to "Hester," Box 26, Folder 4, John Howard Lawson Papers.

16. Dalton Trumbo, *The Time of the Toad: A Study of Inquisition in America* (New York: Harper and Row, 1972), 38.

17. Quoted in *New York Times Magazine*, 25 March 1973.

18. Robert Rodgers Korstad, *Civil Rights Unionism: Tobacco Workers and the Struggle for Democracy in the Mid-Twentieth-Century South* (Chapel Hill: University of North Carolina Press, 2003), 340.

19. Howard Fast, *Being Red: A Memoir* (Boston: Houghton Mifflin, 1990), 78–79. However, Lawson's son Jeffrey asserts that Fast has exaggerated the size and nature of the Lawson abode: See Jeffrey Lawson to Gerald Horne, 17 March 2005 (in possession of author).

20. *Hollywood Citizen-News*, 24 October 1947.

21. Ella Winter, *And Not to Yield: An Autobiography* (New York: Harcourt Brace, 1963), 233–34.

22. Lester Cole, *Hollywood Red: The Autobiography of Lester Cole* (San Francisco: Ramparts, 1981), 199–200.

23. *Los Angeles Times*, 14 September 1951.

24. *Hollywood Citizen-News*, 30 April 1957.

25. Jon Lewis, *Hollywood vs. Hard Core: How the Struggle over Censorship Saved the Modern Film Industry* (New York: New York University Press, 2000), 30.

26. Steven Alan Carr, "The Hollywood Question: America and the Belief in Jewish Control over Motion Pictures before 1941" (Ph.D. diss., University of Texas–Austin, 1994), 114.

27. Evan Mawdsley and Stephen White, *The Soviet Elite from Lenin to Gorbachev: The Central Committee and Its Members, 1917–1991* (New York: Oxford University Press, 2000), 16.

28. Quoted in Joseph W. Bendersky, *The "Jewish Threat": Anti-Semitic Politics of the U.S. Army* (New York: Basic Books, 2000), 204.

29. L. W. Neustadter to B'Nai B'rith, 19 April 1940, Box 55, Folder 11, Papers of the Community Relations Committee, Jewish Federation Council, California State University–Northridge (hereafter cited as CRC, JFC Papers).

30. L. W. Neustadter to Leon Lewis, Box 55, Folder 11, CRC, JFC Papers.

31. Max Vorspan and Lloyd P. Gartner, *History of the Jews of Los Angeles* (San Marino, Calif.: Huntington, 1970), 202, 205–6, 239, 241.

32. Transcript of interview with John Howard Lawson, June 1961, Box 135, Collection No. 100, UCLA.

33. George F. Custen, *Twentieth Century Fox: Darryl F. Zanuck and the Culture of Hollywood* (New York: Basic Books, 1997), 295.

34. Felicia Herman, "American Jews and the Effort to Reform Motion Pictures, 1933–1935," *American Jewish Archives Journal* 53, nos. 1 and 2 (2001): 11–44. See also Charles Higham, *Cecil B. DeMille* (New York: Scribner's, 1973), 278.

35. "Summary Report on Activities of Nazi Groups and Their Allies in Southern California," Vol. 4, 1 September 1939, Box 1, News Research Service Papers.

36. Handbill, n.d., Box 2, News Research Service Papers.

37. Ibid.

38. Leon Lewis to Walter Wanger, 9 May 1940, Box 55, Folder 11, CRC, JFC Papers. See also Melech Epstein, *The Jew and Communism, 1919–1941* (New York: Trade Union Sponsoring Committee, n.d.).

39. L. W. Neustadter to "Los Angeles Jewish County Committee," 7 May 1940, Box 55, Folder 11, CRC, JFC Papers. See also Norton B. Stern, *The Jews of Los Angeles: Urban Pioneers* (Los Angeles: Southern California Jewish Historical Society, 1981).

40. *Hollywood Citizen-News*, 24 October 1947.

41. *Los Angeles Times*, 26 December 2002.

42. John Howard Lawson, "Can Anything Be Done about Hollywood?" *Masses & Mainstream* 5, no. 11 (November 1952): 41, 44.

43. *New York Times*, 10 December 1949. Reportedly, the MGM studio decided to go along with the purges because of the "fear of possible federal censorship and a box-office decline of as much as 50 percent."

44. William Wyler to Bosley Crowther, 6 November 1947, No. 685, William Wyler Collection, Academy of Motion Pictures Arts and Sciences, Los Angeles. Wyler had reason to worry after a scrawled sign appeared on a movie palace stating, "Do not attend this theatre as William Wyler is a known Red. . . . do not see this picture." See D. E. Manton to Wyler, 5 January 1952, No. 685, William Wyler Collection.

45. *New Yorker*, 21 February 1948, 37.

46. Joseph McBride, *Frank Capra: The Catastrophe of Success* (New York: Simon and Schuster, 1992), 542–44.

47. Speech by Adrian Scott, n.d., Box 3, Folder 2, Adrian Scott Papers.

48. Adrian Scott to Office of Naval Intelligence, 12 February 1942, Box 3, Folder 40, Adrian Scott Papers: "Because of my training . . . [as] a writer . . . analytical and critical requirements that this field demands." See also, in the same file, Earl Warren to Adrian Scott, 2 April 1946: "in recognition of your service in the California State Guard . . . your service was entirely voluntary."

49. Adrian Scott, "Where Will It End?" *Cine Technician*, U.K., 14, no. 72 (May–June 1948): 80–81, Box 1, Folder 13, Adrian Scott Papers.

50. Adrian Scott to Pauline Lauber, 8 November 1948, Box 5, Folder 14, Adrian Scott Papers.

51. Clipping, n.d., Box 1, Robert Rossen Papers, University of Wyoming.

52. Clipping, the *Mirror,* December 1946, Reel 384, Box 422, National Republic Papers, Stanford University.

53. See Kenneth Gould, Editor-in-Chief of "Scholastic" Magazine, to J. W. Greenberg, 16 December 1947, Box 5, Folder 32, Adrian Scott Papers.

54. Adrian Scott to Harry Miller, 12 November 1947, Box 5, Folder 30, Adrian Scott Papers.

55. Oral history, Joan Scott, n.d., Box 1, Nancy Lynn Schwartz Papers.

56. Oral history, Edward Dmytryk, 1959, Columbia University, New York City.

57. *Film Comment,* December 1987, Box 1, Folder 6, Hollywood Blacklist Collection, Southern California Library for Social Studies and Research, Los Angeles.

58. MPA, "Screen Guide for Americans," n.d., Association of Motion Pictures and Television Producers Collection, Academy of Motion Picture Arts and Sciences.

59. *Los Angeles Times,* 21 May 1951.

60. *Daily Worker,* 26 September 1961.

61. Charlton Heston, *In the Arena: An Autobiography* (New York: Simon and Schuster, 1995), 306, 308.

1. BEGINNINGS

1. Inventory aid of Lawson Papers, n.d., John Howard Lawson Papers. See also John Howard Lawson to Dr. Eberhard Bruning, 7 September 1955, Box 13, Folder 5, John Howard Lawson Papers; Leroy Robinson to John Howard Lawson, n.d., Box 39, Folder 4, John Howard Lawson Papers.

2. John Howard Lawson writings, n.d., Box 92, Folder 2, John Howard Lawson Papers.

3. Jeff Lawson, "An Ordinary Life," in Judy Kaplan and Linn Shapiro, eds., *Red Diapers: Growing Up in the Communist Left* (Urbana: University of Illinois Press, 1998), 54–60; quotation on 58.

4. *Daily Variety,* 9–15 September 1996.

5. *Los Angeles Times,* 15 October 1989.

6. *WGA News,* November 1977, Box 1, Edward Eliscu Papers.

7. See John Howard Lawson writings, Box 2, Folders 2, 4, and 5, John Howard Lawson Papers.

8. *Savitri,* 1908, Box 61, Folder 4, John Howard Lawson Papers.

9. *A Hindoo Love Drama,* 1914, Box 61, Folder 5, John Howard Lawson Papers.

10. John Howard Lawson to Leroy Robinson, 2 January 1964, Box 39, Folder 4, John Howard Lawson Papers.

11. John Howard Lawson autobiography, n.d., Box 92, Folder 1, John Howard Lawson Papers.

12. Leroy Robinson, "John Howard Lawson at Williams College," *Bulletin of the Faculty of Liberal Arts, Nagasaki University Humanities* 20, no. 1 (1979): 1–25; quotation on 5, Clipping File: John Howard Lawson, Billy Rose Library.

13. Writings of John Howard Lawson, various dates, Box 3, Folder 2, John Howard Lawson Papers.

14. *Williams Record*, 17 November 1916, Box 3, Folder 2, John Howard Lawson Papers.

15. Leroy Robinson to Editor, *Jewish Currents*, March 1964, Box 35, Folder 9, John Howard Lawson Papers.

16. Franklin Sargent to John Howard Lawson, 22 March 1915, Box 3, Folder 4, John Howard Lawson Papers.

17. John Howard Lawson to "Mary," 19 July 1916, Box 3, Folder 4, John Howard Lawson Papers.

18. Undated clippings, Box 3, Folder 2, John Howard Lawson Papers.

19. John Howard Lawson autobiography, Box 92, Folder 2, John Howard Lawson Papers.

20. Contract between John Howard Lawson and Dorothy Donnelly, 1 September 1915, Box 3, Folder 2, John Howard Lawson Papers.

21. Undated clipping, Box 3, Folder 2, John Howard Lawson Papers.

22. See S. Forrest of Cohan & Harris, 17 May 1917, Box 3, Folder 2, John Howard Lawson Papers.

23. Passport, ca. 1919, Box 3, Folder 5, John Howard Lawson Papers.

24. John Howard Lawson autobiography, Box 92, Folder 1, John Howard Lawson Papers.

25. *New York Times*, 26 October 1980.

26. John Howard Lawson speech, 12 November 1955, Box 13, Folder 5, John Howard Lawson Papers.

27. Oral history, Kate Drain Lawson, 1976, George Mason University, Fairfax, Virginia. She was an "accomplished theatrical designers of sets and costumes" and worked, inter alia, with Charles Laughton (with whom she had "harrowing conflicts"), Jane Wyatt, Shelley Winters, and Robert Ryan. See Charles Higham, *Charles Laughton: An Intimate Biography* (Garden City, N.Y.: Doubleday, 1976), 146, 163.

28. Alice Walker, *In Search of Our Mothers' Gardens: Womanist Prose* (San Diego: Harcourt Brace Jovanovich, 1983).

29. Statement by Madeleine Borough, 20 June 1965, Box 17, Folder 5, John Howard Lawson Papers.

30. Letter from Sue Lawson's grandfather, 14 June 1849, Box 1, Folder 1, John Howard Lawson Papers.

31. Inventory aid, John Howard Lawson Papers.

32. John Howard Lawson autobiography, Box 92, Folder 1, John Howard Lawson Papers.

33. Ibid.

34. Groucho Marx to "Dear Sam," 6 January 1931, Box 1, Groucho Marx Papers, State Historical Society of Wisconsin.

35. John Howard Lawson to John Dos Passos, n.d., Box 5, John Dos Passos Papers, University of Virginia, Charlottesville.

36. John Howard Lawson autobiography, Box 92, Folder 1, John Howard Lawson Papers. See also Rose Lee Goldberg, *Performance Art: From Futurism to the Present* (London: Thames and Hudson, 2001); Gunter Berghaus, ed., *International Futurism in Arts and Literature* (Berlin: Walter de Gruyter, 2000); Gunter Berghaus, *Italian Futurist Theatre, 1909–1954* (Oxford: Clarendon Press, 1998).

37. Marion Meade, *Bobbed Hair and Bathtub Gin: Writers Running Wild in the Twenties* (New York: Random House, 2004), 74.

38. John Dos Passos, *The Best Times: An Informal Memoir* (New York: New American Library, 1966), 65, 67, 69, 76, 136.

39. John Howard Lawson autobiography, Box 93, Folder 5, John Howard Lawson Papers.

40. *Roger Bloomer*, Box 101, Folder 1, John Howard Lawson Papers.

41. *Minneapolis Tribune*, 11 March 1923.

42. *Nation*, n.d., vol. 116, no. 3011, p. 346, Box 4, Folder 1, John Howard Lawson Papers.

43. *Montreal Star*, 23 June 1923.

44. John Howard Lawson, *Roger Bloomer: A Play in Three Acts* (New York: T. Seltzer, 1923).

45. Ibid., 13, 23, 45, 49, 102

46. *Fort Wayne Gazette*, 11 March 1923.

47. See, e.g., Bram Dijkstra, *American Expressionism: Art and Social Change, 1920–1950* (New York: Abrams, 2003); Rainier Rumold, *The Janus Face of the German Avant-Garde: From Expressionism toward Post-Modernism* (Evanston, Ill.: Northwestern University Press, 2002); Timothy O. Benson, *Expressionist Utopias: Paradise, Metropolis, Architectural Fantasy* (Berkeley and Los Angeles: University of California Press, 2001).

48. Bernard Dick, *Radical Innocence: A Critical Study of the Hollywood Ten* (Lexington: University Press of Kentucky, 1989), 45, 46, 50. See also Mardi Valgemae, "Civil War among the Expressionists: John Howard Lawson and the Pinwheel Controversy," *Educational Theatre Journal* 20, no. 1 (March 1968): 8–14.

49. Comment by John Howard Lawson on manuscript by Jay Leyda, December 1966, Box 44, Folder 3, John Howard Lawson Papers.

50. John Howard Lawson autobiography, Box 93, Folder 5, John Howard Lawson Papers.

51. John Howard Lawson autobiography, Box 94, Folder 1, John Howard Lawson Papers.

52. Jeff Lawson, "An Ordinary Life," 58.

53. John Howard Lawson autobiography, Box 94, Folder 1, John Howard Lawson Papers.

54. John Howard Lawson, *Processional: A Jazz Symphony of American Life in Four Acts* (New York: T. Seltzer, 1925), 16, 39, 45, 58, 183.

55. John Howard Lawson autobiography, Box 92, Folder 1, John Howard Lawson Papers.

56. Transcript of John Howard Lawson, June 1961, Box 135, Collection No. 100, UCLA.

57. John Howard Lawson autobiography, Box 92, Folder 1, John Howard Lawson Papers.

58. Ibid.

59. *New York Times*, 25 December 2003.

60. Christine Stansell, *American Moderns: Bohemian New York and the Creation of a New Century* (New York: Metropolitan, 2000), 90.

61. Kenneth Lloyd Billingsley, *Hollywood Party: How Communism Seduced the American Film Industry in the 1930s and 1940s* (Rocklin, Calif.: Prima, 1998), 48.

62. "Drama Calendar" of New York Drama League, Box 4, Folder 4, John Howard Lawson Papers.

63. *New York Telegram-Mail*, 13 March 1925.

64. Clipping, 5 February 1925, Box 4, Folder 5, John Howard Lawson Papers.

65. Upton Sinclair to John Howard Lawson, 16 March 1925, Box 4, Folder 4, John Howard Lawson Papers.

66. John Howard Lawson to Upton Sinclair, 25 March 1925, Upton Sinclair Papers, Indiana University–Bloomington.

67. Advertisement from unnamed newspaper, 9 March 1925, Box 4, Folder 4, John Howard Lawson Papers.

68. *New York World*, 15 February 1925.

69. John Howard Lawson autobiography, Box 94, Folder 1, John Howard Lawson Papers.

70. Undated clipping, Box 4, Folder 5, John Howard Lawson Papers.

71. *New York Graphic*, 13 January 1925.

72. *New York Times*, 1 February 1925.

73. Ibid.

74. Clipping, 13 January 1925, Box 4, Folder 5, John Howard Lawson Papers. For production costs for *Processional*, see undated folder, Box 80, Theatre Guild Papers, Yale University.

75. Richard P. Benoit, "A Hegemonic Analysis of John Howard Lawson and the New Playwrights Theatre" (Ph.D. diss., Kent State University, 2000), 111. See also Valgemae, "Civil War among the Expressionists," 8–14.

76. *New York Times*, 1 February 1925.

77. John Howard Lawson to Ralph Willett, 25 November 1968, Box 58, Folder 1, John Howard Lawson Papers.

78. John Howard Lawson autobiography, Box 94, Folder 6, John Howard Lawson Papers.

79. John Howard Lawson to Eberhard Bruning, 8 May 1966, Box 38, Folder 2, John Howard Lawson Papers.

2. TOWARD COMMITMENT

1. John Howard Lawson speech at San Fernando State College, 1961, Box 36, Folder 1, John Howard Lawson Papers.

2. "Material for Lecture Publicity," n.d., Box 5, Folder 2, John Howard Lawson Papers.

3. John Howard Lawson autobiography, Box 94, Folder 1, John Howard Lawson Papers.

4. John Dos Passos, *The Best Times: An Informal Memoir* (New York: New American Library, 1966), 136.

5. Jack Sherman to Matthew Josephson, 8 September 1972, Box 20, Folder 478, Matthew Josephson Papers, Yale University. See also *New Yorker*, 17 November 1962.

6. *New Yorker*, 17 November 1962.

7. Tim Page, *Dawn Powell: A Biography* (New York: Holt, 1998), 60–65.

8. Michael Gold, *Change the World* (New York: International, 1936), 135.

9. Tim Page, ed., *The Diaries of Dawn Powell, 1931–1965* (South Royalton, Vt.: Steerforth Press, 1995), 7, 10

10. See, e.g., Mardi Valgemae, *Accelerated Grimace: Expressionism in the American Drama of the 1920s* (Carbondale: Southern Illinois University Press, 1972).

11. John Howard Lawson autobiography, Box 94, Folder 6, John Howard Lawson Papers.

12. John Howard Lawson to "Kreuter," 1 December 1957, Box 39, Folder 5, John Howard Lawson Papers.

13. John Howard Lawson to Otto Kahn, 18 February 1926, Box 5, Folder 1, John Howard Lawson Papers.

14. Playbill, 1926, Box 5, Folder 1, John Howard Lawson Papers.

15. John Howard Lawson, *Theory and Technique of Playwriting and Screenwriting* (New York: Putnam's, 1949), 158, xi, 302.

16. John Howard Lawson, *With a Reckless Preface: Two Plays* (New York: Farrar and Rinehart, 1934), xxi. Harold Clurman castigated *Nirvana* as "the most confused of Lawson's plays because he is a poet and not a thinker," and his "thought seems insufficiently nurtured by concrete experience of the world."

17. Statement, August 1925, Box 67, Folder 2, John Howard Lawson Papers.

18. John Howard Lawson autobiography, Box 94, Folder 7, John Howard Lawson Papers.

19. *New York Times*, 8 March 1926.

20. John Howard Lawson to Richard Brown, Box 39, Folder 4, John Howard Lawson Papers.

21. Eugene O'Neill to Mike Gold, 12 February 1925, in Travis Bogard and Jackson R. Bryer, eds., *Selected Letters of Eugene O'Neill* (New York: Limelight, 1988), 194: "I don't know anything about the 'Processional' production or about the play. Several of our organization read it. I remember but thought it too much German patent American goods. I saw . . . 'Roger Bloomer.' It had fine [points] but as mostly an adolescent's idea of adolescence—which isn't very deep or stimulating."

22. John Howard Lawson autobiography, Box 94, Folder 7, John Howard Lawson Papers.

23. Jay Williams, *Stage Left* (New York: Scribner's, 1974), 19.

24. John Howard Lawson to Richard Brown, 12 June 1964, Box 39, Folder 4, John Howard Lawson Papers.

25. John Howard Lawson autobiography, Box 94, Folder 9, John Howard Lawson Papers.

26. John Howard Lawson to "Kreuter," 1 December 1957, Box 39, Folder 5, John Howard Lawson Papers.

27. Kent Kreuter to John Howard Lawson, n.d., Box 35, Folder 3, John Howard Lawson Papers.

28. John Howard Lawson, *Film: The Creative Process; The Search for an Audio-Visual Language and Structure* (New York: Hill and Wang, 1967), 100. See also Richard Peter Benoit, "A Hegemonic Analysis of John Howard Lawson and the New Playwrights Theatre" (Ph.D. diss., Kent State University, 2000); Richard James Helldobler, "An Analysis of the Dramatic Structures of Traditional and Concept Musicals Based on the Theories of John Howard Lawson" (Ph.D. diss., Bowling Green State University, 1992).

29. John Howard Lawson to Richard Brown, 12 June 1964, Box 39, Folder 4, John Howard Lawson Papers.

30. See, e.g., Paul Avrich, *Sacco and Vanzetti: The Anarchist Background* (Princeton, N.J.: Princeton University Press, 1996).

31. *New York Times,* 22 August 1927, 24 August 1927: Lawson signed the appeal in defense of the imprisoned activists.

32. John Howard Lawson to Richard Brown, 12 June 1964, Box 39, Folder 5, John Howard Lawson Papers.

33. Lawson, *Film: The Creative Process,* 101.

34. John Howard Lawson autobiography, Box 94, Folder 7, John Howard Lawson Papers.

35. John Howard Lawson to Richard Brown, Box 39, Folder 5, John Howard Lawson Papers.

36. John Howard Lawson to Upton Sinclair, 6 April 1926, Upton Sinclair Papers.

37. *New York Times,* 1 May 1979.

38. John Howard Lawson, *Loudspeaker: A Farce* (New York: Macaulay, 1927), vii.

39. *Loudspeaker,* Box 101, Folder 1, John Howard Lawson Papers.

40. Undated clipping, Box 5, Folder 2, John Howard Lawson Papers.

41. Lawson, *Loudspeaker,* 49.

42. John Howard Lawson to Actors' Equity, 7 March 1927, Box 5, Folder 2, John Howard Lawson Papers.

43. Williams, *Stage Left,* 21.

44. John Howard Lawson autobiography, Box 94, Folder 10, John Howard Lawson Papers.

45. Dos Passos, *The Best Times,* 163–64.

46. John Howard Lawson to Kenneth Payne, 9 September 1971, Mike Gold Papers, University of Michigan–Ann Arbor.

47. Lawson, *With a Reckless Preface,* xxi.

48. John Howard Lawson speech, 1961, Box 36, Folder 1, John Howard Lawson Papers.

49. John Howard Lawson to Kenneth Payne, 9 September 1971, Mike Gold Papers. Years later he continued to assert that New Playwrights was "my idea of 'revolutionary theatre.'" It represented a "commitment," a "strong commitment (a commitment I never abandoned)"—"but it was an anarchic and undisciplined view, affected strongly by dada and surrealism." Mike Gold "had a clearer idea of politics," and he was the only member of NP who "wanted or even suggested a close relationship with the Communist Party." Yet Gold, thought Lawson, was

> profoundly mistaken in his view of theatre: he believed that an organizational and political "workers' theatre" could be created. Having much longer and closer associations with Broadway, I knew that it was probably impossible under the conditions of the twenties, to create a truly "people's or workers" theatre in any really fundamental or "revolutionary" sense, it would require a completely new orientation toward composition of audience, . . . organization of the personnel, etc. Mike believed passionately that the New Playwrights could be truly revolutionary and successful, if it followed a good organizational plan. This was a sort of romanticism which I believe was characteristic of Mike throughout his career. He simply had no conception of the aesthetic, psychological problems—real and insoluble problems of class relations and class conflict. The failure of [NP] wounded Mike deeply and to a large extent he blamed me for the dissolution." Gold's subsequent attack on Lawson was "an expression of his deep resentment and hurt about the failure of [NP]. He really believed . . . that intellectuals would naturally turn to a Marxist and 'revolutionary' view. I believe and I still believe it nearly forty years later . . . that the class position of the artist creates barriers which make it almost impossible to abandon one's class affiliations.

50. See, e.g., George A. Knox and Herbert M. Stahl, *Dos Passos and the Revolting Playwrights* (Uppsala, Sweden: A. B. Lundequistska, 1964).

51. *The International,* Box 101, Folder 1, John Howard Lawson Papers.

52. Williams, *Stage Left*, 24.

53. John Howard Lawson autobiography, Box 94, Folder 10, John Howard Lawson Papers.

54. John Howard Lawson to Kreuter, 1 December 1957, Box 39, Folder 5, John Howard Lawson Papers.

55. *Daily Worker*, 16 January 1928.

56. Benoit, "Hegemonic Analysis of John Howard Lawson," 189–90.

57. Joseph Freeman, *An American Testament: A Narrative of Rebels and Romantics* (New York: Farrar and Rhinehart, 1936), 380.

58. John Howard Lawson to Kenneth Payne, 9 September 1971, Mike Gold Papers.

59. Quoted in *New York Sun*, 12 November 1927.

60. Lester Cole, *Hollywood Red: The Autobiography of Lester Cole* (San Francisco: Ramparts, 1981), 126–27.

61. Jay Martin, *Nathaniel West: The Art of His Life* (New York: Farrar, Straus and Giroux, 1970), 347, 102: Filmmaker Michael Blankfort recalled that "there was a kind of bohemianism about West for which the 'serious' Marxist [would] show contempt.. Some Party sympathizers distrusted and resented what they regarded as his failure to 'pull his weight' . . . and at least once he was publicly attacked for this by Lawson." Later Lawson concluded that "'the left underestimated West. They saw his hatred of bourgeois society, but not his talent.'" Lawson described this "switch from the Left Bank to the radical left as 'the logical development of a more political point of view.'" Lawson realized later that "'what I was trying to do in the twenties, unsuccessfully . . . was to discover myself. I'd been running away from myself—the bohemian phase was largely running away: the finding of all sorts of metaphysical outlets for my dilemma that I hated the middle class and was yet part of it.'"

62. John Howard Lawson to Richard Brown, 22 March 1964, Box 39, Folder 4, John Howard Lawson Papers.

3. HOLLYWOOD

1. *WGA News*, November 1977, Box 1, Edward Eliscu Papers.

2. Jeff Lawson, "An Ordinary Life," in Judy Kaplan and Linn Shapiro, eds., *Red Diapers: Growing Up in the Communist Left* (Urbana: University of Illinois Press, 1998), 54–60; quotation on 56.

3. John Howard Lawson autobiography, Box 94, Folder 10, John Howard Lawson Papers.

4. John Howard Lawson to John Dos Passos, 28 November 1928, John Dos Passos Papers.

5. John Howard Lawson, Speech at San Fernando State College, 1961, Box 36, Folder 1, John Howard Lawson Papers.

6. Interview with John Howard Lawson, *Cineaste* 8, no. 2 (Fall 1977): 4–11; quotations on 4.

7. Scott Eyman, *The Speed of Sound: Hollywood and the Talkie Revolution, 1926–1930* (New York: Simon and Schuster, 1997), 177, 212, 229.

8. "A New Era in Motion Picture Writing . . . A Collective Report from the Hollywood Chapter, League of American Writers," n.d., Box 1, League of American Writers Papers, University of California–Berkeley (hereafter cited as LAW Papers).

9. *Daily Worker*, 15 August 1925. See also *Daily Worker*, 23 July 1925.

10. John Howard Lawson, *Film: The Creative Process; The Search for an Audio-Visual Language and Structure* (New York: Hill and Wang, 1967), 100.

11. William MacAdams, *Ben Hecht: A Biography* (New York: Barricade, 1990), 5, 6, 169.

12. Lawson, *Film: The Creative Process*, 106. See also Sergei Eisenstein, "Film Essays," n.d., f1973–008/001, Jay Leyda Papers, York University, Toronto.

13. *New York Times*, 29 January 1928.

14. John Howard Lawson autobiography, Box 94, Folder 10, John Howard Lawson Papers.

15. John Howard Lawson to John Dos Passos, 28 November 1928, Box 5, John Dos Passos Papers.

16. John Howard Lawson to John Dos Passos, n.d., Box 5, John Dos Passos Papers.

17. John Howard Lawson to "Mr. Dreiser," 28 September 1928, Box 1, Folder 1, John Howard Lawson Papers.

18. John Howard Lawson to W. A. Swanberg, 9 August 1963, W. A. Swanberg Papers.

19. John Howard Lawson to H. S. Kraft, 7 November 1928, Theodore Dreiser Papers, University of Pennsylvania.

20. John Howard Lawson to Theodore Dreiser, Theodore Dreiser Papers, University of Pennsylvania.

21. "Letters to John Howard Lawson on 'Sister Carrie,'" *Mainstream* 8, no. 2 (December 1955): 20–22.

22. John Howard Lawson to W. A. Swanberg, 9 August 1963, W. A. Swanberg Papers. See Theodore Dreiser to Ernest Boyd, 23 April 1931, Theodore Dreiser Papers, University of Virginia. Yet Dreiser came to embrace Lawson; it was through him that Lawson came to know Marian Ainslee, "a silent screen captionist"—and "intimate" of Dreiser—"who helped Lawson learn film technique." See Paul Buhle and Dave Wagner, *Radical Hollywood* (New York: New Press, 2002), 35.

23. John Howard Lawson to John Dos Passos, 28 November 1928, Box 5, John Dos Passos Papers.

24. John Howard Lawson, n.d., Box 5, John Dos Passos Papers.

25. John Howard Lawson to John Dos Passos, n.d., Box 5, John Dos Passos Papers.

26. John Howard Lawson to John Dos Passos, n.d., Box 5, John Dos Passos Papers.

27. John Howard Lawson autobiography, Box 95, Folder 1, John Howard Lawson Papers.

28. Lawson, *Film: The Creative Process*, 102, 104.

29. Buhle and Wagner, *Radical Hollywood*, 36.

30. John Howard Lawson to John Dos Passos, 28 November 1928 Box 5, John Dos Passos Papers.

31. Eyman, *The Speed of Sound*, 209.

32. Lawson, *Film: The Creative Process*, 105.

33. Buhle and Wagner, *Radical Hollywood*, 34–35.

34. John Howard Lawson autobiography, Box 95, Folder 1, John Howard Lawson Papers.

35. Buhle and Wagner, *Radical Hollywood*, 36.

36. John Howard Lawson to John Dos Passos, 12 January 1929, Box 5, John Dos Passos Papers.

37. John Howard Lawson to John Dos Passos, 30 August 1929, Box 5, John Dos Passos Papers.

38. Buhle and Wagner, *Radical Hollywood*, 36.

39. John Howard Lawson autobiography, Box 95, Folder 1, John Howard Lawson Papers.

40. John Howard Lawson to John Dos Passos, 12 January 1929, Box 5, John Dos Passos Papers.

41. Buhle and Wagner, *Radical Hollywood*, 35.

42. John Howard Lawson to John Dos Passos, 30 August 1929, Box 5, John Dos Passos Papers.

43. Tim Page, *Dawn Powell: A Biography* (New York: Holt, 1998), 64.

4. FROM HOLLYWOOD TO BROADWAY

1. Interview with John Howard Lawson, *Cineaste* 8, no. 2 (Fall 1977): 4–11, 58; quotation on 4.

2. John Howard Lawson, *With a Reckless Preface: Two Plays* (New York: Farrar and Rinehart, 1934), 29.

3. John Howard Lawson, *Film: The Creative Process; The Search for an Audio-Visual Language and Structure* (New York: Hill and Wang, 1967), 101–2.

4. Lawson, *With a Reckless Preface*, xxii.

5. Bernard Dick, *Radical Innocence: A Critical Study of the Hollywood Ten* (Lexington: University Press of Kentucky, 1989), 51.

6. John Howard Lawson to Jane Merchant, n.d., Box 78, Folder 1, John Howard Lawson Papers.

7. John Howard Lawson to John Dos Passos, ca. 24 August 1939, Box 5, John Howard Lawson Papers.

8. John Howard Lawson autobiography, Box 95, Folder 1, John Howard Lawson Papers.

9. Interview, Ring Lardner Jr., n.d., Box 1, Nancy Lynn Schwartz Papers. See undated notes, Box 2, Nancy Lynn Schwartz Papers.

10. "The Crowned Princes," n.d., Box 2, Nancy Lynn Schwartz Papers.

11. See Tim Page, ed., *The Diaries of Dawn Powell, 1931–1965* (Royalton, Vt.: Steerforth Press, 1995), 29, 30, 34, 36, 38, 52–53.

12. John Howard Lawson autobiography, Box 95, Folder 1, John Howard Lawson Papers.

13. Jonathan Lee Chambers, "Artist-Rebel to Revolutionary: The Evolution of John Howard Lawson's Aesthetic Vision and Commitment, 1923–1937" (Ph.D. diss., Southern Illinois University, 1996), 29.

14. John Howard Lawson autobiography, Box 95, Folder 1, John Howard Lawson Papers.

15. John Howard Lawson to Theodore Dreiser, 6 April 1931, Theodore Dreiser Papers, University of Pennsylvania.

16. Secretary of Theodore Dreiser to John Howard Lawson, 14 April 1931, Theodore Dreiser Papers, University of Pennsylvania.

17. John Howard Lawson to John Dos Passos, n.d., Box 5, John Dos Passos Papers.

18. John Howard Lawson, *Success Story* (New York: Farrar and Rinehart, 1932), 20, 61, 80, 88, 149, 161, 163.

19. Play, n.d., Box 101, File 1, John Howard Lawson Papers.

20. Harold Clurman to John Howard Lawson, 23 May 1930, Box 5, Folder 5, John Howard Lawson Papers.

21. Playbill, September 1932, Box 5, Folder 3, John Howard Lawson Papers.

22. *New York Times*, 2 October 1932. See also *New York Times*, 27 September 1932.

23. *New York Post*, 27 September 1932.

24. Mike Gold critique, *New Masses*, 10 April 1934, Box 5, Folder 5, John Howard Lawson Papers.

25. *New York Mirror*, 17 October 1932.

26. Harold Clurman, *The Fervent Years: The Story of the Group Theatre and the Thirties* (New York: Knopf, 1945), 93, 100.

27. Quoted in Margaret Brenman-Gibson, *Clifford Odets, American Playwright: The Years from 1906 to 1940* (New York: Atheneum, 1981), 212, 223, 234.

28. Marjorie Loggia and Glenn Young, eds., *The Collected Works of Harold Clurman: Six Decades of Commentary on Theatre, Dance, Music, Film, Arts and Letters* (New York: Applause, 1994), 401.

29. Letter from Cecil B. DeMille, 28 February 1933, Box 5, Folder 5, John Howard Lawson Papers.

30. See, e.g., *New York Daily Mirror*, 31 October 1932.

31. Undated clipping, Box 5, Folder 5, John Howard Lawson Papers.

32. Brenman-Gibson, *Clifford Odets, American Playwright*, 239.

33. Kshamanidhi Mishra, *American Leftist Playwrights of the 1930s: A Study of Ideology and Technique in the Plays of Odets, Lawson and Sherwood* (New Delhi: Classical, 1991), 164–65.

34. John Howard Lawson autobiography, Box 96, Folder 1, John Howard Lawson Papers.

35. Paul Buhle and Dave Wagner, *Radical Hollywood* (New York: New Press, 2002), 39.

36. Mick LaSalle, *Dangerous Men: Pre-Code Hollywood and the Birth of the Modern Man* (New York: St. Martin's, 2002), 165–66.

37. Page, *Diaries of Dawn Powell*, 50, 55, 56.

38. Andrea Most, *Making Americans: Jews and the Broadway Musical* (Cambridge, Mass.: Harvard University Press, 2003), 17, 18.

39. John Howard Lawson autobiography, Box 96, Folder 1, John Howard Lawson Papers.

40. Page, *Diaries of Dawn Powell*, 52–53.

41. John Howard Lawson, *The Hidden Heritage: A Rediscovery of the Ideas and Forces That Link the Thought of Our Time with the Culture of the Past* (New York: Citadel Press, 1968), vi.

42. Quoted in Chambers, "Artist-Rebel to Revolutionary," 30.

43. John Howard Lawson, "Communism in Relation to 'Success Story,'" ca. 1930, Box 5, Folder 3, John Howard Lawson Papers.

44. *New York Herald Tribune*, 25 September 1932.

45. Anita Loos to Michael Rosneauer, 3 January 1932, Anita Loos Papers, Yale University.

46. Playbill, March 1934, Box 5, Folder 3, John Howard Lawson Papers.

47. Brenman-Gibson, *Clifford Odets, American Playwright*, 242.

48. Clurman, *The Fervent Years*, 132.

49. *New York World-Telegram*, 23 March 1934.

50. *New York Times*, 23 March 1934.

51. Clurman, *The Fervent Years*, 133.

52. Lawson, *With a Reckless Preface*, 136–37.

53. *The Pure in Heart*, Box 101, Folder 1, John Howard Lawson Papers.

54. *New York Herald Tribune*, 21 March 1934.

55. Lawson, *With a Reckless Preface*, x. xii, xiv, xvii, xxiii.

56. Wendy Smith, *Real Life: The Group Theatre and America, 1931–1940* (New York: Grove Weidenfeld, 1990), 99.

57. Clurman, *The Fervent Years*, 133.

58. Undated clipping, ca. 1932, Clipping File, Billy Rose Library.

59. *New York Herald Tribune*, 12 August 1934: Walter Prichard Eaton maintained stalwartly that "critics cannot make or mar a play. At most they can help a little either way." Lawson's *The Pure in Heart* failed "because it is a bad play"; it was "muddled in idea, it is vitiated by mawkish sentimentality," while his celebrated *Roger Bloomer* "was the drama of a bewildered adolescent. He seems, alas, to be still a bit bewildered, to need a clearer grasp on both his materials and methods." Another irked critic snapped that "the business of using prefaces to plays to attack critics is a tradition of long-standing, brought to fine art by Bernard Shaw." Lawson thought that the "critics become dictators of the theater," but the "trouble with a great many of our playwrights is that they read unfavorable notices of their plays and immediately call to mind the ghost of Clement Scott. But they forget that they are not Ibsens or even Bernard Shaws." See *New York World-Telegram*, 29 June 1934.

60. Page, *Diaries of Dawn Powell*, 56.

61. *New York Evening Post*, 4 August 1934: "When in doubt," snapped one critic, "Lawson swings to the left . . . rather than admit his incompetence as a dramatist, Mr. Lawson lamely belabors a great art." He was no more than an "alibi seeker." "While Ibsen had his Archer, Brieux his Shaw and O'Neill his Nathan, there is not, on the compass of his horizon, a Damon for [Lawson's] Pythias." Yes, Lawson was "America's most promising playwright"; however, "day after day, week after week, month after month, year after year, he keeps promising. And nothing but a *Gentlewoman* or a *The Pure in Heart* comes of it," and "they are not much"; "if he would stop writing reckless prefaces and write a really first-rate play we might take him at his own valuation."

62. Smith, *Real Life*, 167.

63. Eric Bentley, *Bernard Shaw, 1856–1950* (New York: New Directions Books, 1959), xii–xiii.

64. Mishra, *American Leftist Playwrights of the 1930s*, 164–65, 162.

65. Clurman, *The Fervent Years*, 133–34.

66. Mishra, *American Leftist Playwrights of the 1930s*, 168.

67. Page, *Diaries of Dawn Powell*, 85.

5. COMMITMENT

1. Wendy Smith, *Real Life: The Group Theatre and America, 1931–1940* (New York: Grove Weidenfeld, 1990), 167.

2. John Howard Lawson speech at San Fernando State College, 1961, Box 36, Folder 1, John Howard Lawson Papers.

3. Article by Arthur Vogel, n.d., Box 35, Folder 9, John Howard Lawson Papers.

4. Statement by Clifford Odets, n.d., Box 35, Folder 9, John Howard Lawson Papers.

5. Lawson response to 1964 questionnaire on Clifford Odets, Box 39, Folder 3, John Howard Lawson Papers.

6. John Howard Lawson to Margaret Brenman-Gibson, 25 June 1964, Box 39, Folder 3, John Howard Lawson Papers.

7. Quoted in Margaret Brenman-Gibson, *Clifford Odets, American Playwright: The Years from 1906 to 1940* (New York: Atheneum, 1981), 562.

8. John Howard Lawson speech, 1961, Box 36, Folder 1, John Howard Lawson Papers.

9. Transcript of 1961 Interview with John Howard Lawson, Box 135, Collection No. 100, UCLA.

10. John Howard Lawson to John Dos Passos, 9 April 1934, Box 5, John Dos Passos Papers.

11. John Howard Lawson to Richard Brown, 1 November 1967, Box 39, Folder 6, John Howard Lawson Papers.

12. John Howard Lawson to Kenneth Payne, 9 September 1971, Mike Gold Papers.

13. John Howard Lawson, "A Reply to Mike Gold," *New Masses*, 17 April 1934, Box 5, Folder 5, John Howard Lawson Papers.

14. Transcript of interview with John Howard Lawson, June 1961, Box 135, Collection No. 100, UCLA.

15. Undated statement by Lawson, Box 98, Folder 8, John Howard Lawson Papers.

16. John Howard Lawson to Percy Hammond, 25 March 1934, Box 5, Folder 7, John Howard Lawson Papers.

17. John Howard Lawson to Bernard Sobel, n.d., Box 5, Folder 7, John Howard Lawson Papers.

18. *New York Times*, 23 March 1934.

19. John Howard Lawson to John Dos Passos, 9 April 1934, Box 5, John Dos Passos Papers.

20. John Howard Lawson, "A Note on 'New Masses' criticism," ca. 1934, Box 7, Folder 1, John Howard Lawson Papers.

21. See, e.g., Gerald Horne, *Black Liberation/Red Scare: Ben Davis and the Communist Party* (Newark: University of Delaware Press, 1994).

22. John Howard Lawson autobiography, Box 98, Folder 9, John Howard Lawson Papers.

23. John Howard Lawson, "A Southern Welcome (in Georgia and Alabama)," 1934, Box 5, Folder 6, John Howard Lawson Papers.

24. *New York Post*, 29 May 1934; *New York Post*, 28 May 1934; *New York Post*, 11 January 1935.

25. John Howard Lawson autobiography, Box 98, Folder 9, John Howard Lawson Papers.

26. Lawson, "A Southern Welcome."

27. John Howard Lawson article, ca. 1934, Box 88, Folder 10, John Howard Lawson Papers.

28. John Howard Lawson, *Film: The Creative Process; The Search for an Audio-Visual Language and Structure* (New York: Hill and Wang, 1967), 124.

29. *New York Times*, 7 July 1934. See also *Daily Worker*, 18 May 1934.

30. Remarks by John Howard Lawson, 12 November 1955, Box 13, Folder 5, John Howard Lawson Papers.

31. Robin D. G. Kelley, *Hammer and Hoe: Alabama Communists during the Great Depression* (Chapel Hill: University of North Carolina Press, 1990), 72.

32. John Howard Lawson autobiography, Box 98, Folder 9, John Howard Lawson Papers.

33. Kelley, *Hammer and Hoe*, 93.

34. John Howard Lawson to Jeffrey Lawson, date unclear, Box 97, Folder 1, John Howard Lawson Papers.

35. Joseph Breen to Father Tierney, 7 March 1922, Box 10, Folder 7, American Magazine Archives, Georgetown University, Washington, D.C. Here Breen expresses a vile anti-Semitism while visiting Vienna.

36. Joseph Breen to Martin J. Quigley, 1 May 1932, Box 1, Folder 2, Martin J. Quigley Papers, Georgetown University. Breen expresses more anti-Semitism here.

37. Quoted in Felicia Deborah Herman, "Views of Jews: Antisemitism, Hollywood and American Jews, 1913–1947" (Ph.D. diss., Brandeis University, 2002), 9.

38. For further detail on pro-Nazi activity in Southern California, see Reports, 1936–1940, Boxes 1–3, News Research Service Papers.

39. Oral history, Carey McWilliams, 1982, 300/195, UCLA.

40. Memorandum to Henry Hersbrun, ca. 1935, Part 1, Box 1, Folder 1, CRC, JFC Papers.

41. Clipping, 16 June 1935, Box 14, Folder 17, CRC, JFC Papers.

42. *Los Angeles Examiner,* 27 July 1933; clipping, 15 September 1936, Box 30, Folder 13, CRC, JFC Papers.

43. Transcript of John Howard Lawson interview, June 1961, Box 135, Collection No. 100, UCLA.

44. Michael Gold, *Change the World* (New York: International, 1936), 52.

45. John Howard Lawson autobiography, Box 98, Folder 7, John Howard Lawson Papers.

46. Brenman-Gibson, *Clifford Odets, American Playwright,* 367.

47. *New York Times,* 24 July 1935.

48. Lawson response to 1965 questionnaire on Clifford Odets, Box 39, Folder 3, John Howard Lawson Papers.

49. *New York Times,* 16 June 1934.

50. *New York Times,* 29 May 1934.

51. *New York Times,* 13 December 1936.

52. See, e.g., Gerald Horne, *Class Struggle in Hollywood, 1930–1950: Moguls, Mobsters, Stars, Reds and Trade Unionists* (Austin: University of Texas Press, 2001), passim.

53. Oral history, Edmond DePatie, 1965, 300/27, UCLA.

54. Joseph Breen to Martin J. Quigley, 1 May 1932, Box 1, Folder 2, Martin J. Quigley Papers.

55. John McCabe, *Cagney* (New York: Knopf, 1997), 106.

56. Groucho Marx to Sam Goldwyn, ca. April 1931, Box 1, Groucho Marx Papers.

57. Oral history, Robert Pirosh, 1986, 388, Southern Methodist University.

58. John Howard Lawson to John Dos Passos, ca. 1934, Box 5, John Dos Passos Papers.

59. John Howard Lawson to Jane Merchant, n.d., Box 78, Folder 1, John Howard Lawson Papers.

60. Interview with John Howard Lawson, *Cineaste* 8, no. 2 (Fall 1977): 4–11, 58, quotation on 4.

61. Ibid., 8.

62. Minutes of meeting of "Motion Picture Writers," 3 February 1933, Box 5, Folder 4, John Howard Lawson Papers.

63. Undated memorandum, Box 5, Folder 4, John Howard Lawson Papers.

64. John Howard Lawson, "The One Hundred Days," *ICARBS* 3, no. 1 (Summer–Fall 1976): 3, Academy of Motion Pictures Arts and Sciences.

65. John Howard Lawson autobiography, Box 96, Folder 1, John Howard Lawson Papers.

66. John Howard Lawson article, *Writers Forum* 2, no. 9 (July–September 1964), Box 20, Folder 1, John Howard Lawson Papers.

67. Undated document re: Founding of Screen Writers Guild, Michael Cole Papers. I viewed this collection in the Solana Beach, California, home of Michael Cole—son of the screenwriter Lester Cole—and he informed me then, in the spring of 2003, that he intended to deposit this collection at the University of Wyoming.

68. *Screen Guilds' Magazine* 2, no. 9 (November 1935): 5.

69. *Screen Guilds' Magazine* 2, no. 12 (February 1936): 3.

70. *Screen Guilds' Magazine* 2, no. 5 (April 1935): 8.

71. John Howard Lawson to John Dos Passos, 25 March 1934, Box 5, John Howard Lawson Papers.

72. John Howard Lawson autobiography, Box 96, Folder 1, John Howard Lawson Papers.

73. Lawson, *Writers Forum.*

74. John Howard Lawson autobiography, Box 96, Folder 1, John Howard Lawson Papers.

75. Lawson, *Writers Forum.*

76. Lawson, "The One Hundred Days."

77. John Howard Lawson to Edward Childs Carpenter, 13 July 1933, Box 5, Folder 3, John Howard Lawson Papers.

78. John Howard Lawson to Ralph Block, 2 December 1933, Box 5, Folder 3, John Howard Lawson Papers.

79. Undated speech by John Howard Lawson, Box 5, Folder 4, John Howard Lawson Papers.

80. John Howard Lawson to Joachim Albrecht, 25 March 1968, Box 58, Folder 2, John Howard Lawson Papers.

81. Lawson, *Writers Forum.*

82. Lawson, *Cineaste* interview, 8.

83. John Howard Lawson autobiography, Box 96, Folder 8, John Howard Lawson Papers.

84. Lawson, *Cineaste* interview, 8.

85. Ibid.

6. THEORY AND PRACTICE

1. Lester Cole, *Hollywood Red: The Autobiography of Lester Cole* (San Francisco: Ramparts, 1981), 159.

2. Jeff Lawson, "An Ordinary Life," in Judy Kaplan and Linn Shapiro, eds., *Red Diapers: Growing Up in the Communist Left* (Urbana: University of Illinois Press, 1990), 54–60, 54.

3. Paul Buhle and Dave Wagner, *Hide in Plain Sight: The Hollywood Black-listees in Film and Television, 1950–2002* (New York: Palgrave, 2003), 283.

4. Oral history, Philip Barber, 1975, George Mason University.

5. John Howard Lawson autobiography, Box 98, Folder 10, John Howard Lawson Papers.

6. Statement by John Howard Lawson, ca. 1934, Box 7, Folder 1, John Howard Lawson Papers.

7. John Howard Lawson autobiography, Box 98, Folder 10, John Howard Lawson Papers. See also oral history, John Bright, 300/356, 1991, UCLA.

8. Ibid. See also oral history, Edmund Hall North, 1986, 300/270, UCLA.

9. Ethan Mordden, *The Hollywood Studios: House Style in the Golden Age of the Movies* (New York: Knopf, 1988), 185, 186, 70, 179.

10. Interview with John Lee Mahin in Patrick McGilligan, *Backstory: Interviews with Screenwriters of Hollywood's Golden Age* (Berkeley and Los Angeles: University of California Press, 1986), 258.

11. *Variety,* 30 April 1936.

12. *Hollywood Reporter,* 6 May 1936. See *Hollywood Reporter,* 5 May 1936. See also *Variety,* 4 May 1936.

13. *New York American,* 27 April 1936.

14. John Howard Lawson autobiography, Box 96, Folder 1, John Howard Lawson Papers.

15. Quoted in *New York Times,* 26 March 1936.

16. *New York Times,* 5 April 1936.

17. John Howard Lawson to Joachim Albrecht, 25 March 1968, Box 58, Folder 2, John Howard Lawson Papers.

18. *New York Times,* 5 April 1936.

19. John Howard Lawson to Ernest Pascal, 2 April 1936, Box 7, Folder 2, John Howard Lawson Papers.

20. Statement by Dorothy Parker, Nathaniel West, and S. J. Perelman, 31 March 1936, Box 7, Folder 2, John Howard Lawson Papers.

21. Clipping, 3 April 1936, Box 7, Folder 2, John Howard Lawson Papers.

22. John Howard Lawson to Ernest Pascal, 2 April 1936, Box 7, Folder 2, John Howard Lawson Papers.

23. Interview with John Howard Lawson, *Cineaste* 8, no. 2 (Fall 1977): 4–11, 58; quotations on 8.

24. Letter from Harry Cohn et al., Box 7, Folder 2, John Howard Lawson Papers.

25. David O. Selznick to Lloyd Wright, 10 February 1942, Box 321, David O. Selznick Papers, University of Texas–Austin.

26. Harold Clurman, *The Fervent Years: The Story of the Group Theatre and the Thirties* (New York: Knopf, 1945), 158.

27. See *New York Herald Tribune,* 14 June 1936. See also undated review of Lawson book, Clipping File, Billy Rose Library.

28. *New York Herald Tribune,* 28 April 1936.

29. Charmion Von Wiegand, "Playwright into Critic," *New Theatre,* April 1936, Clipping File, Billy Rose Library.

30. *New York Times*, 16 June 1935.

31. *New York Times*, 18 March 1934.

32. John Howard Lawson, "Straight from the Shoulder," *New Theatre*, November 1934, Clipping File, Billy Rose Library.

33. John Howard Lawson autobiography, Box 98, Folder 4, John Howard Lawson Papers.

34. James Murphy, *The Proletarian Moment: The Controversy over Leftism in Literature* (Champaign-Urbana: University of Illinois Press, 1991), 118.

35. John Howard Lawson to John Dos Passos, ca. 1934, Box 5, John Dos Passos Papers.

36. Malcolm Goldstein, *The Political Stage: American Drama and Theater of the Great Depression* (New York: Oxford University Press, 1974), 193. "In 1937 Nykino was superseded by Frontier Films, founded," inter alia, by Lawson. Elia Kazan was on the board.

37. Speech by John Howard Lawson, 12 November 1955, Box 13, Folder 5, John Howard Lawson Papers.

38. Report of LAW conference, 6 December 1936, Box 1, LAW Papers.

39. Report on the Second American Writers Congress, 6 April 1937, Box 1, LAW Papers.

40. Minutes, LAW, 11 March 1937, Box 1, LAW Papers.

41. Minutes, LAW, 8 April 1937, Box 1, LAW Papers.

42. Executive Council Minutes, 17 November 1937, Box 1, LAW Papers.

43. Report by Sonora Babb, n.d., Box 1, LAW Papers.

44. Langston Hughes to John Howard Lawson, 21 July 1936, Box 1, Folder 1, John Howard Lawson Papers. See also Mary Sanders Walden, "John Howard Lawson: Theatre Rebel and Social Critic" (M.A. thesis, George Washington University, 1965).

45. *New York Times*, 18 February 1937.

46. John Howard Lawson, *Marching Song* (New York: Dramatists Play Service, 1937), 54, 61.

47. Clurman, *The Fervent Years*, 187.

48. *New York Times*, 27 December 1937.

49. Paul Buhle and Dave Wagner, *Radical Hollywood* (New York: New Press, 2002), 40–41.

50. Clurman, *The Fervent Years*, 187.

51. Lawson, *Cineaste* interview, 9–10.

52. *San Jose News*, 11 August 1966.

53. Quoted in William Wright, *Lillian Hellman: The Image, the Woman* (New York: Simon and Schuster, 1986), 136.

54. John Howard Lawson, *Film: The Creative Process; The Search for an Audio-Visual Language and Structure* (New York: Hill and Wang, 1967), 124, 125, 126.

55. Joseph Breen to Walter Wanger, 3 February 1937, "Blockade," MPAA Production Code Administration Files, Academy of Motion Picture Arts and Sciences.

56. Joseph Breen to Walter Wanger, 22 February 1937, "Blockade," MPAA Production Code Administration Files.

57. *New York Times*, 26 June 1938.

58. "The Bulletin 1938," publication of the Knights of Columbus, Hollywood Council 2406, "Blockade," MPAA Production Code Administration Files.

59. Joseph Breen to Charles J. Turck, 4 August 1938, "Blockade," MPAA Production Code Administration Files.

60. Will H. Hays, *The Memoirs of Will H. Hays* (Garden City, N.Y.: Doubleday, 1955), 498.

61. Nancy Lynn Schwartz, *The Hollywood Writers' Wars* (New York: Knopf, 1982), 127.

62. *Nation*, 9 July 1938.

63. Undated article of uncertain provenance written by John Howard Lawson, Box 75, Folder 1, John Howard Lawson Papers.

64. *Variety*, 13 July 1938.

65. *Daily Worker*, 10 July 1938.

66. *Variety*, 22 June 1938.

67. John Howard Lawson, *Theory and Technique of Playwriting and Screenwriting* (New York: Putnam's, 1949), 351.

68. Lawson, *Film: The Creative Process*, 127.

69. Circular, n.d., Box 75, Folder 1, John Howard Lawson Papers.

70. John Howard Lawson to Austin Lamont, 22 April 1968, Box 58, Folder 2, John Howard Lawson Papers. See also *New York Times*, 21 July 1938.

71. *New York Evening Sun*, 21 July 1938.

72. Transcript of 1961 Interview with John Howard Lawson, Box 135, Collection No. 100, UCLA.

73. Quoted in *Censored! A Record of Present Terror and Censorship in the American Theatre* (New York: National Committee against Censorship of the Theatre Arts, 1935), 5.

74. Quoted in Samuel Sillen, "Our Time," *Masses & Mainstream* 4, no. 4 (April 1951): 3–9; quotation on 6.

75. John Howard Lawson, "Camera and Microphone," *Masses & Mainstream* 1, no. 3 (May 1948): 36–47; quotations on 37, 39, 41, 43, 44, 47.

7. STRUGGLE

1. Undated notes from Nancy Schwartz, Box 1, Nancy Lynn Schwartz Papers. When the writer Nancy Schwartz came to interview Trumbo in his home "in the hills above Sunset Plaza, on St. Ives Drive," she was stunned. It was "impressive," she thought. "There is a locked outer grillwork door, then the door to the house, and you step into an immense living room foyer with ceilings that must be 25 feet. Magnificent, large canvasses," stood like guards "over the fireplace." Perhaps it was a "Grosz painting"; on other walls there were "faces, almost Cubist, modern, abstract, but humanoid. There [was] almost

something Roman about the place—a great man's home and there [was] marble in the entrance way" to buttress this supposition.

2. Cedric Belfrage, *The American Inquisition, 1945–1960* (Indianapolis: Bobbs-Merrill, 1973), 26. See also David F. Prindle,. *The Politics of Glamour: Ideology and Democracy in the Screen Actors Guild* (Madison: University of Wisconsin Press, 1988), 52.

3. Gerald Clarke, *Get Happy: The Life of Judy Garland* (New York: Random House, 2000), 68.

4. Michael Steinore, "Mary R. Levey, AKA Robert A. Rodson: Great-Grandpa Was a Citizen Spy, Los Angeles, 1911–1918," *Western States Jewish History* 33, no. 4 (Summer 2001): 339–43; quotation on 341.

5. Letter to Joseph Kramer, 3 May 1934, Part 1, Box 13, Folder 21, CRC, JFC Papers.

6. Report, 19 November 1937, Record Group 46, Box 17, R2255, Records of the United States Senate Internal Security Subcommittee, National Archives, Washington, D.C.

7. Report, 15 March 1938, Record Group 46, Box 19, R2440a, Records of the United States Senate Internal Security Subcommittee. See "Two Decades of Progress: Communist Party L.A. County, 1919–1939," Los Angeles: Communist Party, 1939, Record Group 21, Box 1332, Folder 92, Criminal Case 21862–21833, Records of the District Court of the United States for the Southern District of California, Central Division, 1929–1938, National Archives and Records Administration, Laguna Niguel, California.

8. Virginia Gardner, "California Close-Up," *Masses & Mainstream* 1, no. 4 (June 1948): 51–58; quotation on 54.

9. Interview, Philip Dunne, n.d., Box 1, Nancy Lynn Schwartz Papers.

10. Robert E. Burke, *Olson's New Deal for California* (Berkeley and Los Angeles: University of California Press, 1953), 18–19.

11. John Weber, "Communist Influence in Hollywood," 1997, Box 1, Folder 7, Hollywood Blacklist Collection, Southern California Library for Social Studies and Research.

12. Franklin Folsom, who knew both Lawson and Jerome, felt that the latter was "handicapped" in Hollywood, since "he had published very little" and, as a result, "felt insecure with writers. He tried to compensate by being overly assertive." See Franklin Folsom, *Days of Anger, Days of Hope: A Memoir of the League of American Writers, 1937–1942* (Niwot: University Press of Colorado, 1994), 99.

13. Nancy Lynn Schwartz, *The Hollywood Writers' Wars* (New York: Knopf, 1982), 153.

14. Undated memo, Box 619, J. B. Matthews Papers, Duke University, Durham, North Carolina.

15. Schwartz, *Hollywood Writers' Wars*, 153.

16. Neal Gabler, *An Empire of Their Own: How the Jews Invented Hollywood* (Garden City, N.Y.: Doubleday, 1988), 334–35.

17. See, e.g., Samantha Barbas, *Movie Crazy: Fans, Stars and the Cult of Celebrity* (New York: Palgrave Macmillan, 2001). See also Charles L. Ponce de Leon, *Self-Exposure: Human-Interest Journalism and the Emergence of Celebrity in America, 1890–1940* (Chapel Hill: University of North Carolina Press, 2002); Leo Braudy, *The Frenzy of Renown: Fame and Its History* (New York: Oxford University Press, 1986).

18. *WGA News*, November 1977, Box 1, Edward Eliscu Papers.

19. William MacAdams, *Ben Hecht: A Biography* (New York: Barricade, 1990), 178.

20. John Dos Passos, *Most Likely to Succeed* (New York: Prentice-Hall, 1954). See Harold Clurman, *All People Are Famous: Instead of an Autobiography* (New York: Harcourt Brace, 1974), 83.

21. Undated clipping, *Brooklyn Daily Eagle*, Clipping File, Billy Rose Library.

22. Interview, Charles Glenn, n.d., Box 1, Nancy Lynn Schwartz Papers. Red leader Dorothy Healey called Tenney a "typical piecard" who was "involved with labor 'cause it pays," a "radical" in the 1930s who "switched for opportunist reasons." See interview, Dorothy Healey, n.d., Box 1, Nancy Lynn Schwartz Papers.

23. Oral history, Jack Tenney, Vol. 1, 1969, University of California–Berkeley.

24. *Third Report, Un-American Activities in California, 1947, Report of the Joint Fact-Finding Committee to the Fifty-seventh California Legislature* (Sacramento, Calif.: State Legislature, 1947), 260–61. See also oral history, Jack Tenney, Vol. 2, 1969, University of California, Berkeley.

25. *New York Post*, 21 July 1938.

26. *Hollywood Reporter*, 24 June 1938.

27. *San Jose News*, 11 August 1966.

28. John Howard Lawson, *Film: The Creative Process; The Search for an Audio-Visual Language and Structure* (New York: Hill and Wang, 1967), 127.

29. *New York Times*, 15 July 1938. The writer James Cain recalled that he "did the first part" of the screenplay, "a twenty-minute preliminary hit with Casbah gangster types," though he'd "forgotten" when he was "closed out. The director John Cromwell got John Howard Lawson in. He had a certain gift but it was a solemn and humorless gift. There were a lot of laughs in the section I dialogued but not one laugh after that. I took some satisfaction in that." See Pat McGilligan, *Backstory: Interviews with Screenwriters of Hollywood's Golden Age* (Berkeley and Los Angeles: University of California Press, 1986), 118; Roy Hoopes, *Cain: The Biography of James M. Cain* (New York: Holt, Rinehart, Winston, 1982), 289. Charles Boyer's biography goes a step further and alleges that neither Cain nor Lawson—"neither of them"—wrote this screenplay. See Larry Swindell, *Charles Boyer: The Reluctant Lover* (Garden City, N.Y.: Doubleday, 1983), 118, 120, 121. See Lawson's screenplay, n.d., Box 75, Folder 1, John Howard Lawson Papers.

30. *Variety*, 27 July 1938

31. Letter from Gerard Raoul-Duval, 14 June 1938, No. 286, MPAA Production Code Administration Files.

32. Walter Wanger to Gerard Raoul-Duval, 23 June 1938, No. 286, MPAA Production Code Administration Files.

33. Robert Osborne, *Sixty Years of the Oscar: The Official History of the Academy Awards* (New York: Abbeville Press, 1989), 61. The nomination was for the story, which *Boys Town* won.

34. Income tax returns for Walter Wanger Productions, for fiscal year ending 30 June 1941, Producers' Legal Files, Record Group II, Series 3A, Box 38, F4, United Artists Papers, State Historical Society of Wisconsin.

35. See, e.g., Paul O'Brien to H. J. Muller, 8 February 1939, Record Group II, Series 3A, Box 37, Folder 3, United Artists Papers (re: "Mortgage, Pledge and Security Agreement" between Walter Wanger and the Bank of America).

36. Marquis James and Bessie Rowland James, *Biography of a Bank: The Story of Bank of America* (New York: Harper and Bros., 1954), 429.

37. J. H. Rosenberg, Vice President, Bank of America, to H. J. Muller, Record Group II, Series 3A, Box 37, Folder 4, United Artists Papers. For more on the financial relationship between Wanger and Bank of America, see Record Group II, Series 3A, Box 36, United Artists Papers.

38. See data on distribution of films in Germany, 1929–1930, Record Group II, Series 2A, Box 149, Folder 8, United Artists Papers.

39. See O'Brien Legal Files, China, 1930–1937, 1938–1951, Record Group II, Series 2A, Box 58, File 2, United Artists Papers.

40. See, e.g., Edward Jose to Arthur W. Kelly, 2 October 1926, Record Group II, Series 2A, Box 67, Folder 16, United Artists Papers. Writing from Cape Town, Kelly, an agent in the region of UA, says, "The two theatres at Rossettenville and Doonfontein are simply, as everyone knows, nigger theatres. No white man ever goes there."

41. See, e.g., Files on Bulgaria, Record Group II, Series 2F, Box 1, Folder 4, United Artists Papers; Files on Cuba, Record Group II, Series 2F, Box 1, Folders 6 and 7, United Artists Papers; Foreign Correspondence Files, Record Group II, Series 2F, Box 44, United Artists Papers.

42. Joseph Kennedy to "Dear Martin," ca. 1926, Box 1, Folder 10, Martin J. Quigley Papers.

43. Martin Quigley to Joseph Breen, 10 January 1939, Box 1, Folder 2, Martin J. Quigley Papers.

44. See Joseph Breen to Martin J. Quigley, 1 May 1932, Box 1, Folder 2, Martin J. Quigley Papers.

45. Joseph Breen to "Dear Martin," 23 August 1935, Box 1, Folder 2, Martin J. Quigley Papers.

46. See, e.g., Joseph Breen to Martin J. Quigley, 25 September 1937, Box 1, Folder 2, Martin J. Quigley Papers.

47. Joseph Freeman, *An American Testament: A Narrative of Rebels and Romantics* (New York: Farrar and Rinehart, 1936), 380.

48. John Howard Lawson to John Dos Passos, ca. 30 August 1939, Box 5, John Dos Passos Papers.

49. John Dos Passos to Matthew Josephson, 2 August 1953, Box 3, Folder 75, Matthew Josephson Papers.

50. Virginia Spencer, *Dos Passos: A Life* (Garden City, N.Y.: Doubleday, 1984), 383.

51. John Howard Lawson to John Dos Passos, 14 September 1939, Box 5, John Dos Passos Papers.

52. John Howard Lawson to Oswald Garrison Villard, 20 December 1934, Upton Sinclair Papers.

53. John Howard Lawson autobiography, Box 98, Folder 7, John Howard Lawson Papers.

54. John Howard Lawson to Sidney Howard, 13 February 1935, Box 5, Sidney Howard Papers, University of California–Berkeley.

55. John Howard Lawson to Sidney Howard, 28 February 1935, Box 5, Sidney Howard Papers.

56. John Howard Lawson autobiography, Box 98, Folder 4, John Howard Lawson Papers.

57. Lawson, *Film: The Creative Process,* 133.

58. John Howard Lawson autobiography, Box 99, Folder 4, John Howard Lawson Papers.

59. Oral history, Abraham Polonsky, 1974, American Film Institute, Los Angeles.

60. Philip Dunne, *Take Two: A Life in Movies and Politics* (New York: Limelight, 1992), 110–11. Dunne, a lasting symbol of Liberal Hollywood and author of the script for *How Green Was My Valley* and other works, declared: "I do not believe that those who joined the Communist Party did so with the purpose of undermining our form of government, or fomenting violent revolution, or acting as a Soviet agent, or doing any of the other things which a great part of the American public thinks a Communist does." No, he says, "those who joined the American Communist Party of the 1930s had much in common with the Byronesque romantic rebels of the preceding century."

61. John Howard Lawson to John Dos Passos, n.d., Box 5, John Howard Lawson Papers.

62. John Howard Lawson to John Dos Passos, ca. 24 August 1939, Box 5, John Dos Passos Papers.

63. See, e.g., Gerald Horne, *Black and Red: W. E. B. Du Bois and the Afro-American Response to the Cold War, 1944–1963* (Albany: State University of New York Press, 1986).

64. John Howard Lawson to John Dos Passos, n.d., Box 5, John Dos Passos Papers.

65. See case of anti-Semitic firing of a carpenter at Paramount: "Mrs. Leo Strauss" to L. A. Rose, 5 August 1936, Part I, Box 1, Folder 3, CRC, JFC Papers. See the case of writer and director Harry Zutto, "suddenly laid off" from MGM—he was the "only Jew in the department," and this was a plot "to keep

certain departments one hundred percent Aryan." Memo to Fred Pelton of MGM, 27 May 1936, Part 1, Box 1, Folder 8, CRC, JFC Papers.

66. Letter to Henry Hersbrun, n.d., ca. 1930s, Part 1, Box 1, Folder 1, CRC, JFC Papers. Jack Warner and other executives contributed substantially to combating anti-Semitism. See also Memo, 13 March 1934, Part 1, Box 1, Folder 8, CRC, JFC Papers; Fred S. Meyer of Universal Pictures to Leon Lewis, 28 December 1936, Part 1, Box 1, Folder 6, CRC, JFC Papers.

67. *New York Times*, 20 November 1934, Part 1, Box 5, Folder 9, CRC, JFC Papers. See Jack Warner, *My First Hundred Years in Hollywood* (New York: Random House, 1964), 262–63.

68. John E. Moser, "'Gigantic Engines of Propaganda': The 1941 Senate Investigation of Hollywood," *Historian* 63, no. 4 (Summer 2001): 731–51; quotation on 731.

69. Matthew J. Bruccoli, *F. Scott Fitzgerald's Screenplay for "Three Comrades" by Erich Maria Remarque* (Carbondale: Southern Illinois University Press, 1978), 265, 266, 267. See also Greg Lawrence, *Dance with Demons: The Life of Jerome Robbins* (New York: Putnam's, 2001), 56. Similarly, a future president of the guild, Michael Blankfort, had originally been an Orthodox Jew—then he visited the Soviet Union in 1929 and returned pro-Communist. He had rejected Jewish Orthodoxy and now he grasped at the idea of anti-Semitism being an evil function of capitalism and imperialism that would ultimately disappear under socialism—a common view in Communist ranks. Then he did not think "how did we feel as a Jew" but "how did we feel as socialists." See also interview, Michael Blankfort, n.d., Box 1, Nancy Lynn Schwartz Papers.

70. File on John Howard Lawson, Box 619, J. B. Matthews Papers. See also *New Masses*, 22 January 1936, 26 January 1937; *Daily Worker*, 23 August 1937; *Daily Worker*, 6 April 1937.

71. *Los Angeles Daily News*, 3 June 1936.

72. Ella Winter, *And Not to Yield: An Autobiography* (New York: Harcourt Press, 1963), 221:

73. Oral history, Donald Ogden Stewart, 1971, American Film Institute.

74. Report, 20 October 1936, Part 1, Box 30, Folder 13, CRC, JFC Papers.

75. Interview, Sam Marx, n.d., Box 2, Nancy Lynn Schwartz Papers.

76. James Murphy, *The Proletarian Moment: The Controversy over Leftism in Literature* (Champaign-Urbana: University of Illinois Press, 1991), 147.

77. Francis Talbot, S.J., to "George Terwilliger, Supervisor, Amateur Division, Play Bureau, Federal Theatre Project," 9 February 1937, Box 13, Folder 60, American Magazine Archives.

78. See article, ca. 1938, by Westbrook Pegler, Box 20, Folder 1, American Magazine Archives: "Father Coughlin was correct in contending that many Jews have been vigorous Communists in Russia and elsewhere."

79. William Wilkerson to Francis Talbot, 15 April 1938, Box 17, Folder 22, American Magazine Archives.

80. "An American" to Francis X. Talbot, Box 17, Folder 22, American Magazine Archives.

81. Francis Talbot to William R. Wilkerson, 20 April 1938, Box 17, Folder 22, American Magazine Archives.

8. FIGHTING—AND WRITING

1. Quoted in Kenneth S. Lynn, *Charlie Chaplin and His Times* (New York: Simon and Schuster, 1997), 397. See also Charles J. Maland, *Chaplin and American Culture: The Evolution of a Star Image* (Princeton, N.J.: Princeton University Press, 1989), 255; Joyce Milton, *Tramp: The Life of Charlie Chaplin* (New York: HarperCollins, 1996), 449, 191.

2. See, e.g., "Goldie" to "Dear Herbert," ca. 1938, Carton 20, Tom Mooney Papers, University of California–Berkeley. See also Larry Swindell, *Body and Soul: The Story of John Garfield* (New York: Morrow, 1975), 64, 238; oral history, Helen Slote Levitt, 1991, 300/351, UCLA; oral history, Martin Ritt, 1987, 401, Southern Methodist University.

3. Paul Buhle and Dave Wagner, *Radical Hollywood* (New York: New Press, 2002), 87. See also oral history, Guy Endore, 1964, 300/21, UCLA.

4. U.S. Congress, House of Representatives, Committee on Un-American Activities, 84th Cong., 2nd sess., 19 April 1956, "Investigation of Communist Activity in the Los Angeles, California Area—Part 9" (Washington, D.C.: Government Printing Office, 1956), 3828–29.

5. Franklin Folsom, *Days of Anger, Days of Hope: A Memoir of the League of American Writers, 1937–1942* (Niwot: University Press of Colorado, 1994), 100.

6. Larry Ceplair and Steven Englund, *The Inquisition in Hollywood: Politics in the Film Community* (Garden City, N.Y.: Doubleday, 1980), 59.

7. Minutes of Board Meeting, 30 October 1940, Box 1, LAW Papers. See also John Howard Lawson to Lawrence Gellert, n.d., Box 1, Lawrence Gellert Papers, University of California–Berkeley.

8. Interview, Carl Foreman, n.d., Box 1, Nancy Lynn Schwartz Papers. See Howard Koch, *As Time Goes By: Memoirs of a Writer* (New York: Harcourt Brace Jovanovich, 1979), 89.

9. Gerda Lerner, *Fireweed: A Political Autobiography* (Philadelphia: Temple University Press, 2002), 233–34.

10. "The Crowned Princes," n.d., Box 2, Nancy Lynn Schwartz Papers.

11. Description of Schulberg by Nancy Schwartz, n.d., Box 2, Nancy Lynn Schwartz Papers.

12. U.S. Congress, House of Representatives, Committee on Un-American Activities, "Communist Infiltration of Hollywood Motion-Picture Industry—Part I," 8 and 21 March; 10, 11, 12 and 13 April 1951, 82nd Cong., 1st sess. (Washington, D.C.: Government Printing Office, 1951), Testimony of Budd Schulberg.

13. Ring Lardner Jr., *I'd Hate Myself in the Morning: A Memoir* (New York: Thunder's Mouth/Nation Books, 2000), 103.

14. *New York Times*, 24 May 1951.

15. Nora Sayre, *Running Time: Films of the Cold War* (New York: Dial, 1978).

16. Neal Gabler, *An Empire of Their Own: How the Jews Invented Hollywood* (Garden City, N.Y.: Doubleday, 1988), 336. Budd Schulberg, *What Makes Sammy Run?* (1941; New York: Modern Library, 1952), xi.

17. Victor Navasky, *Naming Names* (New York: Viking, 1980), 293.

18. John Howard Lawson to Joachim Albrecht, 21 January 1969, Box 58, Folder 2, John Howard Lawson Papers.

19. Quoted in *New York Times Magazine*, 25 March 1973.

20. John Howard Lawson to Joachim Albrecht, 25 March 1968, Box 58, Folder 2, John Howard Lawson Papers.

21. Schulberg, *What Makes Sammy Run?* 170, 228, 252, 119, 134.

22. Interview, Richard Maibum, n.d., Box 1, Nancy Lynn Schwartz Papers.

23. Interview, Lester Cole, n.d., Box 1, Nancy Lynn Schwartz Papers. See interview, Liz Faragoh, n.d., Box 2, Nancy Lynn Schwartz Papers; interview, Charles Glenn, n.d., Box 1, Nancy Lynn Schwartz Papers.

24. Nancy Lynn Schwartz, *The Hollywood Writers' Wars* (New York: Knopf, 1982), 170, 155, 213, 152.

25. Oral history, Jack Tenney, 1969, vol. 2, University of California–Berkeley.

26. Folsom, *Days of Anger, Days of Hope*, 100–101.

27. Undated notes of Nancy Schwartz, Box 1, Nancy Lynn Schwartz Papers.

28. Lardner, *I'd Hate Myself in the Morning*, 55. See also Ring Lardner Jr. to Ian McLellan Hunter, 25 October 1960, Box 4, Ian McLellan Hunter Collection, Academy of Motion Pictures Arts and Sciences. The prolific Hunter wrote numerous teleplays for such series as *The Defenders* and *The Adventures of Robin Hood* and was known to imbibe various substances. See also Tom Dardis, *The Thirsty Muse: Alcohol and the American Writer* (New York: Ticknor and Fields, 1989). See interview, Elizabeth Glenn, n.d., Box 1, Nancy Lynn Schwartz Papers. See interview, Ring Lardner Jr., n.d., Box 2, Nancy Lynn Schwartz Papers. According to his frequent collaborator, Michael Kanin, Lardner often used scotch and Benzedrine to write. See interview, Michael Kanin, n.d., Box 2, Nancy Lynn Schwartz Papers.

29. Interview, Cleo Trumbo, n.d., Box 1, Nancy Lynn Schwartz Papers.

30. Interview, Paul Jarrico, n.d., Box 1, Nancy Lynn Schwartz Papers. See interview, Jean Butler, n.d., Box 1, Nancy Lynn Schwartz Papers. The Communist screenwriter Waldo Salt, who penned *Coming Home, Serpico,* and *Midnight Cowboy*, "was always late for deadlines," according to his former wife. And "when he wasn't drinking," he "kept going by the amphetamines that kept him awake, and he would work all night long, day after day, and then just sort of collapse." See oral history, Mary Davenport, 1993, 300/391, UCLA.

31. Oral history Ring Lardner Jr., 1985, 317, Southern Methodist University, Dallas. The writer recalls that the producer David O. Selznick "had tremendous energy—part of it chemically induced; he used to take a lot of benzedrine and stuff to keep going and would work fabulous hours."

32. Undated notes of Nancy Schwartz, Box 2, Nancy Lynn Schwartz Papers.

33. Paul F. Boller Jr. and Ronald Davis, *Hollywood Anecdotes* (New York: Morrow, 1987), 103.

34. Oral history, Ring Lardner Jr., 1985, 317, Southern Methodist University.

35. See interview with Buck Henry, *Cineaste* 27, no. 1 (Winter 2001): 4–10.

36. William Froug, *The Screenwriter Looks at the Screenwriter* (New York: Macmillan, 1972), xi, xii, xiii. See also Philip Dunne, *Take Two: A Life in Movies and Politics* (New York: Limelight, 1992), 93, 99; oral history, William Wyler, 1979, 175, Southern Methodist University.

37. Ceplair and Englund, *The Inquisition in Hollywood*, 3.

38. Schwartz, *The Hollywood Writers' Wars*, 96.

39. Schulberg, *What Makes Sammy Run?* 122.

40. George F. Custen, *Twentieth Century's Fox: Darryl F. Zanuck and the Culture of Hollywood* (New York: Basic Books, 1997), 236.

41. Oral history, Robert Pirosh, 388, 1986, Southern Methodist University.

42. See "Conference with Mr. Zanuck," 24 October 1939, Box 76, Folder 2, John Howard Lawson Papers.

43. "Conference with Mr. Zanuck," 24 October 1939, Twentieth Century Fox Collection, University of Southern California.

44. "Conference with Mr. Zanuck," 19 February 1940, Twentieth Century Fox Collection. It is clear from these conferences that the producer and writer mapped out the movie in detail beforehand, making the job simple for any director—and certainly calling into question the idea that movies are "authored" by this contractor. There is much attention here given to "dissolve," "camera . . . pans," etc. See also "Conference with Mr. Zanuck," 22 May 1940, Twentieth Century Fox Collection. See also the story conferences of 15 November 1940, 16 December 1940, and 23 January 1941.

45. "Conference with Mr. Zanuck," 16 November 1939, Twentieth Century Fox Collection.

46. Transcript of 1961 interview with John Howard Lawson, Box 135, Collection No. 100, UCLA.

47. Interview with John Howard Lawson, *Cineaste* 8, no. 2 (Fall 1977): 4–11. See oral history, Philip Dunne, 1983, 291, Southern Methodist University; interview, Milton Sperling, n.d., Box 2, Nancy Lynn Schwartz Papers.

48. Undated letter from the "Progressive Caucus" of SWG, Box 26, Ella Winter Papers, Columbia University.

49. Schulberg, *What Makes Sammy Run?* 142, 171, 190. See also William E. Barret to James Cain, 17 January 1947, Box 2, James Cain Papers, Library of Congress, Washington, D.C.

50. Claude McKay, *A Long Way from Home* (Orlando, Fla.: Harcourt Brace, 1970), 273. See also Laurie Caroline Pintar, "Off-Screen Realities: A History of Labor Activism in Hollywood, 1933–1947" (Ph.D. diss., University of Southern California, 1995).

51. Interview, Carl Foreman, n.d., Box 2, Nancy Lynn Schwartz Papers.

52. Interview, Larry Beilenson, n.d., Box 2, Nancy Lynn Schwartz Papers.

53. Oral history, Philip Barber, 1975, George Mason University.

54. John Howard Lawson to Joachim Albrecht, 25 March 1968, Box 58, Folder 2, John Howard Lawson Papers.

55. "Analysis," 1940, Box 8, Folder 4, John Howard Lawson Papers.

56. F. Scott Fitzgerald, *The Last Tycoon* (New York: Scribner's, 1941), 120, 126–27.

57. Robert Rossen et al. to Executive Board of Screen Writers Guild, 6 October 1941, Michael Cole Papers. These papers are in the possession of Michael Cole, son of Lester Cole, University of California–San Diego, to be deposited at the University of Wyoming, Laramie.

58. David O. Selznick memo, 17 May 1940, Box 321, David O. Selznick Papers.

59. "Official Program" of American Writers Congress, May–June 1939, Box 1, LAW Papers.

60. Ella Winter, *And Not to Yield: An Autobiography* (New York: Harcourt Brace, 1963), 237.

61. Oral history, Carey McWilliams, 1982, 300/195, UCLA.

62. Dunne, *Take Two*, 113.

63. Report of CP-LA meeting, 23 December 1939, Record Group 46, Box 24, R3278, Records of the United States Senate Internal Security Subcommittee. See also interview, Charles Glenn, n.d., Box 1, Nancy Lynn Schwartz Papers; interview, Donald Ogden Stewart, n.d., Box 1, Nancy Lynn Schwartz Papers. Stewart also said that "he never joined [the] CP."

64. Minutes of National Council, 29 June 1938, Box 1, LAW Papers.

65. Upton Sinclair to League, 21 October 1939, Box 1, LAW Papers.

66. "Writers Take Sides on the Question: Are You For, or Are You Against Franco and Fascism?" [418 U.S. Writers Respond], 1938, Box 1, LAW Papers.

67. Report of National Board and New York Chapter Meetings, 2 October 1940, Box 1, LAW Papers.

68. Minutes of National Board and New York Chapter Executive meeting, 27 June 1940, Box 1, LAW Papers. Contrary to her subsequent recollection, Ella Winter at this meeting felt that the United States should not intervene in the European conflict; Albert Maltz opposed her.

69. Minutes of Joint Board Meeting of the National Board and New York City Chapter, 24 July 1940, Box 1, LAW Papers.

70. Minutes of Meeting of National Board and Congress Committee, 30 April 1940, Box 1, LAW Papers.

71. Minutes of Meeting, January 1940, Box 1, LAW Papers. Stone had proposed that "any matter pertaining to international situation be referred to membership before Board permitted to take any action, or make any public statement in relation to international situation."

72. Minutes of Meeting, 11 January 1940 (listed erroneously as 28 December 1940), Box 1, LAW Papers.

73. Interview, Lionel Stander, n.d., Box 2, Nancy Lynn Schwartz Papers.

74. Minutes of Meeting, 24 January 1940, Box 1, LAW Papers.

75. Report, 18 July 1940, Box 1, LAW Papers.

76. Undated clipping, Box 1, LAW Papers.

77. *Motion Picture Herald,* 14 June 1941.

78. *Daily Worker,* 25 June 1940.

79. "Bulletin" of "The Exiled Writers Committee of the Hollywood Chapter of the League of American Writers," June 1941, Box 1, LAW Papers. Lawson chaired this committee and also served as vice president of the overall LAW, with Dreiser as honorary president, Hammett as president, and Richard Wright as vice president.

80. "Minutes of Meeting," 16 May 1935, Box 1, LAW Papers. See "Report on 'Improving the Economic Status of the Dramatist.'"

81. Minutes of Executive Committee, 8 September 1936, Box 1, LAW Papers. "It is proposed that two members be added to the present editorial staff of 'Partisan Review' . . . that the League purchase subscriptions to 'Partisan Review' for its membership."

82. Minutes of Executive Committee, 15 October 1936, Box 1, LAW Papers.

83. See, e.g., Minutes of Meeting of National Board and Congress Committee, 3 June 1941; Minutes of National Board Meeting, 24 April 1941; Minutes of the Joint Meeting of the National Board and the New York Executive, 21, March 1941, LAW Papers.

84. Meeting of American Writers Congress, 4 June 1937, Box 1, LAW Papers.

85. See "We Hold These Truths . . . ," March 1939, Box 1, LAW Papers.

86. Wendell Wilkie to Senator Gerald Nye, 8 September 1941, Box 7, Folder 8, Adrian Scott Papers.

87. Ceplair and Englund, *The Inquisition in Hollywood,* 65.

88. *New York Times,* 26 July 1939.

89. Axel Madsen, *William Wyler: The Authorized Biography* (New York: Crowell, 1973), 169–70.

90. *Variety,* 7 July 1939.

91. Buhle and Wagner, *Radical Hollywood,* 147, 213. The 8 June 1940 *New York Times* said of *Four Sons* that "neither in its performance nor its writing does the film ever rise to any passion and the direction is pedantic and aimless." Of *Earthbound,* the 27 June 1940 *New York Times* said that it possessed "more than a nod to the shade of Sir Arthur Conan Doyle"; it was a "macabre little fancy" and a "solemn piece of foolishness so preposterous that it borders on farce."

92. *Hollywood Reporter,* 5 June 1940.

93. *Los Angeles Times,* 28 May 1940.

94. *Los Angeles Examiner,* 28 May 1940.

95. *Moscow News,* 3 October 1942.

9. WRITING—AND FIGHTING

1. Oral history, Helen Slote Levitt, 1991, 300/351, UCLA.

2. Julian Mayfield to John Howard Lawson, Box 35, Folder 1, John Howard Lawson Papers.

3. See Gerald Horne, *Race War! White Supremacy and the Japanese Attack on the British Empire* (New York: New York University Press, 2004).

4. John Howard Lawson, *Film: The Creative Process; The Search for an Audio-Visual Language and Structure* (New York: Hill and Wang, 1967), 141. See also column by David Platt, *Daily Worker*, ca. 1 December 1943, Reel 8, 100–138754A, *Communist Activity in the Entertainment Industry: FBI Surveillance on Hollywood, 1942–1958*, ed. Daniel J. Leab (Bethesda, Md.: University Publications of America, c1991).

5. *Los Angeles Times*, 30 July 1995.

6. Report on "Sahara," 1 February 1943, Record Group 208, Box 1453, Records of the Office of War Information, National Archives and Records Administration, College Park, Maryland.

7. Joseph Breen to Harry Cohn, 1943, MPAA Production Code Administration Files.

8. James Agee, *Agee on Film: Criticism and Comment on the Movies* (New York: Modern Library, 2000), 36. See also the positive review in the 9 December 1943 *Los Angeles Daily News*.

9. See *Daily Worker*, 3 November 1947.

10. Rochelle Larkin, *Hail, Columbia* (New Rochelle, N.Y.: Arlington House, 1975), 23.

11. John Howard Lawson, *Theory and Technique of Playwriting and Screenwriting* (New York: Putnam's, 1949), 436.

12. NCASP, "Policy and Program for 1948," Box 3, Edward Mosk Papers, Southern California Library for Social Studies and Research.

13. Quoted in Steven Ross, *Working-Class Hollywood: Silent Film and the Shaping of Class in America* (Princeton, N.J.: Princeton University Press, 1998), 242.

14. Joseph Breen to Jack Warner, 11 August 1942, MPAA Production Code Administration Files.

15. Joseph Breen to Jack Warner, 18 August 1942, MPAA Production Code Administration Files.

16. Joseph Breen to Jack Warner, 16 April 1943, MPAA Production Code Administration Files. See also Joseph Breen to Harry Cohn, 6 February 1940, Box 4, Folder 29, Adrian Scott Papers.

17. Report, 10 July 1943, 100–138754, Reel 1, *Communist Activity in the Entertainment Industry*. See also *Peoples World*, 27 March 1943, 3 June 1943.

18. *Daily Worker*, 13 June 1943.

19. Lawson, *Film: The Creative Process*, 141. See also Raymond Massey, *A Hundred Different Lives: An Autobiography* (Boston: Little Brown, 1979), 282.

20. Interview, Michael Kanin, n.d., Box 1, Nancy Lynn Schwartz Papers.

21. Lawson, *Theory and Technique of Playwriting and Screenwriting*, 371.

22. Aljean Harmetz, *The Making of Casablanca: Bogart, Bergman and World War II* (New York: Hyperion, 2002), 299–300. See John Howard Lawson to Arbitration Committee, SWG, 18 September 1942, Box 76, Folder 2, John Howard Lawson Papers. See also Felix Risenberg to John Howard Lawson, n.d., Box 27, Folder 3, John Howard Lawson Papers.

23. *PM*, 23 May 1943.

24. *Daily Variety*, 17 May 1943. For other positive reviews, see *New York World-Telegram*, 22 May 1943; *New York Post*, 22 May 1943; *New York Sun*, 22 May 1943.

25. Paul Buhle and Dave Wagner, *Radical Hollywood* (New York: New Press, 2002), 234.

26. "Hollywood Writers Mobilization Communique," 8 June 1942, Box 1, Folder 2, Robert Shaw Papers, Southern California Library for Social Studies and Research.

27. Clayton R. Koppes and Gregory D. Black, *Hollywood Goes to War: How Politics, Profits and Propaganda Shaped World War II Movies* (New York: Free Press, 1987), 70. See also oral history, Paul Jarrico, 1991, 300/360, UCLA. This writer wrote *No Time to Marry* in 1938 where the Communist actor Lionel Stander idly hums a few bars from the Red anthem "The Internationale." As a result, the film was "banned in Brazil, banned in Argentina, banned in Bolivia, banner here, banned there."

28. Gerda Lerner, *Fireweed: A Political Autobiography* (Philadelphia: Temple University Press, 2002), 225. See also Patrick McGilligan and Paul Buhle, *Tender Comrades: A Backstory of the Hollywood Blacklist* (New York: St. Martin's, 1997), 103. See Bernard Gordon, *Hollywood Exile or How I Learned to Love the Blacklist* (Austin: University of Texas Press, 1999), 21; see Michael Drosner, *Citizen Hughes: In His Own Words—How Howard Hughes Tried to Buy America* (New York: Holt, Rinehart, Winston, 1985), 173.

29. Alvah Bessie, *Inquisition in Eden* (New York: Macmillan, 1965), 93. See also McGilligan and Buhle, *Tender Comrades*, 334. See also oral history, Paul Jarrico, 1991, 300/360, UCLA.

30. Oral history, Michael Wilson, 1982, 300/196, UCLA.

31. Oral history, Helen Slote Levitt, 1991, 300/351, UCLA. See also oral history, Guy Endore, 300/21, UCLA.

32. Report, date unclear, Serial 1003, (Part 2), Part 9 of 15, File 100–138754, Communist Infiltration, Motion Picture Industry, FOIA Documents, FBI.

33. *Hollywood Reporter*, 26 August 1946.

34. See Russell Holman, Eastern Production Manager for Paramount, to Lowell Mellett, Chief, Bureau of Motion Pictures, 17 December 1942, Record Group 208, Box 1433B, Records of Office of War Information, National Archives and Records Administration; Foreign Minister of the Republic of China to Lowell Mellett, 6 November 1942, Record Group 208, Box 1433B, Records of Office of War Information. See T. K. Chang, Consulate in Los Angeles of Republic of China, to Lie Chieh, Chinese Embassy in United States, ca. 1942, Record Group 208, Box 1433B, Records of Office of War Information. See also *Washington Post*, 25 October 1942. Fervent concern is expressed here about films concerning China.

35. See Lowell Mellett to Samuel Goldwyn, 9 December 1942, Record Group 208, Box 1433B, Records of Office of War Information. See also Manuel Quezon, President of the Philippines, to Lowell Mellett, 17 August 1942, Record Group 208, Box 1433B, Records of Office of War Information. See Low-

ell Mellett to Samuel Goldwyn, 20 August 1942, Record Group 208, Box 1433B, Records of Office of War Information. Ardent concern is expressed here about movies concerning the Philippines.

36. See Lowell Mellett to Vladimir Bazykin, First Secretary of USSR Embassy, Washington, ca. 1942–43, Record Group 208, Box 1432, Records of Office of War Information. See also David Culbert, ed., *Mission to Moscow* (Madison: University of Wisconsin Press, 1980).

37. Report by Marjorie Thorson, 29 September 1942, Record Group 208, Box 1440, Records of Office of War Information. See also Report, 9 March 1943, Record Group 208, Box 1556, Records of Office of War Information.

38. See "Confidential" Report, 19 January 1943, on *Cabin in the Sky,* Record Group 208, Box 1440, Records of Office of War Information.

39. Report on *For Whom the Bell Tolls,* 13 October 1942, Record Group 208, Box 1440, Records of Office of War Information. See Report, 22 October 1942, Record Group 208, Box 1440, Records of Office of War Information.

40. See Report, "The Enemy in the Movies," 25 November 1942, Record Group 44, Box 1845, Records of the Office of Government Reports, U.S. Information Service, Bureau of Intelligence, Office of War Information, Reports and Special Memoranda, National Archives and Records Administration.

41. See, e.g., W. N. Castle, U.S. Department of State, to Will Hays, 28 January 1928, Box 781, Folder 1, Cecil B. DeMille Papers.

42. Dorothy B. Jones, "Communism and the Movies: A Study of Film Content," February 1956, Box 85, Folder 8, Fund for the Republic Papers, Princeton University, Princeton, New Jersey. See letter from Theodore Dreiser, n.d., Theodore Dreiser Papers, University of Texas–Austin. The U.S. government monitored Dreiser's funeral, noting that Lawson provided the main eulogy. See *Daily Worker,* 3 January 1946, Record Group 233, Box 949, Records of the House Un-American Activities Committee, National Archives and Records Administration, Washington, D.C. See oral history, Helen Slote Levitt, 1991, 300/351, UCLA. See also oral history, John Bright, 1991, 300/356, UCLA.

43. During the war, Washington did seek to encourage pro-Soviet films; after the war, Red Hollywood was blamed for this. See Lionel Mellett to Lillian Hellman, 8 September 1942, Record Group 208, Box 1433B, Records of Office of War Information. See Lowell Mellett to Samuel Goldwyn, 3 August 1942, Record Group 208, Box 1433B, Records of Office of War Information.

44. Undated history, Box 1, Folder 1, Hollywood Democratic Committee Papers, State Historical Society of Wisconsin.

45. Report, 18 February 1943, Serial 4, Part 1 of 15, 100–138754, Communist Infiltration, Motion Picture Industry, FOIA Documents, FBI.

46. Report, ca. 1942, Communist Infiltration, Motion Picture Industry, FOIA Documents, FBI.

47. Report, 2 March 1944, Record Group 46, Box 50, R6822a, Records of the United States Senate Internal Security Subcommittee.

48. Report, 29 February 1944, Record Group 46, Box 50, R6864, Records of the United States Senate Internal Security Subcommittee.

49. Report, 24 May 1944, Record Group 46, Box 53, R7110a, Records of the United States Senate Internal Security Subcommittee.

50. Report, n.d., Record Group 46, Box 56, R7425a, Records of the United States Senate Internal Security Subcommittee. In this undated report from C. F. Truitt of San Diego, there is discussion of Lancelot Pinard, "half-French, half-Negro, a native of Trinidad . . . a singer of his native Calypso music . . . had a small role in 'I Walked with a Zombie' and another in 'To Have and Have Not' with Humphrey Bogart. Pinard spoke highly of Bogart."

51. Report, 24 February 1945, Record Group 46, Box 57, R7569b, Records of the United States Internal Security Subcommittee.

52. Report, "Confidential," 9 June 1945, Record Group 46, Box 64, R8342c, Records of the United States Senate Internal Security Subcommittee.

53. *Los Angeles Times,* 14 October 1944. See also Report, ca. 1944, Record Group 46, Box 54, R7245a, Records of the United States Internal Security Subcommittee.

54. Oral history, Carey McWilliams, 1982, 300/195, UCLA.

55. Report, 11 October 1947, Serial 251X1, Part 7 of 15, 100–138754, Communist Infiltration, Motion Picture Industry, FOIA Documents, FBI.

56. L.A.-FBI to J. Edgar Hoover, 14 April 1951, 100–15732, Vol. 28, Reel 5, *Communist Activity in the Entertainment Industry.*

57. Report, ca. 1947, Serial 1003, Part 9 of 15, 100–138754, Communist Infiltration, Motion Picture Industry, FOIA Documents, FBI.

58. See Hearing Transcripts, before Assembly Fact Finding Committee on Un-American Activities in California, 1–5 December 1941 and 23–24 February 1942, Open Session, Box 29, Miscellaneous, Ac. No. 93–04–12, Records of Un-American Activities Committee, California State Archives, Sacramento.

59. Oral history, Jack Tenney, 1969, vol. 3, University of California–Berkeley.

60. Hearing Transcripts, Box 30, Records of Un-American Activities Committee, California State Archives.

61. Ibid.

62. Nancy Lynn Schwartz, *The Hollywood Writers' Wars* (New York: Knopf, 1982), 217, 213.

63. Oral history, Robert Kenny, n.d., Box 1, Nancy Lynn Schwartz Papers.

64. Memoir of Charlotta Bass, 296, Box 1, Folder 3, Charlotta Bass Papers, Southern California Library of Social Studies and Research.

65. Jeffrey Lawson remarks, "Memorial Services for our Distinguished Colleague and First President," *WGA News,* November 1977, Box 1, Edward Eliscu Papers.

66. John Howard Lawson to "Dear Ladle," ca. 1940–44, Gaylor Wood Papers.

67. U.S. Congress, House of Representatives, Committee on Un-American Activities, 82nd Cong., 1st sess., "Communist Infiltration of Hollywood Motion-Picture Industry—Part I" (Washington, D.C.: Government Printing Office, 1951), 223.

68. Barbara Zheutlin and David Talbot, *Creative Differences: Profiles of Hollywood Dissidents* (Boston: South End Press, 1978).

69. Report, 2 March 1944, Record Group 46, Box 50, R6822a, Records of the United States Senate Internal Security Subcommittee.

10. RED SCARE RISING

1. Betty Friedan, *The Feminine Mystique* (New York: Norton, 1963). See oral history, Helen Slote Levitt, 1991, 300/351, UCLA.

2. Patrick McGilligan and Paul Buhle, *Tender Comrades: A Backstory of the Hollywood Blacklist* (New York: St. Martin's, 1997), 311.

3. Norma Barzman, *The Red and the Blacklist: The Intimate Memoir of a Hollywood Expatriate* (New York: Thunder's Mouth Press, 2003), 443. See Lawson Memorial, 8 September 1977, KZ0347a, Pacifica Radio Archives.

4. Contract with Dorothy Parker, 20 August 1945, Box 91, Folder 28, Walter Wanger Papers, .

5. Ed Cooke to John Tracy, 28 May 1946, Box 91, Folder 28, Walter Wanger Papers. In this same file, see also the 7 January 1946 letter from Wanger to Lawson.

6. Robert LaGuardia and Gene Arceri, *Red: The Tempestuous Life of Susan Hayward* (New York: Macmillan, 1985), 56.

7. *Reader*, 21 July 1989, "Smash-Up Clippings File," Academy of Motion Picture Arts and Sciences.

8. Memo from Joseph Breen, 17 April 1946, Box 91, Folder 28, Walter Wanger Papers.

9. Joseph Breen to Walter Wanger, 10 May 1946, Box 91, Folder 28, Walter Wanger Papers.

10. Joseph Breen to Walter Wanger, 21 June 1946, Box 91, Folder 28, Walter Wanger Papers.

11. Memo from James J. Rieden of "Arthur H. Samish and Associates," 14 November 1946, Box 91, Folder 26, Walter Wanger Papers.

12. David Susskind to Maurice Bergman, 8 January 197, Box 91, Folder 26, Walter Wanger Papers.

13. LaGuardia and Arceri, *Red*, 63. See also Beverly Linet, *Susan Hayward: Portrait of a Survivor* (New York: Atheneum, 1980), 103.

14. Paul Buhle and Dave Wagner, *Radical Hollywood* (New York: New Press, 2002), 402.

15. *Los Angeles Herald-Express*, 12 May 1947. But see Bosley Crowther's contrary review in the 11 April 1947 *New York Times*.

16. Bernard Dick, *Radical Innocence: A Critical Study of the Hollywood Ten* (Lexington: University Press of Kentucky, 1989), 60, 63. See also oral history, Dorothy Healey, 1982, 300/179, UCLA.

17. *Daily Worker*, 1 June 1945.

18. James Agee, *Agee on Film: Criticism and Comment on the Movies* (New York: Modern Library, 2000), 148.

19. File on "Counter-Attack," 1945, Box 43, Folder 1, Records of Columbia Pictures, University of Wyoming.

20. Clipping, *New York Times*, ca. 27 July 1945, Box 7, Folder 3, John Howard Lawson Papers.

21. *New York Daily News*, 17 May 1945.

22. *Time*, 30 April 1945.

23. *Hollywood Reporter*, 2 April 1945.

24. *Variety*, 2 April 1945.

25. *New Yorker*, 24 May 1945.

26. Clayton R. Koppes and Gregory D. Black, *Hollywood Goes to War: How Politics, Profits and Propaganda Shaped World War II Movies* (New York: Free Press, 1987), 217.

27. See, e.g., Minutes of Executive Board of HDC, 4 May 1943, Box 1, Folder 6, Hollywood Democratic Committee Papers. Typically, most of the motions made and carried at this meeting were by Lawson.

28. Program of HWM, 1 October 1943, Box 71, Emmett Lavery Papers, UCLA.

29. "Hollywood for Roosevelt" included Wanger, Edward G. Robinson, Dore Schary, Humphrey Bogart, and others who had worked alongside Lawson. See "Hollywood for Roosevelt," Personal File, 7024, Franklin D. Roosevelt Papers, Franklin D. Roosevelt Library, Hyde Park, New York. See their advertisement in the 30 October 1940 *New York Times*. Others in this group included Douglas Fairbanks Jr., Dorothy Lamour, Leo Carillo, William Wyler, Walter Huston, and Rosalind Russell. Others within this circle included Groucho Marx, James Cagney, Charles Boyer, Desi Arnaz, Joan Bennett, Claudette Colbert, Bob Hope, and Merle Oberon. See invitation, 30 April 1942, Box 103, Office of Social Entertainment, Franklin D. Roosevelt Papers.

30. Jack Warner, *My First Hundred Years in Hollywood* (New York: Random House, 1964), 285, 290. Lawson's favorite producer, Walter Wanger, was also in frequent contact with Henry A. Wallace, then vice president. See, e.g., Walter Wanger to Isador Lubin, 20 November 1944, Box 93, Henry A. Wallace Papers, Franklin D. Roosevelt Library. The mute comic Harpo Marx was among those organizing in 1939 on behalf of the "concerted peace efforts to insure the passage of President Roosevelt's peace program." See Harpo Marx to Leon Lewis, 21 August 1939, Box 17, Folder 18, CRC, JFC Papers.

31. Sidney Hook to Stephen Early, 1 February 1940, President's Personal File, 5259, Franklin D. Roosevelt Papers. See also letter from Clifford Odets, 25 April 1938, President's Personal File, 5976, Franklin D. Roosevelt Papers. See also FDR to Odets, 6 May 1939 [sic], in the same file.

32. Everett Wile to John Howard Lawson, 3 March 1944, Box 8, Folder 4, John Howard Lawson Papers.

33. *Cineaste* 8, no. 2 (Fall 1977): 58, 11.

34. John Houseman, *Front and Center* (New York: Simon and Schuster, 1979), 154–55, 156.

35. Paul Buhle and Dave Wagner, *A Very Dangerous Citizen: Abraham Lincoln Polonsky and the Hollywood Left* (Berkeley and Los Angeles: University of California Press, 2001), 104.

36. Houseman, *Front and Center*, 156.

37. California State Legislature, *Sixth Report of Un-American Activities in California, 1951: Report of the Senate Fact-Finding Committee on Un-American Activities to the 1951 Regular California Legislature*, Sacramento, 1951, 51, 55.

38. California State Legislature, *Third Report on Un-American Activities in California, 1947: Report of the Joint Fact-Finding Committee to the Fifty-seventh California Legislature*, Sacramento, 1947, 47, 105, 260–61.

39. Minutes of Meeting, 12 December 1944, Box 1, Folder 6, Hollywood Democratic Committee Papers.

40. Minutes, 10 December 1946, Box 101, Folder 3, Dore Schary Papers.

41. Minutes, 30 April 1946, Box 1, Folder 7, Hollywood Democratic Committee Papers.

42. Minutes, 10 December 1946, Box 101, Folder 3, Dore Schary Papers.

43. Minutes, 11 June 1946, Box 1, Folder 7, Hollywood Democratic Committee Papers.

44. Minutes, 3 July 1946, Box 1, Folder 7, Hollywood Democratic Committee Papers.

45. Ronald Reagan with Richard G. Hubler, *Where's the Rest of Me?* (New York: Duell, Sloane and Pearce, 1965), 166–67.

46. Ibid., 168, 169.

47. Minutes, 3 July 1946, Box 101, Folder 3, Dore Schary Papers. See undated memo from Emmett Lavery, Box 72, Emmett Lavery Papers. See *Hollywood Reporter*, 5 November 1945.

48. Minutes 30 July 1946, Box 1, Folder 7, Hollywood Democratic Committee Papers.

49. Minutes, 6 August 1946, Box 1, Folder 7, Hollywood Democratic Committee Papers.

50. See letter to Senator Frederick Van Nuys, 27 October 1943, Box 7, Folder 2, Hollywood Democratic Committee Papers.

51. Crank letter, 7 August 1946, Box 6, Folder 1, Hollywood Democratic Committee Papers.

52. Minutes, 23 July 1946, Box 101, Folder 3, Dore Schary Papers. See also James Spada, *More Than a Woman: An Intimate Biography of Bette Davis* (New York: Bantam, 1993), 389; Clive Hirschhorn, *Gene Kelly* (New York: St. Martin's, 1984), 134.

53. Letter from Chuck Jones, 19 November 1946, Box 101, Folder 3, Dore Schary Papers.

54. Report, 7 June 1945, Record Group 46, Box 59, R7815c, Records of the United States Senate Internal Security Subcommittee.

55. Report, 24 January 1945, Record Group 46, Box 57, R7550e, Records of the United States Senate Internal Security Subcommittee.

56. Report, "Confidential," 17 December 1945, Record Group 46, Box 62, R8173, Records of the United States Senate Internal Security Subcommittee.

57. Report, 18 March 1946, Record Group 46, Box 64, R8343, Records of the United States Senate Internal Security Subcommittee.

58. Report, 29 June 1946, Record Group 46, Box 66, R8601, Records of the United States Senate Internal Security Subcommittee.

59. Report, 5 March 1943, Record Group 46, Box 42, R6204a, Records of the United States Senate Internal Security Subcommittee.

60. See, e.g., Eugene Block to Leon Lewis, 16 September 1942, Box 18, Folder 8, CRC, JFC Papers.

61. George F. Custen, *Twentieth Century Fox: Darryl F. Zanuck and the Culture of Hollywood* (New York: Basic Books, 1997), 295.

62. Report, 17 June 1946, Record Group 46, Box 65, R8547a, Records of the United States Senate Internal Security Subcommittee.

63. Virginia Gardner, "California Close-Up," *Masses & Mainstream* 1, no. 4 (June 1948): 51–58; quotation on 52.

64. Report, 29 June 1945, Record Group 46, Box 60, R7848·, Records of the United States Senate Internal Security Subcommittee.

65. Report, 18 July 1945, Record Group 46, Box 60, R7891c, Records of the United States Senate Internal Security Subcommittee.

66. Report, 23 July 1945, Record Group 46, Box 60, R7891·, Records of the United States Senate Internal Security Subcommittee.

67. Report, "Communist Infiltration of Motion Picture Industry," 24 May 1947, 100–138754, Serial 157x1, Part 3 of 15, Communist Infiltration, Motion Picture Industry, FOIA Documents, FBI.

68. James Cain to Mr. William Donahey, 11 November 1946, Box 1, James Cain Papers.

69. Report, 24 May 1947, Serial 157x1, Part 3 of 15, 100–138754, Communist Infiltration, Motion Picture Industry, FOIA Documents, FBI.

70. *Hollywood Reporter*, 16 April 1946.

71. Minutes of Executive Board of SWG, 20 August 1945, Record Group 233, "SWG File," Records of House Committee on Internal Security, National Archives and Records Administration.

72. Minutes of Executive Board of SWG, 8 October 1945, Record Group 233, "SWG File," Records of House Committee on Internal Security.

73. "Screen Writers' Guild History, 1945–1947," 8 October 1945, Box 72, Emmett Lavery Papers.

74. *Hollywood Reporter*, 14 August 1946. See also *Hollywood Reporter*, 20 August 1946 and 21 August 1946.

75. Eric Johnston to Emmett Lavery, 8 August 1946, Record Group 233, "Screen Writers Guild File," Records of House Committee on Internal Security.

76. Speech by Eric Johnston, 2 March 1947, Box 93, Folder 2, Dore Schary Papers.

77. *Hollywood Reporter*, 14 August 1946.

78. California State Legislature, *Third Report on Un-American Activities in California*, 142.

79. Eric Johnston to "Dear Cecil," 18 December 1947, Box 915, Folder 6, Cecil B. DeMille Papers.

80. FBI Report, 24 May 1947, Serial 157x1, Part 3 of 15, 100–138754, Communist Infiltration, Motion Picture Industry, FOIA Documents, FBI.

81. Diana McLellan, *The Girls: Sappho Goes to Hollywood* (New York: St. Martin's, 2000), 207.

82. Quoted in *Los Angeles Times*, 1 October 1946.

83. Quoted in *Hollywood Reporter*, 3 December 1946.

84. Bob Thomas, *King Cohn: The Life and Times of Harry Cohn* (New York: Putnam, 1967), 299.

85. Oral history, Helen Slote Levitt, 1991, 300/351, UCLA.

86. D. M. Ladd to J. Edgar Hoover, 2 October 1947, Serial 251x1, Part 6 of 15, 100–138754, Communist Infiltration, Motion Picture Industry, FOIA Documents, FBI. See also "Communist Infiltration of the Motion Picture Industry," 13 October 1944, Reel 11, *Communist Activity in the Entertainment Industry: FBI Surveillance Files on Hollywood, 1942–1958*, ed. Daniel J. Leab (Bethesda, Md.: University Publications of America, c1991).

87. Report, 14 August 1947, Record Group 233, "SWG File," Records of House Committee on Internal Security.

88. Report, 4 June 1945, 100–138754, 100–22916, Reel 2, *Communist Activity in the Entertainment Industry*.

89. Memorandum, n.d, Box 31, Folder 1, John Howard Lawson Papers.

90. See Gerald Horne, *Class Struggle in Hollywood, 1930–1950: Moguls, Mobsters, Stars, Reds and Trade Unionists* (Austin: University of Texas Press, 2001), passim.

91. *Screen Guilds' Magazine* 2, no. 12 (May 1947): 15.

92. Lester Cole, *Hollywood Red: The Autobiography of Lester Cole* (San Francisco: Ramparts Press, 1981), 176.

93. Testimony of Edward Dmytryk, U.S. Congress, House of Representatives, Un-American Activities Committee, 82nd Cong., 1st sess., 17, 23–25 April, 16–18 May 1951, Box 30, Folder 11, Edward G. Robinson Papers.

94. U.S. Congress, House of Representatives, Committee on Un-American Activities, "Communist Infiltration of Hollywood Motion Picture Industry— Part I," 8 and 21 March; 10, 11, 12, and 13 April, 1951, 82nd Cong., 1st sess. (Washington, D.C.: Government Printing Office, 1951), 252, 221.

95. Interview, Jean Butler, n.d., Box 1, Nancy Lynn Schwartz Papers.

96. U.S. Congress, House of Representatives, Committee on Un-American Activities, 83rd Cong., 1st sess., 2 December 1952; 17 February, 12 and 27 March, 7 and 13 April 1953 (Washington, D.C.: Government Printing Office, 1953), 947.

97. David Caute, *Joseph Losey: A Revenge on Life* (New York: Oxford University Press, 1994), 100.

98. Oral history, Richard Collins, 1990, 474, Southern Methodist University.

99. McGilligan and Buhle, *Tender Comrades*, 695.

100. Report, 13 June 1944, Record Group 46, Box 52, R6983e, Records of the United States Senate Internal Security Subcommittee.

101. Report, ca. early 1945, Record Group 46, Box 56, R7468a, Records of the United States Senate Internal Security Subcommittee.

102. Report, 17 June 1946, Record Group 46, Box 65, R8502, Records of the United States Senate Internal Security Subcommittee.

103. Nemmy Sparks to "Dear Comrades," 16 August 1946, Record Group 21, Box 1332, Folder 82, Records of the District Court: "decided that Ed Robbin, formerly of the Los Angeles staff of the Daily Peoples World, was not to be re-registered in the Party at this time . . . [not a] stoolpigeon" but awfully close, they conclude.

104. "Delegates Book, Communist Party, Los Angeles County," 15 September 1945, Record Group 21, Box 1347, Folder 143, Records of the District Court.

105. Report, 28 January 1947, Record Group 46, Box 67, R8887, Records of the United States Senate Internal Security Subcommittee.

106. Transcripts of Hearings, 7–10 October 1946, California State Legislature, Box 30, Records of Committee on Un-American Activities, California State Archives.

107. M. Nelson to Earl Warren, 23 January 1947, Federal Files, Communism, f3640: 17294, Earl Warren Papers, California State Archives.

11. INQUISITION

1. *Washington Daily News*, 27 October 1947.

2. "Knute" to "Dear Thorg," 13 November 1947, Files on the "Hollywood Blacklist," Writers' Guild, Los Angeles.

3. *Washington Star*, 26 October 1947.

4. *Hollywood Reporter*, 20 October 1947.

5. *Washington Daily News*, 27 October 1947.

6. Interview, Nunnally Johnson, n.d., Box 1, Nancy Lynn Schwartz Papers.

7. John Howard Lawson statement to HUAC, 1947, Box 27, Folder 2, John Howard Lawson Papers.

8. *PM*, 27 October 1947. See also Howard Koch, *As Time Goes By: Memoirs of a Writer* (New York: Harcourt Brace Jovanovich, 1979), 167, 166.

9. HUAC Testimony, Jack Warner Collection.

10. *PM*, ca. 18 April 1948, Reel 9, *Communist Activity in the Entertainment Industry: FBI Surveillance Files on Hollywood, 1942–1958*, ed. Daniel J. Leab (Bethesda, Md.: University Publications of America, c1991). The writer Robert Sherwood asserted, "I go along" with "Arthur Schlesinger, Jr." when "he said, 'many conservatives are happily pouncing upon the Communist scare as an excuse for silencing all critics of business supremacy.'" See *Screen Writer*, December 1947.

11. Clipping, *PM*, 22 October 1947, Reel 384, Box 422, National Republic Papers.

12. Notes on Samuel Ornitz, n.d., Box 3, Nancy Lynn Schwartz Papers; *Sentinel*, 6 November 1947, Box 5, Folder 27, Samuel Ornitz Papers, State Historical Society of Wisconsin. See oral history, Samuel Rosenwein, 1989, 300/315, UCLA.

13. Philip Dunne, *Take Two: A Life in Movies and Politics* (New York: Limelight, 1992), 204, 211, 119.

14. Lester Cole to Waldo Salt, 10 March 1979, Box 77, Folder 19, Waldo Salt Papers, UCLA. One of the nineteen, Bertolt Brecht denied he was a Communist, though he quickly left the country after testifying. See "Brecht in Hollywood," BC0451b, Pacifica Radio Archives. Howard Koch was one of the nineteen, though—by his own admission—"not a party member." See Koch, *As Time Goes By*, 167, 166.

15. *Hollywood Reporter*, 4 November 1947.

16. *Hollywood Reporter*, 20 November 1947.

17. *Hollywood Reporter*, 28 November 1947. See also *Hollywood Reporter*, 17 December 1947.

18. *Hollywood Reporter*, 17 December 1947.

19. Memo by Emmett Lavery, ca. 1953, Box 72, Emmett Lavery Papers.

20. *Hollywood Reporter*, 10 September 1947.

21. *New York Times*, 3 April 1962.

22. Memorandum, 25 August 1947, uncertain provenance, Box 72, Emmett Lavery Papers.

23. Remarks of Cecil B. DeMille, 21 February 1947, Box 1154, Folder 28, Cecil B. DeMille Papers. See also his remarks located in Folder 29.

24. Raymond Chandler to George Harmon Coxe, 9 April 1939, in Frank MacShane, ed., *Selected Letters of Raymond Chandler* (New York: Columbia University Press, 1981), 6.

25. Raymond Chandler to Charles Morton, 18 December 1944, in MacShane, *Selected Letters of Raymond Chandler*, 37–38.

26. Raymond Chandler to James Sandoe, 17 January 1948, in MacShane, *Selected Letters of Raymond Chandler*, 106–8. See Letter, 4 January 1948, Laurence Avery, ed., *A Southern Life: Letters of Paul Green, 1916–1981* (Chapel Hill: University of North Carolina Press, 1994), 472–73.

27. *Los Angeles Examiner*, 22 September 1953.

28. Thomas memoir.

29. *Hollywood Reporter*, 21 October 1947.

30. *Hollywood Reporter*, 24 October 1947.

31. "Knute" to "Dear Thorg," 13 November 1947, Files on the "Hollywood Blacklist," Writers' Guild. For an account of the CFA press conference, see A. M. Sperber and Eric Lax, *Bogart* (New York: Morrow, 1997), 377, 378. Charles Higham and Roy Moseley, *Cary Grant: The Lonely Heart* (San Diego: Harcourt Brace Jovanovich, 1989), 189. But see also Graham McCann, *Cary Grant: A Class Apart* (New York: Columbia University Press, 1996), 134, 135, 161. See also Charles Higham, *Errol Flynn: The Untold Story* (Garden City, N.Y.: Doubleday, 1980). See *PM*, 28 October 1947.

32. Dunne, *Take Two*, 204–5.

33. David O. Selznick to John Huston and William Wyler, 24 October 1947, Box 2356, David O. Selznick Papers. See also David O. Selznick to John Huston, 18 October 1947, Box 2356, David O. Selznick Papers.

34. *New York Times*, 22 October 1947.

35. U.S. Congress, House, Committee on Un-American Activities, 80th Cong., 1st sess., 20–24, 27–30 October 1947 (Washington, D.C.: Government Printing Office, 1947), Box 61, Folder 9, Jack Warner Collection.

36. *New York Sun*, 22 October 1947. See HUAC Testimony, Jack Warner Collection.

37. *Hollywood Reporter*, 23 October 1947.

38. HUAC Testimony, Jack Warner Collection.

39. *Los Angeles Examiner*, 18 May 1947.

40. *Daily Variety*, 23 October 1947.

41. *Hollywood Citizen-News*, 23 October 1947.

42. *Los Angeles Examiner*, 24 October 1947.

43. *Hollywood Reporter*, 7 April 1948.

44. *Los Angeles Times*, 16 May 1947.

45. Quoted in *Los Angeles Herald Express*, 10 November 1947.

46. HUAC Testimony, Jack Warner Collection.

47. "Motion Picture Artists Benefit," 7–20 October 1945, Box 61, Folder 10, Jack Warner Collection. Lawson was a sponsor of this event, and Lardner's name was circled.

48. Telegram, 9 October 1945, Box 61, Folder 10, Jack Warner Collection.

49. Jack Warner to John Cromwell, 15 October 1945, Box 61, Folder 10, Jack Warner Collection.

50. Sidney Sutherland to Jack Warner, 11 October 1945, Box 61, Folder 10, Jack Warner Collection.

51. Stella L. Lombard to Dore Schary, November 1947, Box 100, Folder 2, Dore Schary Papers.

52. "Common Sense: America's Newspaper against Communism," 15 January 1963, Box 93, Folder 9, Dore Schary Papers.

53. "Hollywood Close-Up," 6 June 1963, Box 93, Folder 9, Dore Schary Papers. One can find in this collection folder upon folder of "crank" mail. See also Box 93, Folder 10, of this collection: "Nationalist Summary," 21 October 1955: "Two hundred *Red Stars* in Hollywood-Exposed!" Included were both Schary and Lawson.

54. Adrian Scott to "Dear Charles," Box 2, Folder 23, Adrian Scott Papers.

55. David Caute, *Joseph Losey: A Revenge on Life* (New York: Oxford University Press, 1994), 100.

56. Joseph Losey to "Dear Adrian," 28 November 1947, Box 5, Folder 19, Adrian Scott Papers.

57. Elia Kazan to Adrian Scott, ca. 1947, Box 5, Folder 6, Adrian Scott Papers.

58. Bernard Fein to Adrian Scott, Box 3, Folder 45, Adrian Scott Papers.

59. *Los Angeles Herald-American,* 5 November 1947.

60. Jack Moffitt, "The Muse Discards Her Mask," *Esquire,* August 1947, Box 43, File A6, Jack Warner Collection.

61. See, e.g., *Chicago Tribune,* 23 November 1946, 9 November 1946.

62. *Hollywood Reporter,* 18 November 1947.

63. *Hollywood Citizen-News,* 6 December 1947.

64. Statement by Humphrey Bogart, October 1947, Box 2, Folder 3, Gordon Kahn Papers, State Historical Society of Wisconsin.

65. Memo from Humphrey Bogart, 3 December 1947, No. 217, Hedda Hopper Collection, Academy of Motion Picture Arts and Sciences.

66. Jeffrey Meyers, *Bogart: A Life in Hollywood* (Boston: Houghton Mifflin, 1997), 206. See Arch Reeve to "Publicity Directors," 14 August 1944, Association of Motion Pictures and Television Producers Collection, Academy of Motion Picture Arts and Sciences. See also Maurice Ries to Cecil B. DeMille, 8 March 1956, Box 1146, Folder 4, Cecil B. DeMille Papers. Hopper was also a buddy of FBI director J. Edgar Hoover: J. Edgar Hoover to Hedda Hopper, 10 August 1946, No. 1153, Hedda Hopper Collection.

67. Walter Wanger to Hedda Hopper, 9 October 1939, Hedda Hopper Collection. See also Walter and Joan Wanger to Hedda Hopper, 12 January 1940, Hedda Hopper Collection.

68. Oral history, Ben Margolis, 300/250, 1987, UCLA. See the contract with writer Win Brooks for "$750.00" to write "'Shadow on the Heart,'" 30 October 1947, Box 8, Folder 16, Argosy Pictures Papers, Brigham Young University.

69. Oral history, Robert Kenny, 1964, 300/19, UCLA.

70. "Congressional Investigation of Communism in Hollywood," 17 December 1947, Box 8, Folder 1, Kenny-Morris Papers, State Historical Society of Wisconsin.

71. *Atlanta Journal,* 28 October 1947.

72. *Denver Post,* 22 October 1947. For editorial comment, almost uniformly critical of HUAC, see, e.g., *New York Herald Tribune,* 22 October 1947, 1 November 1947; *New York Times,* 23 October 1947, 2 November 1947; *Washington Post,* 5 November 1947, 21 October 1947; *Pittsburgh Post-Gazette,* 23 October 1947; *Detroit Free Press,* 23 October 1947; *New York World Telegram,* 28 October 1947; *Miami Herald,* 1 November 1947; *Orlando Sentinel,* 1 November 1947; *Boston Herald,* 22 October 1947, 27 October 1947; *St. Louis Post-Dispatch,* 22 October 1947; *Toledo Blade,* 29 October 1947; *Des Moines Register,* 23 October 1947; *Chicago Sun,* 23 October 1947; *Christian Science Monitor,* 27 October 1947; *Atlanta Journal,* 28 October 1947.

73. *Tampa Morning Tribune,* 23 October 1947.

74. Interview, Sylvia Jarrico, n.d., Box 1, Nancy Lynn Schwartz Papers.

75. Ring Lardner Jr., "What Is Our Crime?" *Masses & Mainstream* 3, no. 3 (August 1950): 85–88; quotation on 87.

76. John Howard Lawson, "Your Trial," *Masses & Mainstream* 1, no. 5 (July 1948): 3–6; quotation on 3.

77. Otto Friedrich, *City of Nets: A Portrait of Hollywood in the 1940s* (Berkeley and Los Angeles: University of California Press, 1997), 424.

78. *PM*, 11 January 1948.

79. John Howard Lawson, "Deadline for Writers," *Masses & Mainstream* 3, no. 7 (July 1950): 8–13; quotation on 11.

80. Brief in District Court for the District of Columbia, "U.S. vs. John Howard Lawson," et al., Cr. No. 1352–47, Box 15, Margolis-McTernan Collection.

81. Trumbo vs. U.S., Court of Appeals, "Joint Appendix," ca. 1948, Box 20, Margolis-McTernan Collection.

82. *Variety*, 16 April 1948.

83. Oral history, Ben Margolis, 1987, 300/250, UCLA.

84. Carey McWilliams to Robert Kenny, 21 April 1949, Box 9, Folder 1, Kenny-Morris Papers.

85. Dorothy B. Jones, "Communism and the Movies: A Study of Film Content," 1956, Box 85, Folder 8, Fund for the Republic Papers, Princeton University.

86. Nora Sayre, *Running Time: Films of the Cold War* (New York: Dial, 1978), 68–69.

87. John Howard Lawson to Robert Kenny, 5 August 1948, Box 8, Folder 7, Kenny-Morris Papers.

88. Charlotta Bass Memoir, 313, Box 1, Folder 3, Charlotta Bass Papers.

89. Quoted in undated minutes of Board of Directors, PCA, Box 3, Edward Mosk Papers.

90. Minutes of Board of Directors Meeting, PCA, 22 April 1947, Box 3, Edward Mosk Papers.

91. Undated clipping, Box 2, Folder 1, Gordon Kahn Papers.

92. Kate Buford, *Burt Lancaster: An American Life* (New York: Knopf, 2000), 98.

93. William Wyler to "Mr. and Mrs. Hopkins," 6 May 1948, No. 685, William Wyler Collection.

94. List of Acceptances, 15 May 1948, No. 685, William Wyler Collection.

95. Anne Edwards, *Remarkable Woman: A Biography of Katharine Hepburn* (New York: Morrow, 1985), 252. See also Christopher Andersen, *An Affair to Remember: The Remarkable Love Story of Katharine Hepburn and Spencer Tracy* (New York: Morrow, 1997), 189, 190; Report, 19 May 1947, Box 69, R9091a, Records of the United States Senate Internal Security Subcommittee.

96. Lauren Bacall, *By Myself* (New York: Knopf, 1979), 160.

97. Dore Schary to Howard Estabrook, 30 March 1948, Box 17, Howard Estabrook Collection, Academy of Motion Picture Arts and Sciences. Schary, according to the FBI, "advised that he had been acquainted with [Lawson] for a period of years and he knew him to be a very able man who could argue calmly and well under adverse conditions. He stated that he himself had argued with Lawson on more than one occasion at various meetings in Hollywood on various issues" and was "forced to the conclusion that that has been a studied action on the part of Lawson to create a definite impression," i.e., his "'blow up'" in 1947. See Memo from FBI-L.A., 13 January 1951, 100–15732, Vol. 25, Reel 5, *Communist Activity in the Entertainment Industry.*

98. A. A. Heist, Southern California branch of ACLU to Roger Baldwin, 3 October 1947, Box 859, Folder 1, American Civil Liberties Union Papers, Princeton University.

99. Roger Baldwin et al. to Eric Johnston, 9 December 1947, Box 859, Folder 7, ACLU Papers.

12. JAILED FOR IDEAS

1. Sue Lawson to John Howard Lawson, n.d., Box 10, Folder 10, John Howard Lawson Papers.

2. Oral history, Mary Davenport, 1993, 300/391, UCLA.

3. See oral history, Helen Slote Levitt, 1991, 300/351, UCLA.

4. Report, 11 November 1955, 100–138754, Reel 7, Communist Activity in the Entertainment Industry.

5. Adrian Scott to Allan Scott, 31 August 1966, Box 6, Folder 3, Adrian Scott Papers.

6. *Nation*, 19 November 1949, Vertical File, "Hollywood Blacklist," h729-bl, University of Wyoming.

7. Alvah Bessie, *Inquisition in Eden* (New York: Macmillan, 1965), 204.

8. U.S. Congress, House of Representatives, Committee on Un-American Activities, "Hearings Regarding the Communist Infiltration of the Motion Picture Industry," 80th Cong., 1st sess., October 1947 (Washington: U.S. Government Printing Office, 1947), 323.

9. Donald M. Nelson to "All Members," 1 December 1947, Folder 2, Society of Independent Motion Picture Producers Collection, Los Angeles. See the *New York Sun*, 28 October 1947. See also oral history, Paul Jarrico, 1991, 300/360, UCLA.

10. Joseph McBride, *Searching for John Ford: A Life* (New York: St. Martin's, 2001).

11. Harry Belafonte to Louis K. Sidney, 30 July 1952, Box 694, J. B. Matthews Papers. Here the famed performer proclaimed his Catholicism and denied contact with Paul Robeson. In this same box, see similar letters from, e.g., Marlon Brando and Kirk Douglas. For more in this vein, see, e.g., Allan Scott to Spyros Skouras, 2 April 1952, Box 18, Ralph De Toledano Papers, Boston University. See William Wyler to Y. Frank Freeman, 3 May 1954, No. 685, William Wyler Collection. As for Paul Henreid, see his 28 February 1955 recantation in Box 22, Paul Henreid Collection, Academy of Motion Picture Arts and Sciences.

12. See Leonard Monson Penn to B. B. Kahane, 12 October 1952, Box 695, J. B. Matthews Papers. In this same box, see letters from, e.g., Ruth Gordon, John Huston, and John Houseman. The letter of Garson Kanin—thirteen pages in length—is notably interesting.

13. Bob Condon to Walter Winchell, 30 October 1950, Box 619, J. B. Matthews Papers. Attached to this letter is the cited letter from Canada Lee.

14. *Philadelphia Evening Bulletin*, 16 May 1952.

15. Clipping, 25 April 1948, Box 28, Folder 4, John Howard Lawson Papers.

16. Interview, Charles Katz, n.d., Box 2, Nancy Lynn Schwartz Papers.

17. Brief in Case of Lawson et al., October Term 1949, Box 1, Folder 10, Adrian Scott Papers.

18. Albert Lewin to John Howard Lawson, 20 February 1948, Box 1, Folder 4, John Howard Lawson Papers. See Durand van Doren to Lawson, 29 October 1947, Box 24, Folder 2, John Howard Lawson Papers.

19. John Howard Lawson to Durand van Doren, 16 January 1966, Box 24, Folder 2, John Howard Lawson Papers. See Testimony of Michael Blankfort, 4 April 1951, Box 5, Michael Blankfort Collection, Academy of Motion Picture Arts and Sciences. See memo to J. Edgar Hoover, 14 April 1951, 100–15732, Vol. 28, Reel 5, Communist Activity in the Entertainment Industry.

20. Affidavit, Circa 1961, Box 31, Folder 5, John Howard Lawson Papers.

21. Philip Dunne, liberal icon, opined, "'I'm always scared, having lived through'" the Red Scare. "'if anybody is a victim of a witch-hunt,'" he argued, "'then everybody becomes a potential victim.'" *Los Angeles Times*, 4 June 1992. See, e.g., the *Los Angeles Times*, 19 February 1952, where Ronald Reagan complained that "motion picture freedom is slowly being nibbled away by political censorship. . . . 'Hollywood,'" he said, "'is not the Babylon it has been made out to be. . . . our divorce rate,'" said the divorced actor "'is 29.9% while nationally divorces average 40%.'" As for "'communism,'" it was "'infinitesimal in the motion picture industry. They ask us to fire people,'" he lamented, "'because of their political beliefs which happens to be against the law. . . . then when we did fire some Communists, our own courts awarded two of them $90,000 damages.'"

22. *PM*, 15 May 1947.

23. Sean O'Casey to "Dear Sir," Spring 1951, in David Krause, ed., *The Letters of Sean O'Casey*, vol. 2, *1942–1954* (New York: Macmillan, 1980), 783.

24. Statement by O'Casey, in Krause, *Letters of Sean O'Casey*, 198.

25. Eugene O'Neill to "My Dear Sean," 5 August 1943, in Krause, *Letters of Sean O'Casey*, 41–42.

26. Sean O'Casey to Mr. Dickson, 11 May 1945, in Krause, *Letters of Sean O'Casey*, 239.

27. Ibid.

28. Rupert Julian to John Howard Lawson, 20 October 1947, Box 27, Folder 3, John Howard Lawson Papers.

29. Lawson speech, 29 June 1949, Box 9, Folder 7, John Howard Lawson Papers.

30. John Howard Lawson speech, December 1947, Box 11, Folder 8, John Howard Lawson Papers. See *Cine Technician* 14, no. 70 (January–February 1948): 14–15, 27, 15, Box 1, Folder 13, Adrian Scott Papers. See Adrian Scott to "Dear Marian," 13 February 1949, Box 4, Folder 5, Adrian Scott Papers.

31. For samples of these and other items of hate mail, along with the cartoon noted, see Box 27, Folder 3, John Howard Lawson Papers.

32. See, e.g., Thelma E. Gonyaw to J. B. Matthews, 30 November 1951, Box 716, J. B. Matthews Papers.

33. See "ADL Bulletin," April 1955, Box 10, Harold Keith Thompson Papers, Stanford University.

34. Andrea Most, *Making Americans: Jews and the Broadway Musical* (Cambridge, Mass.: Harvard University Press, 2003), 20, 22, 153. See also Gerald L. K. Smith, "Is Communism Jewish?" ca. 1946, Box 1, 73043–10, Glen A. Chandler Papers, Stanford University.

35. American Jewish Committee, "Anti-Semitic Activity in the United States," 1954, Box 10, Harold Keith Thompson Papers.

36. *PM*, 13 June 1948.

37. John Howard Lawson, "Deadline for Writers," *Masses & Mainstream* 3, no. 7 (July 1950): 8–13; quotation on 11.

38. John Howard Lawson, "The Promise of a People's Theater," *New Masses* 38, no. 9 (18 February 1941): 29–30; quotation on 29.

39. John Howard Lawson, *The Hidden Heritage: A Rediscovery of the Ideas and Forces That Link the Thought of Our Time with the Culture of the Past* (New York: Citadel Press, 1968), vi, vii, ix, x, 42, 154, 227, 231, 253, 257, 261, 262, 264, 333, 376, 429.

40. Doxey Wilkerson review of *The Hidden Heritage*, *Masses & Mainstream* 4, no. 1 (January 1951): 91–96; quotation on 91.

41. See, e.g., Angus Cameron of Little, Brown publishers to John Howard Lawson, 20 January 1950, Box 12, Folder 5, John Howard Lawson Papers: "Negative." In the same folder, see also critical evaluations from Lawson's comrade Sidney Finkelstein, 20 June 1951 and 25 June 1951, and "Bernie" to Lawson, 12 June 1947. Apparently the publisher Knopf asserted, "'it is glaringly apparent that he is not a professional historian. . . . it is astonishing how little special attention is given to workers' and peasants' revolts.'" See also the 27 July 1949 *People's Daily World*.

42. *Daily Worker*, 16 November 1948.

43. Clipping, 2 November 1947, Reel 384, Box 422, National Republic Papers.

44. SAC, Boston, to J. Edgar Hoover, 1 February 1950, Vol. 20, Reel 4, Communist Activity in the Entertainment Industry: FBI Surveillance Files on Hollywood, 1942–1958.

45. *People's Daily World*, 9 December 1949.

46. *San Francisco Chronicle*, 12 December 1947.

47. Quoted in *Oregon Journal*, 16 December 1947.

48. *Seattle Post Intelligencer*, 14 December 1947.

49. John Howard Lawson speech, 26 March 1949, Box 12, Folder 1, John Howard Lawson Papers.

50. Dalton Trumbo to Albert Maltz, 12 January 1972, Box 11, Albert Maltz Papers, Boston University.

51. Albert Maltz to Dalton Trumbo, 23 December 1972, Box 11, Albert Maltz Papers.

52. Lester Cole to Albert Maltz, ca. March 1977, Box 11, Albert Maltz Papers.

53. Dalton Trumbo to Ring Lardner Jr., 24 June 1970, Folder 190, Ring Lardner Jr. Collection.

54. John Willett, ed., *Bertolt Brecht Journals* (New York: Routledge, 1996), xiii.

55. James K. Lyon, *Bertolt Brecht in America* (Princeton, N.J.: Princeton University Press, 1980), 14, 289, 290. 305.

56. Lester Cole to Ring Lardner Jr., 31 March 1978, Folder 181, Ring Lardner Jr. Collection, Academy of Motion Picture Arts and Sciences. "My regard for you altered but did not turn to the bitterness and scorn I felt for such egocentric self-praising opportunists as Maltz."

57. Alvah Bessie to Ring Lardner Jr., 30 March 1978, Folder 161, Ring Lardner Jr. Collection: "If there is any way that Cole can disagree with and/or take offense at anything written and/or spoken by anyone in the entire world, he will find a way to do so."

58. Alvah Bessie to Ring Lardner Jr., 12 February 1977, Folder 161, Ring Lardner Jr. Collection. Here he refers to "bastards, finks and stoolpigeons like Dmytryk and others of his ilk. That character turned up twice when I was working" in San Francisco, and "both times said 'hello, Alvah' to which I made no reply. Both times I returned to my office boiling with rage."

59. *Hollywood Reporter*, 29 May 1951. See also Maltz to Adrian Scott, n.d., Box 5, Folder 21, Adrian Scott Papers. See also *Film Comment* 3, no. 4 (Fall 1965), Box 100, Dore Schary Papers. Dmytryk spoke of an unnamed member of the Ten as "a mother's boy. He's not a homosexual, but he's soft. When I was a kid, [we] would have called him a sissie. As a result, he's always looked for the mother image and he married a woman about 15 years older than he is. This woman is a dedicated Communist." See oral history, Edward Dmytryk, 1959, Columbia University.

60. Dalton Trumbo to Ring Lardner Jr., 16 November [year unclear, ca. 1951], Folder 161, Ring Lardner Jr. Collection.

61. Dalton Trumbo to Albert Maltz, 7 February 1973, Box 11, Albert Maltz Papers.

62. Charles Katz to Albert Maltz, 23 August 1976, Box 11, Albert Maltz Papers.

63. Ben Margolis to Albert Maltz, 6 April 1973, Box 11, Albert Maltz Papers. Attorney Robert Kenny argued that the "Ten stoutly maintained that they were *not refusing* to testify. They merely wanted to answer the Committee in their own way. This created a jury issue." See Robert Kenny to Albert Maltz, 22 March 1973, Box 11, Albert Maltz Papers. See oral history, Carey McWilliams, 1982, 300/195, UCLA. Though the Ten were thought by some to be "Fifth Amendment Communists," this constitutional protection was hardly preeminent in their defense. See, e.g., the cartoon in the *Los Angeles Times*, 22 September 1951: Parrots on a perch chirp "Fifth Amendment!" with signs attached reading "Communist Hollywood" and the caption "Party Line" as an eagle stares at them.

64. Charles Katz to Albert Maltz, 2 April 1973, Box 11, Albert Maltz Papers.

65. Alvah Bessie to "Dear Poor Law Student," 19 March 1979, Box 1, Alvah Bessie Papers, Columbia University. See also oral history, Howard Koch, 1974, American Film Institute.

66. Ben Margolis to Albert Maltz, 6 April 1973, Box 11, Albert Maltz Papers.

67. *New York Times,* 14 August 1948.

68. Gerda Lerner, *Fireweed: A Political Autobiography* (Philadelphia: Temple University Press, 2002), 284.

69. Barbara Zheutlin and David Talbot, *Creative Differences: Profiles of Hollywood Dissidents* (Boston: South End Press, 1978), 30–31.

70. Ring Lardner Jr. to Alvah Bessie, 8 February 1977, Folder 181, Ring Lardner Jr. Collection.

71. Quoted in Ellen Schrecker, *Many Are the Crimes: McCarthyism in America* (Princeton, N.J.: Princeton University Press, 1998), 326.

72. Walter Bernstein, *Inside Out: A Memoir of the Blacklist* (New York: Knopf, 1996), 197.

73. U.S. Congress, House of Representatives, Committee on Un-American Activities, "Communist Infiltration of Hollywood Motion Picture Industry—Part I," 8 and 21 March; 10, 11, 12, and 13 April 1951, 82nd Cong., 1st sess. (Washington, D.C.: Government Printing Office, 1951), 251.

74. See, e.g., ibid., 426.

75. Oral history, Alice McGrath, 1987, 300/269, UCLA.

76. Oral history, John Bright, 1991, 300/356, UCLA.

77. Lawson statement, ca. 1946, Box 9, Folder 2, John Howard Lawson Papers.

78. Albert Maltz to John Howard Lawson, 4 March 1947, Box 9, Box 1, John Howard Lawson Papers.

79. Zheutlin and Talbot, *Creative Differences,* 8.

80. Ibid., 35.

81. U.S. Congress, House of Representatives, Committee on Un-American Activities, "Communist Infiltration of Hollywood Motion Picture Industry—Part I," 8 and 21 March; 10, 11, 12 and 13 April 1951, 82nd Cong., 1st sess., 417.

82. *Los Angeles Daily News,* 28 March 1951; SAC, Los Angeles, to J. Edgar Hoover, 17 April 1951, Vol. 28, Reel 5, Communist Activity in the Entertainment Industry: FBI Surveillance Files.

83. Memo to J. Edgar Hoover, 14 April 1951, 100–15732, Vol. 28, Reel 5, Communist Activity in the Entertainment Industry: FBI Surveillance Files.

84. Edward Dmytryk, *Odd Man Out: A Memoir of the Hollywood Ten* (Carbondale: Southern Illinois University Press, 1996), 20, 21, 36, 115–16.

85. John Howard Lawson, "Return to the 'Free World,'" *Masses & Mainstream* 4, no. 6 (1951): 9–17; quotation on 14.

86. U.S. Congress, House of Representatives, Committee on Un-American Activities, "Communist Infiltration of Hollywood Motion Picture Industry," 19 May 1952, 83rd Cong., 1st sess., 3488. See Clifford Odets to John Howard Lawson, 28 December 1948, Box 40, Folder 2, John Howard Lawson Papers.

87. Howard Fast to "Dear Jack," 8 February 1952, Box 12, Folder 2, John Howard Lawson Papers. See also Howard Fast, *Being Red: A Memoir* (Boston: Houghton Mifflin, 1990), 299, 300.

88. However, note that Lawson's opinion of Fast was not exactly positive. See John Howard Lawson to Holland Roberts, 2 April 1957, Box 14, Folder 2, John Howard Lawson Papers.

89. Quoted in *New York Times Magazine*, 25 March 1973.

90. See oral history, Guy Endore, 1964, 300/21, UCLA.

91. Letter from E. S. Sachs, 23 January 1948, Box 29, Folder 5, John Howard Lawson Papers. The National Federation of Practical Agriculture Students, representing three thousand in Mexico, and the Mexican Youth Federation representing ninety thousand, wrote President Truman demanding freedom for the Ten. See Letter, 5 December 1950, Official File 470, Harry S. Truman Library, Independence, Missouri. The United Nations Commission on Human Rights was petitioned by the Ten. The delegation included Lawson, Fast, William Patterson, and others. See *New York Times*, 11 May 1950. The All China Federation of Literature and Arts and the All China Association of Cinema Workers both backed the defendants: *Daily Worker*, 19 May 1950. Mulk Raj Anand to Henry Pratt Fairchild, Box 1, Folder 3, Ring Lardner Jr. Papers, State Historical Society of Wisconsin. The Ukrainian delegate at the UN railed similarly, adding "'this is a strange freedom,'" in Hollywood, "'where people are being hailed [*sic*] before congressional commissions for films . . . friendly to the Soviet Union and to the stand of the Red Army at Stalingrad.'" *Film Sense* 1 no. 2 (December 1949), Box 1, Folder 5, Adrian Scott Papers. See also *Los Angeles Times*, 27 October 1947. The British press of the "left, center and right alike used such terms as 'Hollywood's witch-hunt,' 'nauseating spectacle' and 'antics of a circus load of film stars'. . . . the 'Spectator.' conservative weekly, said the state cannot impose restraint art 'as in Russia' without making both state and art look ridiculous.'" *Los Angeles Times*, 27 October 1947.

92. John Murray to Adrian Scott, Box 5, Folder 33, Adrian Scott Papers. One British writer asserted, "With the big U.S. companies making more and more 'British' quota pictures over here, I do not think that a blacklist of men of noble opinions and ideals is quite so remote." Chris Brunel, "The Hollywood Ten," *Cine Technician* 16, no. 87 (November–December 1950): 172–73; quotation on 173.

93. Arthur Miller to William Wyler, 10 October 1950, No. 685, William Wyler Collection.

94. Janette to John Howard Lawson, 4 March 1950, Box 12, Folder 3, John Howard Lawson Papers. The writer added, "Let's face it—this is America! Two German refugees can't be alone on a program talking about our civil rights! Even two such great men."

95. Pearl Buck to "Mrs. Lawson," 1 November 1950, Box 1, Folder 3, John Howard Lawson Papers.

96. Oscar Hammerstein II to Committee, 31 October 1950, Box 1, Folder 3, John Howard Lawson Papers.

97. Letter from Gladys MacDonald, ca. 1950, Box 1, Folder 3, John Howard Lawson Papers.

98. SAC, Los Angeles, to J. Edgar Hoover, 19 March 1951, Vol. 28, Reel 5, Communist Activity in the Entertainment Industry: FBI Surveillance Files on Hollywood, 1942–1958.

99. See the speech by Samuel Ornitz, n.d., Box 5, Folder 28, Samuel Ornitz Papers.

100. See *Hollywood Review*, no. 2 (September–October 1955), Box 2, Folder 2, Adrian Scott Papers.

101. *Hollywood Review*, January 1953.

102. Memorandum for the Files, 15 September 1950, Official File 470, Harry S. Truman Library.

103. Herbert Biberman to "Sonya and Edward and Soni," ca. June 1950, Vertical File, Folder 412, Herbert Biberman Letters, Academy of Motion Picture Arts and Sciences.

104. "Petition for Executive Clemency," November 1950, Box 12, Folder 3, John Howard Lawson Papers.

105. Undated, unsourced statement, Box 12, Folder 3, John Howard Lawson Papers.

106. *Daily Worker*, 16 April 1951.

107. John Howard Lawson to Victor Grossman, 10 December 1967, Box 60, Folder 1, John Howard Lawson Papers.

108. *People's Weekly World*, 30 June 1950.

109. *Daily Worker*, 22 June 1950.

110. Dalton Trumbo on Lawson, n.d., Box 17, Folder 5, John Howard Lawson Papers. See Herbert Biberman to Gale Sondergaard, 16 July 1950, Vertical File, Folder 412, Herbert Biberman Letters.

111. John Howard Lawson, "Return to the 'Free World,'" *Masses & Mainstream* 4, no. 6 (June 1951): 9–17; quotation on 9.

112. Herbert Biberman to "Edward," 3 July 1950, Vertical File, Folder 412, Herbert Biberman Letters: "The fact that such a man as I am imprisoned for being a serious citizen is the calamity—the actual imprisonment itself, because its basis is understood, is not at all difficult. . . . the political fact is the monstrous fact—the physical fact is puny in comparison."

113. Herbert Biberman to Gale Sondergaard, 12 July 1950, Vertical File, Folder 412, Herbert Biberman Letters.

114. Bruce Cook, *Dalton Cook* (New York: Scribner's, 1977), 209, 213.

115. John Howard Lawson to Peggy and Jeff, 17 August 1950, Box 12, Folder 3, John Howard Lawson Papers.

116. John Howard Lawson to Sue Lawson, 14 August 1950, Box 12, Folder 3, John Howard Lawson Papers: "It would be a good idea for you to send or bring me an extra pair of reading glasses."

117. John Howard Lawson to Sue Lawson, 5 November 1950, Box 12, Folder 3, John Howard Lawson Papers.

118. John Howard Lawson, *Film in the Battle of Ideas* (New York: Masses and Mainstream, 1953), 23.

119. John Howard Lawson to Sue Lawson, 31 July 1950, Box 12, Folder 3, John Howard Lawson Papers.

120. John Howard Lawson to Sue Lawson, n.d., Box 12, Folder 3, John Howard Lawson Papers.

121. Janet to Sue Lawson, 23 June 1950, Box 12, Folder 3, John Howard Lawson Papers.

122. R. O. Culver to Sue Lawson, 1 March 1951, Box 12, Folder 3, John Howard Lawson Papers: "I must return the enclosed letter to you."

123. Carl Marzani, *The Education of Reluctant Radical, Book 5: Reconstruction* (New York: Monthly Review Press, 2001), 113. 130, 139.

124. Thomas memoir. "Upon passing through two sets of iron gates, twenty feet high, with automatic locks and spiked at the top," he recalled. "I got my first look at the inside of a federal prison and believe me, it was no 'pretty picture,' cold, dreary and walls—walls—walls." His "first instruction" was "to remove my clothing, then to take a shower, after which I was thoroughly deloused, as if I'd had the scabies. . . . next I was handed some old clothes. I don't know how many inmates before had worn those clothes," he noted bitterly, "but I suspect many, for they were frayed from one end to the other." His view of prison, as luck would have it, mirrored Lawson's. It was a "'little Siberia,'" he observed without irony, "dreary, dark and dirty without a breath of warmth. It's a combination of a Russian Labor camp and a New Deal Welfare State" and a "stinking cesspool for future crime." "Immorality and thievery were rampant," while the "whole place was enveloped in an atmosphere of sin." The food was terrible—a "'flop house' on the Bowery never gave out poorer fare." There was segregation, of course, "Negroes, with few exceptions, were segregated both in the dormitories and in the mess hall. Jews were assigned to Vermont House, giving it the name of 'Israel House.'"

125. Laura Foner to "Dear Jack Lawson," 7 July 1950, Box 12, Folder 3, John Howard Lawson Papers.

13. "BLACKLISTED"

1. *Daily Worker*, 8 June 1951.

2. Carl Marzani, *The Education of a Reluctant Radical, Book 5: Reconstruction* (New York: Monthly Review Press, 2001), 15.

3. Lawson had another problem, however. He was trying to hide his association with a film, *The Jolson Story*. John Howard Lawson to Jane Merchant, n.d., Box 78, Folder 1, John Howard Lawson Papers. See Bernard Dick, *Radical Innocence: A Critical Study of the Hollywood Ten* (Lexington: University Press of Kentucky, 1989), 61. See also interview, Cleo Trumbo, n.d., Box 1, Nancy Lynn Schwartz Papers.

4. See, e.g., Sidney Poitier, *This Life* (New York: Knopf, 1980), 149.

5. Undated letter from John Howard Lawson, Box 40, Folder 1, John Howard Lawson Papers.

6. George Willner to Sue Lawson, 11 January 1951, Box 12, Folder 3, John Howard Lawson Papers. See Notes, n.d., Box 1, Nancy Lynn Schwartz Papers.

7. Peter Davis, *In Darkest Hollywood: Exploring the Jungles of Cinema's South Africa* (Athens: Ohio University Press, 1996), 39, 46.

8. *Daily Compass,* 24 January 1952.

9. *New York World Telegram,* 24 January 1952.

10. *New York Times,* 24 January 1952.

11. *New York Daily News,* 24 January 1952.

12. *New York Journal American,* 24 January 1952.

13. *New York Herald Tribune,* 24 January 1952.

14. *Sunday Tribune,* 18 November 1951.

15. Speech by John Howard Lawson, 26 March 1949, Box 12, Folder 1, John Howard Lawson Papers.

16. John Howard Lawson to Lawrence Hill, 3 September 1956, Box 40, Folder 7, John Howard Lawson Papers.

17. John Howard Lawson, "Hollywood: Illusion and Reality," *Masses & Mainstream* 5, no. 7 (July 1952): 21–33; quotation on 32–33.

18. See letter from John Howard Lawson, 18 February 1956, Box 30, Folder 9, John Howard Lawson Papers.

19. Victor Navasky, *Naming Names* (New York: Viking, 1980), 293.

20. *Hollywood Review,* November–December 1954, Box 39, Folder 8, Dorothy Healey Papers, California State University, Long Beach. Despite Lawson's curt dismissal of Kazan, it was reported that the famed director contributed $500 to the fund-raising committee for the Hollywood Ten. See *Chicago Daily Tribune,* 12 April 1952.

21. Report, 2 June 1951, 100–50870, Reel 6, *Communist Activity in the Entertainment Industry: FBI Surveillance Files on Hollywood, 1942–1958,* ed. Daniel J. Leab (Bethesda, Md.: University Publications of America, c1991).

22. Oral history, Guy Endore, 1964, 300/21, UCLA.

23. Gerda Lerner, *Fireweed: A Political Autobiography* (Philadelphia: Temple University Press, 2002), 288, 369.

24. Undated memo, Box 31, Folder 1, John Howard Lawson Papers. By way of comparison, in 1935 Trumbo signed a contract with Warner's at a salary of $100 per week; in 1945 Bessie was making $425 weekly with the same company. See Trumbo contract, 1259 0a, 16 September 1935, and Bessie contract, 67262, 15 January 1945, Warner Brothers Archives, University of Southern California. See also the *Washington Herald,* 23 October 1947. Lawson's salary is reported as "about $1500 a week."

25. Undated memo from John Howard Lawson, Box 30, Folder 9, John Howard Lawson Papers.

26. James Lorence, *The Suppression of Salt of the Earth: How Hollywood, Big Labor and Politicians Blacklisted a Movie in Cold War America* (Albu-

querque: University of New Mexico Press, 1999), 65, 92. See undated note by Lawson, Box 40, Folder 4, John Howard Lawson Papers: "I was not closely associated with 'Salt of the Earth' but it was made by my friends."

27. See contract, 2 January 1958, Box 30, Folder 10, John Howard Lawson Papers.

28. Memo, ca. 1949, File 100–138754, Serial 1003, Part 2, Communist Infiltration, Motion Picture Industry, FOIA Documents, FBI.

29. D. M. Ladd to J. Edgar Hoover, 27 June 1949, Reel 2, Volume 18, 100–138754–524, *Communist Activity in the Entertainment Industry.*

30. "Plaintiffs vs. the Blacklist," ca. 1961, Box 31, Folder 5, John Howard Lawson Papers. Guy Endore argued that the "'blacklisted'" were "'rated like steeplejacks and gangsters; they must pay an additional 50 percent premium'" on insurance "'because their chances of living out a normal life are that much lower than the average.'" See undated article by Guy Endore, Vertical File, "Hollywood Blacklist," University of Wyoming.

31. Elizabeth Poe, "A New Attack on an Old Evil," *Frontier,* February 1961, Box 31, Folder 4, John Howard Lawson Papers.

32. Dalton Trumbo's son, Chris, argues that there was no "de jure" victory over the "blacklist," but "sixteen straight cases" lost in court before a de facto victory as it slowly crumbled. *Exodus, Spartacus, The Brave One, Friendly Persuasion, The Bridge on the River Kwai, Lawrence of Arabia,* and numerous other award-winning films were written by "'blacklistees.'" See "Hollywood's Eden," Kz0377.01, Part 5.05, Pacifica Radio Archives. But see *Variety,* 9 January 1952. Banned writers "accepted $107, 500 in settlement of damage suits . . . coin was anted by four studios while . . . others who were likewise defendants . . . stood on their determination to fight. . . . they believe that with the present tenor of public opinion on communism, they have virtually a 100% chance of coming out of court with a 'not guilty' decision . . . clause [in settlement] will keep the 'Nine' [litigants] from further work on the lots. . . . originally 10 but Edward Dmytryk subsequently recanted." See also *New York Times,* 29 April 1952. Federal judge "set aside a jury verdict awarding back salaries totaling $84,3000 to Adrian Scott" in suit against RKO but "upheld the jury's award of $20,000 to Ring Lardner [Jr.]." Interestingly, when President Ronald Reagan met Soviet leader Mikhail Gorbachev in the Kremlin in 1988, he gave him a copy of *Friendly Persuasion* and praised it lavishly. See Joseph Dombrowski, "The 'Friendly Persuasion' (1956) Screenplay Controversy: Michael Wilson, Jessamyn West and the Hollywood Blacklist," *Historical Journal of Film, Radio and Television* 22, no. 4 (2002): 491–514.

33. Thurman Arnold to Frances Inglis, 10 September 1952, Box 72, Emmett Lavery Papers. See also material on antitrust lawsuit contesting the vertical integration of the industry in Box 68, Thurman Arnold Papers, University of Wyoming. See also Paul Jarrico to Waldo Salt, 17 April 1952, Box 80, Folder 20, Waldo Salt Papers.

34. Speech by Richard M. Nixon, 3 April 1952, PPS 208 (1952).8, Speech File, Richard M. Nixon Papers.

35. Elizabeth Poe, "The Hollywood Story," *Frontier* 5, no. 7 (May 1954): 6–25, Box 1, Folder 16, Adrian Scott Papers. See also *Hollywood Review,* September–October 1955, Box 2, Folder 2, Adrian Scott Papers. The "blacklist" included "some 214 motion picture craftsmen and professionals . . . 106 writers, 36 actors, 3 dancers, 11 directors, 4 producers, 6 musicians, 4 cartoonists, 44 other craftsmen and professionals."

36. Oral history, Abraham Polonsky, 1974, American Film Institute.

37. "Breaking the Blacklist," 1976, Iz0036a, Pacifica Radio Archives.

38. See, e.g., Albert Maltz to Edward G. Robinson, 1 June 1950, Box 30, Folder 14b, Edward G. Robinson Papers. See also Trumbo to "Dear Bob," 11 December 1947, Box 30, Folder 14e. See, e.g., Darryl Zanuck to Robinson, 29 January 1951, Box 30, Folder 14bx; Bert Allenberg to Robinson, 31 March 1952, Box 30, Folder 14e.

39. Undated note from John Howard Lawson, Box 14, Folder 2, John Howard Lawson Papers. See Adrian Scott to Robert Jennings, 27 June 1967, Box 46, Folder 4, Columbia Pictures Collection, University of Wyoming.

40. Affidavit by John Howard Lawson, ca. 1961, Box 31, Folder 5, John Howard Lawson Papers. Lawson's "front," Edward Lewis, "wrote and produced" films and "co-produced several films with Albert S. Rogell," and "Jack Warner . . . built film studios for Pepsi-Cola" and "produced over 100 Faye Emerson Shows. Produced Schlitz Playhouse of Stars," etc. See memo, ca. 1955, Box 30, Folder 9, John Howard Lawson Papers.

41. See Albert Maltz to Adrian Scott, 28 March 1953, Box 5, Folder 21, Adrian Scott Papers. The "relationship between me and *The Robe,*" which he wrote, "is entirely satisfactory. . . . there has been no chisel. . . . there will be no screenplay credit for anyone, only an adaptation credit." See also Adrian Scott to "Dear John," 12 September 1957, Box 5, Folder 32, Adrian Scott Papers.

42. Quoted in *Hollywood Reporter,* 12 April 1956.

43. Report, ca. 1948, 100–138754, Serial 1103, Part 11 of 15, Communist Infiltration, Motion Picture Industry, FOIA Documents, FBI.

44. Roy Brewer to Jay Lovestone, 1 November 1951, Box 295, Jay Lovestone Papers, Stanford University.

45. *Los Angeles Examiner,* 8 September 1950.

46. Roy Brewer to "Dear Jay," n.d., Box 295, Jay Lovestone Papers.

47. Art Arthur to "Dear Irving" [Brown], 28 September 1951, Box 295, Jay Lovestone Papers.

48. M. E. Joyce to "My Dear Dick and Pat," 8 November 1952, PPS 16.1544, 1–2, Richard M. Nixon Papers.

49. Speech by Richard M. Nixon, 26 June 1952, PPS 208 (1952), 25, Richard M. Nixon Papers.

50. J. Edgar Hoover to "Dear Dick," 27 June 1952, Box 540, Richard M. Nixon Pre-presidential Papers.

51. Adele Buffington to John Wood, 9 June 1952, Record Group 233, 1.169–75, Records of House Committee on Internal Security, National Archives and Records Administration. See also *Variety,* 9 June 1952.

52. Elizabeth Poe, "The Hollywood Story," *Frontier* 5, no. 7 (May 1954): 6–25, Adrian Scott Papers.

53. Undated letter from "Progressive Caucus" of SWG, Box 26, Ella Winter Papers.

54. Oral history, Ray Bradbury, 1965, 300/28, UCLA.

55. Interview, Emmett Lavery, n.d., Box 1, Nancy Lynn Schwartz Papers.

56. Interview, Alexander Knox, n.d., Box 1, Nancy Lynn Schwartz Papers. This veteran actor saw no issue of principle involved in the "blacklist" but viewed it—along with the Red Scare itself—as just another ruse for the GOP to return to power and smear the Democrats as "soft on communism."

57. Bernard Gordon, *Hollywood Exile or How I Learned to Love the Blacklist* (Austin: University of Texas Press, 1999), 68. See also Robert Lees to Writers' Guild, 2 June 1980, Robert Lees–Fred Rinaldo Collection, Los Angeles.

58. Robert Muckler to Bernard Brennan, 22 August 1951, PPS 288.179.2, Richard M. Nixon Papers.

59. *Hollywood Citizen News*, 28 October 1947.

60. Marty Ford to Richard M. Nixon, 5 November 1952, PP6, 16.236, Richard M. Nixon Papers.

61. Richard M. Nixon to Dana C. Smith, 25 April 1952, PE 247, Richard M. Nixon Papers.

62. See "Guest List for Mervyn Leroy Dinner for RN," 4 May 1961, Box 798, Richard M. Nixon Pre-presidential Papers.

63. Louis B. Mayer to Richard M. Nixon, 28 August 1957, Box 485, Richard M. Nixon Pre-presidential Papers.

64. Report, 16 July 1956, 100–138754, Reel 7, *Communist Activity in the Entertainment Industry:* "Marilyn Monroe Productions is filled with Communists and money from MM Productions is finding its way to the CP. . . . the source stated that 'there is probably not one person in the company who is not a Commie.'" But see a revealing anecdote about Monroe and imperialism in Indonesia in oral history, Ralph Clarkson, n.d., No. 343, Eastern Washington State Historical Society, Northwest Museum, Spokane. See also oral history, John Ruffato, 1978, No. 348, same site.

65. Report, 5 August 1949, R10034a, Box 75, Records of the United States Senate Internal Security Subcommittee.

66. *Variety*, 11 October 1948.

67. Report, 15 June 1947, Box 69, R9071, Record Group 46, Records of the United States Senate Internal Security Subcommittee.

68. Report, 15 July 1947, Box 69, R9132, Record Group 46, Records of the United States Senate Internal Security Subcommittee.

69. Report, 18 June 1950, Box 77, R10340, Record Group 46, Records of the United States Senate Internal Security Subcommittee.

70. Report, 2 December 1951, Box 78, R10482, Record Group 46, Records of the United States Senate Internal Security Subcommittee. See NCASP, "Policy and Program for 1948," Box 3, Edward Mosk Paper. See oral history, Edmund Hall North, 1986, 300/270, UCLA. See oral history, William Fadiman, 1996,

300/478, UCLA. Meanwhile, in Memphis the children's series *Our Gang* was barred, since "the shorts featured a Negro child playing with white children." See *Hollywood Reporter*, 21 October 1947.

71. Report, ca. 1948, 100–138754, Serial 1103, Part 11 of 15, Communist Infiltration, Motion Picture Industry, FOIA Documents, FBI.

72. H. B. Fletcher to D. M. Ladd, 21 July 1949, 100–138754, Serial 1003, Part 8 of 15, Communist Infiltration, Motion Picture Industry, FOIA Documents, FBI.

73. Report, 6 April 1951, Box 79, R10619, Record Group 46, Records of the United States Senate Internal Security Subcommittee.

74. Report, 3 August 1951, Box 80, R10793, Record Group 46, Records of the United States Senate Internal Security Subcommittee.

75. "Communist Infiltration of Intellectual Groups," 15 July 1953, 100–138754, Serial 1003 (Part 2), Part 9 of 15, Communist Infiltration, Motion Picture Industry, FOIA Documents, FBI.

76. Report, 13 December 1951, 100–15732, Reel 6, *Communist Activity in the Entertainment Industry.*

77. *Hollywood Reporter*, 13 June 1952.

78. Report, 15 December 1953, 100–138754, Reel 7, *Communist Activity in the Entertainment Industry.*

79. Report, 15 May 1956, 100–138754, Reel 7, *Communist Activity in the Entertainment Industry.*

80. Memorandum, "Communist Infiltration of Intellectual Groups," 1 January–30 June 1955, Reel 14, *Communist Activity in the Entertainment Industry.*

81. D. M. Ladd to J. Edgar Hoover, 13 July 1945, 100–138754, Reel 2, *Communist Activity in the Entertainment Industry.*

82. See, e.g., Franklin Folsom, *Days of Anger, Days of Hope: A Memoir of the League of American Writers, 1937–1942* (Niwot: University Press of Colorado, 1994), 118.

83. See salute to John Howard Lawson, 12 November 1955, Box 13, Folder 5, John Howard Lawson Papers.

84. Harry Hay to Paul Jarrico, n.d., Box 13, Folder 5, John Howard Lawson Papers.

85. Statement by Walter Lowenfels, n.d., Box 13, Folder 5, John Howard Lawson Papers.

86. Report, ca. 1956, 100–14732, Serial 1106, Part 12 of 15, Communist Infiltration, Motion Picture Industry, FOIA Documents, FBI.

87. Ibid., Report, 14 May 1957, 100–15732, Serial 1118, Part 13 of 15, FBI.

88. Ibid., Report, 14 November 1958, 100–137754, Serial 1126, Part 15 of 15, FBI.

89. Ben Dobbs, Report for Southern California District of Communist Party, 1 November 1957, Box 21a, Dorothy Healey Papers.

90. Report, 15 June 1956, 100–138764, Serial 1106, Part 12 of 15, Communist Infiltration, Motion Picture Industry, FOIA Documents, FBI.

91. Report, date unclear, ca. 1956, 100–14732, Serial 1106, Part 12 of 15, Communist Infiltration, Motion Picture Industry, FOIA Documents, FBI.

92. See series of articles by John Gates in *New York Post*, 20–26 January 1958, Box 2, Folder 8, Celeste Strack Kaplan Papers, Southern California Library for Social Studies and Research.

93. See, e.g., letter, 26 March 1958, Box 2, Folder 8, Celeste Strack Kaplan Papers. Similarly, in 1968 the Southern California District Committee of the Party, led by Dorothy Healey, Ben Dobbs, and "other members" of this body, "by majority vote" opposed the Warsaw Pact intervention in Czechoslovakia. The "secretariat" of the national Party said this was a "violation of democratic centralism and a frivolous use of the Party's constitution"—by a 61–7 vote. See Daniel Rubin to Dorothy Healey, 23 October 1968, Box 3, Folder 32, Paul Novick Papers, Center for Jewish History, New York City.

94. Report, 13 November 1957, 100–138754, Reel 7, *Communist Activity in the Entertainment Industry*.

95. Report, 14 November 1958, 100–138754, Reel 7, *Communist Activity in the Entertainment Industry*.

96. Report, 14 November 1958, 100–138754, Communist Infiltration, Motion Picture Industry, FOIA Documents, FBI.

97. SAC, Philadelphia to J. Edgar Hoover, 12 December 1949, 100–244991, Reel 4, Volume 19, *Communist Activity in the Entertainment Industry*.

98. Clipping, ca. 1950, Hollywood Ten Clipping File, Academy of Motion Picture Arts and Sciences.

99. Oral history, Paul Jarrico, 1991, 300/360, UCLA.

100. Theodore Ward to John Howard Lawson, 3 August 1940, Box 34, Folder 4, John Howard Lawson Papers.

101. Charlotta Bass to John Howard Lawson, 4 November 1954, Box 15, Folder 4, John Howard Lawson Papers.

102. Julian Mayfield to John Howard Lawson, n.d., Box 15, Folder 4, John Howard Lawson Papers.

103. John Howard Lawson to Anold Perl, 30 August 1953, Box 35, Folder 1, John Howard Lawson Papers.

104. Joan to John Howard Lawson, 19 June 1955, Box 35, Folder 1, John Howard Lawson Papers.

105. Alvah Bessie to John Howard Lawson, 24 March 1953, Box 35, Folder 1, John Howard Lawson Papers. In this same file, see also the letters sent to Robeson from Lawson.

106. V. J. Jerome to John Howard Lawson, 10 July 1954, Box 5, Folder 92, V. J. Jerome Papers.

107. John Howard Lawson to V. J. Jerome, 16 September 1954, Box 5, Folder 92, V. J. Jerome Papers.

108. John Howard Lawson to Julian Mayfield, 16 September 1954, Box 35, Folder 1, John Howard Lawson Papers. See Barbara Zheutlin and David Talbot, *Creative Differences: Profiles of Hollywood Dissidents* (Boston: South End Press, 1978), 83.

109. See, e.g., John Oliver Killens to John Howard Lawson, 27 July 1955, John Howard Lawson Papers.

110. John Howard Lawson to Adele, 2 April 1955, Box 35, Folder 1, John Howard Lawson Papers.

111. John Howard Lawson to John Oliver Killens, 12 June 1955, Box 35, Folder 1, John Howard Lawson Papers.

112. Transcript of interview with John Howard Lawson, June 1961, Box 135, Collection No. 100, UCLA.

113. John Howard Lawson to Bella, 30 January 1964, Box 43, Folder 3, John Howard Lawson Papers.

114. John Howard Lawson to Mildred Stockman, 8 October 1967, Box 43, Folder 3, John Howard Lawson Papers.

115. J. W. K. Vaughan to John Howard Lawson, 16 June 1966, Box 43, Folder 3, John Howard Lawson Papers. Lawson also "submitted ideas" of a "planned t.v. series" which "was to be done in England" called "'Women in Love.'" See prefatory note by John Howard Lawson, ca. 1959, Box 43, Folder 3, John Howard Lawson Papers.

14. THE FALL OF RED HOLLYWOOD

1. Clipping, ca. 27 December 1950, Reel 385, Box 423, National Republic Papers.

2. Undated memoir, Box 63, Folder 1, Herbert Biberman and Gale Sondergaard Papers, State Historical Society of Wisconsin.

3. *Los Angeles Mirror*, 17 October 1961.

4. *New York Post*, 25 June 1951.

5. *Mirror*, 17 September 1951, Box 2, Folder 26, Civil Rights Congress Papers, Southern California Library for Social Studies and Research.

6. *Mirror*, 19 September 1951.

7. Virginia Gardner, "California Close-Up," *Masses & Mainstream* 1, no. 4 (June 1948): 51–58; quotation on 52.

8. Report, 1 February 1949, Record Group 46, Box 74, 49814a, Records of the United States Senate Internal Security Subcommittee.

9. Letter to CEDC-L.A., 6 September 1951, Box 4, Folder 4, Smith Act Collection, Southern California Library for Social Studies and Research.

10. "The Key," 24 April 1950, Box 1, Hollywood Blacklist Collection.

11. *Washington Daily News*, 30 October 1947; *Washington Times Herald*, 30 October 1947.

12. Oral history, Alice McGrath, 1987, 300/269, UCLA.

13. *New York Journal American*, 31 August 1947.

14. *Mirror*, 20 September 1951.

15. Report, 1 February 1949, Record Group 46, Box 74, R9814a, Records of United States Senate Internal Security Subcommittee.

16. *Variety*, 19 March 1952.

17. Statement by Ben Margolis, 28 July 1952, Record Group 21, Box 1316, Folder 13, Records of the District Court.

18. See Exhibits, Box 1338, Folder 105; Box 1345, no folder.

19. Dorothy Healey and Ben Dobbs to "Dear Comrades," 11 August 1950, Box 1331, Folder 13, Dorothy Healey Papers. See John Howard Lawson to Hester Sharnoff, 23 December 1968, Box 57, Folder 6, John Howard Lawson Papers. See also John Howard Lawson to Hester Sharnoff, 2 February 1969, Box 57, Folder 6, John Howard Lawson Papers.

20. Gerda Lerner, *Fireweed: A Political Autobiography* (Philadelphia: Temple University Press, 2002), 349.

21. Undated note by John Howard Lawson, Box 75, Folder 4, John Howard Lawson Papers.

22. Victor Navasky, *Naming Names* (New York: Viking, 1980), 345.

23. United Artists to Stan Margulies, 28 April 1959, Box 31, Folder 1, John Howard Lawson Papers.

24. John Howard Lawson et al. to Kirk Douglas et al., n.d., Box 31, Folder 2, John Howard Lawson Papers.

25. John Howard Lawson to Ed Lewis, 8 June 1959, Box 31, Folder 1, John Howard Lawson Papers.

26. See Lawson note, n.d., re: "lawsuit and settlement with Edward Lewis . . . growing out of Black Market work, 1956–1960," Box 31, Folder 3, John Howard Lawson Papers.

27. Memo from John Howard Lawson, 4 December 1960, Box 31, Folder 3, John Howard Lawson Papers.

28. John Howard Lawson to Karl Tunberg, 4 November 1965, Box 36, Folder 3, John Howard Lawson Papers.

29. George Weltner to Barney Balaban, 19 April 1956, Box 1, George Weltner Papers, University of Wyoming.

30. George Weltner to Barney Balaban, 15 February 1956, Box 1, George Weltner Papers.

31. Adrian Scott to George Weltner, 12 February 1957, Box 4, Folder 33, Adrian Scott Papers.

32. George Weltner to Barney Balaban, 11 December 1957, Box 1, George Weltner Papers.

33. George Weltner to Barney Balaban, 19 December 1957, Box 1, George Weltner Papers.

34. Frank Freeman to Barney Balaban, 23 May 1958, Box 1, George Weltner Papers.

35. George Weltner to Barney Balaban, 11 April 1957, Box 1, George Weltner Papers.

36. George Weltner to Barney Balaban, 31 January 1958, Box 1, George Weltner Papers.

37. Eric Johnston to Y. Frank Freeman, 15 March 1963, Box 6, Folder 28, Eric Johnston Papers, Eastern Washington State Historical Society, Northwest Museum.

38. Eric Johnston to Christian Herter, 4 February 1963, Box 6, Folder 30, Eric Johnston Papers.

39. George Weltner to Barney Balaban, 20 May 1958, Box 1, George Weltner Papers.

40. Confidential memorandum to Barney Balaban, 20 November 1962, Box 1, George Weltner Papers.

41. Oral history, Edward Dmytryk, 1979, 179, Southern Methodist University. According to Dmytryk, Harry Cohn "had always been against" the "Inquisition"; "most of the executives were," he said. Cohn "wasn't even going to cooperate with the others, but they forced him into the Waldorf Declaration." Strikingly, Cohn was said to have a "big picture of Mussolini hanging on the wall" behind his "desk." *Hollywood Reporter*, 27 September 1951.

42. Oral history, Philip Dunne, 1971, American Film Institute, Los Angeles. After Lardner was ousted from Fox, his fellow screenwriter Philip Dunne "drove on the lot at 9 in the morning that day," as he "was called to Zanuck's office" who "said, 'I'm against this, I don't believe it,'" referring to the "blacklist." "'I want you to know I had nothing to do with it.'" Dunne thought this was "probably true. The story was that the New York banks were pressuring the studios to conform."

43. Marquis James and Bessie Rowland James, *Biography of a Bank: The Story of Bank of America* (New York: Harper and Bros., 1954), 430. Ned Young, a "blacklisted" writer who wrote the striking classic *The Defiant Ones*, saw this ban "breaking" in 1959; "there were many reasons" for this, he thought, but "most important of all" was the "splitting up of Hollywood into scores of independent producing companies, each vying for good stories." See transcript, KABC-TV, 9 January 1959, Box 9, Folder 5, Nedrick Young Papers, State Historical Society of Wisconsin.

44. Dalton Trumbo to Michael Wilson, 24 February 1959, Box 46, Folder 10, Michael Wilson Papers, UCLA.

45. *Hollywood Reporter*, 28 March 1960.

46. Albert Maltz to "Marty and George," 26 April 1960, Box 11, Albert Maltz Papers. See clipping, *Daily American* [Paris], 15–16 May 1960, Box 11, Albert Maltz Papers.

47. Interview, Paul Jarrico, n.d., Box 1, Nancy Lynn Schwartz Papers.

48. Quoted in *Los Angeles Times*, 3 September 1967.

49. "Plaintiffs vs. the Blacklist," ca. 1961, Box 30, Folder 5, John Howard Lawson Papers.

50. *Los Angeles Herald-Express*, 30 December 1960.

51. Fred Rinaldo to John Howard Lawson, 7 May 1965, Box 30, Folder 7, John Howard Lawson Papers.

52. Ben Margolis to John Howard Lawson, 3 June 1965, Box 30, Folder 7, John Howard Lawson Papers.

53. Albert Maltz to *San Francisco Chronicle*, ca. 15 January 1964, Box 39, Folder 43, Dorothy Healey Papers.

54. Quoted in *Los Angeles Times*, 3 September 1967.

55. John Howard Lawson to Richard Brown, 24 June 1964, Box 39, Folder 4, John Howard Lawson Papers.

56. *Los Angeles Times,* 3 September 1967.

57. John Howard Lawson to V. J. Jerome, 10 December 1957, Box 5, Folder 92, V. J. Jerome Papers. See leaflet, ca. 1957, same box and folder. See also transcript of John Howard Lawson interview, June 1961, Box 135, Collection No. 100, UCLA.

58. Colonel Joseph Owen to Richard M. Nixon, 11 June 1948, PPS 205.612, Richard M. Nixon Papers.

59. George Murphy to Richard M. Nixon, 5 November 1951, Box 540, Richard M. Nixon Pre-presidential Papers.

60. Statement by Clayton Thomason, representative of International Alliance of Theatrical Stage Employees, Scenic and Title Artists, Local 816, to Richard M. Nixon, 19 October 1962, Box 101, Richard M. Nixon Pre-presidential Papers.

61. Statement by Richard M. Nixon, 19 October 1962, Box 101, Richard M. Nixon Pre-presidential Papers.

62. See, e.g., John Howard Lawson, *Film in the Battle of Ideas* (New York: Masses and Mainstream, 1953), 14.

63. S. Chernikova, executive secretary of "Foreign Literature," 8 January 1960, Box 13, Folder 4, John Howard Lawson Papers: "carrying your new article on the new trends in Hollywood." In same folder see also Chernikova to Lawson, 15 May 1959, where reference is made to "money transactions."

64. Chen Ping-yi, Vice-Editor-in-Chief, Chinese Writers Union, Peking, to John Howard Lawson, 25 September 1957, Box 17, Folder 1, John Howard Lawson Papers.

65. Nobuyuki Masugi to John Howard Lawson, 17 April 1958, Box 13, Folder 4, John Howard Lawson Papers.

66. Mr. Akira Iwasaki to John Howard Lawson, 12 December 1955, Box 35, Folder 1, John Howard Lawson Papers.

67. Akira Iwasaki to John Howard Lawson, 26 March 1956, Box 35, Folder 1, John Howard Lawson Papers.

68. John Howard Lawson to Peter Vassilev, Bulgarian Embassy, Washington, D.C., 12 December 1964, Box 17, Folder 2, John Howard Lawson Papers. See John Howard Lawson, "Styron: Darkness and Fire in the Modern Novel," *Mainstream* 13, no. 10 (October 1960): 9–18; quotation on 10.

69. Maxim Lieber to John Howard Lawson, 23 March 1969, Box 91, Folder 1, John Howard Lawson Papers.

70. John Howard Lawson to Max Lieber, 11 February 1965, Box 38, Folder 8, John Howard Lawson Papers.

71. John Howard Lawson to Julio Garcia Espinosa, Instituto Cubano del Arte & Industria Cinematografico, 4 August 1960, Box 17, Folder 1, John Howard Lawson Papers. See John Howard Lawson to Carlo Salinari, "Il Contemperaneo," Rome, 2 July 1964, same box, same folder; see also John Howard Lawson to Georges Sadoul, ca. 1954, same box and folder.

72. Alfredo Guevara, ICAIC, to John Howard Lawson, 1 September 1960, Box 17, Folder 1, John Howard Lawson Papers.

73. Jack Warner, *My First Hundred Years in Hollywood* (New York: Random House, 1964), 323.

74. See remarks by John Howard Lawson, 12 November 1955, Box 13, Folder 5, John Howard Lawson Papers. See John Howard Lawson to Lawrence Hill, 12 May 1960, Box 35, Folder 10, John Howard Lawson Papers. See also John Howard Lawson, *Film: The Creative Process; The Search for an Audio-Visual Language and Structure* (New York: Hill and Wang, 1967), xxviii, xxvi, xxvii, xxix, 21, 76. See John Howard Lawson to Sidney Finkelstein, 7 May 1959, Box 18, Folder 2, John Howard Lawson Papers.

75. John Howard Lawson to "George," 3 January 1964, Box 17, Folder 1, John Howard Lawson Papers. Lawson was similarly critical about the state of the theater. Edward Albee was "[in] over his head," he thought, while Arthur Miller—a frequent target of his, perhaps because he expected more of him—was "afraid to break free from old forms." See *San Jose News,* 11 August 1966.

76. Abby Mann to John Howard Lawson, 29 April 1968, Box 58, Folder 2, John Howard Lawson Papers.

77. John Howard Lawson to "Lee and Tammy," 25 October 1966, Box 17, Folder 1, John Howard Lawson Papers.

78. John Howard Lawson to V. J. Jerome, 7 March 1958, Box 5, Folder 92, V. J. Jerome Papers.

79. John Howard Lawson to V. J. Jerome, 10 December 1957, Box 5, Folder 92, V. J. Jerome Papers.

80. John Howard Lawson to Richard Brown, 1 March 1964, Box 39, Folder 4, John Howard Lawson Papers.

81. John Howard Lawson to V. J. Jerome, 12 August 1963, Box 5, Folder 92, V. J. Jerome Papers.

82. John Howard Lawson to V. J. Jerome, 10 December 1957, Box 5, Folder 92, V. J. Jerome Papers.

83. *Los Angeles Times,* 3 September 1967.

84. John Howard Lawson to Sidney Finkelstein, 6 February 1966, Box 20, Folder 3, John Howard Lawson Papers. See Sidney Finkelstein to John Howard Lawson, 12 February 1966, same box and folder.

85. John Howard Lawson to Sidney Finkelstein, 22 November 1965, Box 21, Folder 3, John Howard Lawson Papers. One conclusion that jumps off the page of this study is that there was more flux ideologically—certainly contentious debates—among Communists in the United States than has been detailed previously. The contention among the Hollywood Ten, most of whom were Reds, has been noted, and Lawson's edgy debates with the Communist Finkelstein signal this as well. Lawson's unique viewpoint—critical of Stalin and Soviet intellectuals critical of Stalin alike—was not the norm within Red ranks, for example. With the Soviet experience still fresh in his mind, he wrote a piece for the avowedly pro-Moscow, New York–based journal *New World Review* that the editor, Jessica Smith, rebuked: "I believe you are even stricter in

your position than some of the Soviet ideological leaders. Since we ourselves are not completely in accord with your position . . . important as your views are, they are not the only ones held seriously, even [by] many people in the USSR. . . . would there be any objection to publishing an article by [Mike Gold] which would take a somewhat different view than you in the same issue?" See Jessica Smith to John Howard Lawson, 25 November 1963, Box 15, Folder 3, John Howard Lawson Papers.

86. John Howard Lawson to Leo and Peggy, 10 January 1966, Box 43, Folder 43, John Howard Lawson Papers.

87. See *New York Times Book Review,* 28 March 1965, Box 24, Folder 3, John Howard Lawson Papers.

88. John Howard Lawson to Art Shields, 16 May 1964, Box 17, Folder 2, John Howard Lawson Papers.

89. John Howard Lawson to Maxwell Geismar, 25 June 1965, Box 1, Folder 4, John Howard Lawson Papers.

90. John Howard Lawson to James Allen, 10 January 1967, Box 26, Folder 5, John Howard Lawson Papers.

91. Navasky, *Naming Names,* 301.

92. John Howard Lawson to Richard Brown, 1 November 1967, Box 39, Folder 6, John Howard Lawson Papers.

93. John Howard Lawson to Jessica Smith, 5 December 1963, Box 16, Folder 3, John Howard Lawson Papers.

94. John Howard Lawson to Sidney Finkelstein, 22 November 1965, Box 20, Folder 3, John Howard Lawson Papers. See also James Murphy, *The Proletarian Moment: The Controversy over Leftism in Literature* (Urbana: University of Illinois Press, 1991), 147. See John Howard Lawson to Joseph North, 24 December 1965, Box 18, Folder 1, John Howard Lawson Papers. See also John Howard Lawson, *The Hidden Heritage: A Rediscovery of the Ideas and Forces That Link the Thought of Our Time with the Culture of the Past* (New York: Citadel Press, 1968), xi.

95. Lawson, *Film: The Creative Process,* xxix, 256.

96. John Howard Lawson to Joseph North, 24 December 1965, John Howard Lawson Papers. See John Howard Lawson to Durand Van Doren, 16 January 1966, Box 24, Folder 2, John Howard Lawson Papers.

97. John Howard Lawson to Sidney Finkelstein, 22 November 1965, Box 21, Folder 3, John Howard Lawson Papers. See John Howard Lawson to James Allen, 10 January 1967, Box 26, Folder 5, John Howard Lawson Papers.

98. John Howard Lawson to Max, 29 August 1966, Box 38, Folder 8, John Howard Lawson Papers.

99. John Howard Lawson to V. J. Jerome, 2 July 1958, Box 5, Folder 92, V. J. Jerome Papers.

100. John Howard Lawson to Joseph Freeman, 9 January 1965, Joseph Freeman Papers, Stanford University.

101. John Howard Lawson to V. J. Jerome, 17 January 1962, Box 5, Folder 92, V. J. Jerome Papers.

102. John Howard Lawson to Jessica Smith, 5 December 1963, Box 16, Folder 3, John Howard Lawson Papers.

103. Speech by John Howard Lawson, 16 June 1963, Box 16, Folder 1, John Howard Lawson Papers.

104. Lawson, *Film: The Creative Process*, 268, 271

105. Sue Lawson to "Dear Alice and Jerry," 3 February 1963, Box 5, Folder 92, V. J. Jerome Papers.

106. See undated remarks by Lawson, Box 15, Folder 3, John Howard Lawson Papers.

107. Sue Lawson to "Dear Alice and Jerry."

108. John Howard Lawson to Art Shields, 16 May 1964, Box 17, Folder 2, John Howard Lawson Papers.

109. *Daily Worker*, 10 January 1964.

110. Esther and Art Shields to Jack and Sue, 4 January 1964, Box 17, Folder 2, John Howard Lawson Papers.

111. John Howard Lawson to Esther Shields, 24 January 1964, Box 17, Folder 2, John Howard Lawson Papers.

112. John Howard Lawson to Richard Brown, 12 June 1964, Box 39, Folder 4, John Howard Lawson Papers.

113. John Howard Lawson to Hester, 1 May 1968, Box 57, Folder 6, John Howard Lawson Papers.

114. John Howard Lawson to Hester, 20 November 1968, Box 57, Folder 6, John Howard Lawson Papers.

115. John Howard Lawson to Hester, 23 December 1968, Box 57, Folder 6, John Howard Lawson Papers.

116. Bob Shaw to John Howard Lawson, 17 March 1965, Box 43, Folder 2, John Howard Lawson Papers.

117. John Howard Lawson to V. J. Jerome, 30 August 1963, Box 5, Folder 92, John Howard Lawson Papers.

118. Herta to "Susie and Jack," 6 January 1963, Box 16, Folder 2, John Howard Lawson Papers.

119. John Howard Lawson to "Lee and Tammy," 25 October 1966, Box 17, Folder 2, John Howard Lawson Papers.

120. Letter to Wilbur Smith, 10 December 1967, Box 26, Folder 8, John Howard Lawson Papers.

121. John Howard Lawson to Ralph W. Bushee, 26 January 1965, Box 26, Folder 8, John Howard Lawson Papers.

122. *San Jose News*, 11 August 1966.

123. John Howard Lawson to Max, 23 October 1965, Box 38, Folder 8, John Howard Lawson Papers. Lawson was not just a man who handled words. See John Howard Lawson to Max, 27 June 1967, Box 38, Folder 8, John Howard Lawson Papers.

124. John Howard Lawson to V. J. Jerome, 8 September 1964, Box 5, Folder 92, V. J. Jerome Papers.

125. John Howard Lawson to "Lee and Revels," ca. 1967, Box 26, Folder 7, John Howard Lawson Papers.

126. Misha to John Howard Lawson, 18 October 1966, Box 19, Folder 1, John Howard Lawson Papers.

127. John Howard Lawson to Archibald McLeod, n.d., Box 38, Folder 2, John Howard Lawson Papers.

128. John Howard Lawson to "Dear Jackie," 11 March 1969, Box 58, Folder 1, John Howard Lawson Papers.

129. See Lawson's final examination for the summer class he taught at Stanford in 1966, 11 August 1966, Box 37, Folder 1, John Howard Lawson Papers: "Compare 'Caligula' and 'Mother Courage'—again, in terms of theme, characterization, and structure. How are these two plays related to the theatre of the sixties?" Also consider the "influence of Chekhov in Odets' 'Awake and Sing.'"

130. John Howard Lawson to Nat and Janet, 11 February 1965, Box 57, Folder 6, John Howard Lawson Papers.

131. John Howard Lawson to Goldie and Harry, 10 May 1967, Box 26, Folder 7, John Howard Lawson Papers.

132. Quoted in *College Times*, 11 March 1966, Box 36, Folder 7, John Howard Lawson Papers.

133. Dalton Trumbo to John Howard Lawson, 18 December 1956, Box 1, Folder 4, John Howard Lawson Papers.

134. Joseph Freeman to John Howard Lawson, 20 January 1965, Box 1, Folder 4, John Howard Lawson Papers.

135. John Howard Lawson to Durand Van Doren, 24 December 1965, Box 24, Folder 2, John Howard Lawson Papers.

136. See John Howard Lawson to Earl Robinson, 15 December 1972, Box 2, Folder 16, Earl Robinson Papers, University of Washington, Seattle: "I have been hurt—really wounded in spirit—by characters like [Eric] Bentley—not as a purely personal matter, but as an indication of shallow thinking about complex and important developments of art in our time. I have tried to make some sense out of the tangled history, but I don't think I or anybody has placed the twenties—fifties, seventies cycle of history in any understandable perspective."

137. John Howard Lawson to Mike Davidow, 4 November 1965, Box 36, Folder 3, John Howard Lawson Papers.

138. *New York Times Sunday Book Review*, 15 November 1964. According to one analysis, Kael, "who started her career on the Bay Area left Pacifica radio station KPFA," was "paying penance ever since." See Paul Buhle and Dave Wagner, *A Very Dangerous Citizen: Abraham Lincoln Polonsky and the Hollywood Left* (Berkeley and Los Angeles: University of California Press, 2001), 196.

139. Alvah Bessie to John Howard Lawson, 10 December 1964, Box 43, Folder 2, John Howard Lawson Papers.

140. *Punch*, 3 March 1965.

141. John Howard Lawson to Bella, 9 September 1966, Box 43, Folder 3, John Howard Lawson Papers.

142. John Howard Lawson to V. J. Jerome, 3 August 1964, Box 5, Folder 92, V. J. Jerome Papers.

143. John Howard Lawson to V. J. Jerome, 11 January 1954, Box 5, Folder 92, V. J. Jerome Papers.

144. John Howard Lawson to Sidney Finkelstein, 22 November 1965, Box 21, Folder 3, John Howard Lawson Papers.

145. John Howard Lawson to Max, 9 January 1967, Box 38, Folder 8, John Howard Lawson Papers.

146. John Howard Lawson to John Gassner, 26 September 1966, John Gassner Papers, University of Texas–Austin.

147. John Howard Lawson to Angus Cameron, 7 January 1964, Box 91, Folder 1, John Howard Lawson Papers.

CONCLUSION

1. John Howard Lawson to B. Leontiev, 9 March 1956, Box 17, Folder 1, John Howard Lawson Papers.

2. John Howard Lawson to Mike Gold, 17 May 1960, Mike Gold Papers.

3. Paul Patek to John Howard Lawson, 7 June 1960, Box 15, Folder 7, John Howard Lawson Papers.

4. John Howard Lawson to Lee and Revels, 24 January 1969, Box 57, Folder 6, John Howard Lawson Papers.

5. John Howard Lawson to Claire Hartford, 28 March 1969, Box 57, Folder 6, John Howard Lawson Papers.

6. John Howard Lawson to "Ladle," n.d., Gaylor Wood Papers.

7. Letter from John Howard Lawson, 22 June 1975, Gaylor Wood Papers.

8. John Howard Lawson to Alvah Bessie, 4 January 1972, Box 7, Folder 1, Alvah Bessie Papers.

9. *Time*, 24 January 1977.

10. *New York Times*, 26 August 1977.

11. *Los Angeles Times*, 13 November 1994.

12. Sheridan Gibney, "What Is Screenwriting?" *Screen Writer* 2, no. 12 (May 1947): 10–14; quotation on 10.

13. *Guardian* [U.K.], 9 July 2003.

14. Quoted in *New Yorker*, 20 October 2003.

15. *New York Times*, 27 July 2003.

16. *New York Times*, 25 April 2003.

17. Paul Buhle and Dave Wagner, *Hide in Plain Sight: The Hollywood Blacklistees in Film and Television, 1950–2002* (New York: Palgrave, 2003), x.

18. Quoted in *New York Times*, 6 January 2004. See also *Los Angeles Times*, 7 January 2004.

19. See review of *The Majestic*, *Journal of American History* 89, no. 3 (December 2002): 1171–72.

20. Ben Barzman to Adrian Scott, 21 May 1960, Box 4, Folder 8, Adrian Scott Papers.

21. Adrian Scott to Ben Barzman, 6 June 1960, Box 4, Folder 8, Adrian Scott Papers.

22. See Gerald Horne, *Race War! White Supremacy and the Japanese Attack on the British Empire* (New York: New York University Press, 2004), 326–27.

23. *New York Times,* 5 May 1978.

24. Lester Cole to Editor of "New York Times," ca. March 1978, Folder 183, Ring Lardner Jr. Collection.

25. Lester Cole to Ring Lardner Jr., 16 April 1978, Folder 183, Ring Lardner Jr. Collection.

26. Bennett Cerf to Adrian Scott, 2 December 1952, Box 4, Folder 23, Adrian Scott Papers.

27. *New York Times Magazine,* 25 March 1973.

28. Quoted in Buhle and Wagner, *Hide in Plain Sight,* 246.

Index

Text: 10/13 Aldus
Display: Aldus
Compositor, printer and binder: Sheridan Books, Inc.